FEB   2009

THE
ENTITY

Also by Eric Frattini

THE
ENTITY

FIVE CENTURIES
OF SECRET VATICAN
ESPIONAGE

ERIC FRATTINI

Translated by Dick Cluster

ST. MARTIN'S PRESS ❧ NEW YORK

www.stmartins.com

Library of Congress Cataloging-in-Publication Data

Frattini, Eric.
    The entity : five centuries of secret Vatican espionage / Eric Alonso Frattini ; Translated by Dick
Cluster.
        p. cm.
    ISBN-13: 978-0-312-37594-2
    ISBN-10: 0-312-37594-8
    1. Espionage—Vatican City—History. 2. Intelligence service—Vatican City—History. I. Title.
    UB271.V38F73 2008
    327.12456'34—dc22

                                                                                      2008025769

First published in Spain by Espasa Calpe under the title *La Santa Alianza*

First U.S. Edition: November 2008

10 9 8 7 6 5 4 3 2 1

To Hugo, the most valuable to me

thanks to his constant presence and for the love

that he gives me every day of his life . . .

To Silvia, for her love and her unconditional support in everything I do . . .

To my mother, for always supporting and encouraging me . . .

CONTENTS

Contents

ACKNOWLEDGMENTS

To *the sources* who have provided invaluable aid whose names I prefer not to have appear in this book.

To *the sources* who have provided invaluable aid who have asked that their names not be cited in this book.

To *the archivists and librarians* of more than thirty-nine institutions in fourteen countries who I have consulted. Without many of the documents to which they gave me access, I could not have written this book.

To *Tuhviah Friedman,* director of the Institute of Documentation for the Investigation of Nazi War Crimes, in Haifa (Israel), for providing all the documentation about Vatican relations with Nazi Germany, the information about members of the Vatican hierarchy's roles in the escape of Nazi war criminals, and the original files on high-ranking Nazis who had contact with Pius XII during the occupation of Italy.

To *Alison Weir,* for her magnificent documentation on Mary Stewart's reign and her era.

To *Dorothee Lottman-Kaeseler,* director of the Active Museum of German Jewish History in Wiesbaden, German Federal Republic.

To *David Álvarez,* professor of politics at St. Mary's College, California, for what I have learned from reading his marvelous books. Without doubt, a true maestro.

To *Manuel Fernández Álvarez,* a true maestro and authentic tower of knowledge on Philip II's reign and era. I have learned so much from reading his *Felipe II y su tiempo (Philip II and His Time).*

To the *Office of Information of the Central Intelligence Agency* (CIA) in Langley

Acknowledgments

(Virginia); to the administrators of the *National Archives and Records Administration* (NARA) and the *National Security Archives* of George Washington University, for giving me access to their documents on the U.S. intervention in Poland under the Reagan administration.

To *David M. Cheney,* for allowing me to review his magnificent and well-documented historical archives on the Catholic hierarchy and the Roman curia. Without these, I would have found it very difficult to write this book.

To *Dick Cluster,* for the arduous task of having to translate my book into English, surely not a simple one.

To *Phil Revzin,* my editor, for believing in this book and in me.

And finally and especially, an acknowledgment to all the people and organizations who erected obstacles, barriers, and stumbling blocks to prevent this book from becoming what it is today. They sharpened my curiosity and, therefore, my research as well.

To all the above, my most humble and sincere thanks. Part of this book belongs to all of you.

In every espionage operation there is an above the line and a below the line. Above the line is what you do by the book. Below the line is how you do the job.

—*John le Carré,* A Perfect Spy

THE
ENTITY

INTRODUCTION

The papacy, the supreme authority at the head of the Catholic Church, is the oldest established institution in the world. It was the only institution to flourish during the Middle Ages, a leading actor in the Renaissance, and a protagonist in the battles of the Reformation, the Counter-Reformation, the French Revolution, the industrial era, and the rise and fall of communism. For centuries, making full use of their famous "infallibility," popes brought their centralized power to bear on the social outcomes of unfolding historical events. The historian Thomas Babington Macaulay, in his study of the history of Protestantism, asserted that the popes knew how to place the Church in the center of events, just as they knew how to mitigate its role. He stressed the pontiffs' ability to co-opt new social movements that kept arising over the course of centuries, or to adapt the Church to them.

The emperor Napoleon Bonaparte regarded the papacy as "one of the best jobs in the world." Adolf Hitler called it "one of the most dangerous and most delicate in international politics." Napoleon likened the power of a single pope to that of an army of 200,000 men. Really, throughout history, the papacy has always displayed two faces: that of the worldwide leadership of the Catholic Church and that of one of the planet's best political organizations. While the popes were blessing their faithful on the one hand, on the other, they were receiving foreign ambassadors and heads of states and dispatching legates and nuncios on special missions.

This power has led many to see the popes more as the "priests of princes" than as the "vicars of Christ." From the eighth century on, the supreme pontiffs sought primacy and universal jurisdiction for their pronouncements until in 1931, with the creation of Vatican Radio, they gained uninterrupted contact with the world, which made this desire a reality. During the Reformation, Martin Luther attacked the papacy as an unnecessary human evil. The Catholic historian Lord Acton criticized the papacy's excessive centralization and, after a trip to Rome, declared that "power corrupts, and absolute power corrupts absolutely."

The history of the Holy Alliance (in 1930 renamed The Entity), the Vatican's spy service, cannot be told without telling the history of the popes, nor can the history of the popes be told without telling the history of the Catholic Church. It is clear that without Catholicism there would be no pope, and, as Paul VI wrote in his encyclical *Ecclesiam suam,* "Take away the sovereign Pontiff and the Catholic Church would no longer be catholic." Without the actual power that the popes have possessed, neither the Holy Alliance nor the counterespionage unit *Sodalitium Pianum* would exist. Both have formed part of the machinery that they have also helped to create: the Holy Alliance since its foundation in 1566 by order of Pope Pius V, and the *Sodalitium Pianum* (S.P.) since its foundation in 1913 by order of Pius X.

Carlo Castiglioni, historian and author of one of the best encyclopedias on the papacy, wrote: "Without any doubt, the triple crown worn by the popes symbolizes the power they exercise in heaven, on earth, and in the underworld." That statement is easy to explain. In heaven, the pope has God; on earth, the pope has himself; in the underworld, the pope has the Holy Alliance.

In spite of the fact that papal authority has been changed by modernization and renewal, by politics and economics, the interests of the Church have always determined the actions of the Vatican's spies. Experts on the Vatican assure us that the Church and its papal structures have never abandoned their imperial image. Rather, attributes of an emperor have simply been transferred to the pope.

Forty popes have governed or, better put, "reigned" since the creation of the Holy Alliance, from Pius V to John Paul II. They have had to confront de-Christianizations and schisms, revolutions and dictatorships, colonizations and expulsions, persecutions and attacks, civil wars and world wars, assassinations and kidnappings. Papal policies have always set the objectives; the Holy Alliance has been a powerful instrument for carrying them out.

From the sixteenth to the eighteenth century, the enemies the papacy and the Holy Alliance had to confront were liberalism, constitutionalism, democracy, republicanism, and socialism. In the nineteenth and twentieth centuries, these enemies became Darwinism, Americanism, modernism, racism, fascism, communism, totalitarianism, and the sexual revolution. In the twenty-first, they will be scientific intrusion in religious questions, the unipolar power bloc, overpopulation, feminism, and social agnosticism.

These examples serve to demonstrate that often the Vatican's political activity and its secret service have operated in parallel fashion, using different methods toward the same objective. On one hand, popes have negotiated to roll back or neutralize certain measures directed at Rome; on the other, the Holy Alliance and the "Black Order" have intervened to destroy the enemies of the Church.

David Rizzio, Lamberto Macchi, Roberto Ridolfi, James Fitzmaurice, William Parry, Marco Antonio Massia, Giulio Alberoni, Alexander de' Medici, Giulio Guarnieri, Tebaldo Fieschi, Charles Tournon, John Bell, and Giovanni DaNicola have been among the Holy Alliance agents whose operations changed the course of history from the mid-sixteenth century to the twenty-first.

Ludovico Ludovisi, Lorenzo Magalotti, Olimpia Maidalchini, Sforza Pallavicino, Paluzzo Paluzzi, Bartolomeo Pacca, Giovanni Battista Caprara, Annibale Albani, Pietro Fumasoni Biondi, and Luigi Poggi have been some of the powerful chieftains of the pontifical espionage apparatus who, always in defense of the faith, have planned and ordered covert operations, political or state-sanctioned assassinations, and mere "liquidations" of secondary players who got in the way of the policies of the pope of the moment, the policies of God on earth.

Kings have been killed, diplomats poisoned, and one or another among feuding factions supported, all as a norm of papal diplomacy. Blind eyes have been turned to catastrophes and holocausts. Terrorists have been financed, as have been South American dictators, while war criminals have been protected, Mafia money laundered, financial markets manipulated, bank failures provoked, and arms sold to combatants even as their wars have been condemned. All this has occurred in the name of God, with the Holy Alliance and the *Sodalitium Pianum* as His tools.

Since the inquisitor Pius V (sanctified years later) founded the Vatican espionage service in the sixteenth century with the sole objective of ending the life of the heretic Elizabeth I of England and supporting the Catholic Mary Queen of Scots, the Vatican state has never admitted the existence of the

Holy Alliance or of the counterespionage arm *Sodalitium Pianum,* although it can be said that their operations have been an open secret. Simon Wiesenthal, the famous Nazi hunter, declared in an interview that "the best and most effective espionage service I know in the world belongs to the Vatican." Cardinal Luigi Poggi, nicknamed "the Pope's Spy" (John Paul II being the pope in question), carried out one of the largest modernizations of the Holy Alliance by taking advantage of his close contacts with the Israeli Mossad. Thanks to His Eminence, the Israeli secret service was able to foil a planned attack against Prime Minister Golda Meir during her visit to Italy. Poggi would also be in charge of channeling the necessary Vatican funds, by way of Paul Marcinkus's Vatican bank, the Institute for Religious Works, to finance the Solidarity trade union led by Lech Walesa. That would be a joint operation between the Holy Alliance and William Casey's CIA.

Through its five centuries of history, the long shadow of the Holy Alliance has been visible in plots against Elizabeth I of England and in the St. Bartholomew's Eve Massacre in France; in the adventure of the Grand Armada and the assassinations of the Dutch prince William of Orange and the French king Henry IV; in the War of the Spanish Succession and the confrontation with Cardinals Richelieu and Mazarin in Paris; in the attempted assassination of King Joseph I of Portugal; in the French Revolution and the Battle of Austerlitz, the rise and fall of Napoleon; in Cuba's war against Spain and the South American secessions; in secret relations with Kaiser Wilhelm II during the First World War, Adolf Hitler during the Second, and the Nazi-related affairs of "Croatian Gold" and the "Odessa" organization immediately after; in the fights against the terrorist group Black September, Carlos the Jackal, and communism; in the obscure finances of the Institute for Religious Works and its still more obscure ties to Freemasons, Mafiosi, and arms traffickers; in the creation of financial companies in fiscal paradises and in the funding of right-wing dictators like Anastasio Somoza and Jorge Videla.

During these five centuries, secret societies answering to the Holy Alliance—like the "*Octogonus* Circle" or the Black Order—have carried out covert operations for other countries' spy services, including the Mossad and the CIA. While in such cases the target has been a clear enemy, such as Arab terrorism or the "evil" of communism, the Holy Alliance has known how to adapt to any time and situation because, as the all-powerful Cardinal Paluzzo Paluzzi, head of the Holy Alliance in the mid-seventeenth century, once remarked, "If the Pope orders the elimination of someone in defense of the faith, this is carried out without question. He is God's voice and we [the Holy Alliance] are his right hand."

This book, far-ranging though it may be, is just a small exploration of five centuries of history by way of the covert operations of the powerful spy service of the city-state called the Vatican. The priest-agents of the papal espionage service, the Holy Alliance, and the counterintelligence, the *Sodalitium Pianum,* have killed, robbed, conspired, and betrayed by command of the supreme pontiff in the name of God and the Catholic faith. The pope's spies have been the perfect symbol of the symbiosis under whose slogan they have acted: "With the Cross and the Sword." All events narrated in these pages are real. All individuals mentioned are real as well.

El Tamaral, Spain

2004

1

BETWEEN THE REFORMATION
AND A NEW ALLIANCE (1566–1570)

For many, as I have often told you and now tell you even in tears, conduct themselves as enemies of the cross of Christ.

—Philippians 3:18

There are various stories as to who actually founded the Holy Alliance, the Vatican's espionage arm. But it was surely Pope Pius V (1566–1572) who in 1566 organized the first papal espionage service with the goal of fighting Protestantism as represented by Elizabeth I of England.

Protected by the powerful cardinal Giovanni Pietro Caraffa (the future Pope Paul IV), Miguel Ghislieri had been summoned to Rome to take charge of a special mission. Ghislieri was instructed by His Eminence to create a sort of counterespionage service. Organized in the shape of a pyramid, it had the task of collecting information about anyone who might violate papal directives or Church dogma, so that they might then be judged by the Inquisition, or "Holy Office."

The young priest was fond of secret societies, and for him the Holy Office was one of the most powerful "secret societies" of its time. The work carried out by Ghislieri's agents in the regions of Como and Bergamo caught the attention of the powers-that-be in Rome. In less than a year, almost twelve hundred people ranging from peasants to nobles were judged by Inquisitorial courts. More than two hundred, after undergoing terrible tortures, were found guilty and executed.

The rope torture consisted of tying the presumed heretic's hands behind his or her back and then lifting the prisoner by a rope hanging from the ceiling. Once the prisoner was suspended in this way, the rope would be released for an instant so the body would fall by its own weight, and then the fall would be broken while the prisoner was still a few feet above the floor. The violent motion would dislocate the suspected heretic's extremities.

Another frequent tool was the water torture. The torturers would lay their victim in a wooden trough and stuff a soaked cloth in his or her throat while covering the nose to prevent breathing. When Inquisition doctors would halt the torment, many of the captives were already dead.[1]

In 1551, under the papacy of Julian III (1550–1555), Miguel Ghislieri was promoted by Caraffa, for services rendered, to the position of commissary general of the Congregation of the Holy Office of the Inquisition, as the chief official of the Roman Inquisition was known. As such, Ghislieri set about improving the Holy Office so it could better fulfill its objectives. In the first place, he reformed its governing council, and the pope named a group of cardinals to control it. In the case of important figures of Roman society being brought up for judgment, these cardinals served as both judges and papal counselors.

It was also Ghislieri who, early in 1552, established the seven classes of criminals who could be judged by the courts of the Holy Office: heretics; suspected heretics; those who protected heretics; magicians, witches, or sorcerers; blasphemers; those who resisted the authorities or agents of the Inquisition; and those who broke, disrespected, or violated the Holy Office's seals or emblems.

In that same year, Ghislieri began to assemble a true network of spies all over Rome. They operated everywhere, from the city's brothels to the kitchens of its noble palaces. The information of all sorts that they collected was delivered personally to Ghislieri in one of two ways: by word of mouth or by the so-called *Informi Rosso* (Red Report). The latter was a small piece of parchment rolled up inside a red ribbon bearing the emblem of the Holy Office. According to the laws in effect, breaking of this seal was punishable by instant execution. In these reports, Ghislieri's agents wrote down all the charges, often without a shred of proof, against Roman citizens thought to have violated Church precepts and so be susceptible to investigation by a tribunal of the Holy Office. The *Informi Rosso* was deposited in a small bronze mailbox dedicated to this purpose in the Roman headquarters of the Inquisition.

For years, the general of the Inquisition created one of the biggest and most effective spy networks and one of the best archives of personal data about the citizens of Rome. Nothing was said or done in the lanes or squares of the city without Ghislieri's knowledge. Nothing was said or done in the interior of the Vatican, either, without the general of the Inquisition knowing about it.

On May 23, 1555, after the brief papacy of Marcellus II, which lasted for less than a month, seventy-two-year-old Cardinal Giovanni Pietro Caraffa was elected pope without opposition from either the faction favoring the Holy Roman Empire or that favoring France. The Venetian ambassador, Giacomo Navagero, described the new pontiff this way: "Caraffa is a pope of violent and fiery temperament. He is too impetuous to manage the affairs of the Church and, of course, this aged pontiff does not tolerate anyone contradicting him."[2]

Caraffa, now Pope Paul IV, came to fear the unprecedented power of Miguel Ghislieri, whom the Roman populace called "the shadow pope." In spite of everything, however, the pontiff bestowed the title of cardinal on him. From then on, Ghislieri the Inquisitor became ever more dangerous and powerful. Many members of the College of Cardinals did not want to let him chart the future of the Catholic Church from his post atop the feared Inquisition.

Ghislieri's agents did as they pleased, spreading terror through the streets of Rome. The cardinal's spies, known as "black monks," chose a victim and waited for him to go walking down some lonely street. At that moment he would be attacked, spirited into a closed carriage, and taken to one of the compounds of the Inquisition. A friar who was witness to the arrival of such captives described it this way, as published in Leonardo Gallois's *Historia General de la Inquisición* in 1869:

> The victim was taken to the ground floor, just off an inner courtyard near the main entrance. There began his initiation, in a circular room where ten skeletons hung from the walls to announce that in this abode the guests were sometimes nailed there alive to calmly await their deaths. After such a holy warning, the victim came upon two more human skeletons in an adjoining gallery, not on their feet as if receiving visitors, but spread out like a mosaic or carpet. On the right side of the same gallery, a grease-stained oven could clearly be distinguished. It was the secret replacement for the bonfires in public plazas which had fallen into disuse in this corrupt century. . . .

Few cells, properly speaking, could be found here on the first floor, but on the second floor, to the right, was the chamber of the Holy Tribunal flanked by two doors. Above one was a sign proclaiming *stanza del primo padre compagno* and above the other, *stanza del secondo padre compagno*. Thus were named the two inquisitors in charge of the double mission of helping the Suprema to uncover criminals and turn them definitively into convicts.[3]

Cardinal Ghislieri's situation, however, changed completely when Pope Paul IV died suddenly on the night of August 18, 1559. As word of his death spread, sedition spread, too, through the Roman streets. Hunting down Ghislieri's agents became one of the main pastimes of the aroused masses. Many of those who had loyally served the Holy Inquisition were killed by the crowds and their bodies thrown into the sewers. The disorder did not end there. The Roman masses attacked the palace that housed the Tribunal of the Inquisition and toppled the statue of the late pope.[4]

Cardinal Ghislieri and some of his men managed to preserve a large part of the secret archives, which accompanied them in eight carriages in their flight from Rome.

At last, normalcy returned when, on December 25, 1559, Cardinal Giovanni Angelo de' Medici, enemy of the late pope, became his successor under the name of Pius IV.

This pope was a man of firm character, a skilled diplomat determined to cleanse the Catholic Church of all traces of Paul IV. To this end, he surrounded himself with two loyal cardinals who were also his nephews, Mark Sittich von Hohenems and Carlo Borromeo. The first was a master swordsman, skilled in all the arts of war. The second was a master diplomat.

Borromeo had been Archbishop of Milan, papal legate in Bologna and Romagna, head of government in the papal states, and finally the pope's private secretary. As a first measure, the cardinals Carlo and Alfonso Caraffa were arrested and confined in the castle of Sant'Angelo. So were Giovanni Caraffa (the Duke of Paliano) and other gentlemen of the duke's court who were accused of the murder of his wife.

As his second measure, following the advice of Carlo Borromeo, Pope Pius IV decided to rehabilitate Cardinal Morone and Bishop Fiescherati, who had been accused of heresy by the Holy Office on Paul IV's orders. His third measure was to send Cardinal Ghislieri into exile and dissolve his network of black monks.[5] His Eminence, who had taken refuge in an isolated monastery, thus returned to his duties in his former bishopric, which was well regarded when the College of Cardinals assembled once again after Pius IV's death on December 9, 1565. Curiously, after three weeks of deliberations, Pius IV's key advisor, Cardinal Carlo Borromeo, decided to support the candidacy of Ghislieri, which was backed by King Philip II of Spain. For years, Ghislieri had been collecting an annual subsidy of eight hundred ducats from the Spanish crown.[6]

On January 7, 1566, Cardinal Ghislieri was elected pope. He adopted the name Pius V. The Spanish ambassador reported, "Pius V is the pope whom the times require." Philip II also approved of his ally's ascension to the Throne of St. Peter. His selection represented a victory for all the forces who wanted a pontiff who was austere and pious but simultaneously able to fight and act energetically against the Protestant Reformation. What was surely true was that Pius V would use his broad experience as head of the Inquisition to create an effective espionage service, implacable and operating with blind obedience to the orders of the pope.

The first function of the agents of the Holy Alliance—a name bestowed by the pope himself on his secret service in honor of the alliance between the Vatican and the Catholic queen Mary Stuart—was none other than that of obtaining information about possible political movements and intrigues directed from the court of London. The reports they assembled were sent to the powerful monarchs who supported Catholicism and papal power against the rising Protestant tide. The main responsibility of the papal spies was to lend their services to Mary Stuart (Mary Queen of Scots) with the aim of restoring Catholicism to Scotland, which had declared itself Presbyterian in 1560, and to fight against Protestantism in general. Pius V understood that his main enemy was the schismatic Church of England, represented by Queen Elizabeth I, the daughter of Henry VIII and Anne Boleyn.

Henry VIII had broken with the Catholic Church in 1532, when he asked Pope Clement VII (November 19, 1523–September 25, 1534) for permission to divorce his queen, Catherine of Aragon, daughter of the "Catholic Monarchs" Ferdinand and Isabella of Spain and aunt of the Holy Roman Emperor Charles V, who was also King Charles I of Spain, so as to marry his lover, Anne Boleyn.[7] The pontiff studied the letter sent him by the English king, an old parchment measuring sixty by ninety centimeters and bearing the supporting signatures of seventy-five leading personalities of the realm. Seventy-five red silk ribbons hung from the document, with seventy-five wax seals.[8]

In his petition, Henry VIII expressed the desire to marry his lover, and he requested the pope's permission to divorce his current queen, Catherine of Aragon. The petition was denied by Clement VII, which provoked Henry's rage and rejection of the Catholic Church. The King of England decided to marry Anne Boleyn. In spite of Rome's rejection, he ordered his marriage to Catherine annulled.

The definitive schism was provoked on January 15, 1535, under the papacy of Paul III, when, in order to give juridical legitimacy to his new ecclesiastic supremacy, Henry VIII summoned the clergy and the scholars of all the universities of his realm to publicly declare that the Roman pope had no divine right or other authority over England. The new church was to be a Catholic-Anglican institution under the authority of the crown.

The five-year reign of Mary Tudor, which came to an end with her death on November 17, 1558, was nothing if not intense. Wars, executions, internal rebellions, coups d'etat, and religious conflicts were the order of the day. The night Mary died, her sister, Elizabeth, was proclaimed Queen of England.

A great part of the English populace received the new queen's ascension with joy. In part, this reaction stemmed from their painful memories of the reign of her sister, popularly nicknamed Bloody Mary. At her ascension to the throne, Mary had decided to restore Catholicism whatever the cost—a policy supported by Pope Paul IV but opposed by the Spanish ambassador. A precondition of this policy was to cut off the heads of all those who had defended the Reformation.

Many of the Protestant bishops (castigated by Mary as "bad shepherds who have led their flocks to damnation")[9] were the first to be burned at the stake for the crime of heresy. The former bishop of London, Nicholas Ridley (the same who had shortly before judged Mary Tudor a bastard and proclaimed Lady Jane Grey Queen of England in her place), was burned alive on October 16, 1555, in a public square in Oxford. Hugh Latimer, the ex–bishop of Worcester, accompanied him in the flames. Another execution ordered by the queen, to the surprise of both Rome and the English Parliament, was that of the ex–bishop of Canterbury, Thomas Cranmer, who was condemned on March 21, 1556. Cranmer had pronounced the annulment of Henry VIII's marriage to Catherine of Aragon and consummated the definitive break with papal power in Rome.

On January 15, 1559, Elizabeth was crowned Queen of England, and on May 8, Parliament opened its new session at which she proposed new laws permitting the reestablishment of Protestantism throughout the kingdom and its possessions. Rome and its Catholic Church, led by Paul IV, an old man of eighty-three, lacked the strength to resist the renewed religious shift in England.[10]

What the pontiff knew for sure was that the only way to at least maintain a Catholic enclave in Protestant England was to support the Queen of Scotland, Mary Stuart. Over the years that followed, she would become a puppet in conspiracies hatched by Paul IV and his successors along with the powerful and monastic King Philip II of Spain, the capricious King Charles IX of France, the insignificant and uncultured Ferdinand I of Austria, and Mary's own son, Prince James, who would eventually betray her and inherit her throne.

The circle began to close around Mary Stuart when the two men closest to her became spies for powers with important interests in Scotland. On July 29, 1565, she married the Catholic Henry Darnley. The new king-consort of Scotland was tall, strong, blond, and attractive to women, but unlearned and possessed of little culture. Furthermore, Darnley, though the new Scottish monarch and the bedmate of its queen, was himself a puppet in the hands of Sir Francis Walsingham, the head of Elizabeth's spy network, and in those of the Scottish nobles. Darnley was a coward above all.[11]

A few months later, toward the end of 1565, Mary developed a friendship with a young dark-skinned Italian from the Piedmont region, David Rizzio. Rizzio came to Scotland as a member of the retinue of the visiting Marquis of Moreta, ambassador from Savoy.[12] He was twenty-three years old and had round green eyes that caught the attention of a queen much attracted to men's appearances. Rizzio was skilled in music and poetry, in the lute and the making of verses. He was also a priest and one of the most active spies in the recently created Holy Alliance.[13]

Mary Stuart asked the ambassador of Savoy to cede young Rizzio for her personal enjoyment. Little by little, the Piedmontese courtier worked his way up in her entourage. Within a few days he rose from being a mere singer at the queen's pleasure to a post as a personal attendant with a salary of seventy-five pounds a year. Thanks to this position close to the queen, Rizzio gained access to her most private papers.

The queen found in the Italian everything her husband, Henry Darnley, lacked. Rizzio had clear ideas and wide knowledge of the arts; he knew Latin, spoke perfect French and Italian, and was fluent in English, too. Despite his newfound royal favor, the spy continued to eat at the servants' table, but a chance to alter this situation appeared when the queen fired her private secretary, Raulet. Though Raulet had been her most trusted assistant, she fired him when she discovered that he had been ignoring several Scottish nobles' assertions about English "bribes." Walsingham, head of the Elizabethan spy network, devoted significant crown funds to bribes with which to acquire the services of infiltrators in the Scottish court.

So Raulet's desk was occupied by David Rizzio instead. In spite of being a loyal defender of the Counter-Reformation and informing Pope Pius V of all English and Scottish doings, Rizzio now dedicated body and soul to the service of Mary Queen of Scots.

The Holy Alliance's spy was gaining more and more power, and Darnley knew it. The queen's husband, however, knew that if he wanted to get rid of Rizzio, he needed to first consult Walsingham, who in turn needed to consult Elizabeth I. He knew that only thus could he be safely covered if his wife were to get wind that he was responsible for the assassination of the Piedmontese.

David Rizzio and his brother Joseph, whom he had brought with him from Italy, had become part of the Holy Alliance's circle of spies in Scotland. Their mission, by order of the pope, was to collect information about John Knox, a former student of John Calvin's, who surpassed his master in orthodoxy and fundamentalism. For Pius V, Knox was the only obstacle to Scotland's returning to the bosom of the Catholic Church. According to the reports of papal spies, Knox was a former obscure Catholic priest who had decided to plunge into the Reformation. Calvin and George Wishart had been his teachers until the Scottish queen regent Mary of Guise (mother of Mary Stuart) had decided to burn Wishart at the stake. That was the act that engendered Knox's dogmatic fundamentalism, as well as a deep and visceral hatred toward the Stuarts.

On the death of his teacher, John Knox became the leader of the so-called Rebellion against the Regent. French troops who landed in Scotland to support Mary of Guise captured Knox and sent him to the galleys.[14]

After he was freed, Knox took refuge in Calvinist lands, where he learned how to preach and solidified his implacable hatred of sumptuous display. Almost as soon as he reached Scotland, he succeeded in winning both the lords and the people to the cause of the Reformation. Joseph Rizzio informed the pope of Knox's activities, writing in one document:

> Converted into a Scottish prophet, he thunders every Sunday from his pulpit in St. Giles, casting hatred and damnation on all who do not heed his word. Like a child, he celebrates every defeat suffered by a Catholic or by any adversary of a different religion. When an enemy has been killed, Knox speaks of God's hand. Every Sunday at the end of his sermon he praises God and asks Him to soon do away with the reign of the usurping Stuarts and thus with the queen who occupies an undeserved throne.[15]

David Rizzio himself informed Pius V about the encounter between Knox and Mary Queen of Scots:

"This meeting between the faithful Catholic queen of Scotland and the fanatical Protestant John Knox took place in Edinburgh. The preacher turned impolite and held the Roman Catholic Church responsible for a whore who could not be the bride of God. These words offended Queen Mary."[16] The Holy Alliance told the Rizzio brothers to reinforce their security measures. Apparently they had made too many enemies in a very short time, and the pope's network did not want to lose such precious agents. Two of the main enemies of the pair of Italians and of the Counter-Reformation in Scotland were the queen's chancellors: Moray (her illegitimate stepbrother) and William Maitland, both Protestants.

Soon the spies of the Holy Alliance discovered, through a traitor, that Elizabeth I of England had been bribing Chancellor Moray and several lords to promote a rebellion against Mary. The pope could only inform the Spanish king, Philip II, who in turn sent word to the English court, through his ambassador, that if this were to happen, perhaps he would find himself obligated to send help to the Catholic queen. The ambassador made no mention of Pius V's letter to Mary Stuart on January 10, 1566: "My dear daughter: We have heard with great joy that you and your husband have given great proof of your diligence by restoring in your kingdom the true religion of God," though he must have been aware of it.[17]

The ever-closer relationship between Mary Stuart and her secretary, David Rizzio, began to make many of the powerful men around the Scottish queen uncomfortable. Her marriage to Henry Darnley went from bad to worse.

Darnley felt rejected by his wife, not only as a husband but also as a king. He felt disappointed that he had not been proclaimed King of Scotland with full rights and duties but only by honorific title.

Philip II, meanwhile, had written to his ambassador Guzmán de Silva, telling him "he should let the queen of Scotland know she should act with moderation [toward Rizzio] and avoid anything that could irritate the queen of England." This message fell into the hands of Elizabeth I thanks to an infiltrator in the Spanish ambassador's household who was loyal to Randolph, the English ambassador. In fact, Philip II did not understand Mary Stuart's temperament, which put the pope's spy in serious jeopardy. During an episode of pillow talk between Rizzio and Mary, the Italian had told the queen of his discovery that the English were paying Scottish rebels.[18]

The English ambassador, for his part, did not know that David Rizzio and his brother had discovered in early February 1566 that the escape of Scottish rebels who had risen against the queen the year before had been financed through Randolph. Thanks to the Italian spies, Mary had a lengthy report on the English diplomat's role in the Scottish unrest of the previous year. Armed with Rizzio's report, Mary Stuart summoned the English ambassador to her presence on February 20, 1566.

Even today, expelling an ambassador is no simple matter. It was all the less simple in the sixteenth century if one wanted to escape the consequences of such an act, and Mary Stuart did not give the consequences enough thought. On the day after ordering Randolph's expulsion, Mary sent Elizabeth I a letter absolving her of any responsibility, in spite of knowing that Elizabeth was the intellectual author of the operation and Randolph her executing arm. Even the nearly three thousand escudos used by Walsingham's men to bribe those who aided the escape of the Scottish rebels had come from the English queen's private coffers, but the Scottish sovereign always remembered the words of her Spanish counterpart about avoiding any action that could upset Elizabeth.[19] On February 21, 1566, Mary Stuart wrote Elizabeth I, in courtly French:

Lady, my good sister: In accord with the sincerity I always have practiced toward you, I believe I must write these words in which you shall be informed of the wrong actions and behavior of Randolph, your minister here. I have been told on good authority [by Rizzio and the Holy Alliance] that, in the most dangerous of the disturbances carried out by my rebels against me, the said Randolph supported them with the sum of three thousand escudos to win the favor of individuals and to strengthen my enemies' hands. As a consequence, I immediately removed this thorn from my side, calling Randolph before me and my council and demanding that he admit to whom he had conveyed this sum. I dare to hope that, he having been sent by you to lend us his good offices but having devoted himself to the contrary task, you will deem him unfit to be shielded by your authority. However I do not wish to deal with him more harshly than to return him to you with letters that will convey my accusation in greater detail.

On March 1, 1566, Ambassador Randolph departed Scotland with his retinue, but he left the blow against Pius V's spies almost fully prepared. One of his most valuable allies in this vengeance would be the queen's husband, Henry Darnley.

In his return voyage to London, Ambassador Randolph stopped in the city of Berwick to await orders from his queen. From there he sent a letter to Elizabeth:

A matter of no small consequence is about to take place in Scotland. Lord Darnley is furious with the queen, because she has denied him the crown matrimonial and he has assured knowledge of such usage of herself [her relationship with David Rizzio] as altogether is intolerable to be borne. . . . He [Darnley] has decided to free himself of the cause of this scandal [the agent of the Holy Alliance]. The execution and performance of these matters will take place before the session of Parliament, as near as it is.[20]

Darnley was no longer invited to the special sessions of the Council of State, he was denied use of the royal arms of Scotland, and he found himself reduced to a mere prince-consort. The contempt shown to Mary Stuart's husband came not only from the queen herself but also from her closest courtiers. David Rizzio, as her private secretary, no longer showed Darnley official documents. He wielded the so-called Iron Stamp (the royal signature) himself, without consulting Darnley. The English ambassador no longer addressed Darnley by the title of Your Majesty, and coins bearing the faces of Mary and her husband and the legend *Henricus et Maria* were recalled from circulation; they were replaced with new coins bearing the legend *Maria Regina Scotiae*. To all this were added the rumors about

Mary's relations with her secretary, now become *maître de plaisir,* or "pleasure master," to the queen.

Thanks to his ability to please Mary Stuart, the Holy Alliance's agent had taken on princely gestures and was arrogantly carrying out maximum duties of state, when only a few months before he had been eating with the servants and sleeping above the stables. The nobles, many of them Protestants, knew that Rizzio was only a pawn of Pope Pius V in his plan to make Scotland a Catholic nation within the great plan of Counter-Reformation being carried out by Rome.[21] Apparently Mary Stuart had agreed with Pius V to make Scotland the first country to abandon the Reformation and return to the great Catholic union.

The pontiff had given orders to his agents to protect Mary Stuart from any danger that could impede such an important step. The Scottish nobles, for their part, regarded David Rizzio as the secret orchestrator of that design. Ambassador Randolph had already let his sovereign know this when he wrote in his letter from Berwick, "Either God will give him [David Rizzio] a quick end or they [the Scottish nobles] will make his life unbearable."

In spite of their hatred for the Italian spy, the nobles did not want to confront their queen. They knew the harshness with which she had repressed the previous rebellion. Nor did they want to accompany Moray into the fate of an English exile. They reasoned that if they won the support of Henry Darnley, this would change the character of an assassination of Rizzio. Rather than being a simple crime of envy—and, as such, an act of rebellion against the queen—it would become a patriotic act in defense of the true faith (the Protestant one).

To lure Darnley to their cause, the conspirators would have recourse to something as simple as his jealousy of the Italian. They didn't know that Rizzio, on the pope's orders, had kept Mary from conceding the matrimonial crown and associated rights of rule to Darnley. Pius V wanted to avoid at all costs the possibility that, if something happened to the queen, Darnley as regent could change his mind about making Scotland a Catholic nation. But none of this bothered Darnley as much as the fact that his wife didn't let him touch her, while she allowed the spy of the Holy Alliance to spend long evenings with her in her room.

Mary Queen of Scots was now pregnant with the child who years later would become James VI of Scotland and James I of England. The conspirators had, for the first time in the history of Scotland, a king's permission to rebel against their sovereign. The conspiring nobles promised to seize power from Mary and give it to Darnley as the new Scottish king. For his part, he promised to grant them amnesty and to reward them with new lands once he assumed the throne. Walsingham's spies informed him that "the queen [Mary Stuart] repents her marriage to Henry Darnley, but some talk of awarding him the crown of Scotland whether the queen likes it or not. I know that if that thing should take effect which is intended, David [Rizzio], with the consent of the king, shall have his throat cut within these ten days."[22]

Darnley did not want the pope's spy dead for political reasons; he wanted him dead out of simple jealousy of the man who had made off with his wife's trust and his royal seal. Moray prepared for his return to Scotland once the coup had been carried out, and the fanatic John Knox had already written a sermon praising the death or, better put, execution of a miserable Catholic.[23]

It was March 9, 1566, in the afternoon, in Holyrood Castle. That very morning David Rizzio had received a warning from one of his spies, but he paid no attention. He knew he would be spending the whole day at the queen's side and so nothing could happen to him, because no one would dare raise a weapon or even a hand against him in Mary's presence. However, he was wrong.[24]

The day went by quickly. Mary Stuart was reading in the chamber attached to her bedroom, on the fourth floor of the tower. Henry Darnley invited Rizzio to play cards there. The Italian suspected nothing. Several nobles sat down around the table in the royal chamber, along with the queen's stepsister and, across from her, Rizzio, dressed in a damask gown. The conversation was pleasant, and music filled the small room. A miniature door in the rear, hidden by a curtain, opened to admit Darnley. The door had intentionally been left unlocked. The consort sat down next to his wife.

Seconds later, the curtain flew open again and the conspirators appeared in the room, swords and knives in hand. The first to enter with unsheathed sword and be recognized by the queen was Lord Patrick Ruthven.

The queen stood up, knocking over her chair, and chastised Ruthven for coming into her presence with his sword out of its scabbard. The Scottish noble told her not to fear, because his intrusion would affect only the Italian spy. Rizzio had gotten to his feet, but he was unarmed. Only the queen could protect him. Darnley stepped back to get away from the imminent fight. Mary Stuart stepped in front of Ruthven, whose eyes were fixed on Rizzio, and demanded that he relinquish his weapon. The Scot replied, "Ask your husband."

The queen turned to her husband, who was hidden behind a curtain. He managed to reply, between stammers, "I know nothing of the matter."

Now Ruthven was joined by more of the conspiring nobles, likewise with swords in hand, who had mounted the narrow spiral staircase leading to the queen's bedroom. Rizzio tried to escape, but the Scots grabbed his arm.

The rebels shouted to the queen that Rizzio was a spy of the pope and for this he deserved to die. Mary Stuart replied that if David Rizzio was to be charged, Parliament should do it. Ruthven held the Italian's arms while another conspirator bound him with a rope. As he was dragged away, he grabbed at the queen's dress, which ripped under the pressure of his terrified fingers.

Mary continued to protest. One of the rebels leveled a pistol at her. Ruthven brushed the pistol away with his hand so the shot passed above the queen's head and buried itself in the wall. Darnley held the queen, who was sinking toward the floor. The others dragged Rizzio's body down the narrow stairway, banging his head against the steps.

Once outside the royal presence, the conspirators pounced upon the Holy Alliance spy. The first thrust entered through his left side. The second pierced his right hand when he tried to cover his face and passed through into his neck. Bleeding, he tried to rise, but another thrust cut his jugular vein. A cry drowned in blood before it could exit from his mouth. Then Ruthven's well-aimed thrust pierced his heart. Rizzio was dead.[25]

Mary Stuart, still held by her husband, kept on shouting at the conspirators and her traitorous spouse. Darnley, his mouth to her ear, reproached her for having banished him from her bed in favor of Rizzio, while Ruthven returned to the room with his sword still dripping the Italian's blood. In a voice deep and low, Mary repeated over and over that the pair of them had signed their own death sentences. Her vengeance would be terrible.[26]

The cries and the sounds of swordplay attracted the attention of James Bothwell, head of the queen's guard, but he found the door locked. After a brief reconnaissance, Bothwell and his second-in-command, Huntley, leaped in through a window, swords in hand. Henry Darnley calmed them by saying what had happened was the killing of a spy sent by Pope Pius V, whose mission was to prepare a landing of Spanish troops in Scotland. Thus Rizzio's assassination both separated Mary Stuart from the Scottish crown and cut the direct line of communication between queen and pope.

A little more than three months later, on June 19, 1566, the new heir to the crown of Scotland was born. That Mary gave birth to James in the month of June means that he must have been conceived in September of 1565. That was the month of the Scottish rebellion, weeks after Mary Stuart had expelled Henry Darnley from her bed after having married him in July. David Rizzio appeared in the Scottish court in mid-September, which suggests the possibility that James VI was really the son of the Holy Alliance spy. Mary Stuart, very intelligently, pardoned Darnley, which allowed her to recover her crown and her freedom. But the Holy Alliance was not inclined to allow the murder of one of its members to pass without revenge.

The pope gave his agents an express order to identify the conspirator who had directed the murder of Rizzio, and Henry Darnley appeared at the top of their suspect list.[27]

There are various opinions as to who specifically ordered the reprisals against the killers of David Rizzio. Whoever it was, they did not realize that this would be one more step toward the fall of Mary Stuart as the Scottish queen.[28]

Elizabeth I of England had to bring a law of succession before Parliament, which would contain the name of her successor in the event of her death. Mary Stuart hoped to press her claim to the throne, but to win the title of heir, she had to avoid any error that would prejudice her case. The citizens of both Scotland and England tended more and more to see James as the prince of both nations, which displeased Elizabeth. Mary pondered how to break through the circle of enemies surrounding her and avenge the death of her loyal servant Rizzio.

Henry Darnley, her traitorous husband, knew that while Mary was pregnant he could not endanger the baby she carried in her womb. When all was said and done, this child would be the future monarch of Scotland and, with luck, of England as well. Therefore Darnley had ended the queen's enforced seclusion and allowed a doctor and two aides to attend to her. Mary had used one of the nurses to communicate with Bothwell and Huntley, her two trusted men. When Mary managed to win Darnley himself to her cause, the conspiracy weakened still more.

Forty-eight hours after the assassination, all was forgotten. The Holy Alliance spy had been buried in a secret location. Now was the time to plot revenge.

The first four targets were Ruthven, the noble who first seized hold of

Rizzio; Fawdonshide, who aimed and shot at the queen; John Knox, the radical preacher who labeled the queen a bastard; and finally Moray. All four were aware that there would never be a true pardon for them, and at the same time they recognized that the nobles would not lift a finger in their defense, because the child Mary was carrying would be the future ruler of a united kingdom of Scotland and England.

Pope Pius V was not disposed to permit the murder of one of his agents by four Protestants without revenge; the supreme authority of the pontiff required a response. The former head of the Inquisition summoned a priest named Lamberto Macchi.

This young man from Verona, son of an aristocratic family, had joined the priesthood at the age of only fourteen. He was a Jesuit, a member of the order founded by Ignatius of Loyola twenty-six years before. It had been created in 1540 as a rapid-strike force, a corps of soldiers ready to die for the faith and the pope, doing honor to the four Latin words that made up its slogan, *Ad Majorem Dei Gloriam,* "for the greater glory of God."[29]

Ignatius of Loyola had founded the order under three clear premises. The first was to be ready to answer the call of the pope at any time and any place. The Jesuits were, from the start, the "Pope's Men." Second, they were to be the pope's soldiers. Members of the order had to prepare themselves to be devout, but also to be soldiers of God. Jesuits would be hanged in the squares of London, disemboweled in Ethiopia, eaten alive by Iroquois in Canada, poisoned in Germany, whipped to death in the Holy Land, crucified in Siam, left to die of hunger in South America, beheaded in Japan, and drowned in Madagascar, but the spirit of adventure in the name of God was what made the young nobleman Lamberto Macchi join their ranks.

For Ignatius of Loyola, it was very important that his men possess a variety of skills. The founder and his pope needed intellectuals. They needed chemists, biologists, zoologists, linguists, explorers, professors, diplomats, confessors, philosophers, theologians, mathematicians, artists, writers, and architects. They also needed commanders, intelligence agents, spies, and special messengers. Macchi was an expert in these arts. The son of a rich merchant, he had learned swordsmanship while he studied philosophy. He had learned to use explosives while he studied theology. He had learned the art of assassination while he studied foreign languages.

The pope ordered the Jesuit Lamberto Macchi to travel to the court of Scotland with the mission of discovering and revealing Rizzio's assassins. Accompanied by three other Jesuits, Macchi knew what he was supposed to do once he had this list. For him, to snuff out the lives of four Protestants was more a religious issue than a personal one; the order, after all, came from the pope himself. In his bag he carried an *Informi Rosso* that gave him carte blanche for any action in defense of the faith. The name of this document dated from the time when the pope had been commissary-general of the Inquisition in Rome.

Macchi's contact in the Scottish court was none other than Lord Bothwell, head of Mary's personal guard, who now functioned as her advisor and a sort of regent, which displeased the British in general and Queen Elizabeth I of England above all.[30] Some nobles within the realm complained that Bothwell was more arrogant than the Italian David Rizzio, but the difference was that he knew who his enemies were—one of them being Darnley. Moray, on the other hand, was an ally, which placed him in open conflict with Darnley, who had begun to send accusatory letters to Queen Elizabeth in which he proclaimed that his wife, Mary Stuart, was unreliable in religion and that she was offering Scotland to Philip II, the protector of Catholicism.

Toward the end of September, Darnley made the fateful decision to leave Scotland, since the position of king had been denied him. This placed Mary Stuart in a difficult situation. Henry Darnley could not leave Scotland before the heir was baptized in Stirling Castle, especially given the continual rumors about the real paternity of Prince James. He had also not yet decided where to take refuge—in England under the protection of Elizabeth I or in France under that of Catherine de' Medici. As a counterstroke, Mary Stuart sent a diplomatic letter to Catherine in which she accused her husband of possible treason.

While this was going on, the Holy Alliance agent Lamberto Macchi and his three comrades had arrived in Edinburgh, under the roof of one of Bothwell's men, while they waited for a chance to act. Shortly before the end of 1566, Mary Stuart, as advised by both Moray and Bothwell, signed the pardon of the conspirators who had killed Rizzio, but this made no difference to Macchi. The Jesuit had an express order from the pope, and he had to carry it out without discussion or doubt. For Lamberto Macchi, a papal order was a religious truth.

As one of the instigators, Moray was in Macchi's sights. Darnley knew that, in spite of the public proclamation of the royal pardon, he himself would be a prime target of the avengers, so he fled and took refuge in his father's castle in Glasgow.[31]

All Bothwell had to do was put the conspirators within reach of the pope's agents, and they would take charge of the executions. Yet he also knew that he alone would be responsible before God, his queen, and the people of Scotland—a risk and responsibility he was willing to assume.

On January 22, 1567, Henry Darnley fell gravely ill with syphilis, but he remained hidden in Glasgow under the protection of his father, the Earl of Lennox. Meanwhile Mary Stuart, still convalescent, went in search of her husband to get him to return to Edinburgh under her personal escort. Even so, Darnley knew he could be attacked at any moment by Bothwell's followers, by the pope's agents, or by his former coconspirators whom he had left in the lurch and who now were back in Scotland thanks to the royal pardon.[32] Yet Darnley did not know that his return to Edinburgh would be the road to his death. He would not leave the Scottish capital alive.

If the avengers of the Holy Alliance wanted to get all the conspirators who had acted against David Rizzio, they had to do away with the husband of Mary Stuart. Their chosen locale was nothing less than Darnley's own temporary dwelling place, an isolated building of typical Elizabethan construction in the neighborhood of Kirk O'Field, accessible by a dark, narrow road known as "Thieves' Row."[33]

The interior of the house was decorated with an attractive open hallway, ornamented fireplaces, exquisite tapestries, elegant silver tableware bearing the royal seal of Scotland, Persian rugs, and a comfortable bed that Mary Stuart's mother, Mary of Guise, had brought with her from France.[34] Lamberto Macchi and his men were not able to get too close to Darnley, so they had to attack with explosives. The time they chose for this, their first act of vengeance, was the night of Sunday, February 9, and the morning of Monday, February 10, of 1567.

That night the queen gave a grand ball and banquet in honor of the marriage of two of her most faithful servants. Lord Darnley and his retainers were, of course, invited. This gave the Holy Alliance agents time to prepare their attack while the house in Kirk O'Field remained unguarded.[35]

Moray, meanwhile, had mysteriously disappeared from Edinburgh, and Bothwell was nowhere to be found—a fact noted not only by the nobility attending the queen's festivities but also by Darnley, still debilitated by his disease. By 11 P.M., Darnley was worn out and ready to retire, but the queen would not allow him to spend the night in the royal residence of Holyrood. So he set out for his cold mansion in Kirk O'Field.

The executioners of the Holy Alliance, aided by Bothwell, had placed a massive charge of gunpowder in the structural pillars of the house.

At about two in the morning, the Scottish earth trembled. The shock wave could be felt even through the thick walls of the queen's residence. Suddenly the door to Mary Stuart's bedroom burst open, and a servant showing the effects of great exertion informed her that the king's residence in Kirk O'Field had been blown up.[36]

Escorted by armed guards, Mary led a party that quickly arrived at the place where a few hours earlier a lordly mansion had stood flanked by green fields. Now they found only a large crater surrounded by burned and blackened earth. The scattered bodies of Henry Darnley's servants appeared hundreds of yards from the site of the explosion. The king's corpse lay in a creek a few yards away, along with that of a servant and the twisted remnants of his bed, various shards of which were embedded in his flesh. The wounds that the explosion had inflicted on the body of the king-consort of Scotland did not allow its finders to see the marks left by the slim cord with which he had been strangled.

The type of knot used to kill Darnley and his servant was the same one used by the members of a sect in the mountains of Alborz, to the northeast of Tehran and the northwest of Qazvin, called *ashishin*. The explorer Marco Polo had visited the castle of Alamut, headquarters of these *ashishin*,[37] in 1273. In one of his travel diaries he recorded their secrets, their systems, and methods of assassination, including more than thirty-two forms of strangulation.[38] Part of this text was recovered by the Jesuit Matteo Ricci during one of his travels to that part of the world, retracing the steps of the Venetian.[39]

As soon as they had lit the fuses, the four Holy Alliance agents, including Joseph Rizzio, David's brother, left Edinburgh on horseback. The explosion did not even make them turn their heads. Lamberto Macchi knew the result perfectly well. Part one of the revenge had been completed. The supreme pontiff in Rome was so informed.

May 15, 1567, still in mourning, Mary Stuart married Bothwell, whom everyone regarded as the mastermind of Henry Darnley's assassination. On June 6, a group of lords rebelled in the face of Bothwell's possible coronation as King of Scotland. Nine days later, after an inconclusive skirmish at Carberry Hill, Bothwell took flight and Mary Stuart was taken prisoner.[40]

Through a series of events, the relations between Elizabeth I and Philip II went from bad to worse. A report from Pius V, received in Madrid, did nothing to improve them. The report told the powerful Spanish king of the English crown's implication in the recent events in Scotland that led to the ousting of the Catholic Mary Stuart.[41] The year 1568 proved to be the *annus horribilis* of Philip's reign, and the actions of the Holy Alliance did not help. For the great protector of Christianity, that whole affair was really an "English tangle." Still, the Protestant Elizabeth of England was not going to lift a finger against the Catholic Mary Stuart while Spanish armies under the command of the Duke of Alba were in Brussels, so nearby. Thus Philip II displayed his military power.

Meanwhile, Lamberto Macchi and his men had their search for the remaining conspirators firmly in mind. Macchi still carried the red-velvet-wrapped papal document that detailed their mission and conferred the pope's protection. The parchment was to be destroyed once the vengeance was completed or returned to the pope if it were not. The priest's next targets were Lord Patrick Ruthven; Lord Fawdonshide, who had aimed a pistol at the queen; the queen's able if skittish stepbrother Lord Moray; and the radical preacher John Knox.

Fawdonshide was the next to fall. This time Lamberto Macchi and his three followers did not have far to look. Though brave enough to raise his weapon against the queen, Fawdonshide was found hiding in a small house on the outskirts of Lochleven, where he awaited his death in comfort. Putting up no resistance, he was led to a nearby tree and hanged by the neck.[42] The Scottish nobleman was still kicking at the end of the rope when the four horsemen of the Holy Alliance set off in search of their next victim. In the *Informi Rosso,* Fawdonshide's name was crossed out with red blood.

Moray fell next, on January 11, 1570, the victim of a sword thrust through his neck. Macchi wet his finger in the Scotsman's blood and crossed off his name on the parchment, but the avenging of David Rizzio was not over yet. John Knox and Patrick Ruthven remained alive. The *Informi Rosso,* which had been given to Lamberto Macchi in Rome, crowned with a papal seal, could not yet be destroyed.

More than a month later, on February 25, Pius V published the bull *Regnans in Excelsis,* which announced the excommunication of the heretic Elizabeth I of England.[43] Such a sentence was an extremely serious measure in sixteenth-century Europe, and it affected the English people more than it did their sovereign. English Catholics found themselves caught between the loyalty they owed their queen and that which they owed their faith and, therefore, the pontiff of Rome. The English Protestants, on the other hand, had been given a tool to label the pope the "Roman Antichrist."[44] What most worried Elizabeth was not the content of the document as such, but the fact that behind the papal signature probably lay the hand of Philip II of Spain or that of Charles IX of France. However, the Spanish monarch sent a letter to his ambassador in London, Guerau de Spes, in which he showed his surprise:

> His Holiness has promulgated a bull without consulting me or informing me at all. I would, surely, have been able to give him better advice. I fear that all this, far from improving the situation of English Catholics, will lead the queen and her councilors to intensify their persecution.

For the Spanish king, Pius V's bull constituted a grave act of interference in European political affairs. Philip II himself knew that the years when a pope (Gregory VII) could oblige an emperor to humble himself before him, or in which a pope (Urban IV) could award the kingdom of Sicily to a prince, were long since over. The Spanish monarch had no doubt Pius V had mistaken the century in which he lived.

The consequences of the bull would be the martyrdom of thousands of English Catholics and the end of any possible détente between London and Rome. In the short term, the main victim of this declaration would not be Elizabeth I of England but Catholicism itself. The crowned heads of Europe knew this, but Pius V, the inquisitor-monk and creator of the papal espionage service, was not inclined to retreat, even if he had to use the Holy Alliance's assassins in defense of the faith. Dark years lay ahead.

2

DARK YEARS (1570–1587)

Maintain good conduct among the Gentiles, so that if they speak of you as evildoers, your good works may silence the ignorance of foolish men.

—I Peter 2:12 and 2:15

For the great Catholic powers France and Spain and their crowned heads of state, two policy alternatives remained after the excommunication of Elizabeth I. The first was to help the English Catholics get rid of their heretic sovereign however this might be done and, as part and parcel of this approach, replace her with the Catholic Mary Stuart. The second was to look the other way and keep up good diplomatic relations with the London court.

France was on the brink of civil war, with strong Huguenot pressures coming to bear on its own ruler.[1] Therefore the Scottish queen had no choice but to look toward Spain as her only ally and the only possible way out of her situation. In her messages to Pope Pius V and Philip II, Mary Stuart presented herself as the most fervent of Catholics; in her messages to Elizabeth I, as a moderate Protestant; and to Charles IX, as a friend in need.

Pope Pius V needed someone to manage his conspiracy against the heretic Elizabeth, and for this task he chose Roberto Ridolfi. For years, this Florentine banker and Holy Alliance agent had been involved in the intrigues swirling around both the English and the Scottish queens. Short and fat, a good talker, cultured and with important relationships on both sides of the

English Channel, Ridolfi was quite good friends with Guerau de Spes, with whom he shared the need to offer political and economic support to a possible Catholic party in England.[2] Both the agent of the Holy Alliance and the Spanish diplomat were much devoted to secret and coded correspondence, meetings in dark and lonely spots, and other such endeavors.[3]

The plan designed by Roberto Ridolfi and approved by Pius V consisted of organizing a rebellion against Elizabeth in the English interior, supported by a large landing of Spanish troops at several points along the coast. These troops would converge on London and free Mary Stuart with the aid of Holy Alliance agents and men loyal to her, all for the purpose of putting her on the throne of England in place of the Tudor heretic.

Philip II knew that the moment to attempt this design had come, although not in the best of eras. Spain had not yet fully suppressed the Morisco rebellion in Granada and was in the midst of negotiations to cement the Holy League that would fight the Turks in the Mediterranean, where they had lately fortified the island of Cyprus. Perhaps the Spanish king believed the rumors out of London that spoke of an aristocratic conspiracy against Elizabeth.[4] The lords of Norfolk, Westmoreland, Arundel, and Northumberland all had motives to end her reign.

The Duke of Norfolk, the most determined of the four to carry out some type of action to get rid of the English sovereign, had just been released from the Tower of London. Although Norfolk was closely watched, the Florentine Holy Alliance spy and the Spanish ambassador saw him as the best choice to direct the great conspiracy. He had shown great interest in Mary Stuart, and he had let Ridolfi know that he thought it indeed possible that she could assume the English throne. If the Catholic powers, including Pius V, would support his marriage to Mary, Norfolk would convince her to reinstate the Catholic religion throughout the country, within the general scheme of the Counter-Reformation.[5]

Before embarking on this enterprise, Philip II consulted with the Duke of Alba, on January 21, 1570. The brilliant Spanish general saw the "English adventure" across the Channel as a great mistake. But even so, he wrote to the king:

And to reply to what Your Majesty asks me in this dispatch, I say there are three ways to invade the kingdom of England: The first, allying Your

Majesty with the king of France. The second, undertaking the enterprise alone. The third, if some powerful subjects in Scotland or England could secretly foment rebellion, and so open the way.[6]

Ridolfi had already created an authentic network of spies, which reached from Edinburgh to London and from Glasgow to the Netherlands. The papal spy's first contact with the Duke of Norfolk developed toward late November or early December of 1570. The Florentine wanted a firm commitment that once Mary Stuart was enthroned and Norfolk married to her, he would convert to Catholicism and order all the citizens of his realm to do the same.[7] Pius V wanted a commitment from Norfolk before giving his blessing to the whole operation, and he wanted it in writing.

This written commitment made Norfolk a prisoner of the pope of Rome, and likewise of his Holy Alliance agents. If Norfolk signed, he was joined body and soul to the plot against Elizabeth. He knew he would be wagering his head.

Norfolk's first step would be to serve as intermediary in the transmission of large sums of money to Mary Stuart's followers, who were holed up in Dumbarton Castle. Ridolfi managed all his pieces as if he were playing a game of chess. He sent letters to the Duke of Alba, Philip II, the bishop of Ross, and Pope Pius V. He made a secret swing through the Netherlands, Italy, and Spain, accompanied by several agents of the Holy Alliance, including Lamberto Macchi, Darnley's "executioner."

The military plan involved landing some six to ten thousand men who would come from the Netherlands, part of the host of troops under Alba's command. Ambassador Spes considered the plan a masterwork, but the duke, much more expert in military matters, saw things differently. To him, Roberto Ridolfi was an Italian too fond of talk. In spite of a warning letter the powerful general sent to his king, Philip II decided to take the Holy Alliance agent's communications very seriously.[8] The monarch even put a possible assassination of Elizabeth of England before his council. With that decision, this sixteenth-century ruler gave what in the twenty-first would be called an "executive order."

The problem was that in those times it was an extremely complex task to make all the gears of such a piece of machinery mesh perfectly, due in part to the distances separating the plotters and the slowness of their communications. After a time, Elizabeth's secret services began to spot the first telltale threads of the so-called Ridolfi Plot. The first warning sign came to Elizabeth in the month of

May, when the Grand Duke of Tuscany, a Protestant, told London of a "possible" conspiracy against her, organized by a famous Florentine agent of the Holy Alliance by the name of Roberto Ridolfi.[9] Later, several English agents discovered a small chest containing six hundred pounds sterling that had been sent by the Duke of Norfolk to Mary Stewart.[10] On April 11, a Holy Alliance agent had been detained in Dover with letters in code, while in Scotland documents that implicated the plotters were confiscated after the fall of Dumbarton.

The Queen of Navarre, Jeanne d'Albret, confiscated still other letters and reports from a messenger sent by the Duke of Alba. D'Albret lived in France under the protection of the French crown, and these documents were sent on to Elizabeth. By August 1571, the English spy apparatus had the names of all the plotters as well as the functions to be performed by each. The network was nearly complete.

Curiously, in April of that same year, the English queen had taken a step in the direction of granting some freedom of religion, or at least she had tried to do so. She had convoked Parliament to discuss the revolutionary idea of "religious freedom, loyalty to the queen above all." The document presented to Parliament said:

> Her Majesty would have all her loving subjects to understand that as long as they shall openly continue in the observation of her laws and shall not willfully and manifestly break them by open acts, her Majesty's meaning is not to have any of them molested by any inquisition or examination of their consciences in causes of religion. Her Majesty is very loathe to alter her natural clemency.[11]

But for a final decision she needed approval by the clearly anti-Catholic Parliament. The document forwarded by the chamber made its position quite clear to the sovereign:

> This liberty, that men may openly profess diversity of religion, must needs be dangerous to the Commonwealth. One God, one king, one faith, one profession, is fit for one Monarchy and Commonwealth. Division weakens, concord strengthens.

Elizabeth made her dissatisfaction with that answer clear, but the issue was settled and the queen's hands were tied.

The discovery of the Ridolfi Plot and the Holy Alliance's maneuvers to get rid of Elizabeth I put Mary Stuart in the gravest danger. The conspirators' goose was finally cooked by the pirate John Hawkins.[12] This privateer had convinced Roberto Ridolfi that he would be willing to fight for Philip II and Mary Stuart as the commander of an English Catholic fleet. To Ridolfi, that offered an ideal form of propaganda for the idea that a homegrown rebellion against Elizabeth was emerging inside England. What Ridolfi didn't know was that Hawkins, in fact, was working for the English spy service under the command of William Cecil (Lord Burghley), the queen's favorite.

Elizabeth I of England could read John Hawkins's report:

The pretence is that my power should join with the duke of Alba's power which he doth shortly provide in Flanders as well as with the power which cometh with the duke of Medina out of Spain, and so all together to invade this realm and set up the Queen of Scots . . . but God, I hope, will confound them and turn their devices upon their own necks. Signed: from Plymouth the 4th day of September, 1571, your good lordship's most faithfully in my power, John Hawkyns.[13]

On September 7, the Duke of Norfolk was arrested. On the 9th, the bishop of Ross followed, and the next day, Mary Stuart herself was imprisoned in a dismal chamber of Sheffield Castle.

Confined in the Tower of London, Norfolk continued to deny any part in the Ridolfi Plot and even to deny authorship of letters to the papal spy in his own hand. Because the queen personally prohibited any torture of Norfolk, the interrogators concentrated on the bishop of Ross instead.[14]

The bishop, between tortures, cried out that his tormentors had no right to touch the ambassador of a foreign country (Scotland). But to the English, the bishop was merely a plotting priest who represented the interests of his now-dethroned queen, Mary Stuart, and as such had no diplomatic immunity. With his fingernails pulled out, his flesh swollen by torture, and his feet seared by fire, the bishop confessed that the Scottish queen had poisoned her first husband (King Francis II of France), allowed the murder of her second husband (Lord Henry Darnley), married the instigator of that plot (Lord Bothwell), and finally tried to contract marriage with a traitor (the Duke of Norfolk).

When Mary Stuart was told the content of Ross's statement *motu proprio,* she declared that "the bishop is nothing but a terrified and tortured cleric. I have the valor of a queen and trust that my friends in Spain and France will come to free me." Philip II, who did not have much confidence that Ridolfi's plan would work, and the Duke of Alba, who had even less, decided to abandon her and the rest of the conspirators to their fates. The only measure taken by the English against Spain was the expulsion in December 1571 of Spanish ambassador Guerau de Spes. For their parts, Norfolk, Arundel, Southampton, Cobham, and Lumley were locked up in the Tower of London while awaiting trial. On January 16, 1572, the House of Lords sentenced Norfolk to death, a judgment that required Elizabeth's ratification. Norfolk's father, the third Duke of Norfolk, had been beheaded by her father, King Henry VIII, and now she had to sign the death sentence of his son, the fourth duke.[15]

Months went by without the queen signing the execution order. On May 8, 1572, Parliament met again, with only a single item on its agenda: the execution of the Duke of Norfolk. Elizabeth received their message and finally, on June 1, ordered that the document be brought to her. She signed it "Elizabeth R," and then the Lord Keeper of the Great Seal dripped a gob of wax alongside, to which he applied the royal seal.[16]

On the morning of June 2, Norfolk was escorted to the main courtyard of the Tower. Still on his feet, he swore loyalty to his sovereign, Queen Elizabeth, and fidelity to the true Protestant religion of the land. Then he handed a silver coin to the executioner, who accepted it in his glove. Norfolk knelt with his hands behind him, and a single blow of the axe separated his head from his body. Roberto Ridolfi, for his part, managed to flee from England on board a ship that had anchored in a secluded harbor for the purpose of transporting him to France should the plot go wrong.[17]

Only two weeks earlier, after the death of the conspiratorial Pius V on May 1, 1572, the College of Cardinals had chosen a new pope: Cardinal Hugo Boncompagni, who received key support from Philip II.[18] Boncompagni was the son of a wealthy family in Bologna, where he had studied law. After a period as a university professor, he was called to Rome by Cardinal Parisio, under whose aegis he began his career in the Roman curia. In spite of his legal background and reserved nature, he was not immune to the lifestyle of Renaissance Rome.

Pope Pius IV (December 25, 1559–September 12, 1565) then sent Bon-compagni as papal legate to the court of Madrid. There he established close relations with the Spanish monarch, until he was again called to Rome upon the death of Pius IV and the ascension of Pius V to the Throne of St. Peter, this time to take charge of the Secretariat of Papal Briefs (documents and cor-respondence less weighty than bulls).

After the death of Pius V, thanks to Philip II's unconditional support, Hugo Boncompagni was elected pope on May 13, 1572, in a conclave that took less than twenty-four hours. He took the name Gregory XIII in honor of St. Gregory the Great, on whose feast day he had been named cardinal.[19]

The new pope reformed the Trinitarians of Spain and Portugal, confirmed the reform of the Barefoot Carmelites begun by St. Teresa de Ávila, and ap-proved the founding of the congregation of the Oratorio di San Filippo Neri. He also, however, would—with the Jesuits' help—organize the first task force of the Holy Alliance, the papal espionage service founded by his prede-cessor. This force consisted of a small detail of shock troops selected by the Society of Jesus and loyal to papal authority, whose sole objective was assassi-nating Queen Elizabeth, head of the English Protestant Church.

The efforts to overthrow Elizabeth with the aid of Philip II and Irish Catholics were abandoned after the failures of two invasion attempts and an internal conspiracy, but the Holy Alliance would not retreat in its campaign to be rid of the heretic queen.

The results of the Ridolfi Plot, the papal excommunication, and the northern rebellion had broken the unity of English citizens behind their queen. Elizabeth I knew that only a union with France would end Philip II's attempts at military intervention in England. More and more, Charles IX had granted religious liberties to the Protestants, and civil peace with the Huguenots grew to be established policy after the 1570 edict of Saint-Germain-en-Laye, which upset Madrid. Charles IX knew that if he were to marry Elizabeth, the two of them could confront any Spanish attempt at in-tervention and, therefore, any action mounted by Pope Gregory XIII.

Even the Huguenots thought about a possible English-French alliance that could fight against the Duke of Alba in the Netherlands. Egged on by his loyal favorite Gaspar de Coligny, Charles IX took a conciliatory tack toward Elizabeth I, signing the Treaty of Blois on April 29, 1572, in which, at Eliza-beth's insistence, there was no mention of freeing Mary Stuart or of restoring her to the throne of Scotland or even of her name. For years, the issue of Mary

Stuart had soured relations between London and Paris.[20] Now it was time for the political plots and betrayals to play out on new stages, and the same was true for the actions of the pope and his Holy Alliance agents. New situations called for new spies.

While negotiating the English-French treaty, Elizabeth had not stopped keeping her eye on Spain, especially after the expulsion of its ambassador Guerau de Spes for his participation in the Ridolfi Plot. The Spanish crown's affairs in London now rested in the hands of a secretary without diplomatic powers, Antonio de Guaras. At the end of 1572, he had been recruited by the papal espionage service to inform on any action by Elizabeth until the Holy Alliance could infiltrate other agents into the queen's circle. After the Ridolfi Plot, the English secret services had captured and executed a dozen papal agents, but the Jesuit Lamberto Macchi was still active—and now in London.

Elizabeth's first action with respect to Philip II was to expel Dutch privateers from the English ports where they had found shelter and supplies since 1566. This fleet of corsairs, known as the "Sea Beggars," originated from Flemish-Dutch merchant ships that had taken to the sea to escape from Alba's forces and to capture valuable war booty by attacking Spanish ships. Their crews were made up of English and Scottish privateers, Irishmen loyal to Elizabeth, and even French Huguenots. They all carried letters of marque issued by William of Orange in his position as sovereign prince of Orange in Provence.[21] Letters of marque were documents by means of which a belligerent power conceded to private sailors the right to attack and board any ship belonging to an enemy power.

By expelling the pesky Dutchmen, Elizabeth achieved two objectives: to please the Spaniards and to finally eliminate the smuggling trade carried out by the Sea Beggars. But the order provoked an unexpected result. The Holy Alliance reported that William de La Marck, the Sea Beggars' commander, desperately needed a supply port. If he couldn't find one in England or France, he would need to attack Spanish forces in the Netherlands to get one. Rome then gave instructions to its agents to warn Alba's men ensconced in some of the English coastal cities about any movement by warships.

In fact, on April 1, 1572, the Sea Beggars occupied the port and city of Brielle, on the Dutch island of Voorne by the mouth of the Maas River. The Holy Alliance reported that La Marck's privateers would not remain there. A few days later, the ships weighed anchor and occupied the fortified city of

Flushing on Walcheren island, from which they controlled the mouth of Scheldt. There they raised the flag of William of Orange.[22]

The Holy Alliance agents reported to Alba that a wave of joy swept through Protestant England, where talk of the possible fall of the Spanish regime in the Netherlands had begun. This wave provoked the enlistment of thousands of English soldiers and French Huguenots in volunteer units that joined La Marck's privateers in Flushing. The wave ran on, raising the populaces of Flanders, Holland, Zeeland, Guelders, and Frisia against the Spanish authorities. The brilliant spy Lamberto Macchi had reported from London that William of Orange and Louis of Nassau were sending Elizabeth continued entreaties for England to lead the Netherlands' independence movement under the Protestant banner. Macchi wrote the pope:

> Elizabeth has only two options: to remain neutral or to intervene in an open war against Spain on the Continent. She knows this is a very great risk. If the duke of Alba succeeds in recovering control of the rebellious cities, his armies will not stop there and will continue their advance toward London with the blessing of King Philip. Elizabeth cannot put herself in such danger. Nor does it interest her to do away with Spanish power on the other side of the Channel and let William of Orange become such a powerful neighbor.

The Holy Alliance spy knew that although Leicester and Walsingham (now ambassador to Paris) were in favor of intervention, Cecil's opinion in favor of a wait-and-see policy carried more weight at court.[23]

Gaspar de Coligny advised the French king to lead both Protestants and Catholics in a war against Spain as a way to unite his realm and to name the Duke of Anjou viceroy of the Netherlands. That image of greatness appealed to Charles. Until early June, it was believed throughout Europe that a great change in alliances was in the making and that Protestantism would end Catholic Spain's power over the Continent. Nearly fifteen hundred English volunteers had fought alongside the Sea Beggars in the capture of Bruges. This deed put Elizabeth I in dire straits with Philip II.

These first victories that bathed the defenders of the Reformation with glory, however, soon turned to terrible defeats followed by massacres carried out by the defenders of the Counter-Reformation. In mid-June, William of Orange was repulsed by the Spanish armies and pushed back toward Germany with enormous losses. The city of Mons surrendered without knowing that the Huguenot troops coming to its relief from France had been wiped out at Quievrain. This expedition had been commanded by General De Genlis, a relative of Charles IX's advisor Coligny. At Quievrain, Alba had ordered his troops to take no prisoners.

William of Orange became the Holy Alliance's new target. With Philip II's blessing, Gregory XIII ordered him eliminated. The French Huguenots, meanwhile, became the new victims of the Protestant defeat in the Netherlands. To avoid Spanish retaliation, Charles IX had planned to wed François, Duke of Alençon, to Elizabeth. He knew that if he succeeded, Philip II would not dare to jeopardize the fragile stability of Spanish-English relations by attacking France. François was willing to embrace the Protestant faith if that would bring him closer to Elizabeth, and to that end he sent his ambassador Boniface de la Mole to London. Neither the ambassador nor Elizabeth knew that massacres of Protestants in Paris were under way.

Since the first week of August, Charles IX had been maneuvering between two fires. His advisor Coligny continued to urge open war against Philip II. On the other hand, the king was getting opposite pressures from his mother, Catherine de' Medici, his brother Henry of Anjou, the Spanish ambassador Zuñiga, and Pope Gregory XIII's representative in court. Prince Henry, heir to the throne of France and a fervent Catholic, knew that to neutralize his brother's yen to attack Philip II, he had to get rid of Coligny. The heir realized that he had to avoiding bloodying his own hands, so he made the proposition instead to a man sent by the papal nuncio. Apparently, this man was an agent of the Holy Alliance. On the night of August 22, Coligny was riding through the streets of Paris in an open carriage when two closed carriages blocked his way at an intersection. Four men jumped out and tried to skewer the royal counselor with their swords, but a rapid intervention by his guards put them to flight. Gaspar de Coligny suffered wounds in the face and his right arm. It was now clear that someone very close to the king wanted him dead.

Both Prince Henry and Catherine de' Medici knew that Coligny could inflame the Huguenots throughout the country to rise against the king, so they convinced him to mobilize militias throughout Paris. On the night of August 23 and on into August 24, St. Bartholomew's Day, a true bloodbath engulfed the capital. Between five thousand and twenty thousand Huguenots, depending on one's source, were killed in Paris in only two days.[24] The militia had free rein. They invaded the Huguenots' homes, murdered men, raped women, and sliced children's throats. Afterwards, the corpses were thrown into enormous bonfires.[25]

Admiral Gaspar de Coligny fell that same week. After the assassination attempt, he had retreated to his family castle of Chatillon, knowing that he could be killed at any moment if he couldn't make contact with William of Orange. On the night of August 26, three men with daggers made their way into his room and killed him with nine blows. Legend has it Coligny was executed by men of the Holy Alliance, though legend is all this is.

In Protestant capitals, public opinion saw what was henceforth termed the St. Bartholomew's Day Massacre as the result of a plot by Philip II, Catherine de' Medici, the Duke of Alba, and Pope Gregory XIII. What is sure is that for months the Holy Alliance spies had been bombarding Rome with messages about the possible repercussions of the Parisian violence, including the possibility of a massacre of Protestants. Rome did not pass on these warnings to anyone; after all, everyone who died that day—the aged, women, and children included—was a heretic.

Walsingham, the English ambassador, now sent back unequivocal reports: "I do not see how this tragedy can but shock the entire kingdom." Royal guards dispatched by Charles IX from his palace had protected the diplomat from the militias. This protection had in turn allowed him to shelter Englishmen such as Walter Raleigh, who happened to be in Paris on that bloody day. To mitigate the effect of the massacre, Catherine de' Medici herself concocted a version that the king went on to defend before his parliament in Paris and that the agents of the Holy Alliance would spread throughout Europe: "Gaspar de Coligny had contrived a plan to kill the king, his brothers, and the royal family. The government had been informed just in time [presumably by papal spies] thanks to divine mercy, and by order of the king the admiral [Coligny] and his accomplices had been executed to avoid a bloody coup d'etat." So ended discussion of the deaths of thousands of people.

Mary Stuart continued to be the Queen of Scotland, but her support dwindled more and more. Her involvement in the Ridolfi Plot had left her in a difficult position vis-à-vis Elizabeth. France, for its part, was now not so inclined to aid her, because of the projected détente between Paris and London. Even Charles IX's wife, Anne of Austria, had named Queen Elizabeth as godmother of the daughter she had just borne. More and more, the boy prince James of Scotland was recognized as a rightful king.

From London, Macchi informed Gregory XIII that the English were devising a plan against Catholic Scotland. Elizabeth had sent Henry Killigrew to Edinburgh with specific instructions:

> It is evident that the presence of the Queen of Scotland is so dangerous to His Majesty [James] and to the kingdom that it has become necessary to be free of her. Although justice could accomplish this here, for various reasons it appears preferable, nonetheless, to send her to Scotland and there place her in the hands of the regent [Morton] to there face judicial proceedings in such a way that no one may any more be placed in danger by her.[26]

This text clearly demonstrates Elizabeth's interest in sending Mary Stuart to her death. But Morton explained to the emissary from London that if they really wanted to aid Scotland, all they had to do was help get rid of a Catholic thorn embedded in Protestant Scotland: Edinburgh Castle, still in the hands of Mary's supporters. For the English, to recognize James VI as king was one thing, but to intervene openly in Scotland was another.

Charles IX was busy in La Rochelle, and Philip II in the battle for the Netherlands, so Elizabeth was sure that neither of the two would come to Mary's aid. Finally, on April 17, 1573, an English army crossed the Scottish border. Lamberto Macchi had sent an urgent message to Rome reporting that a great number of men and artillery were massing there. His report reached Rome on April 28, already too late. On the morning of May 17, bombardment of Edinburgh Castle began. Twelve days later, the besieged forces surrendered.

The next ten years were an unsettled period throughout Europe, still under the effects of the Ridolfi Plot, the St. Bartholomew's Day Massacre, and the English assault in Edinburgh. France, Spain, and Rome all continued the policies of the past. Four rulers—Elizabeth I in England, Philip II in Spain, Gregory XIII in Rome, and Henry III (who became King of France after his brother Charles's death in 1574)—guided the politics of the end of the sixteenth century and the beginning of the seventeenth.

At the end of 1573, Philip replaced the Duke of Alba with Luis de Requesens as governor and commander in the Netherlands, but Requesens died in 1576 after two years in power. The monarch then sent Don Juan of Austria until his death in 1578, when he was succeeded by his trusted advisor and second-in-command Alessandro Farnese, Duke of Parma.

From their base in Flushing, the Sea Beggars loyal to William of Orange continued punishing the fleets that sailed through the English Channel. Elizabeth by now had threatened William that if the Beggars continued boarding English vessels, she would have to ally herself with Spain to punish them. In 1578, because of the pressures applied by the Spanish armies, William of Orange offered the crown of the liberated areas of Netherlands to Elizabeth, but she knew that her acceptance would put the fragile alliance between London and Spain in danger.[27]

On the other hand, the death of Ignatius of Loyola on July 31, 1556, had left the Society of Jesus without strong leadership for its nearly five thousand members spread throughout the world. In 1581, a thirty-seven-year-old Italian, Claudio Acquaviva, was chosen as superior-general of the order. This marked the beginning of the so-called golden age of the Jesuits. Acquaviva and Gregory XIII formed one of the best partnerships in the entire history of the Catholic Church.[28]

For some time, the Jesuits had understood how Catholic Ireland occupied a strategic place in any serious attempt to reconquer Protestant England by military means. The pope was convinced that support for James Fitzmaurice, the nephew of the Earl of Desmond, could advance the Catholic cause in the British Isles. The Jesuits' idea was to organize a military expedition to Munster, whence Fitzmaurice believed he could lead a rebellion against Elizabeth.

To carry out this plan, the Jesuits and the agents of the Holy Alliance chose Thomas Stukeley, a ruffian, former pirate, and self-proclaimed illegitimate son of Henry VIII. Stukeley, who was well known to the English spy apparatus, had become a super-defender of Catholicism and installed himself in Madrid, where Philip II had named him "marquis of Ireland." Always on the lookout for adventures and honors, before leaving for Ireland, Stukeley decided to join King Sebastian of Portugal in a foolish crusade against the infidels of Morocco. On August 4, 1578, his head was separated from his body in the battle of Alcazarquivir. The Holy Alliance needed a new leader for the Irish rebellion.

Fitzmaurice once again would be at the top of the venture. Gregory XIII was willing to finance and bless the operation, but he determined that a member of the Holy Alliance should accompany Fitzmaurice. This time the choice fell upon an English priest named Nicholas Sanders, who had become famous during Elizabeth's reign for his pamphlets condemning the Anglican heresy.[29]

On June 27, 1579, James Fitzmaurice and Nicholas Sanders set sail for Ireland from El Ferrol under the papal flag. Their troops and crew consisted of fifty men, mostly Italians and Spaniards. On July 17, they landed on the Smerwick peninsula, where they made camp while awaiting reinforcements from Spain. The operation very soon began to take losses. A shot fired by English troops felled James Fitzmaurice. The Earl of Desmond, who had returned to Ireland after serving a prison term in the Tower of London, replaced him. Within a few weeks, all of Munster was in open rebellion against the English.

Meanwhile Nicholas Sanders was touring all the churches in Ireland, preaching the need for the Irish to rebel against the heretic queen, with the text of the bull excommunicating Elizabeth in hand. Protestants took refuge in Dublin and Cork. The Earl of Ormonde assumed command of Irish troops loyal to England. Finally, in September 1580, Spain dispatched support troops, but on the day before their arrival, Elizabeth sent English reinforcements and a large naval fleet to put down the insurrection. By November, the rebel stronghold was besieged by sea and by land.

After several days of negotiations, the Spanish commander asked Lord Grey of Wilton, head of the English forces, for surrender terms. Wilton carried orders from Elizabeth herself demanding the capitulation and annihilation of all the rebels.

On November 10, 1580, the gates of the fort opened to admit the English troops and the Irish ones loyal to Elizabeth. More than fifty men were executed on the spot, as were Irish Catholic civilians—men, women, and children—who had taken shelter inside. Thirty Spanish officers were spared and allowed to return to Spain upon payment of a sizable ransom. An English Catholic and two Irish ones who had come from Spain with Fitzmaurice were tortured and executed.[30]

Nicholas Sanders, who had not been inside the fort, soldiered on as a secret agent of the Holy Alliance in Ireland until 1581, when he died of cold and hunger.[31]

After the Holy Alliance's "Operation Munster," Elizabeth I of England protested to the Spanish ambassador. The English sovereign accused the Spaniards and their king of a hostile act in the form of a landing of troops on soil under English sovereignty. The Spanish diplomat replied that Spain had nothing to do with the venture, which had been planned and financed by Pope Gregory XIII.

The official explanation from the court of Madrid was that "papal ships and papal troops have the right of free passage through the land and ports of the King of Spain, a Catholic prince and defender of the faith." Elizabeth indignantly threatened to send English troops to the Netherlands in response. Ambassador Mendoza again responded with very little diplomacy:

> In your own interest, you must know that if the King of Spain decides to make war upon you, he will do so with such force that you will not even have time to breathe before the blow falls.[32]

The Irish fiasco caused Gregory XIII to turn his eyes to the still-unresolved Scottish question. Elizabeth I and Philip II did the same.

In the seven years since the fall of Edinburgh Castle, Mary Stuart had lost any vestige of power. Thanks to Morton's regency, the Protestants and Queen Elizabeth had Scotland on a very short leash while the teenage James VI grew into his role as a good king. Still, storm clouds gathered over Scotland, a pawn in a game of religious chess.

James VI had made a triumphal entrance into Edinburgh on October 17, 1578. The cheers of the crowds whetted his taste for power. The young monarch was intelligent and knew his responsibilities, just as he knew that he needed an advisor to help him navigate the minefield of Scottish politics. He chose a French cousin on his mother's side, Esmé Stuart, Seigneur of Aubigny, descended from Scots who had taken up residence in the Berry region of France during the Hundred Years' War.[33]

Esmé d'Aubigny was a fervent Catholic who had sworn loyalty to Pope Gregory XIII. He soon became a sort of Holy Alliance free agent in Scotland. From his privileged position, almost better than that of David Rizzio with Mary Stuart, he could persuade the young king to convert Scotland to Catholicism—or at least so it was believed in Rome. Rizzio, after all, had managed only the bedroom affairs of a queen; d'Aubigny managed the political affairs of a king.

The Frenchman arrived at the Scottish court in 1579. A year later he officially embraced Protestantism so as to pass unnoticed among James's courtiers. James made him earl and then Duke of Lennox; he also saw in his distant cousin a possible heir to the throne.[34]

In other European courts, monarchs and their counselors wondered why Esmé d'Aubigny had so much interest in Scotland and James VI. William of Orange thought he was a French pawn. Elizabeth thought he was an agent of Gregory XIII and the Jesuits. In truth, he was just a man in search of his own fortune. D'Aubigny could play the perfect Catholic to the pope and Philip II and the fervent Protestant to Elizabeth I and James VI.

Advised by the Holy Alliance, Esmé d'Aubigny knew that if he were ever to become king in Scotland, he had to get rid of the regent, the powerful Earl of Morton. On December 31, 1580, special guards arrested Morton as he was about to enter the royal residence. The charge was having participated in the assassination of Henry Darnley fourteen years earlier. The ex-regent found himself confined in a dark cell in Edinburgh Castle, awaiting trial.

On hearing this news from Scotland, Elizabeth decided to send her ambassador Thomas Randolph to demand Morton's immediate release. The English sovereign was told that James VI and d'Aubigny were being manipulated by a new papal conspiracy—which was true.

Then Walsingham, who was now not only secretary of state but also head of espionage, advised the queen to do one of two things: either send a fleet of warships to the Scottish coast to intimidate James VI into releasing Morton, or simply order the assassination of d'Aubigny. Elizabeth chose option two. But she specified that the killing of the Holy Alliance agent should not take place in the king's presence.[35]

One night in March of 1581, four men sent by Walsingham intercepted Esmé d'Aubigny, Duke of Lennox. A skilled swordsman, the Frenchman killed his first attacker with a single stroke, while a shot fired by the second English agent wounded him lightly in one arm. The sound of approaching guards then put Walsingham's spies to flight. The attack had failed, but d'Aubigny could not leave things as they stood. To avoid a second attempt, the powerful counselor ordered Morton's execution, which took place on June 2 of that same year.

Meanwhile, another net was being woven around James VI and Esmé d'Aubigny and against Elizabeth I in what became known as the "Throckmorton Plot." The spinners were many: Philip II, Henry III, Gregory XIII, and Mary Stuart. The objective was the same as always: to oust the heretic Elizabeth and replace her with Mary.

In the first months of 1583, Thomas Morgan, then secretary of Mary's embassy in France, recruited a twenty-eight-year-old English Catholic, Francis Throckmorton. Throckmorton was a supporter of the pope and a lover of intrigue. Sent to England, he set about collecting as much information as possible about English defenses—coastlines, strongholds, possible landing points, etc. His two main links with the Continent were Charles Paget, another member of the Holy Alliance in London who traveled frequently to Paris with coded messages, and the French ambassador to Elizabeth's court, Michel de Castelnau de Mauvissière. Throckmorton's dispatches were also sent to the Spanish and French embassies in London and to the Spanish one in Paris. The Spanish ambassadors Mendoza in England and Juan Bautista de Taxis in France informed Philip II about the progress of a conspiracy in which they were not very sure whether to participate.

By the spring of 1583, Walsingham had much of this plan on his desk, including the names of the Holy Alliance's conspirators and spies. Throckmorton did not realize the extent of English infiltration of the French legation in London. Since the beginning of the year, Walsingham had a spy who went by the code name of Fagot in place within the French embassy. Many years later, it would be revealed that Fagot was none other than the famous Italian philosopher Giordano Bruno, as historian John Bossy points out in his magnificent book *Giordano Bruno and the Embassy Affair*.[36] Until recently, it was thought that the real traitor who torpedoed the Throckmorton Plot was the ambassador's secretary, Jean Arnault, Seigneur of Cherelles.[37]

Thanks to the information supplied by Bruno to Walsingham, Throckmorton was arrested on October 12. Before his detention, a servant in the Spanish embassy managed to hide some important papers that directly implicated Spanish diplomats and the Spanish king. The Holy Alliance spy Francis Throckmorton was executed on July 10, 1584.[38] Giordano Bruno—or, better put, Fagot—continued working as an English spy until 1586, when he ceased to live in the French embassy in London.[39]

All the intrigues directed from Madrid and Rome were designed to increase the tension in Scotland. The original idea had been to create a Catholic military force that, after landing in Scotland, would take James VI prisoner and convey him to France, where he would convert to Catholicism either under duress or of his own free will. In the same operation, members of the Holy Alliance aided by English Catholics would free the imprisoned Mary Stuart and restore her to her throne.[40]

The pope's agents were the Jesuit fathers Crichton, Holt, Edmund Campion, and Robert Parsons. Crichton, more loyal to the Jesuit leader Claudio Acquaviva than to Pope Gregory XIII, became an authentic legend in the Holy Alliance until his capture on September 3, 1584. Campion was very cultured, a good conversationalist and diplomat. Parsons was a warrior, skilled with the sword and vehement in speech.[41]

All of them were supposed to travel to Edinburgh and make contact with lords who would lend their support to Mary's cause. The operation was to be financed by Philip II and the pope. Henry III of France, who had appointed himself general of the operation, planned the military aspect in detail. On a map of Scotland he deployed tokens representing twenty thousand troops, an unrealistic number for the era. Mary Stuart planned to send her son, the dethroned James VI, to Spain under the "protection" or, better said, vigilance of Philip II, with the idea that he would there convert to Catholicism.

To avoid such an eventuality, Walsingham staged a counteroperation. In August 1582, he ordered the Earl of Gowrie, an enemy of de Aubigny, to capture James VI and hold him in the castle of Ruthven until the Protestants were securely in power in Edinburgh.

A week after the detention of the monarch, Esmé d'Aubigny, Duke of Lennox, fled Scotland and took refuge in France. Walsingham's agents managed to capture the Jesuit priest Holt. After confessing under torture to his participation and that of the Holy Alliance in the plot, he was hanged without trial. Father Crichton escaped and made his way to Rome. Father Parsons fled to France, where he continued working for the Holy Alliance. Father Campion also escaped from Scotland, but he was caught in England shortly afterwards. Imprisoned in the Tower, he was tortured and executed in Tyburn on December 1.

During 1583, the Scottish problem continued to reverberate through the politics of late-sixteenth-century Europe. On June 29 of that year, James was restored to the throne of Scotland. From that moment on, and knowing that his mother, Mary Stuart, had been involved in the plot to overthrow him, he decided to cut off all contact with her. Officially and in the eyes of England, Scotland broke with its former queen by order of her own son.

Gregory XIII, in weak health at eighty-three years of age, still had the spirit to go out with a bang: he ordered the Holy Alliance to assassinate William of Orange. The Protestant prince had survived one attempt on his life only two years earlier. In late-sixteenth-century Europe, political assassination was less the exception than the rule.

For this operation, the pope turned again to Father Crichton, now in Rome after his successful escape from Scotland. Both the Dutch leader and Protestant queen of England deserved to die in the name of the true faith. Crichton reached Holland in April 1584 and immediately established close relations with Baltasar Gérard and Gaspar de Albrech, two Catholic fanatics from Burgundy, both ready to bring an end to the life of the Protestant hero, even in a suicide mission.

They got their chance on July 10, 1584, in the city of Delft. That morning, William of Orange and some members of his entourage had come to the main square of the town to meet with local authorities. The Dutchman was able to dodge Albrech's attack, but not Gérard's.[42] The United Provinces mourned the death of their leader, because, although the war with Spain was far from over, the new nation of Holland was taking shape in a Europe devastated by war and religious conflict.

On the morning of September 6, 1584, Dutch privateers attacked a ship crossing the North Sea without a flag. After they killed part of the crew and the rest surrendered, the Dutch pirates searched the ship, where they found a man who refused to identify himself. It was Crichton, the Jesuit priest. After the regicide, he had managed to escape any Protestant retribution. The privateers turned him over to English authorities, who shut him in the Tower of London on Walsingham's orders, awaiting interrogation.[43]

The Dutchmen also turned over compromising documents that Crichton had hurled into the sea but his assailants had been able to recover. Those papers, now in Walsingham's possession, demonstrated the usual interest in invading England with a large Catholic army, freeing Mary Stuart, and putting her on the throne instead of the heretic Elizabeth.[44]

Also among the Jesuit's possessions was a letter signed by Cardinal Galli, bishop of Como and Vatican secretary of state. Addressed to Crichton, it said:

> Because this woman is guilty of causing so much harm to the Catholic faith and the loss of so many millions of souls, there is no doubt that whoever removes her from this world with the pious intention of serving God not only will not be committing a sin, but will be deserving of eternal praise.

The next Parliament met November 23, 1584. Several deputies cited the so-called *Complementary law against Jesuits, priests, and other similar and disobedient persons,* promulgated in 1559, which ordered such persons to leave English soil within forty days under pain of death. William Parry, a member known for his Catholic sympathies, attacked the letter of the law and those who wanted to put it into practice, arguing that in England there were many Catholics willing to die for Queen Elizabeth. Few listeners knew that Parry had worked for the English spy services in Europe. Nor did they know that the MP had planned to assassinate Elizabeth I four years before. Parry had discarded that plan at the last minute for reasons of conscience.

At the end of the session, William Parry was arrested, accused of treason, and taken to the Tower. The queen herself ordered his release. He had saved his skin, but not by much.[45]

From the moment of being set free, Parry began to devise a complex scheme to kill the queen. One of those involved in the new plan, Edmund Neville, Earl of Westmoreland, decided to defect and tell all to Walsingham. The news exploded like a bomb among members of court, who had William of Orange's assassination so fresh in their minds. William Parry appeared in the role of chief Catholic conspirator, with the aged Pope Gregory and the Holy Alliance once more pulling the strings.

The idea was to shoot at the royal carriage during New Year's festivities. The plan had been designed by Thomas Morgan, one of Mary Stuart's faithful confidants. During Parry's interrogation, ties emerged as well to Scottish Catholic refugees in France under the protection of the Catholic Henry III. William Parry's trial was quick, and so was his execution on March 2, 1585. Thomas Morgan was confined in the Bastille for his part in the plot and freed four months later. Edmund Neville was released without charges but required to leave England. He died in Rome in 1619 under the protection of Pope Paul V.

On April 24, 1585, the conclave of cardinals selected their Franciscan colleague Felice Peretti as the newest pontiff, after the death of Gregory XIII two weeks before. Peretti, who adopted the name Sixtus V, had been very close to Pius V, thanks to whom he had become an advisor to the Congregation of the Inquisition. His selection as pope had the support of Philip II.

Sixtus would be the pope who established the closest of all ties with the Jesuits and who would use them as a shock force everywhere they were sent to defend the faith, whatever the mission might be.[46] He fully supported their use as a military force, though he did not approve of their theological points of view.

Claudio Acquaviva knew that if Sixtus V wanted to keep using the Jesuits as shock troops for "special missions," he had to give way in theological matters. Sixtus, for his part, was conscious that if he kept up his pressure against the order, Acquaviva would counterattack by asking his members their opinion about the issue of obedience to the pope and about his views. The pope sent a warning signal to the Jesuit superior-general when in 1590 he ordered the name of the order changed from Society of Jesus to "Order of Ignacio." For Sixtus V, the Jesuits' use of Jesus' name was somewhat offensive. This was so for many cardinals of the period, who objected to having to doff their hats or bow their heads when the name of the powerful order was spoken, since it included Jesus' name. In spite of the papal decision, no Jesuit general or Jesuit assembly ever adopted the new name.

In the spring of 1586, the so-called Babington Plot began, once again with the goal of restoring Mary Stuart to the Scottish throne and possibly of ending Elizabeth's life so that the Catholic queen could wear the crown of both realms. Really, for the English and Scots of the last years of the sixteenth century, both Catholics and Protestants, to raise one's hand against a crowned head of state was not just a crime but a sacrilege. Mary Stuart committed such a sacrilege when she joined the Babington Plot. Elizabeth I would do the same if she executed Mary Stuart once the conspiracy came to light.

In August, the plotters were all arrested. Ballard, Savage, and Babington himself were confined in the Tower. Mary Stuart's trial began October 14, 1586, in Fotheringay Castle in the county of Northampton. On October 25, she was found guilty of high treason, sedition, and support for the plotters who wanted to murder Queen Elizabeth. The tribunal sentenced her to death.

Reactions to the sentence were lukewarm. Henry III of France was too busy fighting two other Henrys: Henry of Navarre and his Protestant backers and Henry of Guise and his Catholics. Philip II was bogged down in Flanders, and Pope Sixtus V had decided to look the other way because James VI of Scotland had allowed him to glimpse a possibility that, once named heir to the English throne and following the death of Elizabeth, he would restore Catholicism. This interpretation led Sixtus to recall the agents of the Holy Alliance from England.[47]

On February 1, Elizabeth signed the document authorizing the execution of Mary Stuart, once Mary Queen of Scots. A week later, on the morning of February 8, 1587, the anointed Queen of Scotland entered the great hall of Fotheringay Castle, where the scaffold had been erected. Mary Stuart, a queen from the day of her birth, determined to act the part during her execution. The earls of Shrewsbury and Kent served as Elizabeth's witnesses.

After a short Latin prayer and uttering the words *"In te domine, confido, ne confundar in aeternum,"* she bent her head on the block, which she grasped with both arms. The executioner lifted his axe and let it fall toward the white neck of Mary Stuart. It smashed part of her skull. His second attempt hit her neck full on, but it took a third to separate her head from the rest of her body. The executioner then grasped her head and tried to lift it in the air. He found himself holding a wig, while the nearly bald, graying head of a woman getting on in years rolled on the wooden floor. In the face of such a vision, someone managed to cry out, "God save the Queen!"[48]

Elizabeth I of England had finally ended her Scottish problem, but Philip II and Pope Sixtus V did not take the execution of a Catholic queen lightly. Weapons ranging from an Invincible Armada to the assassins of the Holy Alliance would be put at the service of the faith and wielded against the heretic queen. Times of action were at hand.

3

TIMES OF ACTION (1587–1605)

There will be darkness over the earth, so thick that it may be felt.
—Exodus 10:21

For years, almost since Elizabeth's excommunication in 1570, there had been talk of an open attack upon England by Spain. In spy circles, including those of England, this possible military operation was known by the code word "the Enterprise." Those attempting to persuade Philip II to carry it out included Pope Sixtus V and the Jesuits, for religious reasons; Mary Stuart's backers, the Scottish Catholics, with the goal of restoring her to the Scottish throne; and the English Catholics, with the goal of proclaiming Mary sovereign of England as well, where she could restore Catholicism once the heretic queen had been made to disappear. Another backer of the Enterprise was none other than Philip's half brother Don Juan of Austria, who wanted to marry Mary Stuart and become King of England and Scotland himself.

On the other hand, Philip II did not want to make a bad decision in order to satisfy anyone. The Spanish king had no great desire to put a half-French queen on the English throne. Nor did he want to give a brother whom he didn't particularly trust access to such a queen. Nor, of course, did he especially want to please the pope, since many people might infer that he was acting at the instructions of Rome.[1]

The endless wars in the Netherlands were costing Philip too much treasure, and Rome demanded more and more action without giving much help in return. What London didn't know, however, was that the Spanish monarch saw Elizabeth of England as an aggressor and, therefore, easily attackable from a political point of view. England had openly intervened in the Netherlands with the signing of the Treaty of Nonsuch; she had given the green light, too, to the pillaging of the Spanish coast by pirate ships under the command of Francis Drake.

After Mary Stuart's execution, the Holy Alliance informed the pope that Elizabeth thought that, having eliminated the basis of an alliance between Scottish and English Catholics and the focal point of Spanish intervention plans, now there was nothing to prompt Spain into a military adventure. With Mary gone, there was no door left open to Rome in its desire to restore Catholicism to the isles. James VI would continue to defend Protestantism, despite the timid messages he sent to Sixtus V about his reasons for not condemning Elizabeth on the matter of his mother's execution.

James VI wanted to become Elizabeth's legitimate heir and succeed her on the throne of England. He had persuaded Sixtus V to refrain from stirring up the Catholics until he was named the legitimate successor, arguing that the pontiff should remove from the country and from its court any Holy Alliance agent bent on assassination. James VI had timidly told the pope's agents that perhaps, once he was wearing the double crown, he could return both realms to Catholicism or at least grant more religious freedom to Catholics—something that never occurred.[2]

The first reports of the military Enterprise date from the end of 1585. But it was really early the next year when the English espionage service learned from various sources about the formation of a great fleet to be sent against England.[3] The English ambassador in Paris wrote to Walsingham:

> The Spanish party here in France are boasting that within three months England will be attacked, and that a great armed fleet is being readied for this purpose. I have difficulty believing this, since the time is so short.[4]

Walsingham half believed this report. Elizabeth's spy chief suspected that Philip was building a large fleet, not to send against England but to support the Duke of Parma in the Netherlands. However, perhaps the fleet would sail instead for Scotland or Ireland, in which case England needed to be ready to respond militarily. Philip II, meanwhile, thought that once his great Armada attacked England, a weakened Elizabeth would have to negotiate an honorable way out. Clearly, the Spanish monarch did not understand the temperament of the English queen.[5]

In the spring of 1587, just two months after Mary Stuart's execution, Walsingham was devoting himself to preparing England's defenses. His agents in strategic points of Europe informed him that Philip II had decided to proceed with the Enterprise.

As a countermeasure, Elizabeth authorized her loyal Francis Drake to set sail with a squadron of almost twenty ships charged with preventing the assembly of the Spanish fleets outside their home ports. The English ships were to interrupt their lines of supply and to pursue or sink the Spanish warships if they made for England or Ireland. Holy Alliance agents informed Spain that Drake's fleet was almost ready to embark from Plymouth and, according to their sources, would attack the ports and coasts in the area of El Ferrol.[6]

On the night of April 2, after Drake's squadron had set sail without notice, Elizabeth changed her mind. She asked Walsingham to send an urgent message to Drake telling him not to attack the Spanish ports. The first message reached Plymouth at 3 A.M., when the sails of the English ships were still visible on the horizon. A second messenger sent by Walsingham had been intercepted by agents of the pope. Once they knew what was afoot, they sent their own urgent reports to Madrid and Rome, but by then it was too late for both Elizabeth I and Philip II. Drake had decided to alter his own plans, and, instead of attacking a port in Galicia or Cantabria or in the Antilles, he decided to change course and attack the city of Cádiz.[7] From his flagship, the *Elizabeth Bonaventure,* and the surrounding vessels, Drake directed the bombardment of the fortified city and the entrance to its harbor. In the mere two hours the operation lasted, Francis Drake succeeded in sinking almost thirty Spanish ships that had been preparing to join the Armada and destroyed the naval barracks and armories as well.[8]

When Pope Sixtus V learned of this attack on Spanish power, he declared, "Our king deliberates while the heretic queen attacks."[9]

From any point of view, Drake's "Operation Cádiz" was a master stroke, but in spite of the heavy blow it dealt to Spain's preparations and pride, the raid set the Armada back only a year. Meanwhile, the Holy Alliance's agents continued operating openly in the Netherlands, protected by the all-powerful Duke of Parma.

One of their best operations was that of Geertruidenberg. During the peace negotiations taking place in the spring of 1588, the pope's agents had managed to foment a rebellion among the mercenary troops guarding the fortified city of Geertruidenberg, a strategic point on the south side of the

Maas River. German mercenaries made up the first line of defense, Dutch ones made up the second, and English and Protestant Irish constituted the third. The Holy Alliance spies had managed to undermine the morale of the troops due to the nearly four months they had gone without pay. The papal agents made speeches in the Dutch city's plaza against "those great ones who rest their behinds on the thrones of Europe and look the other way when it comes time to pay those who defend their seats of power."

England was refusing to pay the debt of 210,000 florins or nearly 22,000 pounds owed to the Geertruidenberg mercenaries, alleging that this was the problem of the States-General (the Dutch parliament), while that body in turn responded that the mercenaries recruited by England were more loyally serving the cause of Elizabeth I than that of Protestantism in the Netherlands. Walsingham knew that Sixtus V was behind the rebellion, and the Duke of Parma and Philip II along with him.

The English spy chief was conscious that sooner or later the troops needed to be paid, or else the strategic city would fall into Spanish hands. At last, when lack of payment had the mercenaries on the point of surrendering the city to the Spaniards, a message from the States-General arrived assuming responsibility for the debt. Thanks to the agents of the Holy Alliance, though, the Spanish army had nearly taken an important military objective without firing a single shot.

Philip II could not easily forget the blow Elizabeth had dealt him in Cádiz, and so he hurried the preparation of the Enterprise all the more. The plan was simple. Embarking from Lisbon, a Grand Armada would set sail for the English Channel, evade any encounter with English warships, cross near Calais, and land in Margate, in the northern part of Kent. There they would be joined by Parma's troops, arriving from the Spanish-controlled ports of the Netherlands. In all, some thirty thousand men would defeat the weak English army and march on London.[10] On paper, the plan was clear and simple. In practice, in the years of the late sixteenth century, this was not the case.

The agents deployed in the areas of action expressed their doubts about the military operation. In a document sent to the pope, one agent wondered how the Duke of Parma's troops would get from the Netherlands to England. Sixtus V himself asked Philip what would happen once England was in Spanish hands. None of these questions was answered.

Parma had made clear that he would gather his fifteen thousand men in Dunkirk, Nieuport, and Sluis, but without the Armada's protection it would be almost impossible to transport them across the Channel, which was full of Dutch privateers and Drake's ships as well. So the Spanish governor requested that the king send the Armada to the coast of the Netherlands to protect his troops before striking the main blow against England. But this itself required first capturing a secure harbor in England, such as the port of Dover.[11] According to historian Garrett Mattingly in his book *The Defeat of the Spanish Armada,* that was the weak point of the whole operation.

The Holy Alliance had instructions from Pope Sixtus V to seek support in the English coastal towns for a possible rising against local authorities once the sails of the Armada came into view. The papal agents also had the mission of creating an extensive communication network that would cover the whole eastern coast of England and the western coast of Flanders and France, so as to keep the Spaniards informed of all English movements.

One of the most active agents of the Holy Alliance, the Genovese Marco Antonio Massia, reported to the pope:

> Here in England it is believed that the Spanish will come with their ships' holds packed full of gallows on which to hang all the men, and whips with which to flog the women, and four thousand wet nurses to suckle the babies who will be carried back to Spain in the ships. It is also said that all children from seven to twelve years old will be branded with hot irons. All these things arouse the people to offer resistance to Spain.

To Rome and Madrid it was obvious that such tales, spread by Walsingham's men, would indeed have their impact on the uneducated populace of the late sixteenth century. The truth is that Philip II had no well-developed plan for the English succession after Elizabeth, nor had he given it much thought after the death of Mary Stuart.

For Philip, the Protestant heir James VI of Scotland was not a valid candidate, although it was always possible that Sixtus V could declare him, too, a heretic and excommunicate him. Really, the pope was more and more in disagreement with Philip II because his agents in the court of Madrid had told him of the monarch's desires to be declared King of England himself, by virtue of being descended on his mother's side from the House of Lancaster.[12] Sixtus V would not allow the Spanish king to unite the crown of England with those of Spain, Portugal, Sicily, and Naples, not to mention the other domains under his control in 1588.

To command the Armada, Philip appointed Admiral Álvaro de Bazán, an experienced seaman and military expert who had already defeated the French fleet in 1582 in the Azores. The problem was that the admiral was now quite advanced in years, and the task of preparing the Armada finished him off on March 9, 1588. Philip replaced Bazán with the Duke of Medina-Sidonia, a rich nobleman recommended by nothing more than his great loyalty to the king. He was, as history would demonstrate, pessimistic, wavering, and in fact somewhat of a coward—three bad qualities in an officer in charge of a great enterprise like the Armada. Philip II was perfectly aware of the defects of his inexperienced admiral and therefore wanted to lead the venture himself. Medina-Sidonia was merely his hand on the tiller of the ships.[13]

The pope's spies kept up their steady stream of reports about English preparations. As her Lord Admiral, Elizabeth named Charles Howard, loyal to the queen despite being the younger brother of the Duke of Norfolk executed in 1572. The English squadron based in Plymouth would be led by Francis Drake, whose job was to keep the Spanish galleons out of the Channel. Howard, for his part, was to block any movement of Philip's ships toward the North Sea.

The Genovese Marco Antonio Massia, now infiltrated into England, reported to the pope that the English had set up a system of coastal bonfires to immediately relay the news of the Armada's arrival. Parma's troops were to be blockaded by the Dutch fleet, made up of thirty ships under Justin of Nassau. The Holy Alliance also reported continual movement of troops and warships in several ports of Flanders and Zeeland. By the beginning of July, the English court knew that the Grand Armada had left Spain. The die was cast.

During the preceding weeks, Walsingham's police devoted their efforts to hunting and capturing the pope's spies. Many of the best of them were interned in the Castle of Wisbech, near the fens of Cambridgeshire.

On the diplomatic front, Elizabeth was sure that France would not support Spain. Henry III had already let Madrid know that his delicate situation did not allow him to support the attack on England. James VI of Scotland was another matter. Elizabeth was not so sure that Mary Stuart's son would refuse to support Philip II, if Philip would help him ascend the English throne as legitimate ruler. What James needed was an army with which to prove his valor in an open confrontation with Elizabeth. The Armada's troops could be just that.[14]

Walsingham advised Elizabeth to order the deployment of troops on the Scottish border while explaining to James that this was not a sign of aggression toward his country but rather a means of defense in case the Spaniards chose to invade England by way of Scotland. Elizabeth did in fact fear a possible Spanish-Scottish alliance. As historians Neil Hanson, Colin Martin, Geoffrey Parker, and Garrett Mattingly all agree in their works *The Confident Hope of a Miracle: The Real History of the Spanish Armada, The Spanish Armada: Revised Edition,* and *The Defeat of the Spanish Armada,* the English treated the defense of kingdom against Spanish invaders almost as a joke. Walsingham wrote then: "Our manner of proceeding is so tepid and unconcerned that only the grace of God and a miracle can save us from such a danger." In any case, the miracle did arrive.

The size of the Armada was incredible for its time: 130 galleons divided into eight squadrons carrying thirty thousand men, to be bolstered by the fifteen thousand more under the Duke of Parma who were waiting in Flemish ports to board ship for England.[15] The English defensive fleet had only thirty-four ships and 6,700 men. Spain outnumbered England by nearly four to one in ships and nearly seven to one in troops. Everyone knew the combat about to unfold would pit five Spanish Goliaths against a puny English David.

The huge fleet left Lisbon on June 7. An intense storm stirring up the Atlantic scattered most of the Armada. The battered ships regrouped in La Coruña. The water in their casks was stagnant, the meat was full of worms, and several hundred men who had taken sick were discharged. On July 22, the fleet weighed anchor again, heading north from the Galician coast. On the 29th, it neared the English coast. Walsingham's spies in Cornwall spotted its sails billowing in a strong wind from the west. In crescent formation, with the flagship in the lead, the Armada advanced along the Devon coast. Drake's and Howard's ships began attacking the stragglers on July 31.[16]

On August 4, one of the Spanish galleons was wrecked on the French coast with important documents on board. Two days later the wind shifted, and Medina-Sidonia made a bad decision. He ordered the entire Armada to take shelter in Calais, but the bay was too small to make room for the whole fleet, and the bulk of the ships remained exposed.

Once again, Drake and Howard decided to attack, while the Spanish ships were struggling to stay anchored rather than be pulled into the North Sea. Parma's troops remained nowhere to be seen, and the English-Dutch fleet blocked any Spanish retreat. Soon many of Medina-Sidonia's ships were on fire, sunk, dismasted, or lost.

On August 8, Admiral Howard launched his last great attack on the Armada, eliminating any possibility of counterattack by the Spanish galleons. The military operation planned by Philip II had been flawed from the start, as the spy Marco Antonio Massia reported to the pope. The Spanish monarch had designed the whole operation as a huge landing and invasion of England, but never as a naval battle. Drake's and Howard's ships took care of the rest.

Ten days after this definitive defeat, Philip II read a rosy message sent by his ambassador in London reporting that Medina-Sidonia had sunk fifteen of Drake's ships, including his flagship. Thanks to the effectiveness of the agents of the Holy Alliance, Sixtus V, seated on his throne in Rome, was the first to know all the gory details of the Spanish defeat. The Armada was no more. The crews shipwrecked in Scotland were given aid and shelter and later repatriated by order of James I; those wrecked in Ireland were massacred. Only twenty-seven ships managed to return to Spain. Though Medina-Sidonia was accused of incompetence and cowardice, Philip kept him on as a trusted aide.

England, on the other hand, trumpeted its victory over a now-weakened Spain, and the triumph of the true religion over the darkness of Catholic papistry. By order of Queen Elizabeth, a new coin showed a Spanish galleon struggling against the waves under the legend "VENIT, VIDIT, FUGIT." (It came, it saw, it fled.) Pedro de Valdés, one of Medina-Sidonia's lieutenants who was taken prisoner by Francis Drake, remained confined in the English pirate's house for five years and was displayed to visitors like a humiliated animal.[17]

The Armada, which the English now styled with the sarcastic adjective "Invincible," has passed into the realm of myth, as has the participation of the Holy Alliance's agents, like the Genovese Marco Antonio Massia, before, during, and after the military operation. Many of the pope's spies were used as simple messengers, others as spies in enemy ports, and others as saviors of many of the shipwrecked crews. Massia himself negotiated with James VI the repatriation of nearly 630 Spanish sailors and soldiers wrecked on the Scottish coasts.

Soon afterwards, ironically, the losers found themselves made into heroes, and the winners into losers. While the Spanish survivors were feted as heroes by their people and their king, many of the demobilized English defenders were felled by typhus, hunger, and exhaustion without Queen Elizabeth I offering them any aid. The victors soon forgot their heroes while the losers glorified theirs. Philip II restored his battered finances thanks to the ships full of gold and precious stones arriving from his American possessions, while England had to rely on plunder and piracy.

The last years of the 1580s brought many deaths of the famous. The Earl of Leicester died of a fever on September 4, 1588. The next year brought the death of Walter Mildmay, close counselor to Elizabeth, chancellor of the exchequer, and scourge of the spies of the Holy Alliance; he succumbed to poison administered by the Holy Alliance, or so it was said. Francis Walsingham, spymaster and true founder of the British secret services, died in 1590; so did his antagonist Pope Sixtus V, on August 27, at the age of sixty-nine. The late pontiff was the one who made most use of the Holy Alliance as an instrument of espionage and special operations, including assassination.

In only fifteen months, three new popes occupied the Throne of St. Peter: Urban VII, Gregory XIV, and Innocent IX. During this short interval, there were no known Holy Alliance operations, or at least no documented ones. The election of Cardinal Ippolito Aldobrandini as Pope Clement VIII on January 30, 1592, set the pontifical espionage apparatus back in motion. Once again, the Holy Alliance began intriguing to get rid of the heretic Elizabeth I.

The new pope, who came from an aristocratic Florentine family, had been part of the entourage of Cardinal Miguel Bonelli, *legate a latere*[18] from the Vatican to the court in Madrid. There he had established good relations with Philip II's spies, and in 1571 and 1572, Aldobrandini became a kind of permanent Holy Alliance agent in the capital of the Spanish empire. He reported directly to Pope Pius V, who founded the papal espionage service only six years before.

Aldobrandini's career as a Vatican spy suffered an abrupt setback with the death of Pius V. During the papacy of Gregory XIII, this former agent of Pius V toiled in the management of legal affairs. When Sixtus V ascended the papal throne, his fortunes changed again. Sixtus became his patron, raising him to cardinal and entrusting him with special missions.[19]

Sixtus V knew that Aldobrandini had experience in the espionage world, the diplomatic world, the religious world, and most important, he had good relations with those surrounding Philip II.

The first special mission of the spy Ippolito Aldobrandini took place in May of 1588, when the pope sent him to Poland. The Holy Alliance agent had to try to mediate among the factions supporting two claimants to the crown following the death of King Stephen Bathory. Aldobrandini tried to get the two heirs, Sigismund Vasa and Maximilian von Hapsburg, to reach a peaceful accord but also to extract from them a firm commitment to keep Poland within the Catholic sphere and in strict obedience to the pope. Sigismund acquired the crown of Poland, making a stable and lasting peace with Maximilian on March 9, 1589. The success of his Polish mission made Aldobrandini one of the most prestigious members of the College of Cardinals.

Pope Innocent IX's sudden death on December 30, 1591, required the fourth convocation of the cardinals in seventeen months. Spanish pressure, as so often before, was quite strong. This time Philip II wanted a more tractable pope on the Throne of St. Peter than Sixtus V, whom he had characterized as "too independent and too given to intrigues." At last, thanks to the Spanish monarch's support, Ippolito Aldobrandini, former spy, was named pope on January 30, 1592.

Clement VIII became pope at a very unsettled European moment. The Netherlands were aflame everywhere, and Maurice of Nassau had emerged as an authentic leader in the fight against Spain.

The previous year, Philip II's forces had lost Zuthphen, Deventer, Hulst, and finally the strategic Nijmegen. From then on, the southern flank of the future nation of Holland was secure. In December of 1592, the situation took an unexpected turn with the death of Alessandro Farnese, Duke of Parma. The court at Madrid named a series of successors, but none was more than a witness to the coming of the end. Count von Mansfeld, the Archduke Ernest, the Count of Fuentes, and the Archduke Alberto were some of them.[20] Little by little, the future Holland was establishing its borders: in Nijmegen in 1591, and in Groningen and Geertruidenberg, which were recovered in 1593 after a long siege by Maurice of Nassau's troops.

The same year and rather suddenly, a new front opened in France. Henry of Navarre had become Henry IV of France after the flight from Paris of Henry III. The deposed king was then assassinated in 1589 by a fanatical Dominican friar and, some sources say, agent of the Holy Alliance. Apparently Pope Sixtus V did not want any obstacles in the progress of Henry IV and his kingdom toward Catholicism, and Henry III was one.[21]

Henry of Bourbon, the Calvinist king of Navarre, had previously been one of the greatest defenders of Protestantism and had been condemned as such by Pope Sixtus V. However, Philip II and Clement VIII did not count on the large number of French Catholics who recognized Henry IV as their king.

As his first measure, Henry IV ordered the evacuation of all the Spanish troops from Paris. Philip II took this as a serious warning that could spark an open war between the two countries. Holy Alliance agents had advised Pope Clement VIII to keep himself in the background, because they knew that Henry IV was ready to reject Calvinism and convert to Catholicism, as indeed came to pass. Aware that the only way to put an end to the divisions in the realm was to reject Protestantism, Henry IV decided to convert on July 25, 1593, just as the agents of the Holy Alliance had foreseen.

That same year, the new King of France sent a representative to Rome to persuade the pope to revoke the censures and penalties imposed by Sixtus V, but Clement VIII was unsure. The cardinals seemed inclined to offer Henry IV absolution. To put a stamp of approval on the reconciliation between Rome and Paris, diplomatic relations—broken off in 1588—were restored.

Instead of supporting Madrid, Clement VIII interceded to get Catholic France and Catholic Spain to sign the Peace of Vervins on May 2, 1598, and put an end to the war that had been desolating both countries for three years. Philip II recognized Henry IV as the true king and returned the territories Spain had conquered in northeastern France. Calais came back into French hands after many years of Spanish domination. At the same time, with the Edict of Nantes, Henry IV permanently introduced freedom of religion throughout his realm.

Elizabeth continued to regard the French-Spanish reconciliation with suspicion and described the French king as "that ungrateful Antichrist." Her rejection of a stable peace placed her once again in the sights of the Holy Alliance. Clement VIII, after all, had to keep defending the true faith, even if it meant he had to approve assassination attempts on the heretic queen.

To show that she would not hesitate to repress Catholicism within her kingdom, Elizabeth demonstrated unprecedented cruelty. In the first years of the 1590s, the queen ordered the execution of sixty-one priests and forty-seven laypersons. In 1593, Parliament approved the so-called Act for Restraining Popish Recusants, which barred Catholics from traveling more than five miles from their homes.[22] After the execution of Mary Stuart, English Catholics had become less restive or perhaps had simply accepted their place in history, but the Jesuits, loyal as they were to the pope and to Philip II, continued to be the most implacable enemies of the heretic Elizabeth.

In 1593, a Jesuit sent by the Holy Alliance took ship from somewhere in the Netherlands with the intent to throw a bomb at Elizabeth's royal carriage as it passed.[23] Apparently, Walsingham's agents managed to prevent this. A figure who might have been in a position to kill Elizabeth of England, however, was a doctor, Rodrigo López.

At the beginning of 1594, the English court was still caught up in the atmosphere of suspicion and deception created by an affair that involved the queen's favorite, the Earl of Essex. For some eight years, Elizabeth's personal physician had been Rodrigo López, a Portuguese doctor of Jewish origins converted to Christianity. López had become quite well known among the British aristocracy since his arrival in London in 1558. He numbered among his clientele the most important figures of the court: Lord Burghley (William Cecil), the Earl of Leicester, Burghley's son Robert Cecil, and even Essex himself. Thanks to his service to the queen, the physician had been granted a monopoly on the importation of anise, which had made him very rich. No one was surprised to see him arrive at the royal palace deep into the night, carrying his black cases full of medicines.

Because of his Portuguese origin, López was also in the circle of friends of Dom Antonio, pretender to the Portuguese crown. In reality, he served as a triple agent, spying for the pope, for the Spanish king, and for Burghley, now chief of the English spies. In December 1593, Essex undertook his own investigation of the spy, whom he accused of trying to kill the queen at the behest of Pope Clement VIII and Philip II. In January 1594, Essex sent a report to Anthony Bacon, one of Elizabeth's confidants:

> I have discovered a most dangerous and desperate treason. The point of the conspiracy was her Majesty's death. The executioner should have been Dr. Lopez. This I have so followed that I will make it appear as clear as noonday.[24]

The letter found its way into Burghley's hands. Elizabeth's spy chief doubted the truth of Essex's accusations. What motive did López have to assassinate the queen, who showered him with attention and favors? Essex did not know that López passed on information to Burghley, specifically about actions and plots against the queen originating in Rome and Madrid. As a precaution, however, Burghley ordered López to remain inside his house. He told the queen that the doctor was ill and had confined himself to avoid passing on any contagion. An epidemic of plague had struck London, and the court had moved to Hampton Court Palace. Essex, seeing that his accusation against López was not resulting in any action, decided to tell the queen his suspicions. She ordered him to silence, accusing him of trying to remove a loyal man out of simple jealousy.[25]

Essex, however, did not give up. López was brought secretly to the Tower of London on January 29 to be interrogated by Essex and Robert Cecil. Brutally tortured, López ended up confessing that he belonged to the Holy Alliance under orders of Pope Clement VIII and that he had proposed to poison the English sovereign. As proof, he showed Cecil and Essex the gold ring sent to him by Philip II for future "service," which he in turn had offered as a gift to Queen Elizabeth. The queen had refused to accept it, returning it to the doctor.

The fact was—as a later trial would show—that Rodrigo López had tried to collect from all sides, including a promised fifty thousand crowns from Philip II once the queen was dead. Burghley asked the doctor why he hadn't revealed the plot before. But López knew that even revealing it, he could be condemned to death under the laws approved during the time of Mary Stuart.

The trial of Rodrigo López and Claudio Tinico (a Holy Alliance spy who served as intermediary between López and Rome) took place on March 14. The sentence was death, but curiously enough Elizabeth did not affix her seal to ratify the sentence until June 7. That same night, López and Tinico were brought to the main courtyard of the Tower, hanged by the neck until dead, and their bodies quartered. The queen continued to believe in Rodrigo López's innocence, though none but the executed prisoner would ever know the truth. In spite of his being convicted of high treason, López's goods were given to his widow, and she was granted a pension for life. Elizabeth kept the ring that Philip II had given the doctor, which she would wear on her finger until the day of her own death.[26]

At the end of June, Philip II ordered the transfer of his own court to his palace at El Escorial in spite of the protests of his doctors, Juan Gómez de Sanabria and Cristóbal Pérez de Herrera. The chill of the mountains on these outskirts of Madrid was bad for his health. On September 1, the king, now very weak, officially desisted from all tasks of state. From that day on, only the friar Diego de Yepes, his personal confessor, ministered to his spiritual needs. On September 13, 1598, at 3 A.M., Philip II died peacefully in his bed in the Monastery of San Lorenzo in El Escorial.[27] Thus vanished, too, one of the main spiritual and financial pillars of the papal secret service, the Holy Alliance, founded thirty-two years before.

For Elizabeth, the death of the principal bulwark of the Holy Alliance would not improve her situation or free her from future intrigues—at least, not so far as Pope Clement VIII was concerned. There remained many intrigues to undertake and many plots to organize against the heretic queen.

The next conspiracy against Elizabeth I was hatched in the Netherlands, under the protective hand of the Spanish governor, the Archduke Alberto, an ex-cardinal now married to the beloved daughter of Philip II, the Infanta Isabel Clara Eugenia. Three Jesuits, one of them Father Carew, crossed the English Channel on board a fishing boat. Upon landing in England, they made their way to London. Their goal was to place a powerful explosive under the queen's bed. To gain such access, the trio sent by the Holy Alliance made contact with a Catholic servant working in the royal palace. Days before they were to attempt the assassination, two of the Jesuits were arrested in the inn where they were staying. The third, Father Carew, managed to escape. Apparently, the servant decided to confess the plot to Robert Cecil.[28] The two Jesuits were executed and quartered in the Tower in April of 1602. Father Carew, arrested shortly afterwards, suffered the same fate in February of 1603.

In July 1601, meanwhile, the Spanish siege of Ostend had begun, while English troops were busy fighting a war in Ireland. For the poorly prepared English army, two fronts were too many. Elizabeth therefore decided to negotiate with Henry of France to guard the waters of Calais and prevent the Spanish from invading England by that route.

Henry IV decided to send his close friend the Duke of Biron to speak with Elizabeth and promise not to allow Spanish forces to use Calais as platform for any invasion of English territory.

In March 1602, Henry IV learned from his secret service that the Duke of Biron, his best friend and comrade-in-arms, was working as a Holy Alliance spy in the service of Philip III of Spain. The duke's idea was to turn all the south and east of France over to Spain and be named King of Burgundy and the Franche-Compté in return. The evidence was conclusive. One of the supposed papal spies used by the duke to carry his messages in fact worked for the French, so all his correspondence with Clement VIII and Philip III had come into the possession of Henry IV. On July 31, 1602, the duke was executed in the Bastille, crying fealty to the king, his friend.

In the beginning of 1603, after a forty-five-year reign, the scepter was finally about to pass from Elizabeth's hand. On March 14, her condition improved considerably, so that she was able to receive an ambassador, Giovanni Scaramelli, sent by the Doge of Venice to reestablish diplomatic relations between England and the Serene Republic. The old woman of seventy still found the strength to flirt with the Venetian. On March 16, she suffered a relapse from which she would not recover. Early on Thursday, March 24, 1603, Elizabeth of England died peacefully in her bed, just as her historic enemy Philip II had done five years earlier. As her legitimate heir she left James VI of Scotland, who would adopt the name James I of England.[29] His first measure as the new monarch was to bring the body of his mother, Mary Stuart, from her secluded tomb in Peterborough cemetery to the crypt in Westminster Abbey housing the remains of the kings of England. Elizabeth and Mary now rested together for all eternity.[30]

Rome received the news of the queen's death with joy. Catholicism's great enemy was dead. Clement VIII ordered the bells rung. His joy, however, proved only momentary, for he soon discovered that James I, King of England, Ireland, and Scotland, twenty-fourth King of England in line from William the Conqueror, had not the least intention of making his country into a Catholic realm.

The pope then ordered the creation of a seminary for Scottish priests in Rome and confirmed the English seminaries created in Seville and Valladolid by Philip II, awarding them important privileges and entrusting their direction to the Jesuits. These centers would produce many new agents of the Holy Alliance willing to give their lives in the name of the true faith and in strict obedience to the supreme pontiff. Clement VIII, in fact, made the papal espionage into a true secret service and its members, the majority of them Jesuits, more and more expert in their "executive" missions.

The pontiff also supported the evangelization of America, where he created new dioceses, and of the Far East. Gregory XIII had given his shock troops, the Jesuits, a monopoly on all missionary work in China and Japan, but Clement extended the privilege to all the orders.

On March 5, 1605, Clement died in Rome. However, he left to his successors in this new century all those new horizons to discover, new spaces in which the Holy Alliance could operate. The English heretics were no longer the prime objective above all else.

4

NEW HORIZONS (1605–1644)

His speech is smooth as butter, yet war is in his heart; his words are more
soothing than oil, yet they are drawn swords.

—Psalms 55:21–22

Alessandro de' Medici would go down in history as a brilliant spy
more than he would as a pope. A member of a minor branch of the
illustrious Florentine family, Alessandro became a perfect spy, first
in the service of his cousin the Grand Duke of Tuscany Cosimo I and later
in the service of Pope Clement VIII.

In 1596, the pontiff sent him to France on a mission to get Henry IV to
live up to what he had already agreed when he converted to Catholicism: re-
organizing the Church in France and making peace with Philip II, which
would give rise to the Treaty of Vervins on May 2, 1598, and would end a
war that had been devastating both countries since 1595.[1]

Cardinal de' Medici spent two years directing France's transition to
Catholicism and creating a wide net of spies throughout its territory who
would report to the Holy Alliance. On his return to Rome, he was welcomed
as a true hero by the people and by Pope Clement VIII. The celebrations
lasted six days, all of them well-stocked with wine and food in the highest
Renaissance style.

After Clement's death, three powerful factions contended in the conclave
called to choose his successor: the Spanish faction, the French one, and the
group of cardinals named by the late pope. The last group's candidate did
not win, because the French and Spanish groups elected Alessandro de'

Medici on April 11, 1605, under the name of Leo XI. Seventeen days later, as a result of a fierce cold he caught after his consecration in Letran, the pope died. In the history of the Holy Alliance he left a much deeper mark as Cardinal de' Medici than as Pope Leo XI, because he created one of the best spy networks in France, which would last almost until the Napoleonic era.[2]

His successor on the Throne of St. Peter was Cardinal Camillo Borghese, who adopted the name Paul V. Borghese, originally from Siena, had been sent to Madrid by the pope in 1593 because of his deep knowledge of legal matters. There he established good connections with important members of the court and with Philip II himself. Thanks to these services rendered in Spain, Pope Clement VIII conferred a cardinal's purple robes on him, and in 1603 he became the vicar-general of Rome. After Leo XI's sudden death, the conclave found itself even more divided than before. The Spaniards presented their candidate with French support, but a group of cardinals rejected him. Finally, Camillo Borghese, who, in spite of receiving a pension from Philip II, had stayed in the background, out of the discussions, appeared as the only consensus solution. On May 16, 1605, he was elected pope. The new pontiff was a man of deep reflection, which meant he delayed important decisions for unbelievable amounts of time, something hard to understand in the convulsive European context of the time.

The new pope's policies centered around a sort of neutrality between Madrid and Paris, with continual exhortations for unity directed to French and Spanish Catholics. England obliged all Catholics to swear loyalty to King James I, while in Germany the interreligious conflicts that ignited the so-called Thirty Years' War were breaking out.

In France, meanwhile, things were not going any better for the cause. For years, the monarch had managed to maintain a religious entente cordiale throughout the state. The Huguenots were his, and he had always stayed friendly with them; Protestantism was recognized, as were its churches, since the 1598 signing in Nantes of a royal decree of freedom of worship, subject to a clause requiring fidelity to the king. In the French Counter-Reformation, the old Church won a great victory. The king expelled all the Jesuits, though he would admit them again in 1603.[3]

Henry IV's mistake was to try, in 1610, to assemble a great Protestant force around Catholic France to fight against his country's historic enemy, Spain. Paul V sent a clear message to the Gallic king, urging him to adopt a less warlike stance toward Philip III. After all, Madrid continued to be one of the main sources of finance for the Catholic adventures undertaken by Rome and the Holy Alliance, which had by now become an authentic armed wing of the Church.

In the broadest tradition of political assassination, and as an effective weapon wielded by the Holy Alliance to change the direction of European politics, one attempt on the life of Henry IV had already been made by a friar sent from Rome. Henry had evaded death because the dagger used was a small one that failed to penetrate any vital organs. The king escaped with only a wound in his arm.[4]

In 1604, Denis Lebey de Batilly, a high crown official and president of the Tribunal of Metz, had written a sixty-four-page tract titled *Traicte de l'origine des anciens assains porte-couteaux* and subtitled *With examples of their attempts and homicides against certain kings, princes, and lords of Christianity.*

The book was a reasonably accurate history of the "assassins" and those they had "assassinated." A surprising explanation of the origin of the ancient "assassins," thanks to Lebey de Batilly's lack of historical knowledge, was that their pedigree began with a pre-Islamic sect he described as dating from the time of Alexander the Great. But in spite of those errors, says the historian Edward Burman in his book *Assassins: Holy Killers of Islam,* Lebey de Batilly dared to put forward observations and revelations that contributed to the understanding of the nature of "assassins" in seventeenth-century Europe as well.

The most interesting part of the manuscript recounts how those "assassins" went about killing their victims, from small business owners to great lords. Henry IV's official made the following analysis:

> It will be left to the reader to compare the history of the Assassins with the events of his own age and the miserable effects which men have had to suffer for some time. For unfortunately there exist even in his day religions with *"assasins porte-couteaux"* quite as bad as these medieval fanatics who, encouraged by another "Old Man of the Mountains," are prepared to kill kings and princes who do not belong to the same sect.[5]

One of those leaders was Pope Paul V. While still Cardinal Camillo Borghese and vicar-general of Rome, he managed to get a copy of Denis Lebey de Batilly's manuscript, produced in Lyon, by way of Spain's ambassador to Paris. A year later, now as pope, Paul V transformed the Holy Alliance into a unit specializing in selective assassination.

Paul V's idea was to create a unit of the Holy Alliance willing to kill and be killed in the name of the faith, and to respond without hesitation to orders expressly given by the supreme pontiff in Rome. The pope had been completely captivated by the tales of the *fida'i*[6] told by Lebey de Batilly in his manuscript. In the mind of a seventeenth-century pope, it was completely pardonable for a fervent Catholic to give his own life in the attempt to do away with the existence of a heretic, and if this were a prince opposed to the true faith or its interests, surely the Catholic assassin would arrive quickly in heaven (the Paradise of the Muslims). Pope Paul V was ready to put his corps of *fida'i* Catholics to work through the length and breadth of convulsive Europe.

Paul V was equally fascinated with the legends recounted by Gerhard of Strasburg from his 1175 diplomatic mission to Syria at the behest of Frederick Barbarossa. The emissary wrote in a letter to his emperor:

There is a sect called the *heyssessini* who live between Damascus and Aleppo. Their leader, Prince Sinan, whom the *heyssessini* follow, possesses in the mountains numerous and most beautiful palaces, surrounded by high walls. The leader lives surrounded by servants who have been taught various languages such as Greek, Roman, Saracen, as well as many others. These young men are taught by their teachers from the earliest youth to their full manhood that they must obey the lord of their land in all his words and commands; and that if they do so, he, who has power over all living gods, will give them the joys of paradise. They are also taught that they cannot be saved if they resist his will in anything. Note that, from the time when they are taken in as children, they see no other one but their teachers and masters and receive no other instruction until they are summoned to the presence of the Prince to kill someone. When they are in the presence of this Prince, he asks them if they are willing to obey his commands, so that he may bestow paradise upon them. Whereupon, as they have been instructed, and without any objection or doubt, they throw themselves at his feet and reply with fervor that they will obey him in all things that he may command. Thereupon the Prince gives each one of them a golden dagger and sends them out to kill whichever prince he has marked down.[7]

Five hundred years later, Paul V saw a great historical parallel to the story told by Gerhard in the twelfth century. The pope was a seventeenth-century

Prince Sinan; the priests of his Holy Alliance were his *fida'i* ready to sacrifice their lives to carry out an order from the supreme pontiff. Camillo Borghese saw himself as a sort of "old man" from the mountains of Alamut, the cradle of assassins.

The passage that most pleased Borghese told how each time Prince Sinan galloped through the fields on his horse, he required another man to precede him shouting, "Fly from the man who carries the death of kings and princes in his hands!" Pope Paul V ardently wished to be, or at least to symbolize, that prince of assassins who acted in the name of his faith.

The first death of kings and princes would be that of Henry IV of France. The French monarch maintained a peaceful foreign policy until 1609, but in the beginning of the next year he began preparing to intervene in Germany against the Catholic Hapsburg dynasty—a plan that some French Catholics opposed.[8] Fearing assassination, the king avoided public celebrations for several months; his darkest presentiments soon proved correct.

On the morning of May 14, the king had an early meeting with the Duke of Vendôme, French ambassador to Madrid, and Villeroy, his loyal secretary of state. As they walked through the Tuileries gardens, Henry confessed to the Duke of Guise that he knew he would die soon, because the stars had so indicated, and the king was much devoted to astrology.[9]

When he repaired to his room, the king found a letter lacking any wax seal. Unfolding it, he read, "Sire, under no conditions go out this afternoon." The king ignored the warning and headed out of the palace, escorted by his second-ranking bodyguard, Captain Praslin. Henry IV then rejected Praslin's protection.

Several courtiers, however, did ride with him in his coach: the Duke of Epernon on his right, the Duke of Montbazon and Marshal Laforce on his left, Mirebeau and Liancourt facing him. A horse guard followed the coach, as did several footmen. When they passed the palace of Logueville, the king stuck his head out the door and ordered the coachman to drive to the Saints-Innocents Cemetery. It was a strange place for the king to visit, but the coachman, without comment, turned the horses that way. So far, no one had noticed a large man armed with a double-bladed dagger following the royal coach.[10]

A few minutes later, the coach turned onto the rue de La Ferronnerie and had to slow down because of the narrowness of the street and the group of citizens who halted to salute the king. Though the coachman tried to drive the horses forward, the royal carriage was soon caught between a large wagon full of buckets and another burdened down with hay. When the coachman tried to turn, one of the carriage wheels caught in a rut and remained stuck for several minutes.

The footmen, meanwhile, had taken a shortcut so as to be able to await the king at the cemetery, while the contingent of horse guards had stopped before the group of people cheering the king. Henry IV leaned his arm on Epernon's shoulder while reading an official letter. Just then the man who had been following rapidly neared the carriage, raised one foot onto the running board, and with the finest *fida'i* technique struck at the king with his dagger. This first stroke, however, only inflicted a superficial chest wound.[11]

The king saw a red stain spreading on his jacket and knew he was wounded. The assassin struck again, this time piercing Henry's lung and cutting his aorta. The action was so fast that no one had time to react between blows. The king could only get out the words, "It's nothing," before slumping sideways onto Montbazon with blood pouring from his mouth. It was 4 P.M. on May 14, 1610. The regicide, instead of fleeing amid the confusion, stood by the carriage with the dagger still in his hand. Suddenly, three men who seemed to materialize from nowhere, swords in hand, threw themselves upon the attacker while crying out, "Death to the assassin." The royal guards turned upon these three men and put them to flight.

The Duke of Epernon ordered the assassin brought alive to a secure place away from the fury of the crowd now gathering around the carriage.

The king was rushed to the palace and treated by his private doctor, Dr. Petit, but there was no way to save his life. He had died, in fact, just after the deadly second dagger thrust.[12]

A detachment of the royal guard brought the attacker to the Retz palace near the Louvre. In his pockets they found eight silver coins, a paper bearing the name Beillard, a rosary, and a mysterious octagonal scrap of parchment with Jesus' name on each side and a phrase in the center: "Prepared for the pain of torment, in God's name." The regicide was identified as one Jean-François Ravaillac, who claimed to come from the city of Angulema and to be thirty-two years old. Ravaillac was a big redheaded man with sunken eyes and a long nose. He looked older than his years.[13]

The strangest thing was that Epernon recognized Ravaillac from his time as governor of Angulema. Jean-François Ravaillac had been sent to Epernon by order of a Jesuit priest, Father d'Aubigny. The Jesuits wanted Ravaillac to serve the governor as bodyguard and simultaneously as a Holy Alliance spy.

The interrogators De Jeannin, Buillon, and Loménie told the assassin that the king was merely wounded, and they needed the names of the other conspirators. Refusing to speak, Ravaillac was shackled by his hands and feet and brought to the tower of Montgomery in the Conciergerie. The regicide only repeated, "No Frenchman or Roman [follower of the pope] has participated or given me aid." He was confronted with the Jesuit priest d'Aubigny, without result. After a trial he was sentenced to death.

After Ravaillac's execution, new clues to the plot emerged. A servant of the Marquise of Verneuil accused her employer, the Duke of Epernon, and the Duke of Guise of being instigators of the assassination of Henry IV along with the Jesuits; she claimed to have heard them plotting it some weeks before.

This servant disappeared shortly afterwards, just when the widowed queen was named queen-regent of France until the dauphin should come of age as Louis XIII. In Rome, Pope Paul V held a solemn Mass in memory of the late king, while in some secret part of the catacombs of the Eternal City a Mass was held for the Catholic martyr Jean-François Ravaillac.

Certainly many unanswered questions hung in the air, such as: Where did the three armed men in dark capes come from, who appeared so quickly after the attack? Who were they? Who sent them? Whom did they serve? Did they want to silence the executing arm of the regicide so that the intellectual authors would not come to light? Was the Duke of Epernon involved? What role did the Jesuits play in the plot? Who left the warning note for the king? None of these questions was ever answered.

Be that as it may, years later the French police would discover that Jean-François Ravaillac had been part of a strange Catholic-mystic group called the *Octogonus* Circle[14] or the "8." Its members were Catholic fanatics offering blind obedience to the pope of Rome, with military preparation particularly in the use of special weapons, all prepared to die for the true religion. Its symbol was an octagon with Jesus' name on each side and a legend with the group's slogan: "Prepared for the pain of torment, in God's name," the same as was carried by Henry IV's assassin.

Several books and papers have linked the mysterious and secret *Octogonus* Circle with the Holy Alliance, but without any conclusive proof. The activities and existence of this organization remain shadowy to this day, as do its origins and the name of its founder.

The queen-regent of France decided to fire the previous chief royal minister, the Duke of Sully, and replace him with a Florentine adventurer named Concino Concini, who rapidly became her favorite. This Italian managed to leave his mark on the politics of the decade following 1610, to the point where his contemporaries unanimously described him as wielding considerable power, uncharacteristic for a foreigner in the French court.[15] Concini also became one of Pope Paul V's best sources of information in Paris. He was not a member of the Holy Alliance, but he was one of the most important spies any seventeenth-century pope could have had.

Some historians insist that Concino Concini served under the orders of Cardinal Alessandro de' Medici before he became Pope Leo XI, helping put together the French network of papal spies during the cardinal's mission to France. Whether or not this is true, the Florentine surely made his mark during the regency period as one of the most famous papal spies. Other sources claim that Concini really served no one but Concini, and the goal of his espionage work in France was simply to carve himself out a position of power during the regency.

His power, according to the historian J.-F. Dubost, emerged in three distinct stages: 1610 to 1614, 1614 to 1616, and finally 1617. In the first period, Concino Concini and his wife, Leonora Galigai, concentrated on amassing an important fortune and acquiring land and positions thanks to Leonora's close relationship with the queen-regent. Concini's wife's influence over Marie de' Medici brought great economic benefit to the Florentine spy. In a very short time, he had made his word count in appointments to high positions within the royal house as well as in the selection of bishops. The economic benefits allowed him to become Marquis of Ancre in 1610 and be named marshal in 1613. In only three years, thanks in part to his wife, the Italian had risen from a mere messenger for Cardinal de' Medici and unimportant spy for Paul V to the imposing position of a marshal of France.[16]

That same year, the dauphin came of age and assumed the position of king, with Marie de' Medici as chief of government. The Concinis were thus able to maintain their previous position, but 1616 would be the year of their greatest ascent.

Concino Concini and his wife pushed to manipulate French politics as they chose. It was rumored that Concini had tightened his relations with Paul V. The Florentine saw to it that all the ministers of the assassinated Henry IV lost their jobs, to be replaced by new ones to his and the Vatican's taste. Barbin became minister of finance; Mangot, keeper of the seals; and Richelieu, foreign minister.[17]

The Italian was ever more ensconced in high places thanks to the spy network created in the kitchens of the great houses of France, many of these spies having previously worked for Cardinal Alessandro de' Medici before he had become Leo XI.

Concino Concini, son and nephew of ministers serving the Grand Duke of Tuscany, was a proponent of absolutism. His advice to Louis XIII reinforced that notion of government. Thanks to his proximity to the king, all the small and large affairs of France passed through his hands, from the naming of a new bishop to the documents that discussed possible alliances with other states.[18] All such information was sent on to Rome through the wide spy network Paul V had created in France.

The one who forged a connection with the Holy Alliance was not Concino Concini himself, but his wife. From 1601 on, Galigai had maintained close connections with Queen Marie de' Medici as her lady-in-waiting. Some historians have asserted that Concini's wife was in fact just a link between the queen and Pope Clement VIII's Holy Alliance, although this remains unproved.[19] In 1605, Concini became part of the queen's trusted inner circle, rising within nine years from maître d'hotel to first chamberlain, the position he held at the time of his fall in 1617.

In the first stages of the regency, Concino Concini concentrated on appointments to positions related to French finances. With the formation of a new government in 1616, now under the rule of Louis XIII, Concini plunged deeper into affairs of state. In that year, the Vatican nuncio Bentivoglio wrote the letter that can now be found in the Bibliothèque Nationale de France:

> The marshal [Concini] also spoke to me of these three new ministers as his own men, and showed great pleasure at my praise of Mangot and Luçon, whom I had already visited, and told me that I was to esteem Barbin still more, since he could be the master of the other two in important matters.[20]

Clearly these men were the creatures of the spy Concino Concini, given that they owed their jobs to him, and once appointed, they were subject to the Florentine's decisions.

One of Concini's measures that provoked the most protests and hatred from the citizenry was his establishment of fortresses to withstand not the attacks of foreign aggressors but those of the king's subjects. For Concini, these hulking monuments were a way to display the ruler's true power to the people, even by provoking fear. To carry out this policy, the Marshal of Ancre called on the leading experts, Italian engineers who had served the Spanish armies in Flanders: Pompeo Frangipani, Apollon Dougnano, and Giuseppe Gamurrini. Between 1615 and 1617, with the aid of the three Italians, he began to extend royal power by building such fortresses, an effort that continued even after his death. Striking examples of the policy are the fortifications of Montpellier (1622), the fortress of Saint-Nicolas in Marseilles (1660), and the castle of Trompette in Bordeaux (1675).[21] Curiously, copies of the plans for all these fortifications can be found in the Vatican Secret Archives, cataloged in 1743 by order of Pope Benedict XIV.

In 1617, the Concinis' hour of reckoning came. In October, the Florentine found himself in the eye of a hurricane capable of unleashing a new civil war in France. By that point, and on the nuncio Bentivoglio's advice, Pope Paul V had decided to cut himself off from the Concinis. He had instructed all Holy Alliance agents to cease any actions ordered by the Italian, and from then on any order from Concini to members of the papal espionage system was indeed referred to Rome for discussion. Concino Concini's growing unpopularity compromised not only Marie de' Medici but Louis XIII and the monarchy as well. Little by little, the weight of public opinion and the king's personal dislike of the marshal began to bear fruit among the nobles, who tended to see Concini exclusively as a foreigner and papal spy.[22]

Finally, on April 24, 1617, while Concini made his way on foot to the Louvre palace, he was stabbed to death by three unknown men. The three assassins were members of Louis XIII's royal guard and had acted on his express order. "A man with Concino Concini's power cannot be fired," Cardinal Richelieu would later say. "He has to be killed." Richelieu, of course, would become one of the giants of French politics, and of French intrigue as well.[23]

Concino Concini—Florentine adventurer, Marshal of France, and papal spy who had raised bribery and political intrigue to an art—had become a nuisance to King Louis. The king's only way out was to order his assassination. Concini made three serious mistakes, the nuncio Bentivoglio wrote to Pope Paul V: He displayed the riches he had obtained from the king, he displayed a degree of wealth inappropriate to a man of his humble origins, and the wealth he put on display had been obtained by immoral or at least doubtful means.[24]

The day of Concini's assassination, Louis XIII himself ordered Leonora Galigai's arrest. The monarch could not leave any loose ends, and Concini's wife fell in that category. Apparently the king gave the order to eliminate her to Cardinal Richelieu, who took care of the final act of the drama.

The cardinal's agents began spreading rumors on the streets of Paris to the effect that Leonora Galigai was involved in witchcraft and had bewitched the queen, Marie de' Medici. Soldiers of the royal guard arrested Galigai in her house near the palace while she was writing a letter to the nuncio Bentivoglio pleading for protection in his residence for herself and her servants.[25]

Searching her house, the soldiers found three books with magic characters, five rolls of red velvet for controlling the spirits of the great, and some pendants she wore on her neck. Taken as talismans and amulets for satanic rites, all of these formed part of the evidence for the charge of witchcraft brought against her.[26] Leonora Galigai, wife of Concino Concini, lady-in-waiting to the Queen Marie de' Medici, and spy for Paul V, was found guilty of witchcraft and sentenced to death. The next day, in an unknown place, the same members of the royal guard who had killed her husband decapitated her. Her body was burned in a bonfire in 1617.

The deaths of Concino Concini and his wife opened a new era of intrigues in France, now choreographed by Cardinal Richelieu, star pupil of the Florentine spy and one of the greatest statesmen of his era. But the Holy Alliance had other goals, connected with the Jesuits. Paul V was more interested in using espionage to win souls for the cause of the Catholic faith than to garner more economic or political power in a Europe consuming itself in the Thirty Years' War.

On January 21, 1621, Pope Paul V died. After a three-day conclave, Cardinal Alessandro Ludovisi became his successor, adopting the name Gregory XV. Like Cardinal Maffeo Barberini (who would later become Urban VIII), Ludovisi was an expert diplomat and able spy who had operated in Spain and France. He had negotiated the peace between Philip III of Spain and Charles Emmanuel I of Savoy over a problem involving the marquisate of Monferrato. On September 19, 1616, he was elevated to cardinal and, some evidence suggests, was assigned by Pope Paul V to reform the Holy Alliance, now fifty years old, and to establish a set of rules for its governance.

As pope, Gregory XV surrounded himself with family members whom he appointed to high Vatican posts. One of the most important for the history of the Holy Alliance was his nephew Ludovico Ludovisi. Born in Bologna, like the pope, he became a cardinal when he was only twenty-five, on the day of Gregory's coronation. The pontiff put his young nephew in charge of overseeing religious and political affairs, including espionage operations.

The two years during which Ludovico Ludovisi led the Holy Alliance were marked by the Thirty Years' War (1618–48) and in particular by a disputed succession in Austria and wars in Bohemia and the Palatinate. His agents were tied up in maneuvering to overthrow the Palatine elector Frederick V, head of the so-called Evangelical Union, and in supporting Maximilian of Bavaria (1598–1641).[27]

On July 8, 1623, Gregory XV died, leaving his nephew Ludovisi still in charge of the Holy Alliance, but the installation of a new pope brought his short but intense career as head of papal espionage to an end. Urban VIII, Gregory's successor, sent Ludovisi to Bologna, where he had been archbishop since 1621. Ludovisi remained there until he died, November 18, 1632, at the age of thirty-six. According to some sources, young Ludovico Ludovisi was poisoned by Protestant followers of Frederick V in revenge for his role in the war against Maximilian.

Maffeo Barberini's election as the new pope began one of the darkest and least glorious periods of the pontifical espionage service, from any point of view.

Born to a rich Florentine merchant family who dealt in oriental silks, the future pope was only three years old when his father died, which led his mother to entrust him to the Jesuits of his native city. Soon he was sent to the Jesuits of Rome, and after completing his schooling there he studied law at the University of Pisa. He began his career as a priest under the patronage of his uncle Francesco Barberini, and a brilliant career it soon became. Clement VIII sent him to France in 1601 to congratulate Henry IV on the birth of the dauphin. In 1604, he became papal nuncio in Paris, where he provided great support to the Jesuits.[28]

On September 11, 1606, Paul V made him a cardinal. King Henry IV himself bestowed the cardinal's cap in a solemn ceremony. Two years later, Barberini was named protector of the kingdom of Scotland.[29]

As Urban VIII, however, his pontificate was marred by nepotism and also by his propensity for intrigues, in which he made use of Holy Alliance agents as needed. Like his predecessor, the new pope surrounded himself with a large court of relatives. In 1623, he named his older brother Carlo general of the papal armies and Duke of Monte Redondo. That same year, Carlo's eldest son,

Francesco, became a cardinal at the age of twenty-six, and the following year Francesco's younger brother Antonio was named cardinal penitentiary, head librarian, papal chamberlain, and prefect of the Tribunal of the Signatura.

In spite of the panoply of positions held by the young cardinal and nephew of the pope, Antonio Barberini never gained control of the Holy Alliance. That job belonged to Cardinal Lorenzo Magalotti, who from 1628 combined the direction of the papal secret service with the role of secretary of state.

Really, Magalotti monopolized all the powers belonging to the College of Cardinals, which provoked serious responses from his colleagues. To quiet them, Urban VIII decided to award them new titles: "eminences" and "princes of the Church." But his most difficult task was to confront a true genius of intrigue and one of the greatest conspirators of the seventeenth century, Cardinal Richelieu.

Richelieu had become one of the most powerful men in France. He came from a family of noble lineage but much reduced finances, which impelled him to a career in the Church, where he became a bishop.[30] He soon discovered that absolutely everything around him was a question of state, from the economy to the religious wars. After Henry IV's assassination, in the regency of Marie de' Medici, Cardinal Richelieu had his first moment of glory, always protected by Concini. But when Louis XIII came into power and broke with all the queen's favorites, Richelieu was forced into exile.

In 1624, at the age of thirty-eight and thanks to a series of conspiracies, the cardinal managed to make his way back into Louis XIII's court. Little by little, he took on the reins of government until he was formally named Prime Minister of France. He began a great career in the service of France, employing any and all means, legal or not. Richelieu's chief assistant outside the royal palace was François Le Clerc du Tremblay, also known as Père Joseph, a former Holy Alliance agent and—some say—member of the ultrasecret *Octogonus* Circle to which Henry IV's assassin, Jean-François Ravaillac, belonged. History books have not settled the question of whether Tremblay was Richelieu's brain as well as his eyes and ears or whether he merely carried out the cardinal's orders, but the collaboration between the cardinal and the Dominican priest was one of the most effective in governing a nation and in mounting intrigues on the great chessboard that mid-seventeenth-century Europe had become.[31]

Joseph du Tremblay was born in Paris in November of 1577. He was ordained in 1604, and he journeyed to Rome in 1616, when the pontificate of

Paul V was in its most critical moment. There he made contact with other Dominican members of the Holy Alliance who taught him the espionage systems of the era, such as shadowing, assassination through poison, and techniques of encoding messages. Once back in France, he traveled through various cities until April 1624, when he made his way into Cardinal Richelieu's inner circle. Many assert that in that same year, or perhaps in 1625, Joseph du Tremblay became France's unofficial minister of foreign affairs. He also became one of the most unwavering enemies of the agents of the Holy Alliance.[32]

For Richelieu, the absolute power of the crown was no end in itself. Rather, to him, the king was the leading servant of the state. The cardinal tended to oppose the old European foreign policy, which had been dedicated almost entirely to religious questions, and favor a politics tied to reasons of state. For him, religious questions and state interests were opposed most of the time. The best example was France's opposition to the Spanish-Hapsburg alliance, an opposition seconded in part by Pope Urban VIII's own fear of Hapsburg ambitions in Italy. This provoked a break in Catholic unity and added fuel to the flames of the Thirty Years' War.

One of largest conspiracies knitted by the Holy Alliance in Richelieu's France involved constructing a so-called league of nobles. A large swath of the French Catholic aristocracy opposed Richelieu's policy of allying with Protestant former enemies to fight against Spain, and Cardinal Magalotti did not want to see them persecuted for this position. Magalotti, Urban VIII's trusted lieutenant, assigned a young priest from Siena to create a network of Catholic nobles who opposed Richelieu and his anti-Spanish policy.

Giulio Guarnieri, the priest in question, was the son of an Italian father and a French mother. The father was a wine merchant who traveled throughout France in search of fine varieties to supply the great and noble families of Paris, Siena, Florence, and Rome. This allowed young Giulio to cultivate contacts among the French nobility, and sometimes to earn good money as an occasional messenger between French politicians and those of Mantua who were opposed to Spanish interests.

Magalotti, as head of the Holy Alliance, wanted to always have one foot firmly placed in France in case Urban VIII's support of Richelieu should prove a misstep that soured relations with Spain.[33]

The pope had already declared himself in favor of French goals over Spanish interests in the conflicts of Valtellina and Mantua. In the first case, he supported the Treaty of Monçon in 1626, which separated the Catholic region of Valtellina from the Protestant Grisons. Valtellina, situated at the borders of France, Italy, and Switzerland, was an apparently unimportant region, but Urban VIII and Magalotti wanted to know why Richelieu was so concerned about it. The Holy Alliance agent Giulio Guarnieri, well acquainted with the region, thanks to his travels alongside his father, then wrote to Magalotti:

> Cardinal Richelieu has such interest in Valtellina because of a narrow valley of great strategic value. This valley permits the passage of Spanish troops from Lombardy toward Germany and the Netherlands. If the French were to close it off, the Spaniards could not communicate with the north except by sea.

The strategic region, just as Guarnieri predicted, fell prisoner to religious struggles for control of the valley. The Protestant side sought support in Venice and in Richelieu's France. The Catholic side sought support in Spain and Austria. Finally, in 1620, the Spaniards occupied Valtellina while the Austrians did the same to the valley of Munster. This displeased France, and Cardinal Richelieu resolved the problem in his favor with a clever move. He guaranteed the inhabitants' full autonomy as long as they would practice Catholicism exclusively. That was a success for the pope, who had appointed himself as a mediator in the peace negotiations.[34]

Meanwhile, Guarnieri had his hands free to continue operating within France in concert with the Catholic nobility, always persecuted because of their opposition to Richelieu's anti-Spanish policy. Guarnieri was their only link to the Vatican and Urban VIII.

Pope Urban VIII's attitude during these tragic events was not very clear. His sympathy for France and Richelieu despite their Protestant alliances was criticized by the Holy Roman Empire's representative in Rome, Cardinal Pasmany. A few years later it was revealed that Giulio Guarnieri and perhaps his boss, Cardinal Magalotti, worked for Pasmany, who in turn informed Spain and the Empire about the movements of Protestant troops.

For more than eight years, Richelieu's spies, led by Joseph du Tremblay, vainly sought to discover the identity of Cardinal Magalotti's spy in France. They came to call Giulio Guarnieri the "phantom spy" and even to believe that Magalotti had invented him.

Meanwhile, to reduce the prestige of the House of Austria and increase that of Louis XIII, Richelieu deemphasized religious principles and maintained all of France in permanent fear of war. It was remorse over this contradiction between religious struggle and political compromise that tortured the conscience of Joseph du Tremblay.[35]

The French spy chief died of an attack of apoplexy in 1638 in Richelieu's castle at Rueil. Four years later, Armand Jean du Plessis (Richelieu himself) died as well. His political heir was Cardinal Jules Mazarin, of Italian origin. On July 29, 1644, Pope Urban VIII followed du Tremblay and Richelieu to the grave, in his case a tomb sculpted by Bernini in the Basilica of St. Peter. After twenty-one years as pope, he left a somber memory among Catholics, who accused him of traitorous behavior for his role in the Thirty Years' War.

Guilio Guanieri, the "phantom spy," kept on working for the Holy Alliance in the France of Mazarin and Louis XIV. The dark era when papal espionage had to work for the Protestant cause because of Urban VIII's neutrality came to an end. Thanks to men like Cardinal Lorenzo Magalotti, head of the Alliance, and the spy Giulio Guarnieri, the Catholic cause had been protected in a hungry and war-torn Europe. Now a new era of expansion would begin.

5

ERA OF EXPANSION (1644–1691)

Do not repeat false reports, nor bear false witness for the wicked. Neither shall you follow the multitude in doing evil, nor, when giving testimony, side with the many in perverting justice.

—Exodus 23:1–2

O n the death of Pope Urban VIII, the cardinals met once again to choose a successor. And once again, the conclave found itself divided by clans and disputes. On one side, the Spanish-Austrian party opposed the previous pope's policies and, therefore, any candidate who had been advanced by Urban VIII. On the other side stood the pro-French party, led by Cardinal Antonio Barberini and supported from Paris by Cardinal Jules Mazarin himself.

Spain had given its clear support to Cardinal Sacchetti, proposed through Cardinal Francesco Barberini (Sacchetti's cousin), but he was rejected by Mazarin. A few days later, on September 15, 1644, the Barberinis decided to unite behind the candidacy of Cardinal Giovanni Battista Pamphili, an old man of seventy-two who adopted the name Innocent X.

The new pope followed the custom of appointing family members to the highest spots in the Church hierarchy. The problem he faced was that the family figure best equipped to carry out such a leading role was a woman, his sister-in-law Olimpia Maidalchini.[1]

Olimpia was a strong woman, the widow of the pope's older brother, after whose death she had managed to place all her sons in high social positions. Innocent X awarded a cardinal's purple to his nephew Camillo Pamphili,

Olimpia's oldest son. Thus the new cardinal became a vehicle through whom his mother could direct or counsel the pope.[2]

In a short time, Olimpia Maidalchini became one of the most powerful individuals surrounding the pope, in spite of not even being allowed to have a private conversation with him. All communications and orders passed through her son—the pope's nephew—Cardinal Camillo Pamphili.

During the first three years of this papacy, Olimpia advised the pope only about political issues of minor importance, such as questions relating to the Roman infrastructure, which noble families should be favored, and which should be punished. In January 1647, Camillo Pamphili, the secret channel between Innocent X and Olimpia Maidalchini, renounced his position and his priesthood to marry Olimpia Aldobrandini, niece of Clement VIII and widow of Paolo Borghese. A new messenger was needed—a discreet one, of course.

The pope then granted cardinals' hats to Francesco Maidalchini and Camillo Astalli, both Olimpia's relatives, so they might become puppets for himself and his sister-in-law. It was Olimpia who recommended to the pontiff that he name Cardinal Panciroli as both secretary of state and supervisor of the Holy Alliance. This followed the path of Urban VIII, who had wanted the papal espionage service and the Church's politics to go hand in hand.[3]

By way of Panciroli, Olimpia extra-officially pulled the levers of the Holy Alliance. She not only secretly attended the meetings between Innocent X and his secretary of state but also decided what operations should be mounted. One of the main enemies of the Holy Alliance was still Cardinal Mazarin's France, but Maidalchini managed this situation with a certain feminine touch.

Louis XIII had died a few months after Richelieu and been succeeded by his son Louis XIV. Due to the new monarch's tender age of five, however, his mother, Anne of Austria, ruled as regent. The queen mother named Cardinal Jules Mazarin head of her council. From then on, Mazarin (called by his enemies "the stingy Sicilian" because of his origins and proclivities) was on his way to absolute control of the state power of France.[4]

Mazarin had first developed a close friendship with his patron Richelieu while serving as papal nuncio in France. Then he left the pope's service and became part of the apparatus of state power in Paris. Queen Anne's trust in him and the incapacity of the rest of the royal family did the rest.

Little by little, things deteriorated to the point that the mostly Catholic nobility began to conspire against the increasingly absolutist power of the state.[5] These intrigues were partly supported and allegedly financed by the

Holy Alliance on the recommendation of its shadow chief, Olimpia Maidal-chini.

Cardinal Mazarin had managed to infiltrate spies into the Vatican, who informed him about the pope's maneuvers against France. In response, Maid-alchini created a counterespionage unit within the Holy Alliance, known as the Black Order. Its members' job was to identify Mazarin's agents and exe-cute them on the spot.[6]

To this end, the unit's eleven members, chosen from the ranks of the Holy Alliance by Maidalchini herself, received a pontifical seal engraved in silver with the image of a woman in a toga holding a cross in one hand and a sword in the other. Apparently the Black Order's emblem paid homage to the su-pervisor of papal espionage herself.[7]

One of Mazarin's best spies in the Vatican was a Genovese priest named Al-berto Mercati. He had been recruited during Mazarin's period as papal nuncio in France. On his return to Rome, Mercati had become part of Cardinal Pan-ciroli's circle, assigned to the secretariat of state as an expert in French affairs. Between 1647 and 1650, important documents relating to France passed through Alberto Mercati's hands. He forwarded their contents to Mazarin through a complex system of messengers.

Mercati knew that the monks of the Black Order were on his trail, and that Olimpia Maidalchini herself had promised the capture of whatever mole was operating under the protection of a high church official.[8] For the spy, this contest became a game more than a question of espionage pure and simple. Mercati left false clues at inns and taverns in an attempt to throw the Holy Alliance agents off his trail, but he also knew that sooner or later the Black Order would discover his identity.

One Holy Alliance operation uncovered by Alberto Mercati was the Fronde movement. Anti-Mazarin and anti-absolutist, the movement was created by high-ranking Catholic nobles who had been forced to pay steep taxes that ended up in the coffers of the cardinal and his followers, all with the approval of the regent, Anne of Austria.[9]

The movement's name ("slingshot") came from a seventeenth-century Pa-risian children's game. Many of the Assembly deputies who made up the Fronde refused to accept new taxes without parliamentary approval. They also established that no subject of the king could be detained for more than twenty-four hours without being questioned and sent before a judge.[10]

Thanks to a document sent by a French agent to Cardinal Panciroli, the spy Alberto Mercati learned that the Vatican and Innocent X were involved in the conspiracy against Mazarin. The infiltrator tried to send an urgent message to Mazarin informing him of a plot by an organization called the Fronde to overthrow King Louis XIV, Queen Anne of Austria, and Mazarin, but the message never arrived.[11]

The unsigned message had been given to a member of the pope's Swiss Guard, a Frenchman, in fact. He was supposed to get it to Paris, but the monks of the Black Order intercepted Mercati's coded letter. The papal soldier's corpse was found hanging from a bridge the next day, with his hands cut off. Attached to his garments was a small strip of black cloth with two red stripes, the symbol of the Black Order.

That same day, the head of the Swiss Guard brought the letter to Olimpia Maidalchini to be destroyed, while the uprising in France went forward. Paris soon filled with street fights and barricades. France teetered on the edge of civil war between the followers of Anne of Austria and Cardinal Jules Mazarin on one hand, and on the other hand the backers of the Prince of Condé, Louis de Bourbon, who wanted the cardinal deposed.[12] To support Condé, Innocent X sent Cardinal de Retz, a Gascon who was also Louis XIV's uncle.[13]

The most important members of the Fronde were not very sure of Retz's loyalties, but in spite of everything, he was Rome's envoy and had the favor of Louis de Bourbon and Innocent X.

Within three months, the revolt was snuffed out. A temporary peace lasted until 1650, when Mazarin had Louis de Bourbon arrested, provoking a new "Fronde" that would last until 1652. In fact, the true author of the Prince of Condé's arrest was Anne of Austria, who was tired of the nobleman's insolence, his lust for power, and his longing to replace the cardinal. But the Holy Alliance agents in Paris preferred to make the populace believe that his detention had been part of a plot by the hated Cardinal Mazarin, a device that further fed the flames.[14]

The provinces of Burgundy and Aquitaine rose against Condé's detention, as did the Duke of Lorraine and the Count of Harcourt. The citizens of Paris took up arms while Parliament demanded Mazarin's exile. Mazarin instead decided to release Louis of Bourbon and then to take temporary refuge in Germany.

Meanwhile, in Rome, after the death of Cardinal Panciroli in early 1651, Olimpia Maidalchini held on to control of the Holy Alliance. Innocent X had named Cardinal Fabio Chigi (the future Alexander VII) to replace Panciroli. Chigi wanted to take control of the apparatus of power in the Vatican, including the Holy Alliance. Maidalchini was an obstacle to him.

Finally, with the mediation of Innocent X, Chigi made a deal with Maidalchini that deprived her of control over the Holy Alliance or its agents but left her in charge of the Black Order.[15] The pope's sister-in-law had no choice but to accept. After all, what she most ardently wanted was to arrest Mazarin's mole.

On September 6, 1652, the Genovese Alberto Mercati was found hanging from a beam in his house in Rome. Stuffed in his mouth was a small scrap of black cloth with two crossed red stripes. The long arm of the Black Order had reached one of the most brilliant enemy spies operating in the Vatican. Purportedly before he died the spy accused Cardinal Panciroli of having ordered him to pass information to Mazarin, but this has never been proved.

On January 7, 1655, Innocent X died at the age of eighty-one. His body remained on view for some hours in the Basilica of St. Peter, but since no one knew what to do with it, for a time afterwards it was taken to a dark room where workers stored their tools. Later he was given a modest tomb in the Church of St. Agnes, in the much-visited Piazza Navona. With the death of Innocent X, the last of the Counter-Reformation popes passed from the scene.

Yet again, the great powers of Europe had to decide who would lead the Catholic Church. The best-positioned was Cardinal Sacchetti, one of the great enemies of the Holy Alliance, which he called "an instrument of the devil good for nothing but doing evil from the shadows." Sacchetti had openly declared his doubts about an arm of the Church so powerful that the popes themselves could not control it. He was determined to do away with it, whatever that would cost. This position may have prevented his selection as the successor to Innocent X.

Cardinal Fabio Chigi, who had directed the Holy Alliance since 1651, had no desire to see the demise of the espionage service that had cost so many lives. Therefore he decided on a dangerous game, informing Philip IV of Spain about Cardinal Sacchetti's evidently pro-French activities and his possible friendship with Cardinal Mazarin. With this information in mind, the monarch decided to block Sacchetti and back the loyal Chigi as successor to Innocent X.[16] Finally, after four months in conclave, on April 7, 1655, the College of Cardinals elected Fabio Chigi, who adopted the name of Pope Alexander VII.

His pontificate would become enmeshed in dozens of political conspiracies and in open conflict with France, in part because of the weakness of the papal states after the signing of the "infamous" Peace of Westphalia in 1648.

Alexander VII was a man with obvious diplomatic skills. Breaking with the nepotism of his predecessors, the new pope preferred to make his own decisions after consulting with experts on each matter.

As his first measure, the new pope decided to reform the entire Roman curia, including its secret services. That measure affected Olimpia Maidalchini, who still had the Black Order under her control.[17] The pope made Maidalchini return control of this mysterious organization to the Holy Alliance, dissolve the Black Order, require its members to pledge obedience to the new pontiff, and, finally, herself retire from public life in exchange for a large sum of money.

In obedience to Alexander VII, the still-powerful Olimpia Maidalchini accepted all his demands and retired to her Roman residence until her death in 1657 at the age of sixty-four. Thus ended one of the darkest yet most interesting periods in the history of Vatican espionage. The new leadership of the Holy Alliance fell to Cardinal Corrado, also datary of the Congregation of Immunity.

Cardinal Corrado lacked expertise in politics, and even more so in questions of intrigue, so essential to running an organization as powerful as the Holy Alliance. He was more interested in the study of religion than in something as worldly as a spy service, even one charged with protecting the interests of the pope and the Catholic Church in a continent ever more antagonistic to the papal states.[18]

Relations between Rome and Paris were going through a difficult stage. France had not been able to defeat Spain abroad, and its internal situation remained unstable after the final Fronde. The new strong man, alongside the weakening Mazarin, was the finance minister Fouquet. His ambition and greed surpassed even those of his predecessors, Mazarin and Richelieu. The capital's streets were plagued with religious riots led by the Jansenites, demanding Catholic reform, which began to affect the government and the crown.[19] The Anglo-French friendship treaty signed in 1655 with Oliver Cromwell, Lord Protector of England, gave Mazarin new strength to continue his war against Spain. The Spanish losses of Dunkirk and far-off Jamaica forced Philip IV to sign a treaty of peace.[20]

The negotiations, planned by the French queen, Anne of Austria, and by Cardinal Mazarin, revolved around a possible marriage of the young King Louis XIV and Philip IV's daughter Maria Theresa. Pope Alexander VII and his counselor, Cardinal Sforza Pallavicino, looked favorably on this plan. Pallavicino had become one of the pope's closest advisors, even taking control of the Holy Alliance from Cardinal Corrado. He saw this royal marriage as a means to lessen French aggressiveness toward the weak papal states.

The marriage proposed in 1658 led to the signing of the Peace of the Pyrenees on the Spanish-French border, November 7 of the following year. In this document, which also reflected the input of Alexander VII, France made a number of concessions. Condé, leader of the Fronde, got his possessions back. French troops left Catalunya and a number of smaller districts, all of which returned to Spanish sovereignty. France gave up Portugal, which did, however, maintain its independence from Spain. Spain's power in Italy and in the Franche-Compté of Burgundy remained intact. The Peace of the Pyrenees, like that of Westphalia, was a treaty signed out of exhaustion, but France had the look of a new European power in comparison with the ever-weakening Spain. On March 9, 1661, Cardinal Mazarin died, making way for the absolutist monarchy of Louis XIV and French power over all of Europe.

During these years, Pope Alexander VII was merely an accidental witness to most of the European developments. What the pope in Rome wanted least was to stir up the passions of neighboring and powerful France, but a hidden hand saw to it that those passions would be dangerously stirred up.

Two serious incidents came close to provoking open war between Louis XIV and Pope Alexander VII. The first occurred on June 11, 1662, when France's new ambassador in Rome, the Duke of Crèqui, escorted by two hundred armed guards, tried to force an audience with the pope. Crèqui thought that Alexander VII had to grant him a hearing as representative of Louis XIV, but the pontiff was not so inclined. Cardinal Pallavicino ordered the pope's Corsican Guard to mass in the entrance to the papal residence so as to block any attempt by the French armed forces to penetrate the pontiff's rooms. Ambassador Crèqui then protested to Cardinal Rospigliosi, secretary of state. The duke also told King Louis XIV of the affront he had suffered as representative of the French crown in Rome.

The second incident occurred on August 20, 1662, when four men, apparently Holy Alliance agents, had a run-in with three French diplomats.

What started out as an argument escalated into a swordfight in the street close to the Farnese Palace, which housed the French diplomatic legation. The sound of clashing blades caught the attention of a Corsican Guard patrol assigned to the area, and also of a detachment of French soldiers protecting the diplomatic site. On arriving at the scene, they found two Frenchmen, as well as one of the Holy Alliance agents, mortally wounded. The other agents, after a serious confrontation with the French troops, were arrested by the Corsican Guard and placed in a jail cell in one of their barracks.[21]

The three Holy Alliance agents, however, were set free when they turned out to be former members of the Black Order under Olimpia Maidalchini. Apparently Cardinal Pallavicino had decided to revive the counterespionage service in spite of the contrary instructions from Pope Alexander VII. Sforza Pallavicino wanted to maintain Maidalchini's men as a nucleus of power, as well as hold on to control of the secrets amassed during the years in which Innocent X's sister-in-law had run the papal espionage service.

When news of the second incident reached Paris, Louis XIV ordered the papal nuncio's immediate expulsion. Mobilized French troops occupied Avignon, and the entire army was ordered to prepare for a long punitive campaign against the overproud Vatican state.[22] War was knocking at the gates of Rome, and this time there was not much that the weak Spain of Philip IV could do.

Alexander VII tried to get the duchess-regent of Savoy, Louis XIV's cousin, to mediate, but this effort failed. The pope had to accept the humiliating conditions of the Treaty of Pisa, signed February 12, 1664.[23] Cardinal Imperiali, the governor of Rome, was sent to Paris to apologize to the king. Mario and Agostino Chigi, relatives of the pope, were sent to the Farnese palace to apologize to the French ambassador, the Duke of Crèqui. The members of the Corsican Guard were discharged and their unit dissolved. Cardinal Pallavicino retired from the public eye, although he continued to wield the same power behind the scenes. Meanwhile, Pope Alexander VII won his place in history with the proclamation of a "secret bull" of February 18, 1664, which protested the French impositions and the Treaty of Pisa, signed only six days earlier to save Italy from foreign occupation:

> We declare, in relation to these doings, that we are opposed to violence and force, although we could not resist that which was imposed without our will or consent. I order that the present statement and protest, written

by ourself, should stand in defense of the truth, with all our power, even if we are unable to make it public.[24]

Evidently the brutality shown by Louis XIV toward the pope after the incident of August 20 was only a pretext to humiliate Rome, Alexander VII and his administration, and the Catholic Church. On his deathbed, the supreme pontiff upbraided the Duke of Chaulnes about the mistreatment of the nuncio in Paris and the damage done to the church in France by royal authority. Alexander died on May 22, 1667, at the age of sixty-nine and was buried in the magnificent mausoleum that Bernini had built for him in the Basilica of St. Peter.

Alexander's death provoked a new wave of Holy Alliance operations, this time in Asia.

Beginning in 1668 with the collapse of the Ming Dynasty, European diplomatic legations began to establish themselves in China with the approval of the Qing government. The Dutch went in 1668 and the Portuguese in 1670, followed by the embassies of Russia and of the papal states at the beginning of the eighteenth century. The result was to introduce the political and religious problems afflicting Europe into China, creating a breeding ground for the operations of spies representing all sides.[25]

The first such spy to meet his death in China was a Dutchman named Olfert Dapper, who had arrived in Asia in 1667 under the orders of Van Hoorn. His mission was to reach an accord with high officials of the Qing court that would grant Holland an exclusive commercial concession, freezing out other European powers. The accord would include a tax exemption for all Dutch ships that anchored in Chinese ports.[26]

When Pope Clement IX, Alexander VII's successor, learned of the Dutch designs, he ordered his agents to eliminate any such impediment to the shipping and other interests of Catholic countries in China. On October 11, 1668, Olfert Dapper was found with his head cut off in a slum adjoining the harbor of Canton.

European residents concluded that this had been a settling of accounts between some Chinese faction and Dapper, though inside the legations it was also rumored that the Dutch diplomat and trader had been executed by the alleged *Octogonus* Circle to which Henry IV's assassin, Jean-François Ravaillac, had belonged, or else by the Black Order. In any case, Olfert Dapper's death set back the signing of a Dutch-Chinese commercial agreement by many years.[27]

Clement IX's sudden death on December 9, 1669, made him only a short-term, transitional pope. This time no less than six factions contended in the selection of a pope to succeed him. The Spaniards allied with Cardinal Chigi promoted the candidacy of Cardinal Scipio d'Elce, but the French blocked his way. Cardinal Azzolini presented Cardinal Vidoni, former nuncio in Poland, but he in turn was barred by Spain. Only when the monarchs of Venice, Spain, and France ordered their ambassadors to find a compromise choice did the conclave, after four months of fruitless votes, choose the aged Cardinal Emilio Altieri as the next pope. He adopted the name Clement X in memory of his predecessor, who had granted him the cardinal's purple.[28]

This pope did not consider the Holy Alliance's role in the European chess game to be of much importance. Clement X preferred the subtleties of politics and diplomacy to the rougher methods of the Holy Alliance. The new pontiff chose to delegate his powers, but lacking family members upon whom he could count, he opted for the powerful Cardinal Paluzzi. Politicians and other figures of the era came to refer to Paluzzi as Cardinal Paluzzi-Altieri, playing on the pope's surname.[29] Within a few months, Paluzzi had not only become the supreme pontiff's shadow but had also taken over the reins of the papal espionage network and the affairs of state. No one in Rome, including the secretary of state, did anything without his knowledge.

It is generally thought to be Paluzzi who revived the Black Order as a counterespionage service, although no documentary evidence supports this claim. What is clear is that in the slightly more than six years during which Clement X occupied the Throne of St. Peter, Paluzzi concentrated a degree of power in his own hands that has few equals in the history of the Roman curia. Espionage and counterespionage were just a few of the dangerous weapons at his disposal, but they were weapons he knew how to use, and he was willing to do so.

Relations with France were no better under Clement X than before, especially because of the arrogance with which Louis XIV acted in all affairs related to the pope and Rome. The most serious crisis occurred on May 21, 1670, when the French ambassador, the Duke of Estrées, accused Cardinal Paluzzi of vetoing the appointment of all French or evidently pro-French priests to the rank of cardinal. The powerful Paluzzi denied the accusation, accusing the French king of being anti-pope and anti-Catholic; Clement X, meanwhile, stood up from his throne to declare the audience at an end. The Frenchman grabbed hold of the pope and made him sit down. The pontiff looked the diplomat in the eye and swore he would not permit any more such French affronts. Cardinal Paluzzi took note.[30]

On the night of May 26, five days after that incident, the secretary of Louis XIV's legation in Rome turned up dead.[31] Apparently the young diplomat, after taking leave of his ambassador, left the building and walked to Trastevere, on the other side of the Tiber, an area full of taverns and brothels. While eating dinner there, he met two well-mannered men who said they were students from Florence who had come to Rome to consider joining the priesthood, as their noble families had decreed.

At one point, the Frenchman left the room to urinate. When he returned, the two Italians had disappeared. Estrées's secretary sat down and finished his meal. Afterwards, since it was a balmy spring night, he decided to walk back to his small rented room near the French embassy. Midway, he began to sweat profusely and found it hard to breathe. He sat down by a fountain and never got up. He was dead, poisoned.

The two young Florentines had disappeared into the narrow streets of the Lateran and then climbed over a vine-covered wall. On the other side, Cardinal Paluzzi was waiting. One of the two, actually a priest already, knelt and kissed the cardinal's ring while handing him a small rolled parchment tied up with a ribbon of red silk—the *Informi Rosso*.[32] The job was done.

The next day, while the French embassy was still unaware of the death of the young secretary, Pope Clement X named six new cardinals, none of them French. From then on, relations between France and Rome, and between Louis XIV and Clement X, practically ceased.[33]

Clement X died on July 22, 1676, not without first beatifying Pius V, the great Counter-Reformation pope and founder of the Holy Alliance.[34]

In August, the cardinals went once more into conclave. The leading candidates for the Throne of St. Peter were Gregory Barbarigo and Benedetto Odescalchi, both cardinals who had been close to the late pope.

Barbarigo informed the College that he would not accept the papal crown. This was good news for Paluzzi, because Barbarigo had spoken out on several occasions against the methods of the Holy Alliance. If he were to become pope, spy operations would be reduced to a minimum despite the dangers of a continent in the shadow of a French regime more and more hostile to Rome.

In spite of French opposition, the cardinals voted in Odescalchi on September 21. He adopted the name Innocent XI in honor of Pope Innocent X.

Like Pamphili, the new pope would regard the Holy Alliance as a necessary evil and would support its use throughout the thirteen years of his pontificate. Therefore he left Cardinal Paluzzo Paluzzi in charge of the spy corps but subordinated him to the secretariat of state directed by Cardinal Alderano Cibo. Innocent XI did not deal directly with Paluzzi as his predecessor Clement X had done. Instead, anything related to the espionage service went through Cibo.[35]

Innocent XI's priorities—and therefore the main battlefields of the Holy Alliance—were three: the always conflictual relations with France and its Sun King, the struggle with the Ottoman Empire, and the hope of bringing England back within the Catholic fold. Cardinal Paluzzi's agents centered their activities on France and England.

Innocent XI had no intention of continuing to tolerate Louis XIV's interference in Church affairs. Therefore he decided to send the Sun King three letters—in 1678, 1679, and 1680—requesting that he renounce the extension of the right of "régale."[36]

Louis XIV, fearing that Catholics would feel diminished obligations to the crown, convoked a meeting with French clergy in 1680 to try to head off any danger. In the meeting, all but two bishops apologized to the king for the words of Innocent XI and reaffirmed their loyalty to the crown. A year later, the king called a new assembly, which recognized the régales as a sovereign right. Cardinals Cibo and Paluzzi urged the pope to counterattack, because the French king would not stop there—and they were right about this.

On March 19, 1682, the year when the court moved to the Palace of Versailles, Louis XIV approved the "four articles" of the declaration written by Bossuet that declared the absolute independence of the King of France in temporal affairs, the authority of the Council of Costanza over the pope, the infallibility of the pope conditioned on the consent of his bishops, and the inviolability of the ancient customs of the French church. To underline his position, he ordered the teaching of these four articles in every school in the country.[37]

Innocent XI showed his dissatisfaction with the French bishops' failure to defend the rights of the Church against their king. With respect to the four articles, he preferred not to interfere, but he denied investiture to all who attended the meetings with the king. In 1687, on the advice of Cardinal Cibo, the pope chose the Holy Roman Empire's candidate for Archbishop of Cologne over the candidate advanced by France. On Cardinal Paluzzi's advice, he abolished the right of asylum in foreign embassies in Rome. Spain and Venice submitted to the papal edict, but France refused. This gave rise to an undercover war between France and the papal states, revolving around the so-called Scipio network.

For two years, the Holy Alliance had known that some French agents had penetrated the Vatican secretariat of state. Louis XIV's spies were, in fact, three priests who worked archiving documents, many of them classified as "delicate material." The spies copied these and sent the copies to the French diplomatic legation in Rome. The head of this network was known as Scipio.

Alderano Cibo summoned Paluzzi and ordered him to eliminate the network of French spies within the Lateran, using any means necessary. Paluzzi would indeed use all the means at his disposal, as Cibo had ordered, including the monks of the Black Order.

The first to fall into the hands of the Black Order was a member of the Scipio network. On the morning of May 11, 1687, two Holy Alliance agents followed a scriptor[38] who worked at the Vatican Library. This friar's task was to transcribe and copy documents of the secretariat of state for later distribution among various members of the curia. The Holy Alliance had discovered that certain documents, especially those having to do with France, fell under the purview of this scriptor. The papal espionage service calculated the number of copies made by the friar and the number later distributed. Whenever a document was classified as "delicate material" and dealt with France or Louis XIV, one of the copies failed to be distributed or simply disappeared.

When this case was reported to Cardinal Paluzzi, the espionage chief ordered the monks of the Black Order to capture this scriptor alive. On May 19, the friar was arrested and sent to the Holy Alliance headquarters, where he was interrogated. Under torture, the Scipio spy was persuaded to reveal the names of the other two members of the network that spied for King Louis XIV in Rome.

On May 21, the tortured corpse of the friar appeared hanging from a bridge over the Tiber with a small scrap of black cloth bearing two crossed red stripes. The fearful arm of the Church had struck at one enemy, but two other spies remained at large.

On May 23, in the afternoon, when Holy Alliance agents deployed to arrest a priest who worked under Cardinal Alderano Cibo, the priest managed to escape their net and seek asylum in the French embassy. Applying the abolition of the right of asylum in embassies decreed by Innocent XI, six monks of the Black Order, with masked faces, entered the Farnese Palace and took the priest by force.

Interrogated by the monks, he revealed that behind the code name Scipio hid a monk who some time before had been part of the Holy Alliance and had been recruited by Louis XIV's espionage service because of his French origins. Scipio was the son of a Venetian citizen and a Florentine woman, who had been brought up in Mazarin's France. Apparently he had specialized, within the Holy Alliance, in the elimination of "enemies of the Church" by means of poison.

On May 26, 1687, eight members of the Black Order entered a bedroom in an inn near the papal palace in Rome. From a black carriage with papal emblems on its doors, Cardinals Paluzzo Paluzzi and Alderano Cibo watched the operation unfold. They had previously ordered that no patrol of the Papal Guard should be in the area. There was no need for witnesses to Scipio's elimination.[39]

The first monks were climbing the narrow stairs when Scipio appeared before them, on guard with sword in hand. Thanks to the attackers' numerical superiority, the fight was brief and Louis XIV's spy had to retreat. Trying to escape through a small window, he fell several meters to where another detachment of the Black Order waited. One of these monks put his sword through the neck of the spy who, bleeding heavily, was trying to get to his feet to continue fighting. In that instant, three swords pierced Scipio's body, one of them slicing his heart in two. He was dead before he hit the ground.

Cardinal Paluzzi made the sign of the cross with his gloved right hand and closed the curtain. The carriage moved on. Once again the Church's secrets were well protected from inappropriate eyes. The corpses of Scipio and the priest pulled from the French embassy appeared hanging from a bridge over the Tiber, as a sign for any Roman or foreigner who might doubt the reach of God's judgment or of its tools, the Holy Alliance and the Black Order.

The incursion of Holy Alliance agents into the French embassy provoked serious reactions in the Parisian court. In November 1687, Louis XIV ordered his new ambassador to enter Rome escorted by an armed regiment in full battle dress. Innocent XI decided to excommunicate this emissary and refused to grant him an audience. In the beginning of 1688, the pope, through his nuncio in Paris, let Louis XIV know that both the king and his ministers should consider themselves *incursus* (sentenced) to ecclesiastic censures.[40]

Now in the full splendor of his power, Louis XIV paid the pope's warnings no heed at all. As he had done during the papacy of Alexander VII, Louis ordered his armies to occupy Avignon and the Comtat Venaissin.

The popes' longstanding wish to see a Catholic monarch wear the English crown seemed to strike a more optimistic note toward the end of the seventeenth century. James II, a fervent Catholic, ascended the throne in 1685. He soon sent an ambassador to Pope Innocent XI and allowed the return of the Jesuits to England.[41] The Holy Alliance deployed more agents throughout England. Cardinal Paluzzi knew that sooner or later the religious situation would return to normal—to Protestantism, that is.

James wanted to imitate the absolutism of Louis XIV in spite of the pope's contrary advice. The Protestant reaction was not long in coming. An uprising was delayed, according the reports of the Holy Alliance agents in James's court, because the king lacked sons and his daughters were all married to Protestant princes.[42] So it was only necessary to wait for him to die. But in 1686 the king's second wife gave birth to a male child, which opened the possibility of a Catholic and authoritarian dynasty in the making.

Rebellion followed, and the Protestants offered the English crown to William III of Orange, the husband of James's older daughter. On November 5, 1688, William and his troops disembarked in England, and soon he was in power. James II had to flee to France, where he remained a refugee till the day of his death. Catholicism's defeat in England was complete, and it has lasted down to the present day.

Innocent XI did not witness this, having died three months before. His successor on the Throne of St. Peter was Cardinal Pietro Ottobani, who adopted the name Alexander VIII. This pope would rule for only sixteen months, and he gave way before the despotic passions of Louis XIV until his death on February 1, 1691. His successor, Innocent XII, became the last pope of the seventeenth century; his papacy was in no way quiet, however.

Europe was once again caught up in religious and political wars, and Louis XIV's power and influence remained strong not only throughout France, but also across the Continent. He exercised absolute power during the time of intrigue that soon arrived.

6

TIME OF INTRIGUE (1691–1721)

And now this warning to you, priests. I will break your arms and I will scat-
ter upon your faces the dung of victims sacrificed in your solemnities, and it
shall take you away.

—Malachi 2:1 and 2:3

When the brief papacy of Alexander VIII came to an end on February 1, 1691, the cardinals met to choose a pope who would turn out to be the last pope of the waning seventeenth century. Once again Gregory Barbarigo seemed the strongest candidate, as he had before Innocent XI's election.

Barbarigo was a pious man, but also a dyed-in-the-wool enemy of the Holy Alliance. Just as in 1676, Cardinal Paluzzi—still in control of papal espionage—did not want to have to dismantle such a powerful security service.[1]

The conclave of 1691 turned out to be longest of the century as well as the last. In all, it lasted five months, from the twelfth of February to the twelfth of July. Neither the Spanish nor the French nor the Holy Roman Empire faction wanted to vote for Barbarigo. When the summer heat wave hit Rome, the cardinals found a compromise candidate, Antonio Pignatelli. On July 12, he took the name Innocent XII.[2]

Pignatelli had been born into one of the noblest families of Bari, his father having been Prince of Minervo and a grandee of Spain. His relations with the Roman curia helped him climb the ecclesiastic ladder, moving through such positions as vice-legate in Urbino, governor of Viterbo, nuncio in Florence,

Vienna, and Poland, and inquisitor in Malta. It was in the last position that he had his closest relations with agents of the Holy Alliance and their commander, Cardinal Paluzzo Paluzzi.

An Irish Protestant merchant by the name of William DeKerry was active in Malta at this time. Popular wisdom said he was no simple merchant but also an English spy and smuggler. The English navy allowed DeKerry's ships free passage in exchange for information about the routes and anchorages of ships sailing under enemy flags or those of Catholic nations. Apparently, the Irishman had bribed the port authorities, who passed on to him their knowledge of routes, departure dates, and the cargoes carried in ships' holds.[3]

The inquisitor Antonio Pignatelli reported this to the secretary of state and the papal secret service by way of a letter to Cardinal Paluzzi. In response, the Holy Alliance sent five agents to the island to eliminate DeKerry's network. The monks kidnapped a Maltese port official and, under threat of being turned over to the Inquisition, he confessed to having passed information on port traffic to DeKerry in return for a healthy sum of money. Several cargo agents were also involved.

Paluzzi decided to eliminate the Irishman, cutting off the network's head, and so he informed his agents. One night, while DeKerry was walking to the French ambassador's residence, four men armed with long and short swords blocked his path. Minutes later, the merchant spy's corpse was thrown into the Mediterranean. Once William DeKerry's death became known, the rest of the network ceased operations and the Holy Alliance agents silently left Malta. Once again, the long arm of the Church had been able to reach its enemies.

During Pignatelli's papacy as Innocent XII, Vatican relations with Louis XIV's France improved. The powerful monarch took the first step by rescinding his order to teach the "four articles" in public schools.[4] In reply, the pope finally filled the vacant posts in the French church hierarchy, but on the advice of Cardinal Paluzzi—who had experienced the entire controversy firsthand during Innocent XI's time—the pope also required all eminences of the French church to write a letter explaining their general point of view on the past events. The experts Javier Paredes, Maximiliano Barrio, Domingo Ramos-Lissón, and Luis Suárez, in their *Diccionario de los Papas y Concilios,* insist that this warming of relations was not a case of Louis XIV surrendering to the pope, because his decrees about *régales* were never rescinded, nor did he abolish the "four articles," and so they continued to be taught in universities and other schools.

In any case, Innocent XII continued his crusade against heretics, using Cardinal Paluzzi's Holy Alliance as the long arm of the faith. One such enemy was Charles Blount.[5]

The theory of free inquiry, which arose in the sixteenth century with the Reformation, not only contributed to major divisions within Protestantism but also led to the creation of small sects, one of which was deism. Although the late-sixteenth-century figure Lord Edward de Cherbury tends to be cited as the earliest deist, the first of whom there is documentary evidence in Wetzer and Welte's *Kirchen-Lexikon* (Dictionary-Encyclopedia of Catholic Theology) is Charles Blount, born in the mid-seventeenth century.[6] From his safe haven in England, Blount stood out as a more and more dangerous enemy of the Church of Rome because deism penetrated the borders of the papal states by way of underground preachers. Several of these were arrested by the Inquisition and, under torture, confessed to being followers of Charles Blount.[7]

The pope would not permit this sort of heresy, so he ordered Paluzzi to take action. The aged cardinal decided to send three monks of the Black Order to England.

One morning in 1693, the polemicist Charles Blount's body was found on the grounds of his home with a bullet in the chest. The authorities' explanation was that perhaps Blount had committed suicide because he could not marry his sister-in-law, whom he loved deeply, and so he had shot himself in the heart out of depression. That explanation closed the case, and Paluzzi's monks made their way back to Rome.

The last years of Innocent XII's papacy revolved around the problem of the Spanish succession. King Charles II, who had ruled since 1665, asked the pope's advice, and the pope declared in favor of the four-year-old elector-prince of Bavaria, son of the elector Maximilian Emanuel and the duchess Maria Antonia, granddaughter of Philip IV. In 1696, young Joseph Ferdinand was indeed declared Charles II's successor through the mediation of Mariana of Austria and the pope.

The signing of the Treaty of Partition in The Hague, at the initiative of Louis XIV of France, gave Joseph Ferdinand all the territories of the Spanish peninsula except Guipúzcoa, as well as Spain's American colonies, Sardinia, and the Spanish Netherlands. It reserved the remaining possessions of the Spanish empire for Archduke Charles of Austria or the Dauphin of France. When this news reached Spain, Charles II responded by naming little Joseph

Ferdinand the sole heir of all his kingdoms, principalities, and states, and forbidding the renunciation of any.[8]

Cardinal Paluzzi then advised the pope that for the boy ever to reach the throne he needed to be protected first. The pope's spy chief knew that sooner or later Louis XIV would try something against the heir for the benefit of his grandson Philip of Anjou. Paluzzi never saw his fears fulfilled, because he died on June 29, 1698, at the age of seventy-five, in Ravenna, where he was archbishop emeritus.

Legend has it that Paluzzi, spymaster for almost three decades, helmsman of the Holy Alliance through the papacies of Clement X, Innocent XI, Alexander VIII, and Innocent XII, was poisoned by Louis XIV's agents at a banquet. Cardinal Paluzzo Paluzzi Altieri Degli Albertoni ingested a strong dose of poison hidden in a roasted lamb apparently seasoned with black hellebore leaves. The highly toxic hellebore plant had been used in ancient times to poison water and arrowheads.[9] No one in the cardinal's kitchen taste-tested the dishes served at his last opulent dinner.[10]

A few months later, in the early days of 1699 and in fulfillment of Paluzzi's prophecy, little Joseph Ferdinand of Bavaria suddenly fell ill. The prescribed treatment was of no avail, and on February 5, his condition became dangerously worse, with convulsions and vomiting. He died in the early hours of February 6 at the age of only seven, making way for the replacement of the Hapsburgs by the Bourbons on the Spanish throne, in the person of Philip V. The rumor that the boy had been poisoned on orders from Versailles circulated through the courts of Europe, but, as in the case of Cardinal Paluzzi, nothing could be proved. Louis XIV would stop at nothing, however, to make his grandson King of Spain, even if he had to plunge Europe into a new war.

On September 27, 1700, Innocent XII died at the age of eighty-five, leaving the problem of the Spanish crown to the next pope. His successor on the Throne of St. Peter would have to deal with the so-called War of the Spanish Succession. The arms and intrigues were ready. Louis XIV had several cardinals at his disposal for the approaching conclave in the Vatican.

The College of Cardinals began its secret session on the afternoon of October 9. Opposing the dominant French faction were the Spanish and Holy Roman Empire adherents and the *zelanti,* who wanted a staunch defender of Church rights. Debates, discussions, negotiations, and maneuverings were still under way when, on November 19, news arrived from Spain that Charles II had died. From then on, attention in the Vatican and in every nation focused on the royal palace in Madrid.

Since little Joseph Ferdinand of Bavaria had died or been assassinated, the fatally ill King Charles had decided to sign a last will in which he declared that his throne should pass to the Duke of Anjou, grandson of the powerful Louis XIV of France.[11]

To avoid their common fear that the powerful Spanish empire would pass into the hands of a single dynasty, however, most European nations sought an accord that would divide the territories instead. Holy Roman Emperor Leopold I and the French king Louis XIV had previously, in 1668, signed an accord in Vienna that called for the partition of Spanish territories between Austria and France if Charles died childless, as turned out to be the case. England and Holland also entered the fray, now that they were united under a single king, William III of Orange.[12]

On October 3, 1700, while the conclave was deliberating the identity of the new pope, Charles II composed a last will leaving his crown and all his positions to the second son of the French dauphin. If Anjou did not accept, the crown would pass to Archduke Charles. A few minutes before 3 P.M. on November 1, the last representative of the House of Austria to be King of Spain died. Under his rule, the Spanish empire had declined, and the Spaniards wanted a new king who would bring back the times of Philip II, an era that, in fact, they were destined never to live again.

As war clouds gathered over Europe, and seeing that neither the French faction nor the Spanish-Imperial one could forge an agreement, the *zelanti* group decided to advance the candidacy of Cardinal Giovanni Francesco Albani. When the conclave reached consensus around Albani, he at first refused to accept. He decided to consult a prestigious group of theologians. Finally, on November 23, 1700, Cardinal Albani became Pope Clement XI.

The new pontiff, only fifty-one years old, was both cultured and jovial, but his political decisions were sometimes too slow, especially for his times. One such delayed decision was that of naming a new chief for the Holy Alliance.

Since the possible assassination of the powerful Cardinal Paluzzo Paluzzi by French agents, the pope's spies had been largely inactive. The effect could be seen, eventually, in the workings of the secretariat of state. For example, no one was able to inform the cardinals in conclave about the death of Charles II until eighteen days after the event.[13]

Clement XI took quite a few years to understand the need for an agile information service to keep abreast of the events that were to ravage Europe within only a few months. If other popes had used the Holy Alliance as an important pawn in the great chess game of European politics, the new pontiff did not yet know how, or at least how much, the Vatican spies would help him make good decisions.

The new secretary of state, Cardinal Fabrizio Paolucci, was a skilled man and an expert in politics, but he also did not have much faith in the Holy Alliance's ability to help the pope make foreign policy decisions. In fact, Paolucci was wrong, and the events about to unfold would make this clear.

In accordance with Charles II's will, Philip of Anjou was crowned as Philip V, the new King of Spain, on May 8, 1701, in Madrid. But the Holy Roman Emperor cast doubt on the validity of the late king's will and insisted that his son, Archduke Charles of Austria, had equal rights to the succession.[14]

In an attempt to avoid the outbreak of war between the Empire and France, Pope Clement XI offered himself as a mediator in this dispute. At the same time, on Cardinal Paolucci's advice, he named his nephew Annibale Albani,[15] a diplomatic expert closely linked to the Holy See, as the administrator responsible for the Holy Alliance.

Under the direction of this new leader, the pope's agents began to funnel information to the secretariat of state overseen by Paolucci. Their first reports dealt with the allies that each side was seeking in case of an outbreak of war. The Holy Alliance said that Philip V was pursuing accords with the Dukes of Mantua and Parma, while Archduke Charles was courting the Duke of Modena. Clement XI then wrote to all three noblemen urging strict neutrality. Cardinal Paolucci and Annibale Albani knew that if any of these nobles joined one side or the other, the coming war could seriously affect the papal states.[16]

At that time, among the Duke of Modena's advisors was a Venetian named Vicenzo Lascari. Lascari urged Modena, in the event of an open war with Philip V, to join forces with the Austrian emperor in support of Archduke Charles. The Venetian knew that his employer, the duke, could win important territorial rights if Charles became King of Spain. In spite of the pope's warnings, the Duke of Modena said he would be willing to go to war to support Archduke Charles's cause.[17]

For Cardinal Paolucci and the papal states, Lascari's meddling was dangerous, and so he became a target for elimination. For the officials close to the pope, the prospect of a war lapping at their doors was more dangerous than the prospect of a larger war that would spread across the Continent.

Before making a major decision, Paolucci, as secretary of state, sent a letter to Modena's advisor, trying to convince him of the danger of drawing the imminent war into the heart of Italy. But Vicenzo Lascari chose to ignore the letter, and he continued his policy of openly supporting the archduke's cause. Finally, Annibale Albani's agents acted. On the night of January 11, 1702, they assassinated Vicenzo Lascari when he was about to step into a carriage. That night the loyal counselor to the Duke of Modena had been to visit a courtesan who apparently was in the habit of passing on all sorts of information to the papal spies in the city. On the Holy Alliance's recommendation, she had scheduled an assignation with Lascari at her house. When he left in the predawn hours to return to his own home, the assassins were waiting in the street, daggers in hand. Six blows were enough to finish off the Venetian.

The next day, after hearing the frightening news of the assassination, the Duke of Modena sent a letter to Cardinal Paolucci announcing his inclination to remain neutral in the War of the Spanish Succession. Once again the Holy Alliance had defended the interests of Church and pope.

During the course of 1701, King Louis XIV had militarily occupied Spain's Italian possessions in the name of his grandson, the King of Spain. These included the duchy of Milan, the kingdoms of Naples and Sicily, and the island of Sardinia. He had also sent troops to the southern provinces of the Netherlands, whose capital was Brussels. The rest of the colonies, the Canary Islands, all of South and Central America, the Philippines, and a number of fortifications on the north coast of Africa all put themselves under the orders of King Philip V.[18]

> The present state of the realm is the saddest in the world, for the feeble government of the last few kings, and the base adulation of servants and ministers, have produced a horrible disorder in affairs: justice is abandoned, policy neglected, resources sold, religion distorted, the nobility demoralized, the people oppressed, power decayed, and love and respect for the crown lost,

wrote the Duke of Escalona, Marquis of Villena, to Louis XIV in 1700.[19]

When a powerful Austrian army under command of the general Prince Eugene of Savoy-Carignan crossed into Italian territory, war seemed almost inevitable. At the end of May 1702, the Holy Alliance's agents in Catalunya reported to Rome that King Philip V was readying a naval force made up of French warships to send to Naples. In fact, on April 8, nine ships under the command of the king himself had weighed anchor in Barcelona.[20] Louis XIV knew that in this international situation of impending war, Italy needed a signal from the new king. At that point, France was confronting an alliance made up of England, the United Provinces (the northern Netherlands), and the emperor. Louis XIV could count only on the support of the Duke of Bavaria and the Prince-Elector of Cologne.

The most important defector—said to have changed his mind on the recommendation of Pope Clement XI and the Holy Alliance—was the Duke of Savoy. In October of 1701, while his daughter was marrying Philip V, he swung his troops and his loyalty to the side of the Austrian emperor, to fight against his son-in-law's grandfather.

William III of Orange, who in 1701 put himself at the head of the second Great Alliance and intervened in the War of the Spanish Succession, died on March 19, 1702, before he had a chance to take an active part in the fighting. His successor, as Queen of England and Ireland, was Anne Stuart, his wife's sister.[21]

Philip V arrived in Naples in the nick of time. The Neapolitans were not happy with either Spain or its new king. Only a few months earlier, the Holy Alliance had uncovered a plot to assassinate the viceroy. This "nobles' plot," as it was known in its time, had been orchestrated by a group of mostly Neapolitan noblemen who wanted to revolt in favor of Archduke Charles in the hopes that out of gratitude he would grant them independence. A few days before the assassination was to take place, the incipient rebellion's ringleader was arrested by Spanish agents who had been warned by their counterparts in the papal espionage. The biggest problem facing Spanish spies in this era was that most of them did not speak Italian or did not speak the proper dialect, so their main informants were the Spanish servants working in noble palaces. The pope's agents, on the other hand, hailed from Florence, Siena, and even Naples, so they had access to much broader networks of informants. In only three days, nineteen people involved in the plot were arrested. Most of them were put to death.[22]

On May 15, 1702, at almost the same moment when Philip V was listening to the music of Alessandro Scarlatti and watching his opera *Tiberio,* England, the United Provinces, and the Empire declared war on France, officially beginning the War of the Spanish Succession. What Clement XI had feared came brutally to pass. From this moment on, Annibale Albani and his spies went to work for the sole and exclusive benefit of the Holy See, always in a dangerous position of neutrality, for which the supreme pontiff in Rome paid the price in the end.

Before leaving Naples, the king sent an ambassador to pay his respects to Clement XI as a sign of courtesy. On June 2, the ambassador sailed north with a convoy of twenty ships. Their arrival in Milan was Philip V's first real contact with the war.[23]

When this occurred, the Holy Alliance agents had already reported to the pope about a mysterious incident in the port of Vigo, where English and Dutch ships had taken Spanish galleons loaded with silver from the Americas by surprise. The English sacked the cargoes and sank the ships.[24] Yet nothing was as it seemed.

In February of 1702, Tebaldo Fieschi, a Holy Alliance agent in London, had informed Albani that the English were preparing a large naval operation against Spanish territory, perhaps Cádiz or Vigo. Fieschi, eighteen years old, was a young, elegant, rich silk merchant born in Siena. From his earliest moments, he had lived close to papal power, because his father had served under several popes. Fieschi had refused to serve the Church by joining the priesthood until Cardinal Paluzzi recruited him to serve in the espionage corps. His main business clients were the nobility of the court of William of Orange; the Sienese spy had even met the king himself. One of his clients was Lady Rooke, wife of the admiral Sir George Rooke.

The Italian not only supplied textiles to Lady Rooke but also was her lover, which had given him access to important documents that Admiral Rooke kept in their house outside London. Thus Fieschi learned of the English plans to attack Cádiz, and he informed Cardinal Paolucci. Curiously, Rome did not warn Madrid about the coming attack, perhaps because such a warning would have represented an end to the neutrality so scrupulously defended by the pope.

A few months later, in July, a combined English-Dutch fleet made up of fifty men-of-war under George Rooke's command indeed attacked Cádiz.[25] Resistance by the troops quartered in the city made things difficult for Rooke's troops, who withdrew and, battered by rough seas as well, lifted their siege of the city after a month. Admiral Rooke, however, avoided a defeatist analysis of the incident, as may be seen in his diary, *Journal of Sir George Rooke, Admiral of the Fleet.*[26]

The setback in Cádiz was soon forgotten because of news of the imminent arrival of a large Spanish fleet from America, carrying silver and headed for the port of Vigo. The Spanish ships traveled under heavy French escort, made up of warships under command of Admiral Chateaurenaud.

The first English squadron sent to spearhead the attack was commanded by the admiral Sir Cloudesley Shovell, followed by the fleet of Sir George Rooke, which was supposed to disembark troops to attack the Spanish ships from the land. Once again, Fieschi reported to the Holy Alliance in Rome that a great fleet had set off under Rooke's command, but this time he did not know where they were bound. What Tebaldo Fieschi did know was that Rooke's goal was to intercept the "Silver Fleet" and try to make off with its cargo. The Sienese spy had collected this information during one of his amorous trysts with Lady Elizabeth Rooke, the admiral's wife.

With that information in hand, the secretary of state, Cardinal Paolucci, informed Pope Clement XI, who in turn ordered the news passed on to the Spaniards by way of Holy Alliance agents in Spain. The papal spies turned Fieschi's report over to Cardinal Luis Manuel Fernández de Portocarrero,[27] Philip V's prime minister. On September 23, 1702, the first combat between French-Spanish ships and English ones took place.[28] Within a few hours, several ships took the contents of their holds to the sea floor, while others were captured, their cargoes requisitioned, and then were sunk.

It was true that, in Vigo, the fleet headed by Admirals Rooke and Shovell sank the Silver Fleet from America. Three galleons and thirteen other ships were burned and sunk, while six more were captured and put into English service. The French convoy accompanying the fleet was also annihilated, except for six that were likewise incorporated into the English navy.[29] The second part of the story, however, is that Admirals Rooke and Shovell found only cacao, pepper, and hides in the holds of the Spanish ships—not a trace of silver. Apparently, with the information that the Holy Alliance agent in London supplied to Cardinal Portocarrero, the Spaniards decided to unload all the silver in strictest secrecy and take it to the Alcázar castle in Segovia, where it remained safe and far from English hands.

In February 1703, Philip V issued a decree that said, in view of the criminal attack on his fleet, he had decided to confiscate whatever quantities of silver aboard the sunken ships had been en route to English or Dutch merchants. Also, he decided to take as a forced loan an important quantity of silver that had been on its way to the merchants and to the consulate in Seville.[30] The monarch thus acquired more than half of the silver being carried by the beleaguered fleet. In fact, Philip V had converted a real tragedy into a splendid and lucrative business deal. As Cardinal Portocarrero said, "The economic has saved the political." The papal espionage corps told the whole tale to the Marquis de Louville, the king's tutor who would come to establish important ties to the Holy Alliance.[31]

The king's relationship with the Marquis de Louville was a very close one. Philip V even went to the point of awarding his tutor command of the so-called Tercio Viejo de los Morados. With nearly six thousand men divided into two regiments, one Spanish and one Walloon, that the king brought with him from Barcelona, the Tercio became the palace guard in place of the old companies of Burgundians and Germans from the Austrian period. From this moment on, the Marquis de Louville became the pope's best spy in the King of Spain's court.

Little by little, the War of the Spanish Succession turned into something almost like a world war, not so much in terms of the theater of operations, but because the conflict provoked economic and political reactions from Peru to Moscow, from Jamaica to Rome, from Paris to Madrid.

In September 1703, Emperor Leopold had his second son crowned King of Spain in Vienna. The eighteen-year-old took the name Charles III, and on March 7 of the next year, he sailed into Portugal accompanied by an English squadron under Sir George Rooke and a force of three hundred German soldiers, four thousand English, and two thousand Dutch.

Philip V, on hearing this news, decided to cross the border, provoking a war with Portugal. That same year, Annibale Albani decided to send his best spy Tebaldo Fieschi to Spain, under the same cover he had used in England, that of a silk merchant. With letters of recommendation from nobles in Venice and Rome, Fieschi approached the Princess des Ursins, one of the closest advisors to Queen Marie Louise of Savoy, the wife of Philip V.

From this position of privilege, Fieschi maintained good relations with Jean Orry, sent from France by Louis XIV to reform the Spanish armies. Shortly thereafter, valuable reports on military matters began arriving in Rome.[32] In these texts, the Holy Alliance spy reported that Orry and the French king were urging the replacement of the Spanish troops' antiquated arms, such as pikes and arquebuses, with bayonet-equipped French rifles. At the same time, the Holy Alliance agents in France reported the shipping of innumerable cargoes of pistols, rifles, bullets, uniforms, and tents to Spain.

From the outset of the war, Pope Clement XI tried to avoid allying with either the Bourbons or the House of Austria, but the military pressure from the Hapsburgs in northern Italy, which threatened the stability of the papal states, forced him to choose sides. On January 15, 1709, he issued a communiqué in which he recognized Archduke Charles as a "Catholic king," but without questioning Philip V's right to the crown of Spain.[33]

With this recognition as "Catholic king" of the occupied Hispanic territories, Charles opened a new front in Spain. Clement XI's next step was to send a nuncio to Barcelona, where Charles had established his court. From then on, there were two kings in Spain, and two papal representatives as well—one to Castile and the other to Catalunya. Philip V reacted by withdrawing his ambassador from Rome, expelling the nuncio from Castile, and formally breaking relations with the pope.[34]

The situation deteriorated still more when Philip V decreed a ban on all official communication with Rome or any monetary transactions with the papal states. A tax was also imposed on sums sent to the Catholic Church. As a final measure, the monarch established the so-called *pase regio,* under which any document coming from Rome had to be submitted for censorship that would "determine whether its practice and execution could be inappropriate or could jeopardize the common good or the State."[35]

The desperate situation in France forced Louis XIV to withdraw all his troops from Spain. In a letter to his grandson, the Sun King spoke of hunger, war, and river flooding. The troop withdrawal was a first step toward peace. Although negotiations in Geertruidenberg collapsed, the progress toward a peace was now nearly inevitable.

In April 1711, Emperor Joseph of Austria died after only seven years on the throne. Since he had no heir, he was succeeded by Archduke Charles. From then on, arms made way for diplomacy. On September 27, 1711, the archduke, now Emperor Charles VI of Austria, left Barcelona never to return, on board an English ship commanded by Admiral Rooke.

In the month of August 1712, hostilities among England, Holland, Portugal, France, and Spain came to an end. On April 11, 1713, the parties to the conflict signed the Treaty of Utrecht. Catalunya remained in armed rebellion against Philip V until September 11, 1714, when Barcelona finally surrendered. That same afternoon, Tebaldo Fieschi, the Holy Alliance spy, sent a report to his chief in Rome, Annibale Albani: "A Franco-Spanish army made up of 35,000 infantry and 5,000 cavalry troops has confronted 16,000 soldiers and citizens. Berwick, commanding the armies of Philip V, has ravaged the city with fire and blood." The last chapter of the War of the Spanish Succession would be the surrender of Majorca in June 1715, to an army of ten thousand men commanded by General D'Asfeld. Philip V ordered the lives of the besieged forces to be spared and issued a royal pardon to the entire city. Peace arrived at last, but the monarch, who would never forget the Catalunyan rebellion and its tragic consequences, imposed martial law on the region for years.

Once the war was over and Philip V was recognized as the King of Spain, the cardinal and secretary of state Fabrizio Paolucci attempted an approach by way of Elisabetta Farnese, the monarch's new wife. Clement XI, advised by Cardinal Giulio Alberoni, decided to take control of the negotiations away from Paolucci and ordered Annibale Albani to pull all Holy Alliance agents out of Madrid. Albani, however, kept Tebaldo Fieschi undercover in Spain.

Cardinal Alberoni's rise had been meteoric. In 1702, the Duke of Parma sent him on a diplomatic mission to Louis-Joseph de Bourbon, Duke of Vendôme, the commander in chief of the French army in the north of Italy. Vendôme promptly hired Alberoni as his secretary. He rapidly gained influence in the Spanish court through his negotiation of the marriage of Philip V and Elisabetta Farnese, and in 1717, he was simultaneously named cardinal by Pope Clement XI and prime minister by King Philip V.[36] That showed how highly the pope regarded the valuable reports received through Alberoni the spy, though they were not so well regarded by the Holy Alliance. Annibale Albani (now cardinal as well) thought the reports on the French army received in Rome were, for the most part, false. For example, the papal spy chief received a report from Giulio Alberoni about a possible movement of French troops toward the papal states. Shortly afterwards, this turned out to be false, because Vendôme was sent to Spain to take over the armies of Philip V.

Giulio Alberoni had gone within a few years from being an unimportant spy in the ranks of the Holy Alliance in northern Italy to being in charge of negotiating the restitution of all the rights of the Catholic Church in Spain as Philip V's prime minister. Yet the resulting concordat did nothing for Rome.

In February 1718, just as Paolucci had foreseen, relations between

Madrid and Rome were shattered again. Alberoni proved himself to be a terrible spy and an awful prime minister. His faulty foreign policy and the defeat of Spanish forces during the French-British invasion decided his fate. Cardinal Giulio Alberoni fell into disgrace on December 5, 1719.

The spy Tebaldo Fieschi, now thirty-six years old, became a fixture in Queen Elisabetta Farnese's palace of El Pardo. A woman of unimpeachable intelligence and a lover of art and pleasure, the queen surrounded herself with quite a few Italians—Venetian actors, Florentine musicians, Neapolitan artists, and Sienese merchants—who formed part of her inner circle. Fieschi, the handsome Sienese who had spied for Pope Clement XI in London almost twenty years before, took advantage of this feat to find his way into Elisabetta's circle. Thanks to this privileged position achieved by a Holy Alliance spy, Rome would be well able to witness the events about to unfold in a changing Europe.

Louis XIV, the powerful Sun King, died on September 1, 1715, after a sixty-five-year reign. Louis XV, a child of six, became the new lord and master of Europe's greatest power. Clement XI died on March 19, 1721, and was buried in the Basilica of St. Peter, leaving behind him a society that answered primarily to reasons of state. Philip V abdicated in favor of his son Louis, who reigned only a short time, after which Philip had to take up the crown again.

The ensuing decades, the papacies of Innocent XIII, Benedict XIII, and Clement XII, were times of profound change but, for the papal espionage service, of almost total inactivity. Clement XI's successors saw no need for a spy service in a period when papal power began to sink roots into a new Europe reborn from its ashes after years of war.

7

SOME BRIEF REIGNS (1721–1775)

Woe to you, scribes and Pharisees, hypocrites. You are like whitewashed tombs, which appear beautiful on the outside, but inside are full of dead men's bones and filth. Even so, on the outside you appear righteous, but inside you are filled with hypocrisy and iniquity.

—Matthew 23:27–28

In Rome, the conclave chose Clement XI's successor. The majority of the cardinals had been named by the late pope, and in the first round of voting, Fabrizio Paolucci nearly had the two-thirds majority needed to be elected. For the Holy Alliance, elevation of Paolucci to the papacy meant a chance to extend the reach of its already long arms. Cardinal Annibale Albani knew that if Clement XI's secretary of state became the new pontiff, his spy service would come into an age of glory. But joy turned to sadness when, in the conclave, Cardinal Althan publicly cast the Holy Roman Empire's veto against Paolucci, in part for his role in the War of the Spanish Succession.[1]

With the powerful Cardinal Paolucci out of the running, it took the College of Cardinals nearly six and a half weeks to agree on a new choice. Finally, on May 8, 1721, Cardinal Michelangelo dei Conti was proclaimed pope under the name of Innocent XIII. Conti would be a short-lived pope, governing the Church for only three years. Still, before he died he gave the go-ahead for reprisals against the Jesuits, which would become harsher during the papacies that followed.

Holy Alliance agents in Asia, almost all of them Jesuits, had reported to Rome on the attitude of Chinese Order missionaries in favor of allowing

both Chinese and Catholic rituals. Innocent XIII then ordered the congregation De Propaganda Fide to write a stern letter of reprimand to the superior-
general of the Society.[2]

In general, the Jesuits defended their own, claiming that their missionaries in China had adapted their work to meet papal norms, obeying the pope's
orders. This controversy represented the first raindrops of a great storm that
would descend on the Society of Jesus in times to come.

During the three years Innocent XIII occupied the Throne of St. Peter, the
Holy Alliance carried out no operations, in part because the new pope never
named anyone as chief of espionage for the Vatican. The same pattern continued in the following pontificate. Cardinal Annibale Albani continued as acting
head of the secret service, but with limited power. His only supporter inside
the Vatican was Cardinal Fabrizio Paolucci, who would again be front-runner
for the papacy in the next conclave.

After the death of Innocent XIII, on March 7, 1724, the College of Cardinals met again in Rome. The leading candidates this time were the Cardinals
Piazza, supported by the imperial forces, and Paolucci, supported by Philip V.
Finally, on May 29, 1724, the cardinals elected Pietro Francesco Orsini, who
decided to call himself Benedict XIV. Told that Benedict XIII, known as the
Moon Pope, had never actually been consecrated, Orsini decided to adopt that
name instead.

Three months earlier, in Spain, King Philip V had abdicated in favor of his
son Louis. On February 9, 1724, the Prince of Asturias was named King of
Spain at the age of seventeen. From then on, young King Louis and his wife,
Queen Louise Elisabeth d'Orléans, began to assume the tasks of governing.[3]

Spanish hopes kindled by seeing a Spanish-born king assume the throne
were soon dashed. Really, the reins of power remained in the hands of Philip
V, in his palace of La Granja de San Ildefonso. All decisions made by the
young king had to be ratified by his father, once Philip had discussed them
with the latest strongman of the regime, Marquis José de Grimaldo.[4]

On June 26, Philip V met in La Granja with his son and daughter-in-law.
The conduct of the queen, then fourteen years old, was habitually indecorous
and unacceptable. She generally wore no underwear, and sometimes wore a
nightgown that left nothing to the imagination. Even the Marquis of Santa
Cruz wrote Grimaldo that "the queen is often seen with two Italians in an
indecorous way." One of the Italians may have been Tebaldo Fieschi, the
Holy Alliance's Sienese spy.

Worn out by trying to cope with his wife's behavior, Louis determined to confine Louise Elisabeth to the Alcázar until she would promise to behave properly. After seven days she was released. Two Italians, one of them Fieschi, were expelled from Spain.[5]

But a more serious situation soon added to King Louis's problems. On August 14, he suddenly fell ill. On the 19th, his doctors diagnosed his disease as smallpox. On the 29th, he grew delirious from high fever, and two days later he died after a reign of only seven and a half months. Philip V had to leave his pleasant retirement in La Granja behind and take up the Spanish crown again.[6]

In Rome, meanwhile, the new pope brought trusted subordinates from his previous work in the dioceses of Benevento, Manfredonia, and Cesena to assist him. One of these was Niccolo Coscia, who had been his assistant in Benevento.

Taking advantage of his relationship with the supreme pontiff and his new position as papal private secretary, Coscia exercised a hitherto unprecedented degree of corrupt power. He embezzled enormous sums, putting the entire Vatican budget at risk; he manipulated his close access to the pope for personal gain; he tried to manage the Vatican's foreign relations in the same way; and above all he used the Holy Alliance for the benefit of chosen kings and princes.[7]

In spite of the opposition of a majority of cardinals who hated Coscia, Benedict XIII raised him into their ranks and gave him a position like the ones previous popes had conferred on their relatives. Annibale Albani, who still held some power in the Holy Alliance, reported to Cardinal Fabrizio Paolucci on Cardinal Coscia's maneuvers to take over control of the spy services and its archives. Albani went so far as to urge several cardinals to keep watch on the business activities of the pope's favorite.

While some in the College of Cardinals preferred to close their eyes and ears to Niccolo Coscia's growing power, a faction led by Cardinal Paolucci advised Benedict XIII to exercise more control over what his favorite did.

Coscia tried to work his way into Paolucci's secretariat of state and Albani's Holy Alliance, but neither proved a simple task. Paolucci had too much support in the college—after all, he had twice been a candidate for pope—while Albani directed a branch of the Church in which Benedict XIII did not really want to interfere.[8]

The situation grew tenser when the pope himself accused Paolucci, Albani, and other cardinals of slandering Cardinal Coscia, but both the secretary of state and the head of the Holy Alliance knew that the pope's favorite was taking bribes from several European monarchs. The problem they faced was how to prove Cardinal Niccolo Coscia guilty of these cases of corruption. Albani decided to order an operation dubbed Operation Iscariot, after the apostle who betrayed Jesus Christ. The plan was to introduce "Trojans"[9]— Holy Alliance agents who served as spies within an organization—into the departments led by Coscia.

In February 1726, the trap began to close around Cardinal Coscia. Paolucci was more and more disposed to get rid of the pope's corrupt secretary whatever the cost. Coscia, who knew the Holy Alliance was after him, decided to fire his own warning shot. One day, the corpse of a priest named Enrico Fasano appeared near a bridge over the Tiber. Parts of his body had been amputated during the torture he had undergone.

Fasano was a Holy Alliance agent assigned by Albani to Operation Iscariot. His task was to collect information on the small army of criminals Niccolo Coscia had recruited in the worst low-life districts of Rome. The corrupt cardinal used this force as a sort of shadowy bodyguard, not so much to protect his person as to destroy any trace or trail that might implicate him.[10]

What role, if any, Benedict XIII played in the assassination of Albani's agent remains unclear. In any case, the warning shot did not deter Albani from the task of collecting evidence of the pope's secretary's corruption.

Coscia's next blow fell upon the priest Lorenzo Valdo, a Dominican who had worked in the papal secretariat since the times of Innocent XII. Valdo had never been more than a minor spy, but his position close to Coscia made him a very useful pair of eyes for Annibale Albani.

On the night of June 9, 1726, Valdo left the papal palace carrying a letter on Benedict XIII's letterhead that he was supposed to deliver to an address in Rome. He knew his mission, carrying a papal letter, was the next thing to sacred. When he reached the house to which the letter was addressed, he knocked on the door. It opened, and three men pulled him inside and stabbed him in the neck. Then they threw his corpse into the Tiber.

An investigation carried out by Albani showed that the letter Lorenzo Valdo had been assigned to deliver might have been blank. Someone very close to Benedict XIII, surely Cardinal Niccolo Coscia, had used the papal seal as a ruse to lure the official to his death.

Three days after Lorenzo Valdo's assassination, on June 12, Cardinal Fabrizio Paolucci himself mysteriously died. He had twice been a candidate for pope, served for twenty-four years as secretary of state, and been one of the greatest friends of the Holy Alliance in all its history. His death left Cardinal Annibale Albani to face the pope's favorite, Cardinal Niccolo Coscia, alone.

Another of Coscia's operations uncovered by the Holy Alliance, this one carried out in 1727, was the manipulation of the Church's relations with Victor Amadeus II of Savoy, King of Sardinia. As his ambassador to Rome, Victor Amadeus sent the Marquis d'Ormea, an able, astute diplomat well-versed in how to win privileges for his sovereign from Cardinal Coscia. These included the opportunity to nominate candidates for cardinal, a veto over appointments of bishops in his region, and finally the "right of presentation" (right to appoint priests to open benefices) in all the churches, cathedrals, abbeys, and priories.[11] Apparently Niccolo Coscia got Pope Benedict XIII to sign a concordat to this effect; in return, Victor Amadeus awarded Coscia the title to important lands in the Piedmont.[12]

Another conflict generated by Coscia involved the Jewish community in Rome. Between 1634 and 1790, more than two thousand Roman Jews converted to Catholicism. Benedict XIII baptized twenty-six of them. These conversions were followed by fireworks and religious processions, while in the ghettos, Coscia's personal army reduced the Jews to silence. If any of them should be found lighting candelabras in funerals or placing small stones on the tombs, Coscia's guards or those of the pope were authorized to whip them.[13]

Cardinal Coscia's thugs had free rein on the Roman streets, and some of them spread the myth that any Catholic who succeeded in converting a heretic would gain automatic entry into heaven. During the following months, many Jewish babies were torn from their homes and forcibly baptized in fountains or with rainwater. Supposedly, all of this took place without the knowledge of Pope Benedict XIII.[14]

Early in 1730, the pope grew sick. He lingered feverish in bed until February 21, 1730, when he died at the age of eighty-two. The best historian of the papacy, Ludwig von Pastor, was right when he declared that "being a good monk is not enough to make one a good pope." Benedict XIII serves as a perfect example of this rule. His papacy focused more on religion than on politics, and as a result, a man like Cardinal Niccolo Coscia could worm his way into the heart of the Holy See.[15]

The conclave that followed Benedict's death lasted nearly five long months, from March 6 to July 12. No faction was strong enough to impose its candidate on the College of Cardinals. Finally, the arrival of summer heat and the deaths of several cardinals led Cardinal Álvaro Cienfuegos, of the Imperial faction, to join with those supporting Cardinal Lorenzo Corsini. On July 12, Corsini was elected pope and adopted the name Clement XII.[16]

At the age of seventy-two, the new pope retained his mental acuity. Since his early days filling important positions in the financial and legal bureaucracy of the Holy See, he had shown a great capacity to remain neutral in the fierce internecine struggles with the Church and its curia. Lorenzo Corsini had fully lived both civil and religious life. This would help him in the difficult task of being supreme pontiff.[17]

His first measure, on July 24, 1730, was to demand Cardinal Albani's resignation as head of papal espionage. Pope Clement XII accused Albani of failing to defend the Church's interests during his tenure as chief of the Holy Alliance. The pope characterized Operation Iscariot as inept and ineffective for having cost the lives of two agents, Enrico Fasano and Lorenzo Valdo.[18] After this preparatory move came Niccolo Coscia's turn.

Immediately upon the death of Benedict XIII, Coscia and his friends had attempted to flee from Rome, but when they reached the city's gates, the Swiss Guard barred Coscia's way, because as a cardinal he was required to participate in the conclave to choose his late protector's replacement.

Curiously, during the voting, Niccolo Coscia's own name appeared on one of the ballots, which provoked protests from the rest of the college.[19]

Clement XII's first move against Cardinal Coscia was to order the creation of four ecclesiastical tribunals to judge the corrupt cardinal and his acts. The first was supposed to judge Cardinal Niccolo Coscia himself; the second, to examine the entire trajectory that had led to Coscia's becoming the pope's trusted assistant, in order to assure that it should not be repeated; the third, to study every case of a privilege obtained by Coscia for a European prince; and the fourth, to analyze the state of the Camera Apostolica's finances and find out how much Cardinal Coscia had embezzled.

The cardinal, seeing himself so pursued, sought the intervention of Emperor Charles VI in the hope the emperor could order the trial stopped. When Clement XII learned of this move, he ordered the immediate opening of Niccolo Coscia's trial.[20]

The priest then fled by night and took refuge in Naples, but he was compelled to return to the papal states by a strict written order from the pope himself. The others tried alongside Niccolo Coscia were his brother Filippo (the bishop of Targa) and Cardinal Francesco Fini.

Francesco Fini had been assigned to the secretariat of state, where he had been a confidant of the late Cardinal Paolucci and even a secret messenger between the latter and Annibale Albani. Apparently, he had also been Niccolo Coscia's agent in charge of monitoring actions carried out by Holy Alliance agents and Albani against the corrupt cardinal.

The trial ended on May 22, 1733. The seventeen cardinals making up the commission unanimously approved Niccolo Coscia's conviction, which the supreme pontiff upheld three days later. All of Coscia's goods were confiscated and distributed among the poor. The corrupt priest also had to pay 100,000 escudos in damages into the coffers of the Church and of Rome. He was sentenced to forgo all his honors and Church positions and his right to vote in subsequent conclaves. Finally, he was sentenced to ten years imprisonment, to be served in a cell in the castle of Sant'Angelo.[21]

On completion of this sentence, Pope Clement XII ordered, Coscia would be absolved of his censures, and his right to vote in the conclave would be restored. Once again officially a cardinal, Niccolo Coscia retired to Naples, where he died September 14, 1755, alone and forgotten.[22]

In spite of the pope's good health, two years into his papacy he began to have trouble with his sight. He ended up completely blind, requiring someone to guide his hand so that he could sign documents. Though he continued to be active in directing the Church, he delegated many state affairs to his nephew, Neri Corsini, whom he had raised to cardinal on August 14, 1730. Neri Corsini took the reins of the Holy Alliance after the firing of Cardinal Annibale Albani.

Under Corsini, the Vatican secret service devoted itself more to religious persecution within the Church and persecution of the Freemasons than to involvement in political issues. During these years, relations with Philip V deteriorated significantly. Continued passage of Spanish troops through the papal state, forced recruitment, and the pope's refusal to allow the anointment of Philip V's son Charles of Bourbon as King of Naples brought about a new rupture between Madrid and Rome. Relations were reestablished in 1737 with the signing of a concordat in which, as a key point, Clement XII consented to Charles's coronation in Naples.

A year later, after receiving an important report from the Holy Alliance about the increasing threat from Freemasonry within the Catholic Church, the pope decided to condemn it in the bull *In Eminenti* of April 28, 1738. In this text, Clement XII barred all his subjects from belonging to Masonic orders or attending their ceremonies, under pain of excommunication.[23] For the supreme pontiff, Freemasonry interfered with full integration into the true religion and elevated fidelity to a secret society above loyalty to God.

The Holy Alliance had issued its first major report on Freemasonry in December of 1733, provoking Clement XII to approve a new constitution in the papal state on January 14, 1734. The constitution prohibited all citizens from taking part in Masonic rites under pain of death and confiscation of all worldly goods. The new law ordered all Catholics to report these rites to Church magistrates, along with the names of those participating.

The next pope, Benedict XIV, in his bull *Providas* of May 18, 1751, ratified the conduct of Clement XII. Pius VII in 1814, Leo XII in 1825, and Pius IX in 1865 also condemned Freemasonry and its rites. Pope Leo XIII, in 1884, in the encyclical *Humanum Genus,* ordered all Christians to be on their guard against the advance of the sect known as the Masons.[24]

On February 6, 1740, Pope Clement XII died at the age of eighty-seven, which brought the convening of a new conclave. Cardinal Prospero Lambertini had a reputation as an important expert in canon law and was very well regarded by the other cardinals, but in the conclave that began on February 14, he did not appear on the list of likely candidates.

This was the beginning of one of the longest conclaves in Church history because of the strength of the factions and the evident divisions within the College of Cardinals. The French faction and the Austrian one were united, but so, on the other side, were the Spanish, Neapolitan, Tuscan, and Sardinian ones. Cardinal Neri Corsini, head of the Holy Alliance, led the group of cardinals named by his uncle, Clement XII. The various factions also split along a binary division between the *zelanti*—those who wanted a pope who would be firm and unwavering in his defense of Church rights—and those lobbying for a more conciliatory and diplomatic pontiff.[25]

Votes and calculations followed one after another without any positive result until someone presented the candidacy of Cardinal Prospero Lambertini. Six months after the opening of the conclave, on the morning of August 17, 1740, Lambertini was elected pope and adopted the name Benedict XIV. His first step was to name Cardinal Silvio Valenti as secretary of state and confirm Cardinal Neri Corsini as head of papal espionage.

Benedict XIV went down in history more as the "pope of the concordats" than as a political figure. From the first year of his reign, this pope hurried to resolve issues between the Vatican and other states that his predecessors had left hanging. A new concordat was negotiated with the kingdoms of Sardinia, Portugal, and Spain. Difficult concordats were negotiated with Naples and with Austrian Lombardy. During this time, the agents of the Holy Alliance remained inactive or made political analyses under the orders of Cardinal Valenti.

The inactivity of papal espionage meant, for instance, that news of the death of King Philip took days to reach the Holy See. The Spanish king died on July 9, 1746. As was his custom, the king had met with his ministers overnight in the Buen Retiro palace and gone to bed at seven thirty in the morning. About one thirty in the afternoon, Philip told the queen he felt like throwing up, but the royal physician was not in the palace. In a few moments, his throat and tongue began to swell. When he tried to get up, he fell back on the bed. He was dead.[26]

The king's sudden death at sixty-two, writes the historian Henry Arthur Kamen in his biography *Philip V of Spain: The King Who Reigned Twice,* was a consequence of his physical and mental deterioration. Philip V had not bathed for at least four months, and his condition was such that when servants tried to wash the corpse, their sponges pulled off strips of skin. Finally, wrapped in a shroud of gold and silver, he was buried in the Church of San Ildefonso in La Granja, eight days after death.[27] The Prince of Asturias was proclaimed King of Spain and reigned under the name of Ferdinand VI.

Little is known about Holy Alliance activities during the eighteen years of Benedict XIV's papacy. This might stem from the fact that the papal espionage service had always counted on a large number of Jesuits within its ranks, but the new pontiff was not very sympathetic to that order. In fact, it was Benedict XIV who finally gave the green light to taking action against the Society, in an order given to Cardinal Saldaña, Archbishop of Lisbon. The order specified examining and studying the activities of Portuguese Jesuits. This was a response to pressures from the Portuguese prime minister Pombal.[28]

Benedict XIV died on May 3, 1758, at eighty-three. The next conclave began May 15, twelve days after the late pope's death. Two factions were dominant in the voting, the *zelanti* and the "Crown cardinals." The latter favored continuing the policies of Benedict XIV. Cardinals Corsini and Portocarrero supported

Cavalchini, and on June 28, he was nearly elected pope by a single vote. Cardinal Rodt, representing the Imperial court, and Cardinal Spinelli then decided to support a bid for the office by Cardinal Rezzonico, who would in fact be chosen as pope on July 6, 1758.[29] Carlo Rezzonico, who named himself Clement XIII, was a Venetian who, truth be told, had a complete lack of talent for politics and diplomacy. To fill the gap, the pope named Cardinal Torrigiani—friendly toward the Jesuits and quite authoritarian—as secretary of state.[30]

During this papacy, the war that had been unleashed against the Society of Jesus became more and more obvious, nearly paralyzing the Holy Alliance. The monarchs of the moment—Ferdinand VI in Spain, Joseph I in Portugal, Frederick II in Prussia, Leopold in Tuscany, Joseph II in Austria, and Charles III in Naples and then in Spain—were ever more suspicious and jealous of the growing power of that order. The kings' ministers attacked the Jesuits for their conservative education, their extremism in defending Church intervention in political affairs, and especially their evident subservience to the Holy See.

The beginning of the end for the Society of Jesus dawned in the early hours of September 3, 1758, when King Joseph I of Portugal returned to his palace incognito after spending the night with his mistress, the Marchioness of Távora. When his carriage slowed down on a narrow street, several shots rang out. At first it seemed that the attempted assassination had been the work of the Marquis of Távora, jealous of his wife's relationship with the king. Little by little, an investigation led by Sebastião José Carvalho e Melo, Marquis of Pombal and prime minister, showed that Távora was indeed the mastermind of the plot, but his motives had been political rather than sentimental. For years, both Joseph I and his prime minister, Pombal, had fought for an absolutist monarchy and relegated the nobility to the role of mere witnesses of royal politics, deprived of voice and vote.[31]

On January 12, 1759, the Marquis of Távora and eleven other nobles were tried, sentenced, and executed for attempted regicide.[32] Pombal also showed during the trial that some of the twelve had maintained close relations with the Holy Alliance and all of them had done so with the Jesuits.[33] The official sentence stated that the Duke of Aveiro, with the goal of recovering the nobility's lost influence at court, had reached an agreement with the Jesuits that they would consider the king's assassination to be merely a venial sin.

On January 19, a royal decree ordered the expulsion of the Jesuits and the confiscation of their properties in all the territories of the Portuguese crown. Clement XIII got the official notice the next day. The Holy See's repeated protests to the government in Lisbon provoked the automatic expulsion of the papal nuncio on June 15, 1760. The repression of the Jesuits now spread across all of Europe, and the Holy Alliance suffered a period of great uncertainty, not knowing what to do or whom to inform.[34]

The pope accused his espionage service of failing to inform him of the operations undertaken by Father Lavelette in the West Indies, while the Holy See's spies denied any responsibility, adding that from the beginning of Benedict XIV's papacy their numbers had been cut and, therefore, the Holy Alliance's tentacles had not merely shrunk but come close to amputation.

The third and final act of the Jesuit tragedy came in 1767, on the 27th of March, when, following the Esquilache Riots in Madrid, King Charles III (who had succeeded his stepbrother Ferdinand VI after his death in 1759) decreed their expulsion from "all my dominions and Indies, Philippine Islands, and other adjacent regions . . . and that all their properties be forfeit." The Spanish monarch's decree most heavily impacted the Jesuit missions, but it also decimated one of the Holy Alliance's most widespread information networks abroad. Almost two thousand Jesuits had to leave their foreign missions. On the heels of the Portuguese, French, and Spanish examples, the Grand Master of Malta also signed an expulsion order on April 22, 1768; he told the pope he was doing so by virtue of his commitments to the kingdom of Naples. The same year, the Duke of Parma followed suit.

Clement XIII's formal protests and bulls against these edicts caused French troops to occupy Avignon and the Comtat Venaissin. Naples occupied the papal cities of Benevento and Pontecorvo; Parma threatened His Holiness with an invasion of the papal state if he did not retract the bulls and condemnations. In January of 1769, the French, Spanish, and Neapolitan ambassadors in Rome formally requested that Pope Clement XIII suppress the Society of Jesus entirely. The pope prepared to resist but in a few days fell victim to a stroke. The next pope, Clement XIV, would have to settle the issue.

The conclave of 1769, which followed the death of Clement XIII, was, without doubt, the most politicized in papal history. It lasted three months, surrounded by continual confrontations among not the cardinals themselves but the ambassadors from the Catholic courts of Europe, who were the true referees of the Holy See's ecclesiastic politics. They all wanted a puppet pope, easy to manipulate. Perhaps Clement XIV would be one.[35]

The point was not to select a good pope skilled in canon law or a skilled politician or an experienced diplomat. The point was to settle on a weak personality who, as pope, would declare himself an open enemy of the Jesuits.

The pro-Jesuit party was led by Cardinal Torrigiani, while the opposite side was commanded by the Spanish cardinals Francisco Solís and Buenaventura Spínola de la Cerda and the French Cardinal de Bernis. In the end, on May 19, 1769, after an exhausting conclave full of pressures and intrigues, Cardinal Antonio Ganganelli became Pope Clement XIV. As the researcher and historian Michael J. Walsh writes in his book *The Conclave: A Sometimes Secret and Occasionally Bloody History of Papal Elections,* there was a pact within the conclave to elect Cardinal Ganganelli in return for his ordering the dissolution of the Jesuits once his election was secured.

In 1848, during the papacy of Pius IX, the Holy Alliance revealed the existence of a sheet of paper on which Ganganelli (Clement XIV) had written during the conclave of 1769, confirming his adherence to the anti-Jesuit party. Curiously, the next day the cardinal was elected pope.[36] Cardinal de Bernis always denied that there had been any sort of political intrigue in the conclave that elevated Ganganelli to the papacy.

The new pope began by firing Torrigiani as secretary of state, replacing him with Cardinal Pallavicini. At the same time, he ordered the Holy See's espionage service completely cleansed of infiltration by any member of the Jesuit order. What Clement XIV did not understand, after the Holy Alliance had been in existence for two centuries, was that its central corps of free agents and informers in the major European power centers belonged to the Society.

On July 21, 1773, Clement XIV signed the papal brief *Dominus ac Redemptor,* which suppressed the Society of Jesus. The document, which was not revealed to the superior-general, Father Ricci, until August 16, said:

> We extinguish and suppress the said Society, annul and abrogate all and each of its offices, ministries, administrations, houses, schools, hospices . . . statutes, customs, decrees, constitutions . . . It is our thought and our will that the [Jesuit] priests should be considered as secular clergy.[37]

(Secular clergy here means akin to parish priests, rather than members of a religious order.)

It was truly humiliating to see the way the Papal Guard itself implemented Pope Clement's brief, entering all the Jesuit houses and requisitioning all the documents within. On September 23, Superior-General Lorenzo Ricci and his most trusted collaborators were escorted to the castle of Sant'Angelo in Rome, where they were to be confined. The confinement was so harsh that Ricci did not learn of the death of his secretary Cornolli until six months later, even though they lived in neighboring cells. Most operatives of the Holy Alliance were reduced to the most minimum activity.

The law demanded that Lorenzo Ricci and his aides be freed, but nothing was done, apparently out of fear that the dispersed Jesuits might regroup around their old leader to rebuild their order in the heart of Catholicism.[38] As "compensation" for his work against the Jesuits, Clement XIV won restitution of the papal states of Avignon, the Venaissin, Benevento, and Pontecorvo. The pope lived only fourteen more months after the suppression of the order, dying September 21, 1774, but the Holy Alliance wanted the last word, which would come during the papacy of Clement's successor, Pius VI.

On the death of King Joseph I of Portugal, in February 1777, the Marquis of Pombal had to give up his post. The prime minister retired to his lands in Oyeras, but the Holy Alliance was not going to allow Pombal, the Jesuits' great enemy, to escape without punishment. The nobleman Francisco Coelho da Silva, speaking during the coronation of Queen Maria I of Portugal in the central plaza of Lisbon, dared to declare:

Portugal still has open wounds provoked by the blind and limitless despotism of that fallen minister [Pombal].[39]

Apparently, free agents of the Holy Alliance tied to the Jesuits supplied the kingdom's judges, in some mysterious form, with a report full of substantiated accusations against the Marquis of Pombal. The twenty-eight-page document led to the former minister's being put on trial. On January 11, 1780, Sebastião José Carvalho e Melo, Marquis of Pombal and former prime minister to the king, was found guilty of corruption and illegal enrichment at the cost of the crown. He was sentenced to a serious prison term. On learning of the sentence, Queen Maria granted him a pardon effective January 1, 1781, by reason of his advanced age. The Marquis of Pombal died May 8, 1782, abandoned by all.

The death of Clement XIV left the Holy See in a state of disarray. Many cardinals—the *zelanti*—were unhappy with Ganganelli's ineffective rule and his nearly complete deference to the crowned heads of Europe, but the Bourbons and their allies across the continent were determined not to change their political line with respect to the Church and the papacy. The horizon of the Holy Alliance seemed quite dark in years that would see revolutions and the rise and fall of eagles.

8

THE RISE AND FALL

OF EAGLES (1775–1823)

Lord, Lord, did we not prophesy in your name? Did we not drive out demons in your name, and do many miracles in thy name? . . . Depart from me, you that work iniquity.

—Matthew 7:22–23

On October 5, 1774, the cardinals met in conclave to designate a successor to the controversial Clement XIV. Once again the *zelanti,* the Bourbons, the French, and the Imperials formed separate factions. Paris and Madrid supported Cardinal Pallavicini, Clement XIV's former secretary of state.

Pallavicini was rejected by the Imperial faction, but Cardinal Giovanni Francesco Albani offered the candidacy of Cardinal Braschi, one of the independents. With the support of the Bourbon courts and over Portuguese opposition, Giovanni Angelico Braschi was elected pope on February 15, 1775, under the name of Pius VI, in honor of Pius V, inquisitor and founder of the Holy Alliance.[1] His papacy would unfold in one of the most convulsive periods of history and a time of deep crisis for the Catholic religion, which had to contend first with attack from Enlightenment reforms and then with the effects of the French Revolution.

The second part of Pius VI's long papacy would be the more difficult and painful. In early July of 1789, the people of Paris were afraid. The fear stemmed partly from their own victory, the convocation of a national assembly that defied King Louis XVI's order to dissolve and swore instead to stay in session until it could give France a constitution. It also stemmed from the brigands, or bandits, a product of the great hunger-driven peasant migrations to the cities.[2]

The Parisian bourgeoisie was determined to fight off both monarchy and anarchy, so it needed arms with which to form a national militia. The bourgeoisie and not the proletariat formed the real engine of the French Revolution, because the latter still lacked conscious leaders. The first "revolutionaries" were the Count de Mirabeau and the Marquis de Lafayette; the lawyers Desmoulins, Robespierre, Danton, and Vergniaud; and doctors like Marat.[3] Jacques Necker, the friend whom all of France trusted to solve the economic crisis causing widespread hunger, had been discharged by Louis XVI. That news was the spark of the explosion, as Simon Schama asserts in his book *Citizens: A Chronicle of the French Revolution.* The powder keg was supplied by the revolutionary Camille Desmoulins when he leaped onto a table of the royal palace to cry, "Necker has been fired. This is the signal for a St. Bartholomew's Day massacre of patriots.[4] Tonight the Swiss and German battalions will go forth from the Champs de Mars [site of their barracks] to cut our throats. Citizens! To arms!" The problem was that the much-needed arms were stockpiled in the Bastille, that symbol of royal power, the fortress in the center of Paris whose threatening cannon stood always at the ready, aimed at the citizenry, whom Louis XVI did not trust. And so, on July 14, 1789, the citizenry stormed the Bastille.[5]

The Bastille's governor, de Launey, ordered his troops to open fire on their assailants, but finally the fortress surrendered. A cook named Desnot separated de Launey's head from his body with a butcher's knife. The same fate befell Losme-Salbray, the commander of the fortress's troops, and several other officers. Their heads were paraded through the streets of Paris atop a pike, signaling the end of the absolutist monarchy.

In the earliest stage of the revolution, Pope Pius VI maintained neutrality in spite of the advice of Cardinal Giovanni Battista Caprara,[6] head of the Holy Alliance, whose agents began to see openly anticlerical movements in France. On July 12, 1790, the Constituent Assembly issued the Civil Constitution of the Clergy and required that all clergy must swear obedience to the new law. Two days later, King Louis XVI, Queen Marie Antoinette, and the dauphin swore their loyalty to the nation. In response, on March 10,

1791, Pius VI issued the papal brief *Quod aliquantim,* denouncing any and all laws passed by the Assembly that affected religion. In turn, that May, the new leaders of France decided to expel the papal nuncio, definitively breaking relations between revolutionary Paris and papal Rome. Persecution of priests, the execution of Louis XVI on the guillotine, and the steady de-Christianization of France all widened and deepened the chasm.[7]

The breach between the people and Louis XVI that cost the French king his head had in some part been provoked by agents of the Holy Alliance. For the people to lose any remaining confidence in him, the king had merely to make use of the veto that the new constitution granted. Papal espionage agents had informed the monarch that the National Assembly was planning to institute several reforms, including those affecting the clergy, which would among other things bar them from making the sign of obedience to the pope of Rome. Pius VI's spies urged the king to use his constitutional veto to reject this law, and Louis XVI decided to do so.

April 2 brought the death of Mirabeau, the man who had led France along a path that included both revolution and monarchy. The pope's agents now urged the king to flee Paris along with his troops, so as to later regain his crown and all his rights.

The Holy Alliance and the royalists managed to outwit the revolution's spies long enough to get the royal family into a coach headed for the border. The flight was short-lived, however, because on July 21, 1791, the king and his family were arrested and ordered back to Paris. Now the break between the king and the people was complete.[8] The king once again employed his veto, this time to block the decree against refractory priests, those who refused to swear loyalty to the nation rather than to Pope Pius VI.

The assault on the Tuileries in August of 1792 ushered in the so-called Terror. The guillotine went up on August 22. On January 21, 1793, it was permanently installed in the Place de la Révolution, today the Place de la Concorde. The king prepared himself, put on his hat, and set off for his appointment with death. When he reached the site of the guillotine, he knelt alongside the priest and received the last rites. Samson's assistants tried to tie his hands, but the king refused. The executioners were ready to force him, but the Abbé Edgeworth counseled Louis, "Make this sacrifice, sire. In this further outrage, I see only a final resemblance between Your Majesty and God." The executioners tied the king's hands behind his back with a handkerchief and cut his hair. Leaning on the abbé's arm, he mounted the stairs to the guillotine. At the last moment, Louis changed direction and walked to the edge of the platform, facing toward the Tuileries. "Frenchmen, I am innocent!" he told the crowd. "I pardon those who are the cause of my misfortunes. I pray to God that the shedding of my blood will contribute to the happiness of France and you, unfortunate people."[9]

The four executioners pushed him down onto the guillotine. The king resisted and cried out, but the blade fell with extraordinary speed and cut off his head, splattering blood upon the abbé. Samson grabbed the severed head by the hair and lifted it to show the people. The accomplices, the fanatics, the furious radicals all surged onto the platform and wet their sabers, their kerchiefs, their knives, and their hands in the king's blood. They shouted, *"Vive la nation!"* and *"Vive la république!"* but almost no one responded. Queen Marie Antoinette met the same fate on September 16, 1793.

Pope Pius VI's protests provoked the occupation of Avignon and the Venaissin, this time by a French revolutionary army. Papal diplomats and politicians gave way to Holy Alliance spies, who played an important role in the coming years. One of the most effective was the Abbé Salamon, who served as a sort of underground papal representative in late-eighteenth-century revolutionary France.

Beginning in 1793, Salamon created one of the best information networks and escape routes throughout the length and breadth of France.[10] The National Assembly, the popular convention that had forced King Louis XVI and his ministers from power, had determined on the confiscation of the properties of the aristocracy and the Church. It also enacted the abolition of the monastic orders, a reduction in dioceses, and the institution of a type of civil clergy committed to the new regime. The nuncio had returned to Rome, but Salamon became Pope Pius VI's eyes and ears in Paris during the Terror. From his small house, the abbé kept up a steady stream of information to the Holy Alliance in Rome about rumors of new measures to be adopted by the revolutionary government against the priests of France.[11]

But one story that has passed more into the legend of the Holy Alliance than into actual history is the case of Louis-Charles Capet, son of the executed monarch, whom the monarchists knew as Louis XVII.

On August 3, 1793, little Louis, only seven years old, was taken from his mother, who was soon to be executed, and confined in a somber cell under protection of two guardians. The pope's agents reported that the boy entered prison on August 13, 1792, under the vigilance of a married couple. Abbé Salamon determined to save the child, or at least to try.[12]

There are two versions of the case of Louis XVII. The first says that little Louis, who because of his age took no active part in French politics, died in prison at the age of ten, on June 8, 1795. Some sources assert that he was poisoned, but in any case he died as a victim of his enforced stay in a cell with barely any space to move, lamentable sanitary conditions, and only rats for company.[13] A doctor who visited him in May found little Louis in a state of grave physical and psychological debilitation.[14]

On June 6 and 7, his condition grew critical, and the 8th brought the death of the boy who for some was King Louis XVII and for others was the citizen Louis-Charles Capet. His body was examined and placed in the coffin and then buried in the cemetery of Ste. Marguerite at 9 A.M. Two soldiers stood guard for several days to keep anyone from making off with the remains of the last king of France. But the boy's death fired the imaginations of many about what had really occurred.

At that time, monarchist plots centered around the assassination of all the members of the Committee of Public Safety and subsequent placement of young Louis on the throne. The chief conspirator was Pierre Gaspare Chaumette, who many claim was an active member of the Holy Alliance and had promised Rome that on the monarchy's restoration, the Church, too, would be restored to its former position.

Legends circulating ever since have held that the child who died was not really Louis XVI's son, but another who much resembled him, while the true king was safe and sound in the court of Charles IV of Spain, thanks to a covert operation carried out by the Holy Alliance.[15]

On the other hand, letters in the National Archive of France show that while an attempt was being made to make it appear that the innocent Louis XVII was safe in Spain, King Charles IV was sending letter after letter to the revolutionary authorities, asking them to turn the two children born to Louis XVI and Marie Antoinette over to him. Paris continually refused to do so.

Another Holy Alliance agent, by the name of Frotté, had gotten an order to try to find the young king and save him. After reaching Paris by way of the Vendée, Frotté wrote: "I have suffered the pain of learning that we have been deceived. The monstrous double regicides, after having made him languish for a long period in prison, have brought about his death in his cell.

There is nothing left for us to do but cry." Another, more romantic version that appeared in 1801 tells the story of a member of Abbé Salamon's network named Émile Fronzac.

Apparently, Fronzac had bribed his way into the palace, left an orphan boy in place of the dauphin, and spirited Louis out of Paris inside a toy wooden horse. The coach carrying them toward the lines of the monarchist army was stopped by a group of gendarmes. Before the papal spy could be forced to surrender, a group of Vendéen soldiers came to his aid, killed the revolutionaries, and rescued their legitimate king.[16]

The researcher Deborah Cadbury, in her study *The Lost King of France: A True Story of Revolution, Revenge, and DNA,* wonders where, if this version were true, the king could have ended up. According to a writer of the era who recounted the adventure of the spy Émile Fronzac and the Dauphin of France, Louis XVII was sent off to America, after the death of the revolutionaries, but a French frigate intercepted his ship, and, when the passenger's identity was discovered, the boy was returned to Paris, where he died in his cell after all. Be this as it may, legend or reality gave rise to a most romantic image of the Holy Alliance and its papal spies in the period when Catholic clergy followed the French aristocracy along the path to the guillotine.

The attempted escape of Louis XVI and his family with the aid of agents of Pope Pius VI, along with the continual speeches of the Revolutionary Council equating priests and nobles, led to an outbreak of fury in September 1792, in which more than two hundred priests were killed.[17] Thousands more took flight, and those who stayed in France had to go underground.

Abbé Salamon was one of the most important of those who decided to stay. Daily he traced his routes through the streets, plazas, shops, and taverns of Paris, collecting information for the Holy Alliance in Rome. "Pius's Ears," as he was known in the Holy See in a clear allusion to the pope, developed many contacts with bishops and priests in the provinces as well.

To evade the strict vigilance to which his status as a priest subjected him, Salamon created safe channels for communication with Rome. His eventual unmasking, arrest, and prison sentence saved him from the famous massacre of September 1792.[18] After his release in December 1798, the priest returned to his work in the papal espionage service, rebuilding the network that had been paralyzed during his imprisonment.[19] Other sources claim that in view of his experience in espionage matters, he was recruited by Pope Pius VI to lead the secret service in the Holy See.

The papal state, meanwhile, organized a large campaign to depict the Revolution and its leaders as a creation of Satan and the result of a great anti-Catholic plot. The goal was to be able to call for a "holy war" against France and its armies, in defense of religion. Nothing, however, halted the implacable advance of French troops. Their commander in chief, Napoleon Bonaparte, forced Pope Pius VI to sign the humiliating armistice of Bologna on June 23, 1796, in which the supreme pontiff agreed to renounce his authority over Ferrara, Bologna, and Ancona, to pay twenty-one million escudos in indemnities, and to turn over five hundred manuscripts and a hundred Renaissance art works as well.[20]

Pius VI then requested Austrian aid, which to Napoleon constituted a violation of the Bologna accord, so he ordered his troops to occupy the papal state. This time—in the Treaty of Tolentino—the French leader demanded the permanent cession of Avignon and the Comtat Venaissin, renunciation of the legations of Bologna, Ferrara, and Romagna, and a payment of forty-six million escudos and numerous works of art.[21]

The situation turned tragic when Holy Alliance agents or former members of the Black Order decided to kill General Mathurin-Léonard Duphot, one of Napoleon Bonaparte's most trusted advisors and best strategists. Duphot had taken part in the Savoy campaigns of the Army of the Alps until he left active service on June 13, 1795, but on February 9, 1796, he was recruited again. In August 1796, he fought in the Mantua, Rivoli, and La Favorita campaigns. Promoted to brigadier general by Napoleon on March 30, 1797, he was sent to Rome to accompany Joseph Bonaparte, Napoleon's brother, who had been named ambassador to the Holy See.[22]

On December 28, 1797, a crowd had gathered outside the French ambassador's residence to demand the proclamation of a republic. A detachment of the Papal Guard pushed the multitude back, and many of them took refuge inside the embassy. General Duphot, who was trying to calm the crowd, was stabbed in the side by an attacker whose face nobody saw. He fell to the ground, bleeding, and soon died. When French soldiers succeeded in expelling both the crowd and the Papal Guard from the area, they found an octagonal piece of cloth alongside the officer's corpse. It had Jesus' name on each side, the phrase, "Prepared for the pain of torment, in God's name," in the center, and the symbol of the so-called *Octogonus* Circle.[23]

As a reprisal for General Duphot's assassination, Napoleon ordered General Berthier, commander in chief of the Army of Italy, to attack and conquer Rome.[24] On February 15, 1798, Napoleon's troops occupied Rome, and on March 7 they deposed Pius VI as temporal ruler and proclaimed the Roman Republic. When the first French units reached the Quirinal Palace, they found that the Swiss Guard offered no resistance. Pius VI had ordered them to disarm and refrain from battle. The pope was detained and the papal archives seized and sent to France.[25]

From then on, the Holy Alliance ceased operations throughout Italy, while members of the *Octogonus* Circle and the Black Order carried out numerous attacks on the French invaders.

Ordered into exile, the pope had to leave Rome on February 20, 1798. After a stay in Siena, he was confined to the Carthusian monastery in Florence, where he continued to see to religious affairs. On November 13, he issued the bull *Quum nos,* which established procedures in case of a vacancy in the office of pope and a process to follow in the ensuing conclave.[26]

In March 1799, the pope was transferred to Parma and later to Turin, after an attempt by members of the Holy Alliance to free him. At the end of the year, eighty-one years old and ill, he was transferred again, carried through the Alps to Briançon in a sedan chair out of fear that papal espionage agents would seize him with Austrian aid. The journey ended on July 13, 1799, in the French city of Valence, were he remained confined until his death on August 29. His corpse was sealed in a lead coffin and taken to Rome for burial in February 1802.

On learning of the pope's death, Napoleon Bonaparte wrote: "The pope is dead. The old mechanism of the Church will fall apart by itself." Like all great dictators in history, he firmly believed that his empire would survive him for centuries, something that did not happen, while the empire of the Church, which he expected to dissolve, survived. But first it had to pass through more difficult and fearful moments.

On October 3, 1799, Cardinal Giovanni Francesco Albani, taking refuge with the rest of the cardinals in Venice (which was at that time part of the Austrian empire), decided to convoke the conclave for December 8. Voting went on and on without any of the proposed candidates winning the necessary two-thirds to be elected pope.[27]

Finally, Cardinal Ettore Consalvi broke the logjam by offering the candidacy of Cardinal Barnaba Chiaramonti, who was elected as supreme pontiff on March 14, 1800. Chiaramonti would govern the Church under the name of Pius VII.

Though selected as pope, Pius VII could not move to Rome until July 3. Emperor Francis II tried to convince the pontiff to establish the papal headquarters in some site under Austrian control, but Pius VII stressed the need for a Church that would be free of any interference. He did accept the appointment of a secretary of state with close ties to Austria.

While the conclave of cardinals had been meeting in Venice, events unfolding in Paris changed not only the history of France but also that of all Europe. The Directory gave way to the Consulate. Approval of a new constitution on December 13, 1799, followed by massive support on the part of the French people on February 7, 1800, converted the glorious general Napoleon Bonaparte into the lord and master of the country's destiny.[28]

After liquidating the Revolution, the First Consul turned to the task of normalizing relations between state and church. Napoleon had reached the conclusion that France wanted to go on being Catholic, so he made the first move to approach Pope Pius VII. Napoleon himself had been baptized but was an agnostic. In the depths of his soul, however, he wanted to mollify the strong Catholic monarchies. The rough-hewn Corsican officer wanted to be received and accepted in the courts of Europe.[29]

Napoleon also knew that he needed to find someone who could not only control the functioning of his own secret services but also check any infiltration by the services of other powers, especially those of Austria and Britain and the Holy Alliance. His choice for this task was Joseph Fouché.[30]

From a moneyed family, the spy had studied for the priesthood in Nantes until he became a member of the National Assembly in 1792. A year later he supported the execution of Louis XVI. His political trajectory always saw him choosing the most powerful side. Some of his cruelest acts took place during the rebellion in the Vendée and later in Lyon. In 1795, he temporarily retired from politics while maintaining his friendships with influential figures, until Napoleon named him head of his powerful espionage services.[31] From then on, Fouché became the main enemy of the Holy Alliance.

The first plot he had to unravel/foil was the so-called Enghien Conspiracy, which involved Generals Moreau, Pichegru, and Georges Cadoudal, along with Bouvet de Lozier, a former general in the army of the princes. At the center of the plot stood Louis-Antoine-Henri de Bourbon, Duke of Enghien. Fouché discovered soon afterwards that some of the conspirators had been in contact with Cardinal Caprara, head of papal espionage, and perhaps with an important member of the Holy Alliance in Paris.[32]

The plan was to kidnap and kill Napoleon. General Moreau would replace Bonaparte until the situation was stabilized. After a few months, the Duke of Enghien would don the crown and Pichegru would be named second consul of France. Cadoudal knew that Moreau, a popular and victorious general beloved by his troops, and General Pichegru wanted to topple Napoleon only for their own good.

The first to fall was General Moreau, whom Napoleon ordered arrested. To avoid rumors, the glorious officer would be judged by a civil tribunal. The order against Moreau also stipulated the detention of fifteen other conspirators, including a Swiss citizen tied to the Russian embassy and the papal nunciature.[33] According to Fouché's reports, the Swiss in question had once been a member of Pius VI's Swiss Guard and had been recruited by the Holy Alliance to carry out secret operations in Napoleon's France during the papacy of Pius VII.[34]

The Russian ambassador, Markof, personally requested that Napoleon release the Swiss citizen, but Napoleon refused. In Paris, word of Moreau's arrest was now on everyone's lips.

On the night of February 26–27, 1804, Pichegru was found in a house at 39 rue de Chabanais and placed under arrest. Méhée de la Touche, Napoleon's best spy in Paris, discovered that Cadoudal was still in the capital and might be trying to contact the Duke of Enghien by way of the nunciature or some papal spy.[35]

By this time, Napoleon saw the conspiracy for what it was: a blueblood prince as leader, Generals Moreau and Pichegru as brains, Cadoudal as executer and executioner. On March 9, Cadoudal was located by the spy de la Touche, who called in the gendarmes. Before being taken, Cadoudal killed one agent and mortally wounded another. Now only the prince remained to be arrested, in Ettenheim on the outskirts of Strasbourg. Napoleon and his consuls debated whether to put Louis-Antoine-Henri de Bourbon to death or imprison him for life. Memories of the guillotine severing royal necks were still all too fresh. During the night, Napoleon ordered his loyal war minister Berthier to take charge of Enghien's arrest.

On March 17, Louis-Antoine-Henri de Bourbon was in custody, along with other plotters. Napoleon had decided that Enghien should die. To him, if "a man conspires like any other man, he should be treated like any other man." But Joseph Fouché opposed taking this step. On the night of the 20th, the trial of Louis-Antoine-Henri de Bourbon began, and by the morning of the 21st, the matter was settled. The Duke of Enghien had been shot.[36]

On April 6, 1804, General Pichegru was strangled in his cell. According to one version, the ex-general was killed by Napoleon's followers, but Bonaparte insisted it would have been stupid for him to eliminate his principal witness against Moreau. Another version has it that Pichegru could have been killed by a hand sent from Rome to avoid his revealing the connections between the Enghien Conspiracy and the Vatican.

The last act of the Enghien Conspiracy occurred on June 26 of that same year, when Henri Samson, the same man who beheaded Louis XVI and his wife, Queen Marie Antoinette, operated the guillotine that dispatched Georges Cadoudal and twelve more accomplices, including the Swiss citizen suspected of belonging to the Holy Alliance. Napoleon allowed General Moreau to leave France after surrendering all his properties.

In the month of March 1804, after the shooting of the Duke of Enghien and a letter in which Louis XVIII denounced the usurper, Napoleon knew that in order to avoid new assassination attempts and Bourbon interference, he had to make himself immortal in the eyes of France and the French. He met with Cardinal Giovanni Battista Caprara, head of the papal spies and *legate a latere* in Paris, to communicate his express desire to be crowned Emperor of France by none other than Pope Pius VII. On December 2, Napoleon Bonaparte crowned himself in Notre Dame de Paris, after which he crowned Josephine kneeling before him, just as depicted in the painting by Louis David, with Pope Pius VII as his illustrious witness.

The pope stayed in Paris for four months, returning to Rome on April 4, 1805. In that same year, the emperor Napoleon's armies won their great victory at Austerlitz, thanks in part to reports received by a double agent who had worked for the Austrian spy service, the Holy Alliance, and the Bonapartist espionage as well. His name was Karl Schulmeister.[37]

Born in the city of Baden, Schulmeister grew up in a family of shepherds and then turned to commerce. One day, he decided that the information he was gathering on all of his business trips might yield greater returns than his merchandise—if he knew to whom to sell it. He brought the law of supply and demand into the world of espionage.

After years as an Austrian spy, he was recruited by the Holy Alliance. Schulmeister claimed to be a good Catholic and declared that his religion required him to offer his obedient service to the pope of Rome. In truth, the information that the Alsatian passed to the papal secret services was of minor importance to them, because its real destination was the Bonapartist services.

A few years after the fact, it became clear that Karl Schulmeister had played an important role in the capture of Louis-Antoine-Henri de Bourbon during the Enghien Conspiracy. Apparently Savary, head of Napoleon's security service, planned to kidnap the duke in Baden, where he had taken refuge. But the double agent told Savary that perhaps he could convince the duke to come closer to the French border, thus facilitating his arrest.

Schulmeister knew that the duke had taken a member of Strasbourg's high society, Charlotte de Rohan, as his lover. Forging the woman's handwriting, Karl Schulmeister wrote a letter to Louis-Antoine-Henri de Bourbon requesting a tryst in Ettenheim, near Strasbourg. The rest is history. The Duke of Enghien was arrested and executed.[38]

The operation brought Karl Schulmeister a great fortune from the hands of Napoleon himself, whom he defined as "a man all brain, and without heart." Next, the emperor entrusted Schulmeister with the new campaign against Austria.

As a first step, Schulmeister wrote a letter to Baron Karl Mack von Leiberich, the field marshal in command of the Austrian forces, in which he pretended to be in fear of French hostility due to his alleged aristocratic origins, all of which was untrue. As cover, Karl Schulmeister had bought the titles of the Bierskis, a noble Hungarian family fallen on hard times. He also presented a letter from the Vatican secret service as a reference.

The Austrian espionage apparatus called Schulmeister to Vienna for questioning. His knowledge of French military units, Napoleon's generals, and their military strategies was so broad that Marshal Mack named Karl Schulmeister to a post on the Austrian general staff. Soon after, he became head of military information services. The former Holy Alliance spy gave Mack some French newspapers printed by Savary for the purpose, as well as letters from fictional correspondents, all testifying to the French populace's discontent with their leader. When Marshal Mack von Leiberich decided to undertake the campaign, Schulmeister persuaded him that Napoleon's armies were falling back to the Rhine to stamp out internal revolts. Mack struck first on October 7, falling into the trap set by the double agent. The disaster at Ulm, on the 19th, brought the deaths of ten thousand Austrian soldiers, the disgrace and demotion of Marshal Mack, and a twenty-year prison sentence as well. Napoleon, for his part, lost almost six thousand soldiers.[39]

Taken prisoner by the Austrian spy service, Karl Schulmeister accused Marshal Mack of responsibility for the defeat, for failing to heed his recommendations and the reports of his spy network in France (which did not actually exist). The spy managed to convince the Austrian general staff of his innocence, and he convinced them as well to adopt a new strategic plan against the Napoleonic armies. The key point of the plan centered on a city called Austerlitz.

The battle, one of Napoleon I's greatest military victories, unfolded in the area around Austerlitz (now Slavkov in the Czech Republic) on December 2, 1805, between a French contingent of seventy-three thousand men and 139 cannon and the Austrian-Russian force made up of sixty thousand Russian soldiers and twenty-five thousand Austrians, supported by 278 cannon. Sometimes called the battle of the "three emperors" because of the presence of Napoleon I, Francis II (Holy Roman Emperor and later Francis I, Emperor of Austria), and Alexander I of Russia, it cost the lives of twenty-seven thousand Austrians and Russians and almost eight thousand French.[40]

On the basis of reports received from the Holy Alliance, the Austrian secret service again suspected Karl Schulmeister and was about to arrest him on a charge of high treason when French troops entered Vienna. Napoleon Bonaparte rewarded Schulmeister with large sums of money but never gave him military honors. After the battle of Austerlitz, Napoleon said, "a man who sells his brothers, the men under his command, does not deserve any medals but only thirty pieces of silver," in allusion to the payment the Romans made to Judas Iscariot for turning in Jesus Christ.

Schulmeister went on to become head of Bonaparte's counterespionage, though he later had to resign in the face of growing Austrian influence around the new empress, Marie Louise, daughter of the defeated Francis I of Austria. When Napoleon's marriage to Josephine failed to produce an heir, the French emperor decided to divorce her and marry the daughter of the emperor he had defeated at Austerlitz.[41]

Relations between Paris and Rome grew ever more strained, approaching the break provoked in 1806 when Napoleon ordered Pope Pius VII to expel all citizens of enemy nations from Rome.

Vatican spies informed the pope that French troops were being put on alert for a possible new occupation of Rome. In spite of the Holy Alliance's warnings, Pius VII refused to expel the foreigners or to support the blockade of England. He also refused to permit Cardinal Consalvi's dismissal from his post as secretary of state, likewise demanded by Napoleon.[42]

In open confrontation, Napoleon ordered the occupation of Ancona and Lazio. On February 2, the emperor at last issued the order for General Miollis to enter Rome, disarm the Papal Guard, and occupy the castle of Sant'Angelo. The third corps of his army surrounded the Quirinal Palace and aimed ten cannon at the papal rooms. Pius VII was a prisoner in his own palace. Control of the papal state passed into French administrative hands.[43]

The Holy Alliance was once again dissolved, by order of Cardinals Pacca (named as its head a year earlier) and Consalvi, and its operations prohibited within the papal state now occupied by Napoleon's soldiers. Neither the secretary of state nor the chief of the papal secret service wanted any type of altercation inside Rome that could provoke the French occupiers in the way that General Duphot's assassination had done nine years before.

On June 10, 1809, Napoleon declared Rome an open city and dispossessed Pope Pius VII of all his power. In response, the supreme pontiff issued a bull threatening excommunication of anyone using any sort of violence against the Holy See or its representatives. Napoleon ordered General Radet to take the Quirinal Palace by storm and capture the pope. On the night of July 5 to 6, Radet forced his way into the papal palace, knocking down doors, and found Pius VII seated at his desk with Cardinal Bartolomeo Pacca. Radet then removed the pope from his palace and from Rome, without allowing him to gather any possessions except a small handkerchief.[44]

Proud of having the supreme pontiff of Rome in his power, General Radet was not about to let anyone come between his prisoner and the interests of his emperor. When the Holy Father came down with dysentery, the situation grew more complex. Forty days after the pope's detention in Rome, Radet and his prisoner arrived in Savona, the final way station of their journey. Meanwhile, the Vatican archives had arrived in Paris, a meeting of the College of Cardinals had been convoked in France, and a palace that would serve as Pius VII's residence had been prepared. Napoleon intended to create a new Vatican in Paris, subject to imperial orders. Cardinal Consalvi, however, had ordered Bartolomeo Pacca to be sure that papal spies had first spirited the Holy Alliance archives to some safe place outside Rome. The archives filled thirty-six closed carriages, which took them to a secret spot in Venice. When the French began sifting through the Vatican papers, they realized that not a single Holy Alliance document remained.

On June 9, 1812, the order came to move Pius VII from Savona to Fountainebleau. According to Fouché's agents' reports, a group of friars of the Black Order were trying to rescue the supreme pontiff. The officer in charge of the pope required him to dress completely in black and travel only by night, so that he would not be recognized. The friars of the Black Order reached the site where the pope had been held, six hours after he had left. Ten days later, the pope and his escort reached their destination, where Pius VII managed to regain his health.[45] Between the 19th and 25th of January 1813, Napoleon and the pope met numerous times. They talked not only of politics but also about personal matters.

The course of the war, with continual French defeats on multiple fronts, led to the siege of Paris and the freeing of the pope. On May 24, 1814, he was finally able to return to Rome. The final blow to the great empire built by Napoleon came at a place called Waterloo.[46]

England, Russia, Austria, and Prussia had pledged twenty years of unity to remove Napoleon from power. Bonaparte did not give way, but his maneuvers failed to halt the march of the allied armies, which reached the gates of Paris on March 30 and forced the French capital to surrender. Napoleon's last gasp was a plan to use the remnants of his army to recapture Paris, but his most illustrious marshals, who had accompanied him in a thousand and one battles, now refused to follow and urged him to abdicate instead. Among them were Michel Ney, Lefebvre, and Moncey Oudinot.[47]

The French people, tired of endless war, wanted peace at any price. On April 6, 1814, in Fontainebleau, the same site where Pope Pius VII had been confined, Napoleon Bonaparte signed his abdication. The allies had already forced the Senate to accept a provisional government under Talleyrand. Napoleon's former associate had to keep order in Paris until the arrival of King Louis XVIII, who would restore the Bourbon monarchy to the throne of France. A few days later, on April 10, General Wellington defeated General Soult in the Iberian peninsula; neither side knew that Napoleon had already capitulated.[48]

The man who had been lord and master of the fate of all Europe became a prisoner on the isle of Elba, off the southern coast of Italy, while his wife, Marie Louise, and his son were given the dukedom of Parma. France had to return to its old borders of 1792. Napoleon decided to leave his place of exile, supported by a small group of skilled marshals and generals, in a last campaign known as the "Hundred Days."

The disastrous defeat at Waterloo on June 15, 1815, meant for Napoleon and his family complete repudiation by all the courts of Europe. To avoid any further Bonapartist outbreaks, the allies decided that this time they would confine Napoleon on the island of St. Helena, an isolated stone outcrop two thousand kilometers from the African coast and more than two months' sail from England. There he remained from October 15, 1815, until his death by poisoning on May 5, 1821.[49]

After Napoleon's internment on St. Helena, Pius VII ordered the head of the Holy Alliance, Cardinal Bartolomeo Pacca, to look out for the welfare of the deposed emperor's family. Napoleon's mother, Maria Letizia, took up residence in Rome in a palace on the Piazza Venecia. She died in 1836, still under the protection of a pope, Gregory XVI. Pius VII also sheltered Napoleon's uncle Cardinal Joseph Fesch and his brothers Lucien and Louis Bonaparte (who had been King of Holland). Louis's son Charles Louis-Napoleon, also taken under the wing of Pius VII and the Holy Alliance, would return to govern France years later under the name of Napoleon III.

Shortly before his death on August 20, 1823, Pope Pius VII uttered the names of the cities Savona and Fontainebleau as a symbol of his suffering in the years of the rise and fall of eagles. The coming years would be full of revolts and conspiracies—a true era of spies.

9

AN ERA OF SPIES (1823–1878)

As brigands ambush a man, a band of priests act as assassins on the way to Shechem.

—Hosea 6:9

The year 1823 saw a conclave to choose Pius VII's successor. This time the two factions contending for leadership in the Holy See were the *zelanti* and the *politicanti.* The *zelanti* (zealots or "rigorists") were led by Cardinal Bartolomeo Pacca, head of the Holy Alliance, and Cardinal Agostino Rivarola. Their party favored a severe and conservative administration that would fight any sign of liberalism attempting to raise its head in Rome.[1]

As the *zelanti* saw it, and Pacca especially, revolutionary radicalism had already tried to create a new order even inside the Vatican's walls. Pacca, Rivarola, and the others took the contrary position, that nothing should change.

The *politicanti,* however, accepted the need for evolution within the Church toward a more social order. Cardinal Consalvi, the faction's leader, wanted to take advantage of the collapse of the Church administration during the Napoleonic era to restore an administration based within the papal state but with a reformed structure.

The Catholic countries, most of them ruled by absolutist monarchies, did not look well on Consalvi, whom they accused of having introduced radical measures such as suppressing the nobility's feudal rights or eliminating the privileges of certain cities. The former secretary of state's opponents presented themselves as Italian patriots and accused him of having sold himself and the Vatican to the Austrians. In the conclave, Pacca managed to block any chance of Consalvi's being chosen as supreme pontiff.[2]

The dispute between cardinals Consalvi and Pacca allowed Austria to veto any *zelanti* candidate, "not because of the rigidity of their principles, but because they were too Italian," as the famous French foreign minister Chateaubriand wrote.[3]

At first, Annibale della Genga did not figure among the candidates. In spite of his having been vicar-general of Rome for three years, he was completely unknown to the public. However, on September 28, thirty-four of the thirty-nine cardinal electors cast their votes for him. Della Genga, surprised by his election, said at the time, "You have chosen a cadaver." In the previous three years, Cardinal della Genga had spent more time in bed from various diseases than working at his desk. His first action as the new pope Leo XII was to name Cardinal Giulio Maria della Somaglia, a *zelanti* ally, as secretary of state. He confirmed Cardinal Bartolomeo Pacca to continue as head of the Holy See's spy services.

The post-Napoleonic Holy Alliance had new enemies to confront: bandits and members of secret societies such as the *carbonari*. The latter had organized an uprising in Romagna. To end it, Pope Leo XII decided to send Cardinal Agostino Rivarola as a peace mediator. The pope did not know that Rivarola carried very explicit instructions from Pacca to suppress the rebellion, and that these instructions were supported by the secretary of state, Cardinal Somaglia.

No one truly saw the *carbonari* as common criminals, but since the early nineteenth century, many sects had grown up in Naples, Milan, and Calabria— most of them outgrowths of Masonic lodges and, therefore, banned by various popes as set forth in numerous bulls. The members of the *carbonari, protectores, independientes, calderari, peregrinos blancos,* and *Mafia*[4] were persecuted in the papal states. That persecution took official form through organizations under Vatican control such as the Holy Alliance, and extra-official form through small underground groups of clergy who carried out covert acts of punishment. These underground groups included the Black Order and the *Octogonus* Circle as well as more obscure formations like the "Black Habits," "Society of the Thirteen," and "Followers of Jehu."[5]

Holy Alliance agents knew that the *carbonari* were led by two men named Angelo Targhini and Leonida Montanari. During an attempt to capture them, one papal espionage agent fell dead of a bullet wound while another was gravely injured. Bartolomeo Pacca was determined to find the ringleaders and bring them before a papal court.

On November 20, 1825, Targhini and Montanari were tricked by a papal spy in the guise of a *carbonari* sympathizer. They were arrested by Holy Alliance agents and soldiers of the Papal Guard, taken to Rome on the 21st, tried for rebellion on the 22nd, and beheaded for having offended the supreme pontiff on the 23rd. But the private war between the *carbonari* and the pope's agents did not end there.

Cardinal Rivarola, acting at the behest of Cardinal Pacca, did his utmost to eliminate the rebellion at a single stroke. Making use of the secret society called the *sanfedisti,* Rivarola and the Holy Alliance unleashed a variety of dirty war. Those suspected of being *carbonari* members or supporters were kidnapped, interrogated under torture, and, most often, summarily executed. Some five hundred people went into exile or into papal jails.[6] When Leo XII learned of the Holy Alliance's secret operations against the *carbonari,* carried out with the approval of the secretary of state, he decided to dismiss Giulio della Somaglia while leaving the powerful Pacca in place.[7]

From this moment on, the new secretary of state, Cardinal Tommaso Bernetti, decided to maintain strict control over the espionage service, its operations, its chief, and above all its actions in the war against the *carbonari.* Bernetti's ideological orientation was decidedly moderate, akin to that of Consalvi. Yet the Holy Alliance's clandestine operations against the rebels did not come to an end.

The next two *carbonari* to fall into the hands of the papal espionage service were Luigi Zanoli and Angelo Ortolani. In February 1828, Zanoli intercepted a papal emissary carrying secret instructions from Bartolomeo Pacca to Monsignor Francesco Capaccini, who years later became an important papal spy against the *carbonari* in Holland.[8]

Zanoli had followed the papal emissary as far as the border. Before the messenger could cross it, Zanoli killed him and stole the messages bearing the wax seal of the Holy Alliance. The *carbonaro* hid in a cabin in Romagna until he was found by Pacca's men. During the attack leading to his arrest, a *carbonaro* in league with Zanoli named Angelo Ortolani shot and killed a member of the Papal Guard. Both were arrested, tried, and sentenced to death. Luigi Zanoli was beheaded on the morning of May 13, 1828, while Angelo Ortolani was hanged that afternoon. To the powerful cardinal Bartolomeo Pacca, "an eye for an eye, a tooth for a tooth" was the appropriate law. His agents in the Holy Alliance were ready to carry it out.

The *carbonari* leaders wanted to strike back at the Vatican to avenge their fallen comrades, and their chosen objective was none less than Cardinal Agostino Rivarola, the papal envoy to Romagna.

Gaetano Montanari, Leonida's brother, and Gaetano Rambelli were chosen to kill Leo XII's envoy. The plan went wrong when, two days before the scheduled date, a tailor who was supposed to supply the two *carbonari* with black habits that would allow them to get close to Cardinal Rivarola made the mistake of giving the disguises to two priests, one of whom was a Holy Alliance collaborator. The next day, both conspirators were arrested. Montanari was executed toward the end of 1828 for attempted assassination of Cardinal Agostino Rivarola. Rambelli was hanged the same year for conspiring against the papal state and the pope. Leo XII died on February 10, 1829, but the war still did not end.

In the conclave of 1823, Cardinal Francesco Saverio Castiglioni had been one of the leading candidates to succeed Pius VII. According to an anecdote from the time, the supreme pontiff himself, in a conversation with Cardinal Castiglioni, had said, "Your Holiness Pius VIII [referring to Castiglioni] will settle this affair later."[9] Thus his election as the new pope on March 31, 1829, amidst disagreements between *zelanti* and *politicanti,* came as no surprise.[10]

Though his papacy was a short one, lasting only twenty months, it was full of events that would change the structure of Europe. The revolutions that broke out in the summer of 1830 in France, Germany, Poland, Belgium, and the papal states ended the system installed by the Restoration.

Pius VIII left the reins of papal espionage in the hands of Cardinal Bartolomeo Pacca, now a very powerful figure within the Roman curia. Among the serious problems that Pope Pius—and therefore the Holy Alliance—had to confront were revolutionary movements and secret societies within the papal state, as well as its always problematic relations with Catholic France. One of the most brilliant papal espionage agents in those years was Monsignor Francesco Capaccini.

During his period as papal nuncio in Holland, Capaccini devoted himself to setting up a wide network of informers that stretched from poor neighborhoods to court salons. A stream of highly secret reports flowed into Capaccini's hands. His sources included members of the Estates General, the Dutch parliament.[11]

In Capaccini, Bartolomeo Pacca had found a true gold mine that he was determined to exploit. Thanks to a state councilor loyal to him, Monsignor Capaccini even knew everything about the royal family. Reports of homosexuality, infidelity, and other affairs of members of the House of Orange came to Capaccini and ended up in Holy Alliance archives in Rome.

On several occasions, Pius VIII had called Pacca's attention to the methods being used by the nuncio in Holland. But in the eyes of the head of the Holy Alliance, all methods were acceptable as long as they were used to defend the interests of the Church of Rome, the pope, and the papal states.

One day, Francesco Capaccini alerted the papal spy service to a top-secret affair. "For a few moments I had in my hands a confidential report sent by the Dutch ambassador in the Holy See about movements developing in the papal states," Capaccini wrote to Pacca. Capaccini had managed to read this report during a visit to the headquarters of the Dutch ministry of foreign affairs. While waiting to be received by the head of the ministry's religious affairs department, during an instant when that official's secretary had left the room, the Holy Alliance agent discovered among a pile of folders one that bore the title "Holy See: 'Confidential and Top Secret' Matter." Without stopping to think, the monsignor opened the file and began to read the first page.

Dated in the summer of 1829, the Dutch report detailed a plot organized by a number of individuals in the city of Spa, from which point they planned to undertake subversive operations against the papal states. The conspirators, who had access to sizable funds and a printing press, intended to travel separately to the Tuscan port of Livorno and enter the papal states as pilgrims. Once within the territory of the Holy See, they would distribute anti-papal and revolutionary literature.

This information was passed on to the secretary of state, Cardinal Giuseppi Albani, and to the head of papal espionage, Cardinal Pacca. The Holy Alliance agents managed to get close to the revolutionary group, linked to the *carbonari,* through an artisan involved in the plot.[12] One of the agents noted that this artisan was a young man who might be seeking revenge against another member of the group. Between October and December of 1829, papal soldiers arrested approximately fourteen members of the revolutionary group. Five of these, the main leaders, were sentenced to death and executed.

If all the Holy Alliance's agents had been as efficient as Francesco Capaccini or the Abbé Salamon, the papal state would have been the best informed government of Europe. Unfortunately, the classic spy tactics followed by Capaccini and Salamon were not deemed acceptable by their colleagues in other precincts. Many thought that the task of spying on another state or government fell outside their priestly functions. Quite a few nuncios did not look kindly on the methods used by the Holy Alliance. For his services to the Church, Monsignor Francesco Capaccini was raised to cardinal *in pectore* on July 22, 1844, by Pope Gregory XVI. This brilliant agent of the papal espionage service died the next year, on June 15, 1845.

For the first time in many centuries, the politics of the Holy See and its secretary of state were not under the influence of any European power. Perhaps for this reason, the revolution of 1830 that shook the foundations of France attacked Church and crown with equal vigor. Charles X, brother of the executed Louis XVI, had reigned in France for six years. His strategy had been to link the image of the Catholic Church with that of the absolutist monarchy, which made the Church the enemy of political liberties. The nuncio in Paris had already reported to Albani and Pacca that Charles X's policy tarnished the Church of Rome's image among French citizens, but no one seemed to be listening to him.[13]

Therefore, in July, the revolutionaries of Paris attacked the archbishop's headquarters, the Jesuit novitiate, the seat of Church missions, and the nuncio's legation. Following their example, uprisings in other French cities assaulted churches, convents, and monasteries. Pius VIII, on Albani's recommendation, dissolved the ties between the Church and Charles X's monarchy, recognizing the new king Louis Philippe d'Orléans instead. On Pacca's recommendation, the pope ordered all French bishops and priests to obey the new monarch the nation had chosen. In similar fashion, the Holy See proceeded to recognize Belgium, a new state that emerged in 1830 when Belgian Catholics and liberals joined forces to fight for their independence from the kingdom of the Netherlands. The Protestant king of Holland tried to impose absolutism in all his domains.[14]

On November 30, 1829, Pope Pius VIII died, giving rise to a new conclave to elect his successor. As was to be expected, the conclave went on too long. It took fifty days and a hundred ballots to choose Pope Pius VIII's successor. Cardinal Alberto Cappellari had not figured among the predicted winners, as is evidenced by the fact that he didn't receive a single vote until after the first month of the conclave.[15]

While the final votes were being read out, Cappellari asked the members of the conclave to stop casting ballots for him. Nonetheless, Cardinal Zurla asked him to accept the papal tiara in obedience to the decision of the conclave. On February 2, 1831, he received the symbols of office from Bartolomeo Pacca, head of the Holy Alliance, and adopted the name Gregory XVI.

The new papacy was soon immersed in a revolutionary wave that shook half of Europe. Rebellion broke out in Modena just a day after Gregory XVI's coronation. The first successes led to advances such as the formation of a revolutionary government in Bologna, where the papal representative was taken prisoner and a republic declared. The revolutionary armies continued their unstoppable march, taking control of the Marche and Umbria. The papal armies could not halt this advance, which had now brought the revolutionaries control of 80 percent of the territory of the papal states. Advised by his secretary of state, Tommaso Bernetti, and by espionage chief Bartolomeo Pacca, Pope Gregory XVI decided to ask Austria for military aid to put down the rebellion. By this time, Bartolomeo Pacca had suffered a serious loss of prestige within the Roman curia, because the Holy Alliance had failed to detect the revolutionary movement within the papal borders.[16]

Austrian troops' entry in the papal states quickly provoked French protests. For more than two months, there was nearly constant unrest, including bombings by revolutionary groups. Among the revolutionaries was Louis-Napoleon Bonaparte, future Emperor of France under the name Napoleon III.[17]

Once the rebellion had been suppressed, England, France, Prussia, and Russia convoked a conference in Rome and forced Gregory XVI to introduce a series of reforms that would calm revolutionary passions. None of the European powers wanted to see revolutionaries take power in the papal states, which might provoke an "epidemic" that could spread to the other nations of Europe.

After the withdrawal of Austrian troops, the papal states witnessed a new rebellion in Romagna in 1832. This uprising, like the previous one, was not discovered in time by the pope's secret services. The only arrest the Holy Alliance agents made was of Giuseppe Balzani, beheaded on May 14, 1833, on the charge of committing offenses against the supreme pontiff.

In January 1836, Gregory XVI decided to dismiss Tommaso Bernetti and Bartolomeo Pacca.[18] As his new secretary of state he chose Cardinal Luigi

Lambruschini, a staunch conservative whom he expected to put down with an iron hand revolutionary movements and leaders. One of the most famous revolutionaries of the era was Giuseppe Mazzini, founder of the Young Italy organization, who saw the supreme pontiff as the main enemy of a united Italy.[19]

Lambruschini became the first cardinal in the history of the Holy See to simultaneously direct the secretariat of state and the espionage service. As the conservative cardinal saw it, the powers-that-be needed to wield diplomacy firmly in one hand (the secretariat of state) and a hammer firmly in the other (the Holy Alliance). As secretary of state, Lambruschini had to negotiate an end to the revolts, with the goal of pacifying the Church's domains. As head of the Holy Alliance, he had to eliminate any movement that could endanger the pope's rule over the papal states, which had endured for almost a thousand years.

Be that as it may, Gregory XVI passed into history as one the popes who signed the most death sentences, 110 in all; who imposed an absolute ban on all freedom of expression, whether verbal or written, by any individuals or groups who did not follow the dictates of the Holy Mother Church; who barred the Jews, under dire threats, from carrying out any civil or religious activity outside the ghetto; and who took the first step toward the complete dismemberment of the papal states.

At the beginning of 1846, Pope Gregory XVI began feeling the effects of a cancer that brought about his death on June 1. His passing made way for the longest papacy in Church history—that of Pius IX—and one of its richest eras, historically speaking. Karl Marx, Friedrich Engels, Auguste Comte, Friedrich Nietzsche, Charles Darwin, Cavour, Giuseppe Garibaldi, Otto von Bismarck, and Napoleon III would be some of the figures in the panorama that passed before Pius IX's view. In one way or another, all of them would affect his thirty-two-year reign.

The conclave of 1846 divided into factions backing three different cardinals: Cardinal Ghizzi, the candidate of those favoring a united Italy; Cardinal Giovanni Maria dei Conti Mastai-Ferretti, the moderate candidate; and Cardinal Luigi Lambruschini, the candidate of the *zelanti,* who saw him as the only one able to confront the revolutionaries and garner Austrian support for doing so.[20]

The incessant arguing among the members of the conclave indicated that the election would be long and drawn out, but to the surprise of all, forty-eight hours after the first ballot, Cardinal Mastai-Ferretti managed to assemble the two-thirds vote needed to be elected supreme pontiff. Mastai-Ferretti chose the name Pius IX. His papacy, in a Europe riddled with wars and revolutions, would be a true breeding ground for spies.

One of the great secret agents whom Cardinal Lambruschini's Holy Alliance had to confront was Wilhelm Johann Karl Eduard Stieber. Born in Saxony on May 3, 1818, Wilhelm grew up in the bosom of a Lutheran family not very fond of priests or of Roman power. Transferred to Rome along with his family (his father was an official), he finished his degree in law at the university there. In those years, Stieber became an informer for the Prussian police about doings in the university. He had not yet turned thirty when workers' movements began shaking Europe.[21]

Frederick William of Prussia feared that revolutionary groups like those of Paris, Vienna, and Italy could topple him from the throne. Stieber understood the power he could amass by making use of that fear.[22]

Between 1845 and 1850, Stieber continued to work as a lawyer while turning over abundant information on his revolutionary and intellectual clients to the Prussian secret service. His first contact with the Holy Alliance came on August 11, 1848. That day, Wilhelm Stieber approached a young priest who worked for the papal nuncio in Berlin. The priest was the secretary to Monsignor Carlo Luigi Morichini, the pope's representative in the Prussian court. Stieber decided to make contact with the papal espionage service because of a piece of information that had fallen into his hands. For the Prussian spy, any such information could be sold to an interested party. Though Wilhelm Stieber had no need for the money, he did crave influence and contacts in other secret services.

In his meeting with Morichini, the spy told the nuncio that a Prussian agent infiltrated into a revolutionary group had reported on an assassination attempt under preparation. The target was to be a high Church official, perhaps the pope himself. Morichini immediately passed the news to Cardinal Luigi Lambruschini, head of the papal spy service, and to secretary of state Cardinal Giovanni Soglia Ceroni. It would take a rapid response to determine who the actual target was, given the large numbers of high officials in the Holy See who might potentially be assassinated.

When Pius IX got the news Stieber had dangled, he ordered Lambruschini to send several Holy Alliance agents to Berlin in search of better information. For two months, those papal spies worked with Stieber's help to penetrate Berlin's revolutionary movements, but did not produce any positive results.

Count Pellegrino Rossi, the chief administrator of the papal states at the time, had been born in the Italian city of Carrara on July 13, 1787, and studied law in the universities of Pavia and Bologna. After completing his studies, Rossi began to work for Joachim Murat, the King of Naples, member of the *carbonari,* and defender of an independent and united Italy.

After Murat's defeat at Tolentino, Pellegrino Rossi was forced into exile in France. He returned to Geneva after Napoleon's defeat at Waterloo. Years later, on the basis of his opinions about reestablishing papal authority within a constitutional regime, he was summoned to Rome by Pius IX. But Rossi believed that the freedoms sought by the revolutionary movements should be granted only gradually, within a regime of civil order. That idea earned him a death sentence from the secret societies whose leaders were exiled in Berlin, Paris, Brussels, and other cities.

On November 15, 1848, three months after Wilhelm Stieber met with papal nuncio Monsignor Carlo Luigi Morichini, Rossi spoke to the Legislative Assembly in the Palazzo della Cancelleria to explain his program. The papal states' administrator sat in his carriage, reading his speech aloud, when the door was flung open and a man who had climbed up on the driver's seat drove a dagger into his neck, killing him in the act.[23]

Holy Alliance agents carried out the investigation. Mysteriously, Cardinal Luigi Lambruschini closed the case without any finding. The investigation of Pellegrino Rossi's assassination was over.

While Pope Pius IX declared in public that the late administrator had died as a martyr of the faith, rumors spread that the deed might have been the work of the Black Order or the *Octogonus* Circle, secretly guided by Cardinal Lambruschini. The Holy Alliance chief was a self-declared *zelanti,* or rigorist, someone who did not want to see any move toward liberalization within the Church or the papal states, which were governed by the infallible authority of the supreme pontiff.

Given this ideology, there was plausibility to the rumor that Cardinal Lambruschini had ordered Count Pellegrino Rossi's assassination because of Rossi's ideas about the role the pope should play in Italian unification. The closing of the investigation prevented any conclusion not only about the assassin himself but also about the intellectual authors of the plot. Cardinal

Luigi Lambruschini, head of the Holy Alliance for eighteen years, died April 12, 1854, and he took this secret to his tomb. In any case, for the secret societies, Rossi's assassination became a signal to ignite the flame of revolution that drove Pope Pius IX into exile and led to the birth of the Roman Republic.[24]

The morning after the papal politician's death, demonstrations broke out. They soon turned to riots and rebellions, which in turn led to the assassination of the pope's secretary, Monsignor Palma. In the face of this situation, the supreme pontiff accepted the minister imposed by the people, but another part of the populace demanded the dissolution of the Swiss Guard and the pope's resignation.[25] Finally, on November 17, the Civil Guard took up positions in the Holy See and expelled both the Swiss Guard and the pope, now deemed a prisoner of the revolution. On November 23, 1848, as had happened before with Pius VI and Pius VII, Pius IX was forced to leave Rome, taking refuge in the port of Gaeta in the kingdom of Naples.

The new provisional government was determined to write a constitution proclaiming Rome a republic. A constituent assembly placed executive power in the hands of a triumvirate made up of Mazzini, Carlo Armellini, and Aurelio Saffi.[26] On February 9, 1849, the assembly formally deposed the pope as head of secular government of the Roman state. The decree guaranteed the pontiff full exercise of his spiritual leadership, but stated that the Roman state would be a full democracy under the glorious name of the Roman Republic.[27]

By Spanish initiative, a conference of Catholic powers assembled in Gaeta. France, Austria, Spain, and Naples took part. On July 3, 1849, the French and Spanish generals Nicolas Charles Victor Ouidinot and Fernando Fernández de Córdoba y Valcárcel landed in Civitavecchia with the aid of Holy Alliance agents, breaking through the Roman defense lines commanded by Giuseppe Garibaldi.[28] They took the capital, while the other powers' armies occupied the rest of the papal states. On April 12, 1850, Pius IX was able to return to Rome. Nonetheless, the popes' hold on temporal power had come to an end.

Camilo Benso, Count of Cavour, became the great architect of Italian unity and of the disappearance of the papal states. Prime Minister of the Piedmont since 1852, he had put forward a plan based on two simple points: *"Chiesa libera in Stato libero"* and Rome as the capital of a united Italy.[29]

Victor Emmanuel II of Savoy, King of the Piedmont, began occupying territory on behalf of the new Italy with Garibaldi's support. He asked the pope to grant his new subjects the same rights Piedmontese citizens already enjoyed and to accept the annexation of some of the areas that had been part of the papal states, such as Romagna. Pius IX, advised by Cardinal Antonelli, rejected this request. "I cannot give up what does not belong to me," he explained to Emperor Napoleon III. Another reason was his fear that the lay politics of the government in Turin would spread to the papal states.[30]

In his encyclical *Nullus certi,* proclaimed on January 19, 1860, Pius IX denounced "the sacrilegious attacks on the sovereignty of the Roman Church" and demanded "the return of what had been stolen [Romagna]." The text ended with a threat to excommunicate the usurpers of the rights of the Holy See. By the end of 1860, the pope retained only a third of his former states.[31]

One of the first Holy Alliance agents to understand the complex equilibrium developing among France, Austria, and the Piedmont was Monsignor Antonino de Luca. Papal nuncio in Munich (1853–56) and then in Vienna (1856–1863), he became a rich source of information for the papal spy service during this time.

Well-versed in history, philosophy, and theology, with a wide command of languages, this Sicilian prelate had been called to Rome in 1829 to direct a theological newspaper and consult with several departments of the Roman curia.[32] In 1853, de Luca was sent to Bavaria as nuncio, and three years later came his transfer to Vienna, the most important post in the papal diplomatic service at the time. His brief apprenticeship in Munich served as preparation for his arrival in the Austrian capital.

In February 1859, England's ambassador to France, Lord Cowley, likewise arrived in Vienna. His task was to seek a solution to the war between Austria and France over their competing interests in Italy. Cardinal Giacomo Antonelli, secretary of state and head of papal espionage, wrote to de Luca: "Since Italian affairs are not extraneous to the diplomatic issues, it would indeed be useful to be kept up to date on the negotiations that have taken place there." So it would be.[33]

With the aid of Wilhelm Stieber, who had reappeared in the world of espionage after an attempt by his enemies to bring him before the bar of justice, Bishop Antonino de Luca became an inexhaustible source of information, all forwarded from Vienna to the Holy Alliance in Rome.

Monsignor de Luca's first great success had come during his time in Munich. As nuncio there, he reported that the Austrian spy service (Stieber, in fact) had told him a revolutionary group had identified three priests as Holy Alliance agents and intended to eliminate them. Apparently, one of these agents had been particularly effective in exposing Garibaldi's followers to the papal police.[34] All Holy Alliance agents operating in Italy were put on a state of alert, urged by Cardinal Luigi Lambruschini (still head of the service at that time) to take precautions.

Nonetheless, in spite of all precautions, in early January of 1854, Gustavo Paolo Rambelli, Gustavo Marloni, and Ignazio Mancini walked into a tavern where the three papal spies were meeting. Each attacker had a designated target. Rambelli shot the first Holy Alliance agent, whose back was turned. The spy fell dead at once. Marloni tried to shoot the second agent, but his pistol jammed. The priest leaped at Marloni and managed to take away his gun. Mancini, meanwhile, shot at the third Holy Alliance agent and mortally wounded him.

When Mancini turned around, he saw that Marloni was still rolling on the ground with the second papal spy. Mancini grabbed a dagger and stabbed the agent in the back several times. The first blow was enough. Then the three attackers fled through the narrow streets surrounding the building, before the Papal Guard could arrive.

Seven days later, Rambelli, Marloni, and Mancini were arrested, charged, tried, and sentenced to death for the killing of the three Holy Alliance agents. On January 24, 1854, the three mounted the scaffold for the fall of the executioner's axe. The signer of their death sentences was the powerful cardinal and secretary of state Giacomo Antonelli. In response, years later, Antonelli would suffer an attempted assassination by a Garibaldi follower named Antonio de Felici. But the assassin would succeed only in wounding the cardinal in the right arm and right hand—the same hand with which, a little later, he would sign a new order to execute de Felici.

Once Monsignor de Luca arrived in Vienna—and always aided by Stieber and his wide network of spies—he took more and more interest in serving the Holy Alliance. One of his communiqués reported that traitorous officers of the Piedmontese army had offered him the defensive plans of Romagna, one of the former papal territories annexed by the Piedmontese king in 1860. No one paid attention to de Luca's report at the time, but Wilhelm Stieber would go on to make use of it in the Franco-Prussian War of 1870.[35]

In March of 1861, Victor Emmanuel II proclaimed himself King of Italy. In the ensuing negotiations with the Church, he offered a thousand and one concessions in the spiritual realm in return for cession of territory in the temporal one. The negotiations dragged on until 1864, when King Victor Emmanuel made a commitment to respect the patrimony and territory in which St. Peter had established the Church.[36]

Given the collapse of the Church's former empire, the Holy Alliance in Rome lost nearly all contact with its spies dispersed throughout the world. The papal espionage service, therefore, failed to foresee the war that was coming in the United States.

In 1861, the United States of America (which had been "united" for only a little more than eighty years) were shaken by the Civil War. This was a nation in which two distinct societies had taken shape, each establishing a different social, political, and economic model. At the same time, in the course of four decades, its territory had multiplied many times: through the purchase of Louisiana from France and of Florida from Spain, the annexation of Texas, and the subsequent war with Mexico (1846–48).[37]

The political atmosphere in both Northern and Southern states was shaped by the Southerners' vested interests in their tobacco, sugar, and cotton plantations and in keeping hold of their nearly three and a half million slaves at all costs, while the unionists leaned more toward trade and financial interests and, therefore, toward tariffs. On one side were the Northern creditor capitalists, on the other, the Southern debtor planters.

On November 6, 1860, the Republican candidate Abraham Lincoln—a lawyer who as Congressman had opposed slavery—was elected President of the United States. On December 20, 1860, South Carolina seceded from the union, followed days later by Mississippi, Florida, Alabama, Georgia, Louisiana, and Texas. In early February 1861, representatives of the secessionist states met in Montgomery, capital of Alabama, to form a new nation, the Confederate States of America.[38]

The C.S.A.'s provisional constitution followed the general lines of that of the U.S., which barred the African slave trade but permitted the domestic one. The Southern states had seceded, they claimed, out of grievances against Northern moves on the slavery question. To lead their Confederacy, they chose Jefferson Davis, former secretary of war.[39]

The new Confederate president issued a call for troops, setting a goal of 100,000 volunteers. As part of its defense plan, the Confederacy took over federal arsenals, military installations, post offices, and customs houses throughout the Southern states. Fort Sumter, in Charleston Bay, refused to

surrender to the Southerners. When Abraham Lincoln announced his intention to send reinforcements, the Confederates knew they had to use force. At
4:30 A.M. on April 12, 1861, Southern artillery fired the first shot of the
American Civil War. The Confederacy was the aggressor, as Lincoln had intended.[40]

During the civil conflict that took place from 1861 to 1865, the Holy Alliance relied on Louis Binsse, papal consul in New York. His intelligence reports were neither elegant nor interesting. For example, at the moment of
the outbreak of hostilities after Fort Sumter, Binsse wrote to his superiors in
papal intelligence about what merchant ships were on their way to what
ports of the papal states, and about a citizen with an Italian name who had
come to him in search of a visa.

A study of Binsse's reports shows that the Holy Alliance agent devoted
himself more to momentary political information, mostly extracted from
newspapers, than to the complex work of a spy. He did, however, sometimes
gather important information, such as a piece of news he unearthed in June
1861, nearly by accident.

Louis Binsse had been invited to a reception in New York, held by Union
politicians and officers to raise money for their cause. During the party, some
women approached him without knowing he was a papal espionage agent,
asking him what he thought of Giuseppe Garibaldi. The Union ladies evidently did not know that Garibaldi was an enemy of Pope Pius IX and,
therefore, also of the pope's consul in New York. The Holy Alliance agent,
putting all his charm to work, managed to extract from a general's wife the
news that Abraham Lincoln had invited Giuseppe Garibaldi himself to ad-
vise his general staff on military tactics.[41]

Agent Binsse reported the Union leader's intention to the Holy Alliance
in Rome and to Cardinal Giacomo Antonelli, secretary of state. The news
gave rise to such an outcry from the Holy See that Lincoln had to retract his
offer and formally apologize to Pius IX. Nonetheless, thousands of Garibaldi's
famous "red shirt" troops formed the so-called Garibaldi American Legion, a
group of volunteers who fought bravely alongside Union troops in various
battles. Once that information reached Rome, the New York consulate became a true spy center from which any news supplied by bishops, priests, or
monks "stationed" in any part of the U.S., North or South, was funneled to
the Holy Alliance in Rome.

News of the Union's naval blockade of the Southern states, with the resulting deterioration of the Confederacy's military position, came mixed
with a request for funds from an order of nuns and news of a bishop's death
and a groundbreaking for a new cathedral. Neither the Holy Alliance in
Rome nor Louis Binsse in New York classified the information as important,
unimportant, or completely pointless.[42] The Holy See believed that the way
to filter the news coming from the war-torn United States was to mobilize
tens of thousands of clergy and bureaucrats working for the Roman curia. In
this time of disintegration of the papal states, Pope Pius IX didn't see the
need to waste other resources.

It was another matter, however, for the Vatican and the Holy Alliance to
show support for one or the other of the conflicting sides. The first pressures on
the pope and his secretary of state came from John Hughes, Archbishop of
New York, ten months after the attack on Fort Sumter. Hughes told Pius IX
and Cardinal Antonelli that he served only the Church, not the interests of any
nation. In fact, the Archbishop of New York was an undercover agent and a
propagandist for Washington. Lincoln's administration paid his salary, and
his reports went to Lincoln's secretary of state, William Seward.

Seward entrusted to Hughes the mission of traveling to Rome and winning Pope Pius IX's public support for the Northern cause. Archbishop
Hughes paid a surprise visit to the Holy See, where he claimed that during
his work for the Holy Alliance he had learned of Confederate plans to attack
Mexico and the Catholic islands of the Caribbean.[43]

But Pope Pius IX's and Cardinal Giacomo Antonelli's sympathies for the
North diminished when the Holy Alliance began to get contrary reports in
May of 1863.[44] The new source was Martin Spalding, the pro-secessionist
Archbishop of Louisville, in the border state of Kentucky. Just as Hughes
was Lincoln's agent, Spalding had been secretly assigned by Jefferson Davis
to win the pope's support for the Confederate cause. Spalding's main contact
was Judah Benjamin, the Confederacy's secretary of state.

In his report to the Holy Alliance, Archbishop Spalding insisted that
the emancipation of black slaves was a political maneuver by Protestant
abolitionists, while the people of the South represented true Catholicism.
Monsignor Martin Spalding also claimed, in a report to Antonelli, that
"the negroes were by nature too inclined toward a licentious life and were
not ready for freedom. Besides, their emancipation could provoke social

disorders which would jeopardize the Church's missionary work among the negroes."[45]

John Hughes's and Martin Spalding's reports to the Holy Alliance showed that Catholic bishops were not immune to political affiliations, and that sometimes they had more loyalty to the Union or the Confederacy than to the pope and the Holy See. The unreliable information received by papal espionage agents during the conflict was evidence of a serious fault line in Rome's policy of relations with Washington, capital of the Union, and Richmond, capital of the Confederacy.[46] Pope Pius IX began by showing sympathy for the Northern cause, only to later turn toward the Southern side, and then again back toward the North. It may have been only after 1865—when the war ended with the North's triumph over the South—that the leaders of the Vatican spy service realized the need to train professional espionage agents if they wanted the future Holy Alliance to be a tool that would help popes make the necessary decisions about given political situations.

As a first step, Cardinal Antonelli ordered all administrative divisions of the Church, its legations, and its archbishoprics to prepare weekly political reports that would include political activities in their areas, titles of books deserving of censorship, titles of periodicals and the political ideas they defended, lists of public entertainments, profiles of public officials, surveillance reports on suspicious foreigners and travelers, and especially any information about subversive political movements or groups. These bulletins were sent to the secretary of state, who categorized them as domestic espionage matters of interest only to the Roman police or foreign espionage matters of interest only to the Holy Alliance.

One of the Vatican secret service's most able spies when it came to collecting and analyzing information was surely Monsignor Tancredi Bellà.[47] As a young papal delegate in the small city of Rieti to the north of Rome, he had shown his espionage abilities when he uncovered the activities of a group that called itself *Fidelità e Mistero* (Fidelity and Mystery). This group carried out sabotage operations against the Austrians and against papal authorities until Bellà's information made its suppression possible.

In 1859, as delegate to Ancona when it was about to fall to the Italian patriots, Tancredi Bellà uncovered a larger plot to overthrow papal power in the region, supported by the Piedmontese king. His information was most important. In mid-April 1859, Bellà discovered that a large number of volunteers from all over Italy were gathering in the Piedmont to fight against the Austrians as members of Giuseppe Garibaldi's "Alpine Hunters." He also learned that antipapal exiles were threatening papal police officials and their families in Romagna, within the papal territories, and that France was mobilizing strong concentrations of troops on its Piedmontese border.

Between March and August of 1860, Monsignor Bellà had learned from one of his agents that Garibaldi was in bad health but that, nonetheless, the unification hero was leading a contingent of five thousand men headed for Sicily. A sizable share of these troops belonged to the secret society of *protectores,* who alongside the *carbonari* sparked Garibaldi's liberation of Sicily in 1860.[48]

Tancredi Bellà's information was of such high quality, in part, because his network was outside the control of the Holy Alliance in Rome. His spies therefore could act with more independence. As delegate, Monsignor Bellà controlled between ten and twelve agents, each of whom recruited his own informants. One of these was a police inspector in Pesaro who had previously served in Tuscany and Venice. After the grand duchy of Tuscany's incorporation into the kingdom of Italy in 1860, the policeman decided to move to the Adriatic port of Pesaro. This Holy Alliance agent likewise decided to leave the papal espionage service and join the Neapolitan police, although he continued to supply information to Monsignor Bellà for years.[49]

Another of Bellà's most active agents was a servant who worked for Odo Russell, an English diplomat and operative of his country's secret service from 1858 to 1870. Thanks to this Holy Alliance agent in Russell's house, the secretary of state kept informed about important visitors to Rome, from aristocrats, diplomats, and journalists to clergymen and bankers. Diplomatic mail also became a good source of information for the pope's spies. In 1860, the American ambassador in Rome formally protested to the cardinal secretary of state that mail between the U.S. embassies in Paris and Rome had been opened by papal spies. Two years later, the ambassador reported to his own state department that all mail from Washington arrived in opened envelopes.[50]

On the other hand, when in 1861 the papal telegraphic service discovered coded communications between the Piedmontese representatives in Rome and their foreign minister, Count Cavour, the Holy Alliance did absolutely nothing. The papal espionage service made no effort to break the simple

Piedmontese code, which would have helped to reveal the House of Savoy's intentions for the future of Italy. The dukedom of Rome—the only territory the pope had left—was protected by Napoleon III's army until the Franco-Prussian War broke out on July 19, 1870, and Napoleon III had to pull his forces out of Rome.[51]

When the last French soldier left the papal city, King Victor Emmanuel declared his firm intent to occupy Rome "to maintain order." Pope Pius IX replied, "I give thanks to God, who has allowed Your Majesty to crown the last period of my life with bitterness. Aside from that, I cannot accept the demands contained in your letter nor associate myself with its principles. Once more I commend myself to God and put my cause—which is entirely His cause—in His hands. I pray that he will concede to Your Majesty the mercy you require."[52]

On September 20, 1870, the Piedmontese army under General Cardona entered Rome by the Porta Pia gate without encountering much resistance. The taking of the Eternal City marked the final step in Italy's unification.

The new Italian state tried to resolve the difficult situation through a unilateral Law of Guarantees, passed on May 13, 1871, that recognized the personal inviolability of the Roman pontiff. Pius IX rejected the law, which would have implied his recognition of the occupation of Rome and of the little that remained of the papal states. In response to this papal rejection, Victor Emmanuel II took up residence in the Quirinal Palace, traditional seat of the pontiffs. "We are in Rome," he declared, "and here we will remain."[53]

The pope in turn initiated the policy of *Non possumus* with respect to his lost states, considering himself a prisoner of the House of Savoy in the Vatican. On November 6, 1876, his trusted and powerful aide Cardinal Giacomo Antonelli died at the age of seventy. He had been secretary of state for twenty-seven years and head of the Holy Alliance for twenty-two.

In 1877, when he had reached the age of eighty-six, Pius IX's own health began to deteriorate. The Italian government began planning a papal funeral, but this was premature because the funereal honors of its own sovereign came first. As fate would have it, King Victor Emmanuel II, the pope's great enemy, died on January 9, 1878, four weeks before Pius IX.[54] In early February, the supreme pontiff was still conceding a few audiences, but on the afternoon of February 7, a cold complicated by high fever ended his life. He had been in office thirty-one years, seven months, and twenty-two days.[55]

With the death of Pius IX and the loss of the papal territories, an entire epoch of papal history came to an end. The following popes and Holy Alliance agents would have to live through tragic times. The horseman of war would gallop through the skies of Europe, raining blood and devastation over the land.

10

THE LEAGUE OF

THE IMPIOUS (1878–1914)

*Said the wicked: Let us therefore lie in wait for the just man,
because he tasks us and he is contrary to our doings, and he up-
braids us with transgressions of the law, and holds up to us the
sins of our way of life. For if he be the true son of God, He will
defend him, and will deliver him from the hands of his enemies.
Let us test him by outrages and tortures.*

—Wisdom 2:12 and 2:18

Cardinal Vincenzo Gioacchino Pecci had been one of Cardinal Giacomo Antonelli's harshest critics, which caused him to stay away
from Rome for almost thirty years. But soon after Antonelli's death,
Pope Pius IX summoned him and named him cardinal-chamberlain. The
pope wanted Pecci to take charge of Church administration until the election
of a new pontiff.

The conclave of 1878 was the first to be held after the 1870 declaration of
papal infallibility and the loss of the papal states. It took place during Germany's emergence as a great European power, displacing France, with Japan
abandoning its thousand-year-old traditions to join the modern world, with
the United States making giant strides toward becoming the world's greatest
power, and with Europe launching a new wave of colonization in Africa and
Asia.[1] Thus the papal regime that would emerge from the College of Cardinals' deliberations would be the first of the modern world. Though they had

lost influence and territory, the cardinals felt free of external pressures for the first time in many centuries.

The conclave that began on the morning of February 18 was also one of the shortest in history. After only three ballots, Cardinal Vincenzo Gioacchino Pecci won more than the two-thirds vote needed to be elected as the new pontiff.[2]

The early years of his administration as Pope Leo XIII were marked by instability and uncertainty. No one took the helm of the papal espionage service, which left many of its operatives without specific orders to follow and unsure to whom they were supposed to report. In the political sphere, matters were much the same.

The papal diplomatic corps needed to rise from its own ashes. There was continual confrontation between Leo XIII and King Umberto of Savoy, and continual attacks and provocations of the Holy See by the kingdom of Italy. One of the most serious came on July 13, 1881, when the Vatican tried to transfer Pope Pius IX's remains to the Basilica of San Lorenzo Fuori le Mura.

Two days before, Holy Alliance infiltrators in the revolutionary groups then ranging through the Roman streets had learned that several such groups planned to seize the late supreme pontiff's remains and throw them into the Tiber. The Swiss Guard went on alert, while the new Roman police were also informed. When the pope's body and its escorts passed through a narrow street, revolutionary agents attacked with stones and other heavy objects in an attempt to get control of the corpse.

The Italian police accompanying the procession decided to look the other way, while the Swiss Guard took the body into a nearby inn for protection. Hours later, the coffin holding the supreme pontiff's remains finally reached the crypt of San Lorenzo.

Such attacks on the Holy See convinced Leo XIII to sound out the Austrian emperor Franz Joseph about the possibility of moving Church headquarters to Austrian territory. But Franz Joseph did not want an open breech with the new Italy over something as unimportant as the pope. Austria's refusal led Leo XIII to the decision to fight for the rights of the Church and the Holy See in Rome. However, another battle loomed, farther away.

Chancellor Otto von Bismarck, suspicious of the powerful Catholic centers that had united in the *Zentrum* party, approved a series of new laws between 1871 and 1878. Their sole object was to harass and persecute the Catholic circles opposed to Bismarck's policies.[3]

Bismarck's *Kulturkampf,* or "cultural struggle," ordered the expulsion of all religious orders from Prussia. It also required all appointments of high Church officials to be approved by the government, closed all the seminaries, and ordered the expulsion of all bishops. Leo XIII suddenly found twelve of the sixteen bishops of Prussia with him in Rome. Continuous protests by Catholic circles that supported Bismarck and the work of the Vatican secretaries of state did the rest.[4]

In 1890, Kaiser Wilhelm II decided to dismiss Bismarck, which brought a new golden age to the *Zentrum.*[5]

Leo XIII surrounded himself with efficient leaders of Vatican diplomacy, such as Cardinals Alessandro Franchi, Lorenzo Nina, and Ludovico Jacobini, but none of them felt the need for a spy service like the Holy Alliance to support Vatican policies abroad. Franchi, Nina, and Jacobini all saw the Holy Alliance's intervention in affairs that could be settled through diplomacy or politics as more of an impediment than a help. Doubtless, they were mistaken. Only the arrival of Cardinal Mariano Rampolla in the secretariat of state after the death of Cardinal Ludovico Jacobini restored some of the splendor of the papal espionage.

One attempt to revive the moribund Vatican secret services came in 1898, the year that war broke out between Spain and the United States. The Holy Alliance had been unable to see the war coming that spring.

Spanish–U.S. relations had been deteriorating because of what was going on in the Caribbean island of Cuba. Spanish repression in Cuba provoked a wave of negative reaction among the U.S. public. In February 1898, two events caused the tense relations to worsen still more.[6]

U.S. spies managed to intercept a letter from the Spanish ambassador in Washington, Enrique Dupuy de Lôme, to a friend of his in Cuba. In the letter he openly criticized the expansionist designs of the United States and made fun of President McKinley. The diplomat had to apologize, but the sensationalist press led by William Randolph Hearst whipped up Americans' wounded pride. The second incident leading toward tragedy was that involving the battleship *Maine.*[7]

On February 15, while on a visit to the port of Havana, the warship accidentally exploded and sank. Two hundred sixty-six men lost their lives. The U.S. Congress, press, and public opinion accused the Spanish of an act of sabotage. The United States sought a Spanish exit from Cuba more strongly than before.

Pope Leo XIII and his secretary of state, Cardinal Mariano Rampolla, still denied the need for an active espionage corps. They preferred diplomacy as a way to avoid wars. The supreme pontiff and Rampolla had successfully mediated a German-Spanish dispute over several Pacific islands, and so they saw the possibility of doing the same with Washington and Madrid in the case of Cuba.[8] However, the Vatican lacked diplomatic relations with the U.S.

The Holy Father ordered his Holy Alliance to contact John Ireland, Archbishop of St. Paul, Minnesota. The apostolic delegate was supposed to attempt mediation in Washington, while Ireland was supposed to try to make contact with President McKinley through other channels. But Archbishop Ireland's experience revealed some of the pitfalls of using local agents. John Ireland was not a Holy Alliance agent who would act disinterestedly in a crisis. Pope Leo XIII and Rampolla would have learned as much if they had only read the Holy Alliance's report on the controversial archbishop.

The priest was strongly identified with the Republican Party, then in power in Washington. A few years earlier, he had become so closely tied to McKinley's 1896 election campaign that he embarrassed broad sectors of Catholic opinion in the country. The papal espionage report underlined the fact that Archbishop John Ireland had urged parishioners attending his Masses to vote Republican.[9]

For his part, the archbishop now thought that this special commission from the pope would lead him to a cardinal's purple, and he enlisted the support of important local political figures. He was a nationalist, in favor of political democracy, religious toleration, and economic growth, but he also believed the United States was destined to become the world's leader, outstripping such traditional powers as Spain and the Vatican.

It is hard to determine John Ireland's exact connections with the McKinley administration or how his nationalism influenced the reports he sent to the Holy Alliance in Rome, but it is clear that his loyalties were divided between his nationalist passion for the U.S. president and his obedience to the supreme pontiff. The Vatican's espionage analysts had by now told the pope that, while John Ireland wanted to help him make peace in Cuba, he did not want to make the McKinley administration or the American Protestants feel that an archbishop or a body of Catholic fellow citizens were unpatriotic or pro-Spanish.[10]

There is no doubt that Ireland worked to secure peace, just as the pope had requested. But it is equally clear that his method of doing so was to urge the Vatican to pressure Madrid, not McKinley's administration, to arrange an immediate armistice in Cuba as the first step to resolving the crisis. Holy Alliance agents continued to keep Secretary of State Rampolla informed about John Ireland's intentions. According to the Vatican secret service, the archbishop wanted to ingratiate himself with both sides and not declare himself in favor of one or the other.

Ireland's next move was to send a coded message to Rampolla and Pope Leo XIII listing the points he saw as crucial first steps toward peace: a declaration by Madrid of an immediate cease-fire throughout Cuba; Spanish-Cuban negotiations to quickly disarm the insurgents; and acceptance of the U.S. president as arbitrator in the search for a negotiated settlement. Those proposals would give Washington the right to impose a solution on Spain, one that demanded a series of concessions. The Holy Alliance agents in the U.S. capital told Rome, furthermore, that the proposals had been written by the State Department, not by the priest. If they were accepted by the pope or by Madrid, the agents warned, the result would be Spain's loss of Cuba.[11]

The problem was that the Vatican analyzed only the information sent by Ireland and not that from the Holy Alliance agents or the papal delegate in Washington. Rampolla and his secretariat read only the reports coming from the Archbishop of St. Paul. They took seriously Ireland's claim that President McKinley "desperately wanted to find a peaceful solution to the conflict" and that only Spain's acceding to his desire could calm the war fever in Congress and public opinion. In fact, the United States wanted to control Cuba—among other reasons, because of its strategic position bordering the Gulf of Mexico—and McKinley was willing either to buy the island or to fight for it.[12]

While the Vatican, somewhat misled by Ireland's report, sought a solution in Madrid, on April 11, 1898, President McKinley asked Congress for special powers to declare war on Spain.[13] That same day, the Congress voted that Cuba was free and independent and if Spain would not renounce sovereignty over the island, the president was authorized to use all means at his disposal to bring it about. On April 21, Madrid and Washington broke off relations. On the 25th, the United States declared war on Spain, the first act of which would be a naval blockade of Cuba. The rest is history.

Next came the defeat and destruction of Spain's Cuban fleet in Santiago and its Philippine one in Cavite, the surrender of Spanish forces in Oriente, the invasion of Puerto Rico, and the siege of Manila. Seeing the impossibility of confronting the naval power of the U.S., the government of Práxedes Mateo Sagasta began peace negotiations.

As a result of the disinformation operation carried out by Archbishop John Ireland and the way the pope and his secretary of state followed Ireland's lead in refusing to back Spain in any way, U.S. president Theodore Roosevelt decided to take the first steps to establish diplomatic relations with the Holy See.[14]

Archbishop Ireland's intrigues were revealed by the Holy Alliance agent Monsignor Donato Sbarretti, a papal espionage expert in North American affairs. It took Sbarretti only a few days to see how Ireland had taken advantage of Leo XIII's confidence to assure himself a brilliant future in Vatican diplomacy. Sbarretti also revealed that John Ireland kept the U.S. secret services informed beforehand as to the content of the messages he was about to send to the supreme pontiff and Cardinal Rampolla.

Monsignor Donato Sbarretti further alerted Rome to the danger facing Catholic religious orders working in the Philippines. He reported that many high U.S. officials responsible for Philippine affairs, especially in the War Department headed by Secretary Elihu Root, were openly prejudiced against those orders and had proposed the radical step of expelling all friars from the archipelago. In a final note, Sbarretti wrote, "I sincerely do not believe that the North Americans have the slightest interest in establishing diplomatic relations with the Holy See as the Archbishop of St. Paul, Monsignor John Ireland, claims."[15]

Mysteriously, the Vatican ignored Sbarretti's warnings about John Ireland, and Pope Leo XIII ordered the report labeled "top secret." When on June 1, 1902, William Howard Taft,[16] civil governor of the Philippines, came to Rome at the head of a small delegation on an official visit, he was received at the papal palace with a ceremony of the sort reserved for ambassadors.[17]

The Holy Alliance, by order of Rampolla and of Leo XIII himself, did everything in its power to make the press see the Taft delegation's visit as a clear signal that the U.S. was considering the establishment of diplomatic relations with the Vatican. Actually, both Rampolla and the supreme pontiff continued to trust Ireland's partisan analysis, rather than that of Monsignor Donato Sbarretti.

The U.S. reaction was not long in coming. William Howard Taft did not like discovering that papal espionage agents were circulating the rumor that his visit represented a formal diplomatic initiative on President Roosevelt's part. He stated in response, "We are in Rome only to negotiate the sale of some land."[18] After several weeks, the negotiations broke down and Washington ordered Taft back to the Philippines.

In early June 1903, while meeting with his secretary of state Rampolla, Pope Leo XIII suffered an inflammation of the lungs. On the 7th, his doctors discovered his lungs were full of fluid. His condition continued to be critical until he died on July 20, surrounded by his most loyal followers. With his papacy ended, too, his policy of restricting the activities of the espionage service. For twenty-two years, the Holy Alliance had been largely inoperative, in spite of the fact that in the last ten years the world had been affected by a series of assassinations that could have touched the pope himself.

The president of the French Republic, Marie-François-Sadi Carnot, was assassinated in 1894. Spanish premier Antonio Cánovas del Castillo suffered the same fate in 1898, as did Austrian emperor Franz Joseph's wife, Elisabeth Wittelsbach, or Sissi, in 1898, Italy's King Umberto in 1900, and U.S. president William McKinley in 1901.

On July 31, 1903, the conclave summoned to elect Leo XIII's successor began its deliberations. The best-positioned candidate was Cardinal Mariano Rampolla, the late pope's secretary of state, but he was vetoed by Cardinal Jan Puzyna of Cracow in the name of the Austrian emperor. Franz Joseph saw in Cardinal Rampolla an enemy of the Triple Alliance (Germany, Austria, and Italy) because of his policy of improving relations with France and Russia. On August 4, Cardinal Giuseppe Melchiore Sarto was elected supreme pontiff by fifty of the sixty-two cardinals at the conclave. Sarto chose the name Pius X. In the opening years of the twentieth century, the Holy Alliance would enter one of its most fruitful eras, though not a particularly glorious one.

In this new century, only the Italians had set out to recruit secret agents inside the Vatican. Therefore, when church-state relations became the subject of dispute, many governments had to gather information on papal plans and politics by way of spies.

French-Vatican relations had once again grown tense since the emergence in 1880 of an important anticlerical trend supported by the politicians Jules Ferry and Émile Combes, who were convinced that the pope sought the overthrow of the Third Republic and a return to monarchy. The conflict boiled over with the army's occupation of convents and monasteries and the expulsion of their occupants. In 1904, Paris and the Vatican formally broke off relations, and France proclaimed a "Law of Separation" between church and state.[19]

In the moment of chilliest relations, the French counterespionage services turned to surveillance of the papal nuncio and interception of coded messages between the Vatican and its ambassador. One report decoded by French spies in 1904 spoke of an incident that had occurred on the Avenue Gabriel across from the French president's residence in the Élysée Palace. The vehicle carrying the nuncio, Monsignor Benedetto Lorenzelli, had collided with a bicyclist without major consequences. Containing only minor news of this sort, the letters were not very significant. Potentially more important from an espionage point of view were telegrams exchanged between the papal secretariat of state and its nuncios. French cryptographers who had succeeded in breaking Spanish, Italian, or Turkish codes were unable, however, to decipher the codes invented by the Holy Alliance cryptographic department.[20]

All told, French secret service surveillance of the Vatican was more a question of accident than of efficiently organized operations. In 1913, on the other hand, the Holy Alliance would mount an operation against the French ministry of foreign affairs.

Monsignor Carlo Montagnini, the Vatican's spy in Paris, knew that French espionage chief Stephen Pichon was decidedly opposed to reestablishing relations with the pope. Therefore he organized an operation to depose Pichon. He ordered the falsification of a supposed message from the Italian ambassador in France to his foreign minister in Rome, which would state that Italian secret services had detected the presence of a certain Cardinal Vannutelli in Paris.

The Holy Alliance's counterfeit message explained that Vannutelli had come to France to meet with President Raymond Poincaré and his foreign minister Stephen Pichon, which would be the first stage of secret conversations with the Vatican about reestablishing the relations broken off in 1904.

As expected, the Sûreté succeeded in decoding the false telegram. Interior minister Louis-Lucien Klotz, when informed of this discovery, protested to the president about having been left out of the loop. He went so far as to threaten to resign. Poincaré claimed to know nothing, which was true. As a result of the crisis, Stephen Pichon had to resign, and Klotz barred his secret service from decoding diplomatic correspondence. The Holy Alliance had succeeded in getting the troublesome Pichon out of the way.

Another Holy Alliance operation uncovered by the French was also the work of Monsignor Montagnini. Montagnini had been secretary to the nuncio, Lorenzelli, and when Lorenzelli left Paris after the break in relations, the secretary took his place under the title of "Attache of Religious Affairs and Custodian of the Nuncio's Archives." In truth, Monsignor Montagnini was a Holy Alliance spy, the Vatican's unofficial eyes and ears in France.

Benedetto Lorenzelli's successor was, however, a frivolous and indiscreet man, rather too fond of collecting information at social events. The new Vatican secretary of state, the Spanish cardinal Rafael Merry del Val, was not particularly impressed; he characterized Montagnini as "frivolous, shallow, and a complete muff."[21]

The French spy services were convinced that Montagnini was organizing underground resistance movements to counter the anticlerical laws and was conspiring with conservative politicians to overthrow the Republic, although they did not have sufficient evidence to present.[22]

One afternoon in December, the French espionage service and police decided to storm the papal embassy in Paris and confiscate all the documents they could find inside. Some Vatican documents did demonstrate contacts between French politicians and the Vatican secret service, but the most compromising papers had disappeared. Still, the French made copies of coded messages sent by Monsignor Carlo Montagnini to the Holy Alliance.

One of these, which Montagnini was not able to keep out of French hands, mentioned the possibility of paying significant sums of money to Liberal Action party leader Jacques Piou, and to others by way of him, in return for their blocking new anticlerical legislation under consideration in the parliament. Piou specifically referred to Georges Clemenceau, the politician who would lead France to victory in the First World War, as possibly being susceptible to a bribe.[23]

In the late nineteenth century, many governments experienced significant declines in their intelligence services, but in the case of the Vatican during Leo XIII's papacy, this deterioration was much sharper. The Holy Alliance's capabilities disappeared along with the papal states and the pope's temporal powers. An instrument designed to protect and maintain those powers became nearly superfluous. At the dawning of the twentieth century, the espionage networks of papal delegates were almost a thing of the past. In those years, many experienced agents of the Holy Alliance donned the bright uniforms of the pope's bodyguards, the Holy See's security, or the guardians of palaces and papal offices. Espionage was left to the nuncios, which brought important changes to the philosophy of strategic information gathering for papal diplomacy.[24]

On the death of Pius IX in 1878, the Vatican maintained full diplomatic relations with fifteen countries, seven of them in Europe, with Catholic majorities or with important Catholic communities in terms of numbers and political influence.[25] The rest were in South America, divided among three nuncios. The papal ambassador in Argentina was also accredited in Paraguay and Uruguay; the one in Peru, also in Bolivia, Chile, and Ecuador. The problem had to do with the parts of the world where there were no papal nuncios and that, therefore, had to be covered by experienced Holy Alliance agents—such as London, Berlin, or St. Petersburg.

Papal authorities under Leo XIII, who did more damage to the papal espionage organization than most others during its three centuries of existence, preferred to send "apostolic delegates" rather than spies to nations with whom there were no diplomatic relations. The apostolic delegates funneled better religious information to the Holy Alliance, while the nuncios supplied better political analysis.

In those years, after Pope Pius IX's encyclicals rigorously condemning modernist ideas, progressives and traditionalists contended for power within the Catholic Church. Pope Pius X, defender of the ideas of Pius IX, chose as his secretary of state a Spanish cardinal, Rafael Merry del Val. In a historic moment when the Central Powers and the Entente were about to go to war, Merry del Val showed a marked preference for the German and Austrian monarchies.[26]

The secretary of state's closest collaborators included an Umbrian priest named Umberto Benigni who over time would become one of the pope's best spies and the founder and director of Vatican counterespionage service. Benigni had a perfect profile as an orthodox traditionalist. With a modest reputation as journalist and polemicist, Umberto Benigni had come from Perugia to Rome in 1895 in search of opportunity. A priest employed in the Vatican Library offered him a job worthy of his ambition and ability.[27]

In 1901, Benigni won a post as history professor in the prestigious Roman Seminary, the elite institution attended by all aspirants to careers in the curia. At the same time, he began writing opinion articles in the ultraconservative newspaper *La Voce della Verità*.

His polemical articles and reactionary social and religious viewpoint attracted the attention of the so-called integralists in the court of Pope Pius X. The integralists defended the pope's temporal powers and opposed all political and theological reform. The intelligent Benigni soon became a favorite of the powerful secretary of state, Cardinal Rafael Merry del Val, and of Gaetano de Lai, the influential prefect of the Consistorial Congregation, the Vatican department in charge of choosing bishops.

Benigni was named *minutante* in the Congregation de Propaganda Fide, the department in charge of missionary activity. As a professor, he also taught the priests who would be dispatched to foreign missions. Soon the obscure Umbrian priest became a true celebrity within conservative intellectual circles in Rome, who made up the so-called black nobility around the Throne of St. Peter.

In 1906, Umberto Benigni was catapulted into the heart of the Vatican bureaucracy by his appointment as undersecretary of state for extraordinary affairs.[28] Though he lacked any experience in diplomatic issues, Benigni set about cultivating contacts that would smooth his ascension through the curia. The secretary of state, Merry del Val, had two secretaries directly below him: the secretary of extraordinary affairs, who dealt with relations with foreign states, and the *sostituto,* or "substitute," for ordinary affairs, who saw to the administrative tasks of the Vatican. Benigni's job, therefore, was to assist Monsignor Pietro Gasparri, who had moved from a post as director of the Vatican Seminary to the job of secretary of extraordinary affairs. That was how Gasparri met Benigni, whom he considered most efficient.[29]

When the nuncio's office in Cuba fell vacant, Gasparri offered the post to Umberto Benigni, but the priest had his sights set higher, in the secretariat of state. He had recently seen how the directorship of the Congregation de Propaganda Fide had been denied to him.

In those years, the office of secretary of state for extraordinary affairs was of great importance, yet mysteriously Pietro Gasparri was put in charge of revising and publishing a new code of canon law, a very absorbing task.

With Gasparri so busy, Benigni became Cardinal Rafael Merry del Val's main collaborator. The obscure priest and journalist who had come to Rome to seek his fortune now circulated in the corridors of power. The new undersecretary moved his office to the apostolic palace so as to be closer to the secretary of state and only four doors away from the supreme pontiff's office.[30]

In 1909, Monsignor Umberto Benigni, acting on the orders of Cardinal Merry del Val, created a spy network devoted to identifying all those within the Vatican or Church institutions who preached modernism. Very shortly, Benigni's agents began to denounce clergymen working in universities, communications media, and political institutions in France, Great Britain, Germany, and Italy. Nearly three hundred such names appeared in their reports. The secretary of state, given his complete antipathy toward political and theological innovation, authorized his subordinate to organize a counterespionage service that would operate only inside the Vatican and Church organizations, while foreign espionage would remain the responsibility of the Holy Alliance.[31] The name of the new counterespionage organization was *Sodalitium Pianum* (sodality, or community, of Pius). Within the walls of the Vatican, it was known for short as the S.P.

Sodalitium Pianum's first efforts went toward formulating a set of arguments that could be used to counter modernist ideas and thus dominate any future public debate within the Church or in the larger society. Separately, the S.P. was to carry out secret recruitment of agents in Europe, North America, and South America who would identify modernists, expose their connections and conspiracies, and frustrate their plans. Umberto Benigni applied himself to this task with the zeal of a fanatic. Soon his functions as undersecretary for extraordinary affairs gave way to others, in the espionage sphere, which had to be kept secret from his colleagues in the secretariat of state and even from his immediate superior, Monsignor Pietro Gasparri.

Recognizing the potential influence of the press, Benigni believed the Vatican needed to use it effectively in the battle against modernism and liberalism. The S.P. chief appointed himself unofficial press director of the secretariat of state. For years, he fed the journalists covering papal events the line they should follow in their articles. Benigni labeled the correspondents of liberal newspapers and news agencies as "enemies" and those of conservative media as "friends."

Another important step of the S.P. was to create its own paper, *Corrispondenza Romana,* which Benigni directed through a straw editor. He filled its pages with attacks on modernism and liberal politics, while defending papal prerogatives openly and without pretense. When criticisms began coming in from countries such as France or Italy itself, Pope Pius X denied that the paper was an official Vatican organ or even a semiofficial one. The pope was lying, because he himself had authorized his secretary of state Cardinal Rafael Merry del Val to finance *Corrispondenza Romana.*[32]

Finally, Monsignor Umberto Benigni wrote an article that expressed his "integralist" and conservative perspective on world religious and political affairs. The article was very well written, in truth, and was distributed by S.P. agents to many foreign correspondents. Many of them published the entire article or a summary thereof under their own names, often without citing the source. Benigni's thesis was read by millions in Argentina, Spain, Austria, Belgium, and the United States.[33]

While such propaganda and disinformation operations played their role in discrediting modernism, Benigni and his superiors in the inner recesses of the Vatican also needed to control that movement's influence within secular organizations and religious institutions. The integralists needed to identify the adherents of modernism and oust them from any powerful positions by applying strong papal sanctions. The S.P.'s main sources of information were bishops, apostolic delegates, and nuncios, yet many of these were not eager to name names for the counterespionage service.

What integralists like Merry del Val and Benigni needed was a quality spy network functioning in the heart of the Holy See, but since the loss of the papal states, no such body existed. In fact, Monsignor Umberto Benigni's arrival in the corridors of power brought the operations of the Holy Alliance to a halt, with the two services often acting at cross purposes. Papal counterespionage became the main enemy of papal espionage, because the *Sodalitium Pianum* agents competed for sources with the spies of the Holy Alliance.

In truth, the clandestine S.P. had no official name or official headquarters or nameplate identifying any of its offices or any administrative departments. Its creation received no mention in the *Anuario Pontificio,* the publication containing the Vatican organizational chart. Its expenses were paid out of secret funds that the secretary of state, Cardinal Merry del Val, funneled to Monsignor Benigni. If anyone in authority asked Benigni directly about his activities, the counterespionage chief answered that the only ones who could give an answer were "God, Pope Pius X, and Cardinal Merry del Val." The questioners desisted rather than have to confront any of that trio.

Benigni employed in the Vatican the same techniques used by the intelligence agencies of powers such as Great Britain, France, Germany, or Russia. Only on rare occasions did the S.P. share information with Italian security services.

Espionage, interception of mail and telegrams, and surveillance of individuals were some of the tasks carried out by papal counterespionage agents. From bishops' palaces, priests' sacristies, lecture rooms, seminaries, and nuncios' offices around the world, they kept the S.P. informed about superiors or colleagues suspected of embracing modernism—including some of Benigni's own employees.

One of the *Sodalitium Pianum*'s little-known spy operations took place toward the end of 1909. Through several informants, Benigni learned of a ring of modernist priests in Rome led by a man named Antonio de Stefano, a noted medievalist and former priest then living in Geneva. The S.P. chief sent a young priest named Gustavo Verdisi to penetrate de Stefano's organization. Verdisi, himself close to the ideas of the modernists, informed Monsignor Benigni that the network run from Switzerland had fallen apart, but the counterespionage chief was not satisfied. He decided to send another priest, Pietro Perciballi, who had been a classmate of de Stefano's in the Roman seminary.[34] In those days, Perciballi had also come to know other defenders of modernism, such as Ernesto Buonaiuti, whose books and writings had been declared heretical by the Holy Office, the Vatican department responsible for maintaining Catholic orthodoxy.

Armed with money, a false passport, and a camera, Perciballi traveled to Geneva to renew his old acquaintanceship with de Stefano. In his first report back to Benigni, Father Perciballi emphasized de Stefano's desire to launch a magazine called the *Revue Moderniste Internationale.* The report also explained how Antonio de Stefano had invited the agent to leave the place where he'd taken up residence in Geneva and move into de Stefano's own house. During de Stefano's long absences, Perciballi spent his time photographing the titles of the books in his target's private library and sifting through the papers in his desk. These included correspondence with Ernesto Buonaiuti. When Perciballi returned to Rome, he brought Benigni copies of de Stefano's private correspondence.

The S.P. archives soon became a treasure trove of information on reformist priests, liberal seminary teachers, and suspicious intellectuals and journalists. Among those named in the reports were a number of cardinals: Amette, the Archbishop of Paris; Ferrari, Archbishop of Milan; Mercier, Archbishop of Brussels; Maffi, Archbishop of Pisa; Piffle, Archbishop of Vienna; and Fischer, Archbishop of Cologne. So were the rectors of the Catholic universities of Louvain, Paris, and Toulouse. Another figure punished for his ties with the "modernists" was Cardinal Giacomo della Chiesa, who was dispatched to Bologna as archbishop because Cardinal Merry del Val wanted to separate him from the Roman curia. In 1914, Cardinal della Chiesa would become supreme pontiff after the death of Pope Pius X.[35] Benigni even went so far as to investigate his superior and patron Monsignor Pietro Gasparri, without express orders from either Merry del Val or Pope Pius X.

The S.P.'s daily reports included such information as the development of the Catholic Center Party in the German Reichstag; the Catholic student organization Sillon in France, which defended social reform and Catholic reconciliation with the Third Republic; the inauguration of a new Uruguayan president who proposed to separate church and state and suppress religious festivals; and tensions in Russia arising from Tsar Nicholas II's security forces' persecution of Catholics in Poland and Lithuania.[36]

Soon, high officials of the Roman curia began referring to the S.P. as the "Holy Terror." Among its main defenders, aside from Pope Pius X himself, were Cardinal Rafael Merry del Val, secretary of state; Cardinal Gaetano de Lai, prefect of the Consistorial Congregation; and Cardinal José de Calasanz Vives y Tutó, a Spanish Capuchin in charge of the department of religious orders.[37]

With the knowledge and complicity of Pius X, Monsignor Umberto Benigni acquired tremendous power. His enemies and victims regarded him as "the pope's evil genius." Every week, Benigni handed exhaustive reports to the pope, to Merry del Val, and to Monsignor Giovanni Bressan, the pope's private secretary and one of Benigni's most loyal allies. The counterespionage chief had more protectors in the highest spheres than he had friends, and so there was much surprise in the halls of the Vatican when the newspaper *L'Osservatore Romano,* on March 7, 1911, published the news that Monsignor Benigni was no longer undersecretary for extraordinary affairs in the secretariat of state. His replacement was a young Vatican official named Eugenio Pacelli, who over time rose within the Roman curia until reaching the office of pope twenty-eight years later as Pius XII. Meanwhile, Pope Pius X named Monsignor Umberto Benigni protonotary apostolic[38] and allowed him to remain at the head of the counterespionage unit. To Benigno's "friends," this news implied a promotion and high honor, while to his "enemies," it seemed to mean a fall into disgrace or exile into purgatory.

The rumor mill—as active then as it is today in the halls of the Vatican—held that Benigni had been dismissed from his important post because he had been caught passing secret papal documents to the Russian imperial representative in the Holy See. The only thing known for sure is that Monsignor Umberto Benigni formally requested leave from his responsibilities in the secretariat of state so as to devote more time to the papal secret services.[39]

From then on, the operations, organizations, and agents of the Holy Alliance and the *Sodalitium Pianum* were united toward a single goal: defense of the Church, the Vatican, and the Pope. Monsignor Benigno continued to have access to the documents and staff of the secretariat of state. He requested a salary of seven thousand lire per year and an increase in operating funds to support his intelligence activities.[40] Cardinal Gaetano de Lai became his new chief contact and protector, while his direct contact with Cardinal Merry del Val was limited to responding to requests for information about bishops in line for promotion or other papal honors. In the spring of 1912, Monsignor Eugenio Pacelli, lover of intrigue and espionage, asked his precursor about a priest who was going to be named bishop. Some weeks later, Pacelli again contacted Benigni to let him know that the secretariat of state was preparing a declaration on workers' movements in Germany and that a replacement for a German archbishop was being sought.

Umberto Benigni's problems were only beginning. A former Catholic priest turned Methodist confessed to the journalist Guglielmo Quadrotta that, when he had been Monsignor Umberto Benigni's private secretary, he had served the Vatican counterespionage service by infiltrating certain Italian circles suspected of modernist tendencies. Another brouhaha affecting Benigni's image and that of Vatican intelligence was fomented by a group of Belgian and German liberals.

This group, in carrying out an investigation of the *Sodalitium Pianum,* had infiltrated a Dominican friar, Floris Prims, into the secret agency. The Dominican made friends with a Belgian lawyer named Jonckx who worked in the city of Ghent. Thanks to this connection, Prims learned about the workings of the S.P. in detail and, therefore, about those of the Holy Alliance. Prims, shocked by his findings and believing that Monsignor Umberto Benigni was operating without authorization or protection from above, decided to go to Rome and request an audience with the pope to tell all.

Rafael Merry del Val rescued Benigni by blocking Floris Prims's attempts to see Pope Pius X. He also refused to see the Dominican himself or to accept any of the documentary evidence Prims had gathered.[41] In 1912, the secretary of state cut off financing for the newspaper *Corrispondenza Romana.* Soon afterwards, he ordered Benigni to close it. Evidently, Umberto Benigni's star was losing its luster. If Pope Pius X had publicly recognized the existence of the *Sodalitium Pianum,* that would have conferred invaluable power on the organization and its founder. Instead of legitimizing the S.P., the pope preferred simply to send his "best apostolic wishes"—always by way of Cardinal de Lai—to the counterespionage service and its chief.

As Benigni's life moved further and further underground, he began to suffer from debilitating paranoia. From his small apartment on Corso Umberto I, he tried to keep his network of informers afloat and maintain his contacts in papal circles, but many of the latter had closed their doors to him by now. He came to believe that modernist agents in the postal services of France, Germany, and Italy were intercepting and opening his mail. For fear of his enemies inside and outside the Vatican, Umberto Benigni traveled abroad to meet his informants personally, and he kept all such visits to Brussels, Paris, or Geneva strictly secret.

By early 1914, Benigni was surviving by seeing to minor papal matters. The former spymaster was now a pathetic and paranoid shadow of his past self. His clear-sightedness in creating an intelligence service similar to those of Russian, France, or Germany had turned chimerical. He had personally seen to the recruitment of informants, oversight of their activities, reading of their reports, care of crucial documents, direct reporting to the secretary of state, and carrying out of covert operations. What he had not done was keep a close watch on the ground under his feet.

When Cardinal Giacomo della Chiesa—a victim of repression by the *Sodalitium Pianum*—became Pope Benedict XV, Umberto Benigni departed from Vatican service. He left behind a secret service in ruins, a Holy Alliance whose operations had been reduced almost to nothing, and broken friendships and eternal suspicion among members of the Roman curia, thanks to the history of internecine accusations. Unfortunately, Benigni's[42] outsized vision of an effective papal espionage service remained only a dream. Curiously, the outbreak of the First World War would breathe new life into the Holy Alliance and espionage operations in general.[43] But a unique opportunity had been lost just when the Horseman of the Apocalypse, sword in hand, was about to drive the world into a global conflagration.

11

THE HORSEMAN OF
THE APOCALYPSE (1914–1917)

*When he broke open the second seal, I heard the second living creature cry
out, "Come, and see." And there went out another horse that was red; and
to him that sat thereon was given power to take peace {away} from the
earth, so that people would slaughter one another. And he was given a
huge sword.*

—Revelations 6:3–4

Gavrilo Princip was a product of the years in which the winds of
anarcho-syndicalism whipped through Europe. He was an overly
idealistic Bosnian Serb student who dreamed of fighting great liberation battles. One day, in the streets of Belgrade, the young student read a
headline announcing a visit by the Archduke Franz Ferdinand and his wife,
Sophie von Hohenberg, to the city of Sarajevo. June 28, 1914, was the feast
of St. Vitus, patron saint of Serbia.

For Serbs in general and Princip in particular, Franz Ferdinand, nephew of
the emperor Franz Joseph and heir to the Austro-Hungarian throne, represented Hapsburg power over the Bosnians and southern Slavs who, following
the example of Serbia, sought to win independence from the Central Empire.[1]

To a nationalist like Princip, this visit meant that the highest representative
of the occupying empire was only a gunshot away. The student contacted the
"Black Hand," a Serbian organization that up until then had merely fired
leaflets at the entourage of General Potiorek, governor of Bosnia. Although the

organization refused to help him, Princip decided to persevere. He recruited five other youths to carry out his plans.

That fatal June 28 began early, when the imperial couple reached Sarajevo. From the station they headed toward the city hall in a procession of open motor cars that traveled by way of the Miljacka docks and the old quarter of Sarajevo so as to get to the city museum. When the procession reached the first terrorist, Mohammed Mehmedbasic, he couldn't act, because of the press of the crowd cheering the archduke. The second, Vasco Cubrilovic, was surrounded by police agents and could not act either. The third, Nedjelko Cabrinovic, threw a bomb that exploded under the carriage behind Franz Ferdinand. The three other terrorists—Princip, Cvijetko Popovic, and Danilo Ilic—saw Cabrinovic being arrested and decided to hold back.[2]

Nonetheless, shortly afterwards fate brought Gavrilo Princip and the archduke together again. The Austro-Hungarian heir told General Potiorek that he wanted to visit those wounded in the assassination attempt—Count Boos-Waldeck, Colonel Erik von Merizzi, and the Countess Lanjus—in the Sarajevo hospital. A problem arose when the vehicles ahead of the imperial couple's car suddenly veered from the expected route. General Potiorek ordered the archduke's driver to back up in a narrow street.

Gavrilo Princip couldn't believe that the car maneuvering with such difficulty in the narrow street was truly occupied by the imperial couple. The student grabbed his weapon, rushed into the street, braced himself against the royal car, and fired off two shots. The first killed the Archduke Franz Ferdinand. The second gravely wounded his wife, Sophie, who died minutes later. The assassination, apparently an isolated episode in a war of liberation, in fact opened Pandora's box. The die of war was cast across Europe.

Well before the First World War actually broke out, Pope Pius X feared an ominous sequel to the assassination. Holy Alliance reports already spoke of a "war" that could shake humanity. The pope, in his hatred of the Orthodox church, continually incited Emperor Franz Joseph of Austria-Hungary to eliminate the Serbs. After the events of Sarajevo, Baron Ritter, the Bavarian representative in the Vatican, wrote to his government: "The pope approves of Austria's harsh treatment of Serbia. He has no great opinion of the armies of Russia and France in the event of a war against Germany. The cardinal secretary of state [Rafael Merry del Val] did not see when Austria could make war if she does not decide to do so now."[3]

On August 15, the pope began to feel unwell, and by the 19th, his status was critical. On the 20th, at 1:15 A.M., almost two months after Franz Ferdinand's assassination, he died holding the hand of his loyal collaborator Cardinal Rafael Merry del Val.

In spite of the difficulties imposed by the war, the cardinals were able to assemble in Rome to choose Pope Pius X's successor. On the afternoon of August 31, fifty-seven of the sixty-five members of the College of Cardinals began to meet. On September 3, 1914, they elected Giacomo della Chiesa pope. He chose the name Benedict XV. Curiously, della Chiesa had been raised to cardinal—and thus made eligible to vote in the conclave that elected him—only four months before Pius X's death.[4]

When the first shots of World War I rang out, the two great Central Powers (Austria-Hungary and Germany) confronted the so-called Entente, or Allied, Powers (France, Russia, and Great Britain), which had met in secret on September 5, 1914, to agree that none of them would sign a separate treaty of peace to end the conflict. Thus the division of European nations and empires was already clear, and the two sides began a war that continued in unprecedented fashion over the next four and half years.

While reports of casualties and destruction poured into the secretariat of state from its embassies in Brussels, Berlin, and Vienna, Pope Benedict XV adopted his first measures intended to break with the past. The changes signaled a new course for papal politics.

Cardinal Mariano Rampolla was sent off to direct the insignificant Congregation of the Fabrica of St. Peter's Cathedral. The new pope's favorites gave Rampolla only forty-eight hours to vacate his quarters in the Appartamento Borgia and move to a smaller space in the Palazzina dell'Arciprete. Benedict XV's next move was to dismiss of the powerful Cardinal Rafael Merry del Val from his post as secretary of state, relegating him to running the Abbey of Subiaco. Once Merry del Val was gone, his friends fell into disgrace as well. For example, Cardinal Nicola Canali was dismissed from his post of "substitute" and sent to the less important secretariat of the Congregation of Ceremonies.

But the biggest blow to the anti-modernist fanatics was the supreme pontiff's order to dismiss Monsignor Umberto Benigni[5] as head of the Vatican counterespionage unit *Sodalitium Pianum,* the S.P., and make him a professor of diplomatic protocol at the Academy of Ecclesiastical Nobles. The change in policy grew clear when Benedict XV issued the encyclical *Ad Beatissimi,* which signaled the defeat of the so-called integralists, a word that, of course, did not appear in the document.[6] The S.P. continued to flourish in a world engulfed by war until the publication in 1919 of some documents from its archives that had been found by the German secret service.[7] To the post of secretary of state, the pope named Cardinal Pietro Gasparri, Benigni's old patron who had lately been in charge of the publication of the new Code of Canon Law.

Meanwhile, the First World War unfolded in accordance with the strategy laid out in 1906 in the Schlieffen Plan, a strategic roadmap for German troop movements that appeared to guarantee a quick victory for the German empire. This prediction did not come true. After the battle of the Marne, September 9–12, 1914, the Germans had to pull back their forward troops, which changed the nature of the military conflict.[8] What had been a war of rapid movement and strategic strikes turned into trench warfare—a cruel, long, seemingly endless struggle with attendant loss of human lives. The Holy See and the pope felt a duty to seek a solution. The Vatican thus became an objective, not a military one this time but a strategic location for spies and conspiracies.

Germany and Austria had diplomatic representation in the papal court. Germany had been very well positioned since the nineteenth century, when it could count on two ambassadors, one representing Prussia and the other representing Bavaria. Count Otto von Mühlberg, the Prussian diplomat, was energetic in his work. His Bavarian counterpart, Otto von Ritter, was especially admired by the Vatican administration for his moderate nature. Austria was represented by Prince Schönberg, scion of a noble family who had served state and church for centuries. All three diplomats were experts in relations with the Roman curia, especially with bishops and cardinals, and with the Italian press.[9]

In contrast, the Allies' diplomatic corps were relegated to rubbing shoulders with lower-ranking levels of the papal administration. The only Allied ambassador with any ties in the upper realms of the Vatican was the Belgian envoy, but he preferred the good life to bad diplomacy, which much annoyed his Russian equivalent. Tsar Nicholas II's representative was not so well regarded in Rome, because of his country's religious politics, which made Orthodox Russia one of the great defenders of Protestantism within Catholic Europe.

The main counterweights to the Central Powers' diplomacy were the English Cardinal Francis Aidan Gasquet and his secretary Dom Philip Langdon. The latter actually worked for the Holy Alliance in the capacity of an Allied propagandist.

Langdon was better known as an expert on English monasteries than as a Holy Alliance spy. Though Dom Philip Langdon carried out missions for the papal espionage services, it was said that Cardinal Gasquet was behind these operations and his secretary was merely following his orders. Patriotic and loyal to Benedict XV, Gasquet never doubted the need to support the Allied cause over the warlike Central Powers. With the aid of the loyal Langdon, he gathered information for the Holy Alliance and sent it on to London.

In one such report, Cardinal Gasquet dispatched a letter to the British Foreign Office, by way of Langdon, describing the Central Powers espionage services' efforts to win the Vatican's sympathy to the German-Austrian cause. The letter urged the Foreign Service to immediately name an ambassador to the Holy See. In November 1914, London sent Sir Henry Howard, a retired Catholic diplomat. In his first report back from the Vatican, he described a quite pro-German atmosphere. Cardinal Gasquet, who was in truth a Holy Alliance agent, kept funneling information on everything inside the Vatican that related to the war unfolding outside.[10]

Gasquet lived in the Palazzo San Calisto, a building in the Trastevere district belonging to the Holy See. The Palazzo soon became the center of Allied sympathizers. Pope Benedict XV summoned Gasquet and requested that he keep his meetings more under cover, because if an ambassador of the Central Powers were to learn of the cardinal's doings, papal neutrality in the war would be jeopardized.[11]

The pope also ordered the cardinal to pass on any information on Central Powers spies in the Vatican to the Holy Alliance before sending it to the British. Benedict XV reminded Cardinal Gasquet that his first loyalty was to the papacy, not the English. Gasquet, however, feared that German or Austrian spies might have managed to infiltrate the Holy Alliance or the counterespionage agency *Sodalitium Pianum.*

Both Cardinal Gasquet and Sir Henry Howard were well aware of the Central Powers' efforts to attract the pope's sympathies to their cause and knew they needed to fight against it.

In the first months of the war, Berlin and Vienna had sent not only ambassadors to the Holy See but also large contingents of diplomats and secret agents. The diplomats frequently requested audiences with Benedict XV, held weekly meetings with the secretary of state, Cardinal Pietro Gasparri, organized additional meetings with his aides, and hosted dinners for high-ranking members of the Roman curia and the Italian press.

The German and Austrian spies, just like their diplomats, worked openly to win the pope and his aides to their cause in order to gain justification for their war policy and undermine the Allied Powers opposing them. The spies' furtive encounters in dark Roman alleys soon gave way to social gatherings in palaces and mansions in sympathy with one side or the other.

Early in 1915, the lightning war turned into trench war. Both sides needed new allies to reinforce their defensive lines or simply to provide replacements for troop units that had now spent months fighting under awful conditions. Thus both sides tried to lure Italy into the war. Although Italy was a member of the Triple Alliance, with Germany and Austria, its leaders were determined not to expose their citizens to the hazards of war. In the first months of 1915, the embassies of both sides mounted full-press efforts to win Italy's support for the Entente or the Central Powers.[12]

The Holy Alliance had already reported to the pope and to Cardinal Gasparri about the intentions of Italy's leaders. Papal spies knew of meetings between representatives of the Roman government and the Austro-Hungarian empire to negotiate Italy's entrance on that side. The price of Italian support for Austria and Germany would be the so-called *terre irredente,* the Italian-speaking lands in the Trentine districts that belonged to the Austrian empire. Rome's opportunist position put Vienna in a tight spot.

On the other hand, the Holy Alliance had also reported to the pope about Italian government contacts with the Allies. The papal espionage service had learned that the government in Rome was simultaneously negotiating its neutrality with the Entente. If Italy stayed neutral and the Entente won the war, the kingdom would likewise be rewarded with lands previously belonging to Austria.

Quickly, Pope Benedict XV ordered his spy service and secretariat of state to devote themselves body and soul to preventing Italian entrance into the war in support of Austria and Germany. The pope doubted the Italian state's ability to survive the storm of war either politically or economically, especially if Italy—and therefore Rome—became a target for bombing attacks.[13]

A problem emerged when the Holy Alliance discovered that many high Church officials in Rome favored Italian intervention on the side of the Central Powers, which were the leading Catholic powers in central Europe and a barrier against the advance of the Russian Orthodox religion and pan-Slavism. Those leanings encouraged German espionage to undertake still more intrigues in the Vatican, often with the support of the *Sodalitium Pianum,* the papal counterespionage.

On February 21, 1915, Holy Alliance agents detected the arrival in Rome of Matthias Erzberger, leader of Germany's Catholic Center Party. Erzberger was well respected in the upper spheres of the Vatican, and a familiar figure to Benedict XV as well. Historians do not accept his close connection with the Vatican as a clear explanation for the curia's and the pope's support for the Central Powers during the war, but they do not entirely dismiss it either.[14]

During the spring of that year, Matthias Erzberger visited the Italian capital on several more occasions, maintaining relations in the Austrian and German embassies and keeping up continual visits to Vatican palaces. The German politician did not know he was under strict surveillance not only by the Italian secret services but also by the Holy Alliance (more sympathetic to the Allied cause and the arguments of Cardinal Gasquet) and the *Sodalitium Pianum* (close to the Central Powers). Clearly, Erzberger was in Italy doing covert work for the Central Powers, but only the Holy Alliance knew the true intentions of the leader of the Catholic Center Party and the political organization *Zentrum,* which had been persecuted by Otto von Bismarck for many years.

Matthias Erzberger had come to Rome on Kaiser Wilhelm's orders, to offer Benedict XV the *terre irredente* in return for his convincing Italy to remain neutral in the conflict. Germany and its ruler preferred for Italy not to intervene in favor of Austria, because that would make Italy a theater of war, requiring both the Central Powers and the Entente to divert troops from other fronts. But Kaiser Wilhelm likewise did not want Italy to intervene in favor of the Entente, which would bring an open Austrian-Italian conflict over the Trentine lands.[15]

The formal proposal that the politician and spy Matthias Erzberger brought from Kaiser Wilhelm to Benedict XV was the automatic transfer of Trentino from Austria to the pope himself. This would allow the creation of an independent papal enclave near the Vatican, including a corridor to the sea. The proposal had the support of the S.P., while the Holy Alliance recommended that Cardinal Gasparri reject the proposal.

Both Benedict XV and his secretary of state, Gasparri, knew that saying yes to Erzberger would in fact end papal neutrality in the war. Both the supreme pontiff and Gasparri doubted that, at the end of the war, either Austria or Italy would permit papal representatives to set up Church administration in Trentino. Still, it was now becoming clear that, for the first time since the outbreak of the First World War, Germany and the Vatican had parallel interests.

Matthias Erzberger provided a secure channel for the flow of messages between the Vatican and Berlin. Suddenly, by way of papal diplomacy, the Kaiser's spy had become an ally of the Holy Alliance. Under the protection of the papal spy service by order of Gasparri and perhaps Benedict XV himself, Erzberger carried diplomatic proposals from one side of Rome to another. He also became a source of Vatican financing, because on Kaiser Wilhelm's orders he was contributing sizable sums to the papal treasury as "donations."[16]

This fact has given rise to serious controversy among historians. Since 1914, the Vatican's coffers had been in a sorry state, nearly empty, because of the war's effect on the economies of Europe in general and Italy in particular. The Vatican had categorically rejected the annual indemnity stipulated in the Law of Guarantees of 1871, which the Italian government was supposed to pay the pope in compensation for loss of the papal states. The pope thought that pilgrims' donations and the Obolo di San Pietro ("Peter's Pence," contributions by parishioners abroad) could support not only the Holy See's expenses but also the broad structure of the Church around the world. But the war killed off tourism and interrupted the flow of donations and pilgrims to the Vatican. The few funds still coming in went to war victims and refugees. The Vatican may not have been bankrupt, but it was in delicate financial shape that could endanger the operation of the papal bureaucracy in a not-so-distant future.[17]

Recognizing this opportunity to ingratiate himself with the pope, Kaiser Wilhelm began sending sizable amounts of money by way of Erzberger to give the Vatican treasury some breathing room. What began as small sums turned into millions in "secret funds" coming from several Swiss banks. Cardinal Pietro Gasparri ordered the Holy Alliance to see to it that these funds would show up in Vatican accounts as part of the so-called Peter's Pence to avoid upsetting the nations of the Entente.

As liaison for undercover German finance operations, the Holy Alliance chose Father Antonio Lapoma, a pro-German priest who worked in the city of Potenza. Father Lapoma and the spy Matthias Erzberger joined hands in

"Operation *Eisbär*" (polar bear, the code name by which German espionage agents in Rome referred to Pope Benedict XV).

Operation *Eisbär*'s first step was to raise money for the Vatican from private citizens of the Central Powers. Thus Erzberger went to Berlin to organize a wide network for fund-raising not only among Catholics but also among Lutherans and other Protestants. German citizens were told the money would go to those wounded in the war. Kaiser Wilhelm's government required businessmen, bankers, and even housewives to actively participate in the fund-raising, without their ever knowing that the eventual recipient would be the Vatican, after the funds passed through Swiss banks.

Italian intelligence believed that in 1914, Benedict XV had inherited empty coffers from the papacy of Pius X, yet now, in 1915, they discovered that the new pope had mysteriously rescued the Vatican's finances. They did not know his main source of income was Kaiser Wilhelm and Germany. The Entente's secret service set out to prove their suspicions that the pope had fallen under the sway of the Central Powers, at least economically. The Kaiser, meanwhile, gave Erzberger complete freedom to turn over as much money as he could.

The Kaiser's agent had close ties to a diplomat in Germany's Roman embassy, Franz von Stockhammern, who had taken over direction of his country's intelligence services in Italy when the war broke out. Erzberger and Stockhammern worked closely together, along with the Holy Alliance's Father Antonio Lapoma, on covert operations to keep Italy out of the war. Lapoma was in charge of countering any attempts by politicians, parties, and grass-roots movements or organizations to bring Italy into the conflict on either side.

Pope Benedict XV and his secretary of state, Gasparri, knew that Italy's neutrality brought them millions of German marks. Given the Holy See's neutral position, it was no surprise that Catholic newspapers—proclaiming themselves mouthpieces for the citizenry—should be firm defenders of Italian neutrality.[18] In the beginning of 1915, Austria's Roman embassy reported to Vienna that several Italian Catholic papers—in fact it was close to fifty—were expressing the opinion that Italy, the Central Powers' only friend, opposed entry into the war.

The Austrian spies knew from various informants that Italy's mass media were getting subsidies from mysterious sources and that perhaps the German embassy was involved. In fact, this money came from the same funds sent by

Kaiser Wilhelm to the Vatican through Swiss banks. The Holy Alliance's agent Antonio Lapoma channeled the money from the banks to the newspaper publishers.

Britain's ambassador Sir Henry Howard had received reports (possibly from Cardinal Francis Aidan Gasquet) about sinister meetings in Franz von Stockhammern's private rooms in Rome's elegant Hotel Russie. There the German diplomat wined and dined his guests with French champagne and Russian caviar. These guests included cardinals, abbots of Roman monasteries, and some bishops from important Vatican departments. They undertook to write newspaper articles, and sometimes they advised the German diplomat about the propaganda campaign that formed part of Operation *Eisbär*. This campaign, directed by Franz von Stockhammern of the German espionage service and the priest Antonio Lapoma of the Holy Alliance, brought about a shift in public opinion in favor of the Central Powers and Italian neutrality and opposed to the Entente. Sir Henry Howard presented a formal complaint to the secretary of state, Cardinal Pietro Gasparri, but without much success.

Gasparri promised to ask the publishers for a more measured tone in articles and editorials. Pope Benedict XV had instructed Cardinal Gasparri that, if the press kept attacking the Entente, he should write an article in *L'Osservatore Romano,* chastising the editors and publishers of those media. In fact, the media criticism grew sharper, if anything, although Gasparri occasionally paid small "subsidies" to one paper or another to keep it from publishing particular articles or drawings critical of the Entente. Those funds came from money sent from Germany to the Vatican.[19]

While Franz von Stockhammern worked closely with the press, Matthias Erzberger did the same with Father Lapoma, spreading neutralist propaganda in still more communications media and changing the minds of those who wanted to see Italy enter the war.

In late spring of 1915, papal spies informed the Germans that the Italian prime minister, Antonio Salandra, and his minister of foreign affairs, Sidney Sonnino, were getting ready to pressure the cabinet and parliament to ratify an accord they had secretly signed in London in April. They had agreed to bring Italy into the war on the French and British side. Father Lapoma put Erzberger in contact with Pasquale Grippo, minister of education in Salandra's cabinet.

Father Lapoma had told Matthias Erzberger of his secret meetings with

Grippo in Roman churches, where the education minister revealed that, after Salandra and Sonnino presented their war proposal, several ministers had come out against intervention. These included Vincenzo Riccio, head of the postal service, and Gianetto Cavasola, minister of agriculture. Riccio and Cavasola were both firm defenders of neutrality at any price.[20]

Pasquale Grippo's information suggested to Vienna and Berlin that Italy's government was divided. The German secret service and the Austrian government pinned their hopes on Giovanni Gioliti, an important politician with great influence in other social circles and in parliament. Erzberger maintained that Stockhammern and Father Lapoma had to stall for time or, if necessary, buy it. Berlin sent him five million lire to distribute among Italian parliamentary deputies. The Austrians also had bought several deputies, and the Germans, through Stockhammern, paid various journalists to ratchet up their attacks on the Entente. Father Lapoma was supposed to gather signatures of bishops and cardinals against the war. In this task he had the aid of Father Fonck, director of the Jesuit Biblical Institute and former member of the Vatican counterespionage service, as well as Monsignor Boncompagni, a high Vatican official with important ties in the Roman curia and aristocracy.[21]

Finally, by order of Kaiser Wilhelm, the German embassy reacted as might have been expected. Benedict XV's support was essential, and on the night of May 6, Franz von Stockhammern, with the aid of the Holy Alliance and of the pope's secretary Monsignor Giuseppe Migone, won entry to the Vatican.

Although the Swiss Guard had closed the gates at 9 P.M. and the Italian police and secret service had all entrances under surveillance, Monsignor Migone managed to bring the spy Stockhammern to the pope's residence. Benedict XV was waiting in a small room.

The supreme pontiff thought that Sidney Sonnino, the Italian foreign minister, was playing too dangerous a game with Italy's future in the balance. In this secret meeting, Stockhammern openly offered him Austria's Trentine lands if he could keep Italy out of the war. Pope Benedict XV offered the German spy whatever support the Vatican could muster in the next cabinet meeting. There was no need to mention Pasquale Grippo's name aloud. However, none of the secret maneuvers, clandestine meetings, propaganda operations, or any other efforts by Franz von Stockhammern, Matthias Erzberger,[22] Father Antonio Lapoma, the German spy service, or the Holy Alliance could avoid the inevitable. On May 23, 1915, Italy declared war on Austria.[23]

Soon afterwards, the Italian espionage services discovered the contacts established between the German secret service, the papal one, and Pope Benedict XV himself toward the goal of influencing Italy's political decisions. They took this as evidence of the Vatican's connivance with the Central Powers. When Italy entered the war, Germany and Austria closed their embassies in Rome, recalling their emissaries to Berlin and Vienna. Germany's and Austria's new ambassadors to the Holy See would operate out of the Swiss city of Lugano. Franz von Stockhammern likewise moved his spy operations to neutral Switzerland. From the safety of Lugano, Germany and the Holy Alliance would organize covert operations against Italy and other members of the Entente.[24] One of these took place in Ireland. It was financed with some of the funds Kaiser Wilhelm had sent the Vatican, still in the secret Swiss bank accounts.

The British secret service knew that Roger Casement, a retired consul, had made contact with Count von Bernstorff, the German ambassador in Washington. Born in Ireland in 1864, Casement had served as British consul in various African nations and in Brazil, where he denounced the slavery in which rubber workers lived. In 1911, he was named a knight of the British Empire by King Edward VII. In that same year, he began trying to organize a revolt against Great Britain, the nation he had served for so many years.[25]

The former diplomat proposed to the German ambassador in Washington that Kaiser Wilhelm II should support the Irish cause. Casement's idea was an Irish uprising against British troops. For the Germans, this could constitute an excellent diversionary operation. If the Irish rose in rebellion, London would have no choice but to send combat units to the island, pulling them from the European front.

On November 2, 1915, Roger Casement reached Berlin, where he had a number of meetings. "Operation Eire" was entrusted to Franz von Stockhammern. The German spy heard out Casement's patriotic speeches about the need to expel the British from Ireland, but all that interested him was pulling British troops from the front. If he had to pay the devil himself to accomplish that, he would.[26]

Specifically, Casement proposed to Stockhammern that Germany finance and arm an Irish military unit. This force would be recruited from Irish prisoners who had been serving in the British army and were now in German POW camps. Casement would be in charge of recruitment. Stockhammern would manage the financing and the arms supply.[27]

The weapons for this small Irish army were supposed to come from those captured from the Russians on the eastern front, but the financing was a different question. The German spy remembered the funds Kaiser Wilhelm had sent Pope Benedict XV in return for his support of Italian neutrality. Much of this money remained in numbered Swiss bank accounts belonging to the Vatican. The German espionage chief knew that if the operation were exposed, Germany could simply deny allegations of involvement and point toward the Vatican instead. Franz von Stockhammern thought it would be simple enough to explain Vatican connivance with a rebellion of "Catholic" Irish patriots against the "Protestant" British army, but he did not realize that Pope Benedict XV's perspective in the twentieth century would differ from that of Pope Pius V in the sixteenth.

While Roger Casement, himself a Protestant, scoured German prison camps in search of Irishmen, money that had up to then belonged to the Vatican began to flow into a new secret Swiss bank account in Casement's name. When news of this development reached Secretary of State Pietro Gasparri and Pope Benedict XV, they summoned Franz von Stockhammern to an urgent meeting in the Swiss city of Lucerne. There the pope's emissaries demanded explanations from the German espionage official. Stockhammern replied that he was recruiting Irishmen who hated the English and wanted to fight on the German side.

Casement's group was sent to Zossen, a site to the south of Berlin away from prying eyes. The Irish ex-diplomat formerly in British service also won the freedom of three more Irishmen who had been confined in the Ruthleben camp after being taken prisoner in France. He decided to send them to Ireland by underground routes to sound out Irish revolutionary leaders about his plan, but the British arrested one of his envoys in the city of Cork and sent him to London for interrogation.

In return for being saved from execution and also paid for his service, this man told the British all he knew about Operation Eire, including Roger Casement's ties to the Germans and perhaps the Vatican, although he could not confirm the last point. When Casement heard that one of his messengers had been arrested, he wanted to abort the operation. But Franz von Stockhammern compelled him to go ahead, reminding him of the immense quantity of money spent on the plan.

Fearful of the possible repercussions, Roger Casement kept himself on the sidelines, turning control of the operation over to John Devoy, an Irish revolutionary leader in the United States.[28] Both Devoy and Judge Cohalan, another Irish leader in Washington, wanted German support for creation of a Republic of Ireland, but the Kaiser needed immediate results, not chimeras in which few could believe.

Telegrams between the German embassy in Washington and the spy service in Berlin allowed the British to gather the most important information about the plan—the landing spot on the beaches of Tralee Bay. Casement, informed at the last minute, protested that these beaches were constantly assailed by fierce winds, which would hinder landing men and arms. But it was too late. Roger Casement boarded a submarine that took him to the Irish coast.[29]

In early April, the conspirators and Stockhammern arranged that a ship called the *Aud,* disguised as a neutral Norwegian fishing vessel, would land twenty thousand Russian rifles in Tralee Bay between Friday the 21st and Monday the 24th. The 23rd, Easter Sunday, was the day selected for the rebellion. It appears that the rebels expected much more outside aid than the Germans were in fact willing to provide. Casement, knowing that the Irish leaders were mistaken, wanted to reach Ireland in a German submarine to warn Republican leader Tom Clarke and call off the rising that he was now convinced would fail.[30]

The role of the papal espionage service in the Easter Rising of 1916 has been much discussed ever since. One version, widely repeated, insisted that the Holy Alliance cryptographic department succeeded in breaking German naval codes just two weeks before the war broke out and offered the codes to Winston Churchill, first lord of the admiralty. Other sources say that the Russians broke the codes and gave them to Churchill in Murmansk. In either case, with those codes in their possession, the British navy's secret service discovered that the Germans were planning to send thousands of arms to Irish rebels on board a Norwegian fishing ship called the *Aud.* When British naval units tried to intercept the *Aud* off the coast of Tralee Bay, the German ship hoisted the flag of the imperial navy, and it exploded soon afterward.[31]

Roger Casement landed at dawn on April 21, 1916, Good Friday. Two leaders of the rebellion, Monteith and Casey, rowed the small boat toward shore, but the boat turned over in the high waves. Casement and Monteith managed to swim to shore, reaching the coast half-drowned. Casey, however, perished. While the surviving pair tried to regain their strength, British soldiers who had been lying in ambush surrounded them. The rebellion of which they dreamed would soon have a tragic finale.[32]

All the plans for the rising went wrong. On Holy Saturday, the news spread that the British navy had intercepted the *Aud* and that Roger Casement had been arrested near Tralee in County Kerry. The revolt's leaders knew that the rising was condemned to failure, so at last they sent out an order to cancel it. English authorities in Dublin were pushing for the arrest of sixty to a hundred important members of the Citizen Army and Irish Volunteers, but the necessary authorization from London did not arrive until Easter Monday, too late.

At noon on Easter Monday, April 24, Connolly and Pearse led a group to Sackville Street (O'Connell Street since 1924) and took possession of the post office. James Connolly addressed his men and told them they were not members of the Irish Citizen Army or the Irish Volunteers but the "Irish Republican Army." This was the IRA's first appearance on the scene.[33]

British troops in Dublin were taken by surprise, but they soon mobilized, defeated the Irish forces, and jailed their ringleaders. On May 3, three days after the Rising was defeated, three rebel leaders were executed by firing squad. On May 4 and 5, several more were executed, and on the 8th, another four. Seventy-seven death sentences were issued in all. Although the majority were not carried out, the rebellion's leaders soon passed into history as "true national heroes" rather than "undesirables." On August 3, 1916, Roger Casement was executed as well, in Pentonville prison, at the age of fifty-two.[34]

Some sources in the British espionage service accused their Vatican counterparts of having supported the Easter Rising and the plans of Stockhammern and Casement, at least at first. Other historians, primarily Irish ones, accused Pope Benedict XV, his secretary of state Cardinal Pietro Gasparri, and the Holy Alliance agent Father Antonio Lapoma of having abandoned Catholic Ireland in its struggle against Protestant Great Britain. Several Roger Casement biographers assert that a Vatican agent (supposedly Father Antonio Lapoma) could have turned Casement over to the English in Tralee Bay on orders of the pope or the Vatican secretary of state. Apparently Benedict XV was not very pleased by the German secret service's use of Vatican funds to finance the Irish revolt—funds that had been intended to subsidize the Vatican and its battered finances.

In sum, the involvement of the Vatican, Pope Benedict XV, and the Holy

Alliance in the Easter Rising of 1916 remains one more mystery among the many that surround the Holy See.

Meanwhile, the First World War continued apace, as did the operations of Franz von Stockhammern and the Holy Alliance.

One morning in April of 1916, Italian counterintelligence received a visit from a lawyer named Antonio Celletti, who claimed to be a friend of one Archita Valente. Celletti said that Valente showed great interest in the classified ads of the newspaper *Giornale d'Italia* and in strange packets he received from unknown men.[35]

In May, Valente asked Giuseppe Grassi, whom Celletti also knew, to carry some letters to a Baron Stockhammern in the Swiss city of Lucerne. Ignorant of what Valente might be up to, Grassi mentioned this upcoming errand to Celletti, who volunteered to deliver the letters in his place. With the letters in hand and the sign and countersign he had gotten from Grassi, Celletti traveled to Lucerne to meet with Baron Stockhammern. In Switzerland, he was met by Mario Pomarici, an openly pro-German Italian journalist who had been paid to write several articles opposing Italian intervention in the war.

Pomarici had become one of Stockhammern's most trusted men. He told Celletti that Valente was a German agent in Italy and that his main task was to gather information about relations between Italy and the Entente as well as those between Italy and the Vatican. On his return to Rome, Antonio Celletti told the Italian espionage service about the conspiracy he had unearthed. By June 1916, Italian counterintelligence had sufficient evidence against Archita Valente and Mario Pomarici, but only in November were the courts able to charge both with high treason.

When Rome's intelligence service began to study Valente's coded messages in the *Giornale d'Italia,* they discovered Franz von Stockhammern's communications with a wide network of agents inside Italy and the Vatican. They passed the information on to officials of the Holy Alliance, who in turn passed it on to the counterespionage service, the *Sodalitium Pianum.* In one message, Valente had spoken of a "Mr. A" and a "Mr. G." Interrogated by Italian intelligence, Archita Valente confessed that both "A" and "G" were Giuseppe Ambrogetti, a Roman attorney who had often served as a special messenger for Pope Benedict XV and for certain cardinals and bishops. Ambrogetti was in fact an experienced agent of the Holy Alliance who had been decorated by the pope himself for "services to the Church."[36]

The Italians arrested the papal spy. Perhaps to save his own skin, he confessed that he was in fact "A," but not "G." Ambrogetti said he had infiltrated the German secret service on Holy Alliance orders and that the money he'd received had been deposited in the Vatican. Pressured further, he said that "G" was Monsignor Rudolph Gerlach, a Bavarian priest who had been chamberlain and confidant to Pope Benedict XV.

Archita Valente, meanwhile, said that during the period of Italian neutrality Monsignor Gerlach had acted as a go-between, distributing large sums of money from Franz von Stockhammern to various newspapers and journalists. He said Gerlach had also disbursed funds to Ambrogetti, the Holy Alliance agent. The money received by Gerlach was deposited in numbered Swiss bank accounts. Giuseppe Ambrogetti said the Holy Alliance had put Gerlach under surveillance. The papal espionage service characterized Monsignor Gerlach as an ambitious and very intelligent man, about whom rumors had been circulating since his time in the prestigious Pontifical Ecclesiastic Academy, when his character and the sincerity of his vocation had been doubted. At that point, the S.P. had alerted the Holy Alliance to keep an eye on him.

The first suspicious signs emerged when Rudolph Gerlach was nominated for a post in the nuncio's office in Bavaria. Cardinal Andrea Frühwirth, head of the papal embassy, refused to accept Gerlach, so he stayed on in Rome. In the Eternal City, he developed ties to Giacomo della Chiesa when the then Archbishop of Bologna came to Rome for his investiture as cardinal. As Benedict XV, della Chiesa brought Monsignor Rudolph Gerlach into his service, but that did not satisfy this unscrupulous adventurer.[37]

For the Holy Alliance, the news that Gerlach was a traitor came as no surprise. The *Sodalitium Pianum* had informed them of the Bavarian priest's continual visits to the Austrian and German embassies in Rome during the period of Italian neutrality. The Italians believed Rudolph Gerlach was the key member of the Kaiser's spy corps in the Vatican. The Italian government would have liked to put him and all his associates in front of a firing squad for espionage and high treason, but then the press would have been all over the scandal. The Vatican, and especially the Roman curia surrounding Pope Benedict XV, wanted to quickly turn the page on the Gerlach affair.

The Italian secret service kept the Vatican and the Holy Alliance informed about the progress of their investigation of the former papal chamberlain. Finally, on January 5, 1917, Monsignor Gerlach was conducted to the Swiss border by Italian agents. Archita Valente and Giuseppe Ambrogetti, implicated in conspiracies against the Italian state, went on trial for high treason and espionage that spring.[38] Rudolph Gerlach was not present at the trial, so he could not testify or defend himself. Valente received a death sentence; Gerlach, life imprisonment in absentia; and Ambrogetti, three years in prison. However, thanks to some secret benefactor, possibly the Holy Alliance, Giuseppe Ambrogetti did not serve a day in jail.

The Gerlach affair was one of the biggest scandals in papal history. Proof that Rudolph Gerlach had betrayed the pope and the Vatican sent Benedict XV into a deep depression. The secretary of state, Cardinal Pietro Gasparri, wrote to Gerlach summoning him to the Vatican to answer the accusations, but Gerlach showed no signs of life. He preferred to stay in hiding in Switzerland, safe from the long arm of the Italian secret service.

A military tribunal exonerated the Vatican, Pope Benedict XV, Cardinal and Secretary of State Pietro Gasparri, the Vatican counterespionage *Sodalitium Pianum,* and the Vatican espionage service Holy Alliance of any responsibility for the Gerlach affair. Yet there is no doubt that Holy Alliance spy Giuseppe Ambrogetti's involvement damaged the image of neutrality the Vatican wanted to project. From London, Paris, Rome, and Washington came insinuations that the Vatican sympathized with the Central Powers, using its secret services to work for a German-Austrian victory. For the governments of the Entente, the Rudolph Gerlach case was proof. The former papal chamberlain had used Vatican channels to pass information to an enemy power in time of war. Years later, it would be revealed that the Vatican had paid the lawyer who defended Monsignor Gerlach before the military tribunal that tried him for high treason.

One member of the Holy Alliance even tried, hoping against hope, to persuade General Luigi Cardona, commander in chief of the Italian army, to mediate with the tribunal to retract the accusation against Gerlach. It was also known that Monsignor Federico Tedeschini, who belonged to the secretariat of state, had testified to the Italian espionage service and the military tribunal that, after a review of the Vatican's diplomatic activities and in line with the censorship imposed by the Italian government, the secretariat's correspondence with the nations of the Central Powers had been restricted. Tedeschini admitted that, beginning in late 1915 and early 1916, Monsignor Gerlach had carried on an extensive correspondence with Matthias Erzberger and Franz von Stockhammern, both recognized as German spies, and that this correspondence had been expressly authorized by Pope Benedict XV. The supreme pontiff's explanation was that this authorization had been intended to convince Germany to stop bombarding civilian areas and to allow the transfer of wounded French and German soldiers to Switzerland. Gerlach always denied having carried on any type of correspondence with German agents in neutral countries by order of the pope. He did admit to having passed large sums of money from Berlin to newspapers like *La Vittoria* so they would come out clearly for Italian neutrality. A report by Matthias Erzberger to Berlin said that Monsignor Gerlach was the espionage service's main source of information in the circles close to the pope.

During the last days of Italian neutrality, Erzberger authorized Monsignor Gerlach to distribute about five million lire to members of the curia, journalists, and politicians in an effort to keep Italy out of the war. After the government in Rome had joined the Entente, Gerlach continued to receive enormous sums of money from Stockhammern. In November 1915, German secret services reported having paid around 200,000 lire to Father Lapoma, the Holy Alliance agent, and to Monsignor Francesco Marchietti-Selvaggiani, the papal nuncio in Switzerland. From May of that year on, Monsignor Gerlach was the main German agent inside the Holy See. When the scandal blew up and Italy demanded the Vatican turn over those responsible, Benedict XV's only reponse was that the Vatican had been the main victim.

Gerlach moved to Switzerland permanently and was decorated by Kaiser Wilhelm II of Germany and Emperor Charles I of Austria, who had succeeded his grandfather Franz Joseph I on November 1, 1916. Gerlach soon left religious life. After the war's end, several nations repaid his services with medals.[39]

The Gerlach affair displayed Pope Benedict XV's sympathies for Italy's enemies. The Italian secret services' surveillance of the pope and his closest advisors increased, to make sure that the Central Powers could not use the Vatican as an intelligence source. The Holy Alliance discovered a few months later that the Treaty of London signed by the foreign minister, Sonnino, which formalized Italy's entrance into the war, had included a secret clause, the so-called Article 15, supported by London, Paris, and St. Petersburg, which prohibited intervention by the Vatican, the pope, or any other high official of the Holy See in a future peace conference.[40]

Both the Entente and the Central Powers began to discover, at the beginning of 1917, that only a negotiated solution could end the butchery the First World War had become. The following years would be ones of maneuvers to achieve peace or at least to reduce the number of enemies. From then on, the main function of the secret services, including the Holy Alliance and the *Sodalitium Pianum,* would be to serve as intermediaries in that pursuit.

12

INTRIGUING TOWARD

PEACE (1917–1922)

I do not sit with deceivers, nor with hypocrites do I mingle.
—Psalms 25:4

In the later years of the First World War, Italian intelligence's main targets were Austria and the Vatican. One of the most efficient agents inside the Holy See was Baron Carlo Monti. He also directed the Office of Religious Affairs, the section of the Italian justice ministry that dealt with everything affecting relations between church and state.

Unofficially, Monti became the communication channel linking the government in Rome to the Vatican, and in a way he was also the bridge between the Italian secret services and the Holy Alliance. What helped him play this role was his close relationship with the supreme pontiff, dating back to their school days in Genoa. Monti's work inside the Vatican was completely open, without any sort of subterfuge. The pope's closest collaborators willingly supplied information for Carlo Monti to pass on to the Italian secret service, with the full knowledge of the Holy Father.[1]

The information so transmitted, in the main by way of "free"[2] agents of the Holy Alliance, tended to deal with the papal administration's intentions on one specific issue or another or with information about politicians or with news that papal intelligence had gathered in some foreign capital. Sometimes Baron Carlo Monti had recourse to the Holy Alliance, as occurred in February

1917, when the Vatican alerted the Italian secret services to social deterioration going on in the interior of Tsar Nicholas's Russia. Monti was not even excluded from meetings between Pope Benedict and his cardinals or from secret coded messages sent by the supreme pontiff or his secretary of state to some nunciatures.

The General Directorate of Public Security was the Italian department that kept tabs on the Vatican activities and personnel. Cesare Bertini, the police chief of Borgo, the Roman district that included the Vatican, deployed a significant number of secret agents throughout the Holy See, particularly where they could observe and report on the comings and goings of diplomats, journalists, or high members of the Roman curia.[3] Bertini's agents in civilian dress made daily visit to the barracks of the Swiss Guard and to the Guardsmen's off-duty haunts to collect information.

The main group of informers inside the Vatican was the so-called Vaticanetto. Made up of former high members of the curia during Pius X's papacy, they formed a circle of opposition to Benedict XV, who had ousted them from power. The group was led by Cardinal Rafael Merry del Val, Pius X's secretary of state; Monsignor Nicola Canali, undersecretary of state; and the two papal chamberlains, Monsignor Carlo Caccia-Dominioni and Monsignor Arborio Mella di Sant'Ellia. Vengeance was the watchword of the Vaticanetto circle, and its operations were designed to humiliate the pope, denigrate Vatican policies, obstruct the papal diplomatic service abroad, and expose all Holy Alliance operations to friendly or enemy secret services.[4]

An example of the information gathered by the Vaticanetto and passed on to the Italian secret services was a report dated March 22, 1915, that discussed the Swiss Guard's acquisition of new rifles from a seller linked to the Austrian secret services. Another, dated September 9, 1916, reported that the chaplain of the Swiss Guard was collaborating on espionage matters with the Austrian embassy. Another, from October 1916, warned that Monsignor Gerlach was supplying maps of the ports of Ancona and Bari so they could be attacked by German submarines. Another reported that the director of the Vatican pharmacy was really the Kaiser's spy. These were all false reports, intended to spread a negative image of Benedict XV and his secret as well as diplomatic services.

Other reports, though assumed by the Italians to be false, really were not. An example was the Spanish king Alfonso XIII's invitation to the pope to seat headquarters in Spain, given the Italian government's belligerent attitude toward the Vatican. Another was the disclosure in March 1917 of the Spanish monarch's approach to Emperor Charles I of Austria in March 1917 to try to mediate a separate Austrian peace with the European powers, leaving Germany out.[5]

One important peace feeler went by way of two Holy Alliance agents, Count Werner de Merodè and his wife, Paulina de Merodè. For years this nobleman had served the Holy Alliance as a courier. Both he and his wife, in fact, had worked for the Vatican secretariat of state and its head, Cardinal Pietro Gasparri, carrying papal messages to high Church officials in countries under German occupation.

Early in April 1917, Werner de Merodè was contacted by a Holy Alliance agent close to Germany, possibly Father Antonio Lapoma, who was trying to set up a meeting with Baron von der Lancken, a former Imperial Guard officer, diplomat, and member of the Kaiser's secret service. Merodè belonged to one of the oldest lineages of France, and von der Lancken was head of German intelligence in Belgium.

Werner de Merodè told Baron von der Lancken that some high political levels of the Entente wanted a meeting in a neutral spot such as Switzerland. The German asked Merodè what "high levels" he was talking about, and the Belgian noble uttered three names: Paul Deschanel, president of the French National Assembly; Jules Cambon, secretary general of the ministry of foreign relations; and Aristide Brian, who had been Council president. Von der Lancken in turn informed Franz von Stockhammern, the head of German espionage in Switzerland; Zimmermann, the secretary of state; and Chancellor Bethmann-Hollweg. Then he waited for news.[6]

To the German intelligence service and the Holy Alliance, Deschanel was too anti-Austrian and Cambon was not very discreet. That left only Brian, the political foe of Clemenceau, the most rabid pro-war figure, who opposed any secret negotiations with the Central Powers.

Werner de Merodè proposed to Brian that he meet with von der Lancken in Switzerland, but the French politician, however much of a peace lover he may have been, had to inform Raymond Poincaré, president of the Republic. In spite of the president's warnings, Brian decided to contact the Prime Minister of Belgium, de Brocqueville, so that the latter could accompany him to the meeting, which was supposed to occur on September 22, 1917. On September 9, thirteen days before that date, Brian met with Poincaré again to tell him when and where the meeting would occur. The neutral witness was to be a young monsignor named Eugenio Pacelli, the future Pope Pius XII, who was apparently acting in the name of the Vatican counterespionage, the *Sodalitium Pianum*.

When Brian tried to leave France on his way to Switzerland, his passage was denied. The French secret services warned President Poincaré that the Germans, with help from the Vatican spy services, were readying a trap to spring on the French negotiator. Apparently someone within the Vatican had alerted the Italian secret services, and they had gotten their French opposite numbers to act. Some sources say it was the English cardinal Frances Aidan Gasquet[7] who supplied news of the Brian–von der Lancken meeting in Switzerland to the Italian espionage service. Really, Gasquet worried that the German secret service, supported by the Holy Alliance, would seek a negotiated settlement that could leave Kaiser Wilhelm and Emperor Charles in place, without any kind of reparations from Germany and Austria-Hungary.

Another lover of intrigue made his appearance in the game of mediation and negotiation around the same time. Like the German baron, this high Catholic Church dignitary had the ear of the Vatican secret services. He also had at his disposal perhaps the oldest and certainly one of the best espionage networks in the world. He was Monsignor Eugenio Pacelli, and his service was the *Sodalitium Pianum*.

The Holy Alliance and its counterespionage unit were committed in principle to supporting the actions of the papacy, and they were both heavily dependent on the Holy See. In truth, both intelligence services were Benedict XV's tools to keep himself very well informed about the maneuverings of those trying to broker a peace, and sometimes to give these maneuverings a small nudge, as occurred in May 1917. On the 20th, Monsignor Eugenio Pacelli left Rome for Munich by way of Switzerland. Benedict XV had just named him nuncio to the Bavarian capital.[8]

Pacelli, at forty, had all the earmarks of a humble friar: incipient baldness, a sharp nose, sunken eyes, and an extremely slender frame. His wide knowledge of Vatican diplomacy, especially in regard to European issues, would allow him to carry out the mission Pope Benedict XV had given him. Back in 1914, when he was undersecretary of state in the papacy of Pius X, Pacelli had been sent to Vienna on a secret mission to set up high-level contacts with the help of Monsignor Umberto Benigni, the head of Vatican counterespionage. In January 1917, while the so-called Sixth Negotiation got under way, Monsignor Eugenio Pacelli had his first meeting with Count Golochowsky, the Kaiser's representative.

After having taken up his new post in Munich, the nuncio Pacelli was sent to Berlin on June 26. On the 29th, the papal representative was received by Kaiser Wilhelm II at German general staff headquarters in Bad-Kreuznach. The meeting began on a relaxed note. Pacelli gave the emperor a handwritten letter from Pope Benedict XV in which His Holiness expressed his desire to achieve a stable peace that would bring an end to the disastrous effects of the war. Then Eugenio Pacelli tried to convince Wilhelm II of the need to accept papal mediation between Germany and the Entente.[9]

Pacelli made his arguments in a manner both courteous and unbending, trying to put the Kaiser between a rock and hard place. Von Hertling, the German foreign affairs minister, remembered Pacelli this way: "That Pacelli was worth more than an army." The Kaiser himself wrote in his memoirs, "Eugenio Pacelli was the perfect image of a Prince of the Church."

At the end of the meeting, the papal envoy left with only a formal German promise to study the idea of papal mediation. The next day's meeting was with Charles I, the Austro-Hungarian emperor, who was visiting Berlin. Pacelli met him in the same location where he had met with the Kaiser.

Meanwhile, the reports reaching the S.P. and the pope were full of suggestions, which allowed Benedict XV to prepare an official Vatican note about the goal of finding a negotiated settlement of the conflict.

Eugenio Pacelli delivered this new papal note to Wilhelm II in person on June 24 and found it well received. But without waiting for a response from Berlin, Benedict XV followed Pacelli's advice and ordered his secretary of state, Cardinal Pietro Gaparri, to deliver the same note to the representatives of the Entente. This communication arrived in France and Great Britain on August 9.

During this time, Switzerland had become fertile ground for Italian intelligence operations against the papacy. For years, the Italian secret services had been convinced the alpine country was the covert operations center for the Holy Alliance and the *Sodalitium Pianum*. The Vatican's espionage and counterespionage operations, now directed toward finding a solution to the First World War, were controlled by a sort of triumvirate made up of Monsignor Luigi Maglione,[10] papal delegate in Switzerland; the superior-general of the Jesuits, who had moved from Rome to Switzerland due to the war; and the Archbishop of Coire, a small diocese in Swiss Romagna.

Military intelligence received constant reports about Holy Alliance actions in Switzerland whose goal was to mediate between the contending powers. Especially, Italian spies had detected a flood of messages between the papal representatives and Berlin and Vienna.[11]

On August 23, the British ambassador in Rome gave Pope Benedict XV a request from the King of England, George V, that any negotiations with Germany had to include a solution to the Belgian question. Pacelli could clearly see that the note implied only London and Berlin as parties to such a negotiation, but at least it was a place to begin. When the English proposal reached Kaiser Wilhelm II, however, he rejected it, insisting that Germany was not willing to make the slightest concession to Belgium.[12]

The idea that the pope could be controlling an international conspiratorial triumvirate in Switzerland worried not only the Entente's secret services, but also the main anticlerical circles of Europe. The British ambassador to the Holy See told the Italian government that its military secret services were more concerned "with quantity than with quality" in the gathering of information. He charged that the Italians were most interested in collecting industrial information, but they needed to concentrate on the Vatican, too. In fact, the English knew about the Holy Alliance maneuvers in Vienna and Berlin. They thought the papal secret services had the most direct contacts with Wilhelm II and Charles I, and someone ought to make use of them.

Starting in the summer of 1915, the foreign affairs minister of the Swiss Confederation had offered to send a diplomatic pouch once a week from Berne to the Vatican. Filled with envelopes of all sizes secured by wax seals bearing the image of the keys of St. Peter, this pouch went from the ministry in Berne to the Swiss embassy in Rome. Once it reached Rome, the pouch was collected by a member of the Swiss Guard and two agents of the Holy Alliance.

The Italian secret services wanted access to this pouch, especially whenever they learned that it contained an envelope originating in enemy territory. The contents of such envelopes were hard to read because, shortly before the outbreak of the war, the Holy Alliance had begun to distribute among papal embassies a system of cryptographic codes for top-secret messages.

For centuries, the governments had protected their confidential communications from prying eyes of other governments—or at least tried to do so—through codes and ciphers. The only codes that the secret services of the Entente and Central Powers never managed to decipher were those of the

Vatican and the Holy Alliance, invented by the Vatican's office of cryptography, the *Reparto Crittografico*.[13]

In December of 1915, a few months after war was declared, the Vatican secret services created a special unit of coders, and also one of cryptoanalysts, commonly called code-breakers. The cryptographic system used by the Holy Alliance was quite complex and generally was used in all communications between the secretariat of state and papal representatives around the world. Between 1914 and 1917, every papal nuncio had a codebook designed by the *Reparto Crittografico* that consisted of seven or eight hundred groups of three- or four-digit numbers each. Each one of these numeric groups represented a word or message. For instance, in the sequence "492-7015-119-3683," 492 = message received; 7015 = Switzerland; 119 = agent; 3683 = Lugano.[14]

The problem was, however, that the codebook needed to be changed at certain intervals, in part because terms like *submarines, attack, retreat, armistice, cannons,* and such things needed to be added. Almost at the end of the war, the Italian secret services got hold of one of these books, which allowed them to read important messages between the Vatican and its legations in Austria-Hungary, Belgium, Spain, Switzerland, and the U.S. Reports from the nuncios about political attitudes in the countries where they were stationed, confidential communications among nuncios, politicians, and intellectuals, instructions of the secretary of state to his nuncios concerning policy changes in the Vatican, alerts about military and political news, peace initiatives from the Entente countries or the Central Powers—these were some of the data that the Italians became privy to.[15]

But the situation would change when the Holy Alliance's *Reparto Crittografico* decided to strengthen its security system for telegraph transmissions, on July 29, 1917. Curiously, on August 1, Pope Benedict XV sent to all the contenders in the war, by way of his nuncios, a document calling for peace by way of acceptance of certain concrete points: mutual evacuation and restoration of occupied territories, mutual rejection of war reparations payments, freedom of navigation in all seas, arms reduction, arbitration of disputes, and open negotiations about disputed territories. Benedict XV and his secretary of state Cardinal Pietro Gasparri thought it was necessary to reach a peace accord as soon as possible because Holy Alliance agents had begun to send information about the possible entry of the United States into the war. The Vatican knew that if this occurred, the situation of the Central Powers would grow very difficult. Therefore the pope ordered the secretary of state and the spy services to try to craft a peace accord before the first U.S. soldier could set food on European soil.

The U.S. entrance into the war on the Entente side occurred on April 6, 1917, but getting troops, transport, and armaments to the ground took longer—a lag the Vatican and Central Powers had to try to take advantage of.[16] Things were not going so well for the Entente, either. Several French army units mutinied, refusing to report to the front, while in Russia the government of Tsar Nicholas II was overthrown by a revolution and replaced by a provisional government. The new communist regime promised the Allies it would stay in the war, but continual mutinies, desertions, and insubordination meant that the officials of the Revolutionary General Staff found this promise impossible to fulfill.

That same year, Monsignor Eugenio Pacelli once again told Pope Benedict XV and the Holy Alliance that the German chancellor Theobald von Bethmann-Hollweg wanted to open peace negotiations with the Allies. Pacelli wrote a note in his own hand, which is still in existence in the Vatican archives:

> Bethmann-Hollweg sees an opportunity to achieve peace once the Reichstag is no longer dominated by the pro-war politicians but by others in favor of peace. I think this is the moment to strike, to bring about serious mediation by His Holiness.[17]

The intelligence services of the Vatican, London, Paris, and Rome all learned about the secret meetings between Bethmann-Hollweg and the nuncio Pacelli. The problem was that the nations of the Entente did not share the pope's point of view about a negotiated settlement with Austria-Hungary and Germany after three years of war—and even less so when their secret services warned that Pope Benedict XV, his secretary of state Pietro Gasparri, and his espionage services the Holy Alliance and *Sodalitium Pianum* wanted only to end the European war before the United States and its war machine could intervene.

To the Entente, the supreme pontiff was evidently pro-German, so France made clear it would never accept Vatican mediation. U.S. president Woodrow Wilson told the papal nuncio in Washington that his country would likewise not accept negotiation with two empires that had given no clear signal of a desire for peace during the three years of war. Italy did not even take papal mediation as a serious proposal. From the moment the Gerlach Affair blew up, the Vatican and Pope Benedict XV were seen as open partisans of the Central Powers.[18]

Eugenio Pacelli, however, was thrilled by the results of his meetings with foreign minister Theobald von Bethmann-Hollweg. Even in his coded messages, the nuncio in Berlin described the situation most optimistically. What Pacelli didn't tell the Vatican was that he had made promises to Vienna and Berlin on his own authority—promises he knew could not be fulfilled, due in part to his lack of any support within the Entente governments.

On September 1917, Pacelli mysteriously disappeared from Berlin and surfaced in Rome. He planned to communicate with Sidney Sonnino, the Italian foreign minister, and let him know that both Austria and Germany were willing to restore Belgian sovereignty, pay reparations to Brussels, and recognize Italian aspirations in Trentino. Sonnino already knew this, thanks to interceptions of Vatican telegrams, but what Pacelli didn't know and the Italian foreign minister did was that the nuncio in Vienna had sent a different message, insisting that Emperor Charles would never make any territorial concessions to Italy. To the Italians, this meant that the Vatican and its nuncio in Berlin, Monsignor Eugenio Pacelli, were playing a two-faced game.

For a while, the Vatican did not know about the famous Article 15 of the Treaty of London, in which France, Great Britain, Italy, and Russia excluded the Vatican from any future peace conference. But a Holy Alliance agent in the British Foreign Office discovered the document and passed the information to Pietro Gasparri. From that moment on, by order of Benedict XV, the Church began a fierce campaign within the Catholic communities of the belligerent countries and the neutral ones as well, to get King George V of England to back a retraction of Article 15. But the Jonckx Affair was on the point of exploding, and its shock waves would hurt the Vatican counterespionage unit, the *Sodalitium Pianum*.[19]

In late 1917 and early 1918, the *Düsseldorfer Tageblatt* newspaper published exposés about a conspiracy against the Central Powers in Belgium. Heinz Brauweiler, the paper's editor and an occasional German espionage agent, charged that a group of Catholic integralists supported by Russia were trying to undermine German security. Brauweiler, in the pages of his paper, claimed that a book recently published in France, *La Guerre Allemande et le Catholicisme,* named the German empire as the Catholic Church's true enemy in the world, warning that the Kaiser wanted to replace the pope as the absolutist Church figure in a future Europe.[20] Brauweiler declared that the whole anti-German plot had been organized by the Vatican counter-espionage service, the S.P., and by a certain Jonckx, a lawyer in the Belgian city of Ghent, under German occupation. The *Düsseldorfer Tageblatt* had the documents that the Dominican priest Floris Prims had tried to show Pope Pius X and his secretary of state, Cardinal Rafael Merry del Val.[21]

On February 3, 1918, the German military police and agents of the Kaiser's intelligence service appeared at Jonckx's house. The German version was that the lawyer and Vatican counterespionage agent kept up permanent contacts with one Baron Sonthoff, a Russian spy, to carry out campaigns against Germany and Kaiser Wilhelm II.

The exposure of the Jonckx Affair proved a complete disaster for the *Sodalitium Pianum* and the Vatican. While Benedict XV and his nuncio in Berlin, Eugenio Pacelli, were trying to negotiate peace between the Entente and Central Powers, the supreme pontiff's secret services were carrying out covert operations against one of the sides. This seriously damaged the image of neutrality the pope wanted to present during negotiations. Therefore he ordered his secretary of state, Cardinal Pietro Gasparri, to stop all activities of the *Sodalitium Pianum.* The counterespionage service's operations were suspended, and its personnel absorbed by the Holy Alliance. From then on, by order of the pope, counterespionage operations inside the Vatican and its administrative bodies would be directed by the *Sodalitium Pianum,* but only as a minor department of the Holy See's espionage service.[22]

At the same time, the pope ordered Gasparri to see to it that all young priests in the Pontifical Academy of Ecclesiastical Nobles, the educational institution from which all the high officials of the curia emerged, should be prepared to work as diplomats and—if circumstances so required—even as spies. The academy was instructed to teach law, history, language, and politics so that its graduates could form a papal diplomatic corps.

Benedict XV's decision soon bore fruit, and a new ecclesiastic elite began to occupy the most important nunciatures around the globe. Among this elite of diplomats and spies could be found Giuseppe Aversa and Eugenio Pacelli (the future Pope Pius XII) in Germany, Raffaele Scapinelli de Leguigno in Austria, Francesco Marchetti-Selvaggiani and Luigi Maglione (future secretary of state) in Switzerland, Giulio Tonti in Portugal, and Federico Tedeschini in Spain.[23]

As the war ground on, meanwhile, German losses alone approached two million, and both Woodrow Wilson and the other Entente leaders were no longer willing to sign any negotiated peace with Germany and Kaiser Wilhelm II. On November 11, 1918, Wilhelm II, Emperor of Germany, fled to Holland and abdicated. Prince Max von Baden, the last chancellor of the Second Reich founded by Otto von Bismarck, turned power over to an interim president, the social democrat Friedrich Ebert.[24]

On September 27, 1919, Foreign Minister Hermann Müller announced that the Prussian diplomatic legation in Rome would officially become the German embassy to the Holy See, and that Diego von Bergen would be the first ambassador.

Matthias Erzberger, ex-spy and now minister of the Reich, decided to establish secret contact with Monsignor Eugenio Pacelli through German and Vatican espionage agents. Both Erzberger and Pacelli sought a complete restructuring of the relations between the German state and the Vatican, and if that required activating both spy services to accomplish it, so be it.

The Holy Alliance then informed Pope Benedict XV that Monsignor Pacelli was negotiating without the secretariat of state's authorization, and that the Holy See would appear in a bad light if the nuncio in Berlin did not succeed in establishing a tacit accord with the Reich without offending Catholic Bavaria. The decision to establish a German embassy to the Holy See presupposed the closing of the Bavarian one. Pacelli was not willing to deal with German foreign ministry, which was of Protestant tendency, if that meant closing the clearly Catholic Bavarian legation.[25]

Pacelli wanted two distinct diplomatic delegations. He wanted a German embassy in the Vatican and a nunciature for German affairs in Berlin, neither of which would cover Bavarian affairs; simultaneously, he wanted a Bavarian legation in Rome and a papal nunciature in Munich. Erzberger, pressured by Eugenio Pacelli, decided to support the nuncio's plan. Apparently, Pacelli threatened to reveal to the Allied countries the nature of Matthias Erzberger's former post and some of the operations Erzberger had carried out in Italy during the war.[26]

Finally, the Reich gave in, and Prussia grudgingly accepted that its own embassy in Rome should become the Reich's legation to the Vatican. Enough time had gone by since Erzberger had told Archbishop Giuseppe Aversa that the Kaiser would never accept a former papal nuncio in Bavaria's being named nuncio in Prussia or the Reich, which would be an implied humiliation.

Pacelli delayed the signing of a concordat with the Reich and, in the opinion of historian Klaus Scholder in his work *The Churches and the Third Reich,* "thus created the fatal starting point from which in 1933 Hitler was to force the capitulation of German Catholicism within a few weeks."

In other words, Eugenio Pacelli, as nuncio in Berlin, could have obtained a formal concordat regularizing relations between Germany and the Catholic Church at the beginning of the 1920s, without limiting the political activity of German Catholics. By the early '30s it was already too late, and Hitler, astutely, saw in the signing of the concordat with the Vatican a way to get the German Catholics and the Catholic centrist parties out of the political arena and out of his way. Pacelli, according to political analysts and historians, played into Hitler's hands and helped him shed the burden of the numerous and troublesome political groups of the Catholic center. Adolf Hitler didn't want a confrontation with Pacelli as Vatican nuncio, and much less with Pacelli as pope.

Another situation confronting the Holy Alliance and Eugenio Pacelli as papal nuncio arose in April of 1920. This involved a dispute between Germany and France over the latter's use of African regiments as an occupying force in the Rhineland region.

Pacelli had received protests from his coreligionists about numerous cases of rape of Catholic women and children by African soldiers in the French army. On December 31, Cardinal Adolf Bertram wrote a letter to Secretary of State Pietro Gasparri charging that "France prefers to employ African soldiers, who because of their savage lack of culture and morality have committed unspeakable assaults on women and children of the region, creating a situation known as the 'black shame.'" The French, in spite of German protests, had plans to send more African troops to the region. Pacelli began to urge Gasparri to activate the Holy Alliance to intervene.

The French ambassador denied Pacelli and Bertram's allegations, labeling them "anti-French propaganda." It was true, however, that the men implicated in these cases were soldiers and officers of regiments from North African countries and French colonies in sub-Saharan Africa.

The Holy Alliance decided to send "investigators" to the region to take testimony from those involved. The pope's spies revealed all sorts of aberrations committed against women and children of the Rhineland by French troops: boys less than ten years of age kidnapped and raped; teenage girls raped, tortured, and used as sex slaves; women beaten and raped, and innumerable cases of this sort.[27]

While the agents reported to Pope Benedict XV in Rome, they also did so to the nuncio Pacelli, but one case even further heightened the tension. An eleven-year-old girl named Nina Holbech was kidnapped by three soldiers and two officers from the African regiments. Two days later, her corpse was found tied to a post in an abandoned barn. Nina had been sadistically tortured and raped to death. Germany demanded justice, but a defeated nation that had provoked a world war had no such right. Yet Pacelli decided to grant it.

The agents sent from Rome determined to take action against the attackers. They gathered information about the schedules of the kidnappers and where they went while out on passes. They studied the checkpoints on the highways and secondary roads, and the barracks where the five who had committed the attack on the girl were housed.

The second prong of the papal espionage unit's plan of attack was a widespread publicity campaign in the United States and Britain, denouncing France for attacks on white girls in the Rhineland by soldiers of color belonging to its army units. As a result of the pressures brought to bear in Washington by the papal spy service, Congress decided to create an investigative commission that would travel to Germany. Eugenio Pacelli believed that the U.S. government would, in the end, pressure Paris to end the rapes and attacks on women and children by African soldiers, but the result was quite different. President Wilson's administration advised the committee not to take any measures or actions against France in relation to the complaints coming from Germany and the Holy See.[28]

On March 7, 1921, Eugenio Pacelli again wrote to Pietro Gasparri to inquire about the supreme pontiff's position, but this time the cardinal secretary of state counseled Benedict XV not to intervene in defense of the victimized German children and women. The Holy See's complaints to Paris ceased.

Mysteriously, the three soldiers accused of the rape and murder of Nina Holbech, who were not put on trial by the French military authorities, appeared one day naked and with their hands tied behind their backs. They had been strangled. The two officers, who were also not reprimanded and who had led the attack on the girl, had been hanged to death from a beam in the same barn where Nina's body had been found. The authors of these crimes were never discovered, but the accusations about the so-called black shame inflicted on white women continued until Hitler reoccupied the region years later.

For Eugenio Pacelli, at the time and later, when he was Pope Pius XII, that black shame left its mark on his attitudes toward race and war. Twenty-five years later, when the first Allied units entered Rome after liberating it from Nazi occupation, the supreme pontiff requested through U.S. and British ambassadors in Rome that "there should be no Allied soldiers of color among the units which remain quartered in Rome after liberation."[29]

Meanwhile, in a hall overlooking Milan's Piazza San Sepolcro two years before these events in the Rhineland, Benito Mussolini met with 118 individuals on March 23, 1919, to found the *Fasci di Combattimento*. Their program called for expropriation of all properties of religious congregations and the suspension of the so-called Law of Guarantees. The Holy Alliance immediately alerted Gasparri and Pope Benedict XV about the meeting and even about the possibility that this pompous man might one day gain unprecedented power. What the Church did not know was that ten years later, that same politician would sign the Lateran Pacts creating the Vatican city-state.

In early January 1922, Benedict XV caught a cold that within a few days turned into acute bronchitis. On January 20, his condition took a turn for the worse. Papal doctors then diagnosed the pneumonia that caused his death two days later, at 6 A.M. Shortly after his death, the Turks erected a statue of Benedict XV with a plaque that read, "To the great pope who lived through a world tragedy as a benefactor of all the peoples without distinction of nationality or religion."

The conclave that followed the supreme pontiff's death lasted only four days. On the morning of February 6, 1922, Cardinal Achille Ratti quickly won the necessary two-thirds of the votes. After selecting the name Pius XI, he told the College of Cardinals that it was his intention to safeguard and defend the prerogatives of the Catholic Church not only in Rome and Italy but throughout the world. He intended to proclaim his blessing *Urbi et Orbi,* expressing a desire for lasting peace, from the balcony over the Piazza San Pietro. This represented a departure from the policy followed since the loss of the papal states in 1870, after which the ceremony had always taken place inside. With this gesture, Pope Pius XI made it quite clear that during his papacy he wanted to settle the so-called Roman question.[30]

The death of Benedict XV marked the beginning of a new epoch, a new era. The so-called era of the dictators was in no way propitious for world peace. The Horseman of the Apocalypse got ready to ride again.

David Rizzio (*British Museum*)

Elizabeth I
(*National Portrait Gallery, London*)

Henry Darnley and Mary Stewart (*The National Trust of Scotland*)

Pius V
*(Mosaic
of the Church
of Saint Paul of Rome)*

James I
*(National Portrait
Gallery, London)*

Gregory XIII
(Mosaic of the Church of Saint Paul of Rome)

Clement VIII
(Mosaic of the Church of Saint Paul of Rome)

Père Joseph of Tremblay
(Author's collection)

Cardinal Richelieu *(Louvre Museum)*

Paul V *(Author's collection)*

Top left: Innocent X *(Mosaic of the Church of Saint Paul of Rome)*. *Top right:* Innocent XII *(Mosaic of the Church of Saint Paul of Rome)*. *Lower left:* Pius VI *(Mosaic of the Church of Saint Paul of Rome)*. *Lower right:* Cardinal Giovanni Battista Caprara *(Museo del Risorgimento, Rome)*

Top left: Pius IX *(Museo del Risorgimento, Rome). Top right:* Cardinal Bartolomeo Pacca *(Museo del Risorgimento, Rome). Lower left:* Cardinal Pietro Gasparri *(Museo del Risorgimento, Rome). Lower right:* Cardinal Mariano Rampolla *(Museo del Risorgimento, Rome)*

Cardinal Rafael
Merry del Val
(Author's collection)

Leo XIII *(Author's collection)*

Pius X *(Casina Pio IV,
Vatican City)*

Left: Baron von der Lancken. *Right:* Eugenio Pacelli (at left) *(Both from author's collection)*

Benedict XV *(Author's collection)*

Pius XI *(Author's collection)*

Pius XII *(Author's collection)*

Reinhard Heydrich *(Institute of Documentation in Israel for the Investigation of Nazi War Crimes)*

Father Ivan Bucko *(Commission of Enquiry into the Activities of Nazism in Argentina {CEANA})*

Bishop Gregory Rozman and saluting troops *(Institute of Documentation in Israel for the Investigation of Nazi War Crimes)*

Father Francesco Repetto *(Archivio di Stato di Roma)*

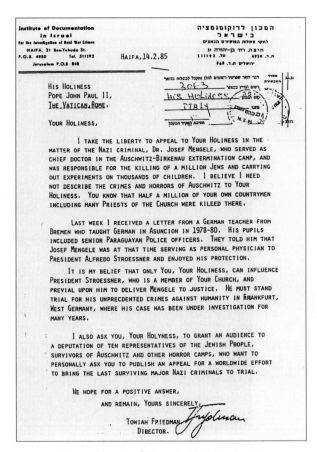

Institute of Documentation
in Israel
For the Investigation of Nazi War Crimes
HAIFA, 31 Ben-Yehuda St.
P.O.B. 4950   Tel. 511192
Jerusalem P.O.B 848

המכון לדוקומנטציה
ב י ש ר א ל
לחקר פשעות הפושעים הנאצים
חיפה, רח' בן-יהודה 31
ת.ד. 4950   טל. 511192
ירושלים ת.ד. 848

HAIFA, 14.2.85

HIS HOLINESS
POPE JOHN PAUL II,
THE VATICAN, ROME.

YOUR HOLINESS,

   I TAKE THE LIBERTY TO APPEAL TO YOUR HOLINESS IN THE
MATTER OF THE NAZI CRIMINAL, DR. JOSEF MENGELE, WHO SERVED AS
CHIEF DOCTOR IN THE AUSCHWITZ-BIRKENAU EXTERMINATION CAMP, AND
WAS RESPONSIBLE FOR THE KILLING OF A MILLION JEWS AND CARRYING
OUT EXPERIMENTS ON THOUSANDS OF CHILDREN. I BELIEVE I NEED
NOT DESCRIBE THE CRIMES AND HORRORS OF AUSCHWITZ TO YOUR
HOLINESS. YOU KNOW THAT HALF A MILLION OF YOUR OWN COUNTRYMEN
INCLUDING MANY PRIESTS OF THE CHURCH WERE KILEED THERE.

   LAST WEEK I RECEIVED A LETTER FROM A GERMAN TEACHER FROM
BREMEN WHO TAUGHT GERMAN IN ASUNCION IN 1978-80. HIS PUPILS
INCLUDED SENIOR PARAGUAYAN POLICE OFFICERS. THEY TOLD HIM THAT
JOSEF MENGELE WAS AT THAT TIME SERVING AS PERSONAL PHYSICIAN TO
PRESIDENT ALFREDO STROESSNER AND ENJOYED HIS PROTECTION.

   IT IS MY BELIEF THAT ONLY YOU, YOUR HOLINESS, CAN INFLUENCE
PRESIDENT STROESSNER, WHO IS A MEMBER OF YOUR CHURCH, AND
PREVIAL UPON HIM TO DELIVER MENGELE TO JUSTICE. HE MUST STAND
TRIAL FOR HIS UNPRECDENTED CRIMES AGAINST HUMANITY IN FRANKFURT,
WEST GERMANY, WHERE HIS CASE HAS BEEN UNDER INVESTIGATION FOR
MANY YEARS.

   I ALSO ASK YOU, YOUR HOLYNESS, TO GRANT AN AUDIENCE TO
A DEPUTATION OF TEN REPRESENTATIVES OF THE JEWISH PEOPLE,
SURVIVORS OF AUSCHWITZ AND OTHER HORROR CAMPS, WHO WANT TO
PERSONALLY ASK YOU TO PUBLISH AN APPEAL FOR A WORLDWIDE EFFORT
TO BRING THE LAST SURVIVING MAJOR NAZI CRIMINALS TO TRIAL.

   WE HOPE FOR A POSITIVE ANSWER,

      AND REMAIN, YOURS SINCERELY,

         TOWIAH FRIEDMAN
         DIRECTOR.

Letter about Josef Mengele (*Author's collection*)

Left to right: Ante Pavelic, Josef Mengele, and Hans Fischbock (*Commission of Enquiry into the Activities of Nazism in Argentina {CEANA}*)

Paul VI and Pasquale Macchi *(Archivio di Stato di Roma)*

Left: Cardinal Paolo Bertoli *(Archivio di Stato di Roma)*.
Right: Father Alighiero Tondi *(Author's collection)*

CERTIFICATO DI MORTE

Certifico che Sua Santità GIOVANNI PAOLO I, ALBINO LUCIANI,
nato in Forno di Canale (Belluno) il 17 ottobre 1912,
è deceduto nel Palazzo Apostolico Vaticano il 28 settembre 1978
alle ore 23 per " morte improvvisa - da infarto miocardico acuto ".
"Il decesso è stato constatato alle ore 6.00 del giorno 29 settembre 1978.

Città del Vaticano , 29 settembre 1978.

(Dott. Renato Buzzonetti)

Visto il Direttore dei Servizi Sanitari
(Prof. Mario Fontana)

Death certificate of John Paul I *(Author's collection)*

John Paul I *(Archivio di Stato di Roma)*

Banco Ambrosiano certificate
(Author's collection)

BANCO AMBROSIANO ANDINO S.A.
L I M A – Perù

Gentlemen:

This is to confirm that we directly or indirectly control the following entries:
- Manic S.A., Luxembourg
- Astolfine S.A., Panama
- Nordeurop Establishment, Liechtenstein
- U.T.C. United Trading Corporation, Panama
- Erin S.A., Panama
- Bellatrix S.A., Panama
- Belrosa S.A., Panama
- Starfield S.A., Panama

We also confirm our awareness of their indebtedness towards yourselves as of June 10, 1981 as per attached statement of accounts.

Yours faithfully,

ISTITUTO PER LE C: :E BI RELIGIONE

IL GIUDICE ISTRUTTORE

Roberto Calvi
(Calvi Family Collection)

Paul VI and
Licio Gelli
(Author's collection)

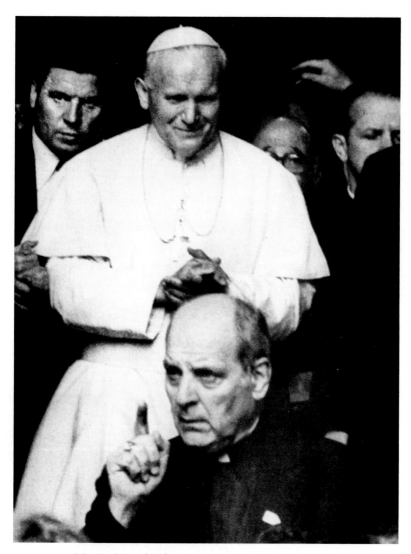

John Paul II and Bishop Paul Marcinkus *(Author's collection)*

Assassination attempt on John Paul II *(Italian Police Department)*

Yvan Bertorello
(Author's collection)

13

ERA OF THE DICTATORS (1922–1934)

There is no sincerity in their mouths; their hearts are corrupt. Their throats are open graves; on their tongues are subtle lies. Condemn them, Lord; make them fall by their own devices, for they have rebelled against Thee.

—Psalms 5:10–11

The Russian Revolution of 1917 gave the Church, Pope Pius XI, and the Holy Alliance espionage service a new enemy: atheistic communism, whose spread threatened to destroy Christianity.

On the morning of April 21, 1926, a modestly clothed figure hurried through the revolving door of the Hotel Moscow en route to the church of St. Louis-des-Français, the only Catholic sanctuary then functioning in the Soviet capital. In his rush, he crossed the plaza facing the Lubyanka, the headquarters, prison, and execution site of the much-feared *Obyeddinenoye Gosudarstvennoye Politicheskoye Upravleniye* (OGPU), the government's political police. Entering the church, he found two people praying at the altar, a middle-aged woman and a well-dressed dark-complexioned man.

Three workers nervously approached the new arrival. Everything was infused with high tension, explicable in a country whose communist regime was hunting, jailing, and even executing those who refused to abandon their religious beliefs. In a whisper, the new arrival introduced himself as Michel d'Herbigny, a Catholic archbishop sent to Moscow by Pope Pius XI on a clandestine mission to set up a secret Catholic hierarchy and an administration that could replace bishops and priests exiled or imprisoned by the communist authorities.[1]

D'Herbigny was not only a fervent Catholic intent on carrying the Church's word to the farthest reaches of the Soviet Union. He was also an expert agent of the Holy Alliance charged by the pope himself with creating a special section of the spy service to prepare the priests who would be sent to Russia to do underground pastoral work.

One of those present in St. Louis-des-Français was Father Eugène Neveu, whom the French ambassador in Moscow had dispatched there on d'Herbigny's request. The recently arrived bishop announced that the Holy Father had appointed Neveu as the first secret bishop and that d'Herbigny had come from Rome to consecrate him. As soon as he left the church, Michel d'Herbigny returned to his hotel. He was told there that he had to report to an office of the Moscow police and that he had to leave the country by nightfall.

First, though, d'Herbigny needed to perform the consecration ceremony for Eugène Neveu as the first Catholic bishop of the Soviet Union. The witnesses would be a woman, Alice Ott, the sacristan of St. Louis-des-Français, and Lieutenant Bergera, military attaché of the Italian embassy in Moscow. Bergera was a personal friend of the pope from their days in Warsaw, when Bergera served as military attaché and the then-cardinal Achille Ratti as papal nuncio.

D'Herbigny gave Neveu a few minutes to prepare. Then the bishop read the document of appointment, in perfect Latin, signed by the cardinal secretary of state, Pietro Gasparri. He placed a ring on Neveu's finger as a symbol of episcopal authority, which would also allow him to ordain priests and consecrate additional bishops.[2]

After the brief ceremony was over, the five people gathered inside the church got ready to depart. Bishop Michel d'Herbigny gave his final instructions to the new bishop Eugène Neveu. The latter had to find the priests Alexander Frison and Boleskas Sloskans, show them his credentials, and secretly consecrate them both as bishops.[3]

Frison was a priest who led a small Catholic congregation in Odessa, on the Black Sea. Sloskans led another in Leningrad. Neveu would always remember the words d'Herbigny whispered in his ear—"remember that now you are a successor to the apostles"—but that did not calm him in the least. After all, some of Christ's apostles had become martyrs in defense of the faith.

From then on, Neveu, Frison, and Sloskans became the leaders of the Holy Alliance network in the Soviet Union, known as *the underground*. Secret missions in enemy territory were nothing new for the Holy Alliance. In recent years, such operations had been mounted in occupied Belgium, in

Turkey, in Austro-Hungarian territory, and even in Germany. In truth, the Vatican had received the first news of Tsar Nicholas's fall with a certain measure of joy, because Nicholas had been a loyal ally of the Russian Orthodox Church against the Roman Catholic one, which had suffered official discrimination and persecution. The tsar's overthrow and the installation of a provisional liberal-democratic government in March 1917 had raised the hopes of the Holy Alliance. Under new legislation, the government moved toward reconciliation with the papacy and with Catholicism in Russia.[4]

All this changed, however, when Vladimir I. Lenin's Bolsheviks took power in November of the same year. The Bolsheviks saw religious belief as a class question. Religion had to be erased from the new society they wished to create.

On January 23, 1918, the Council of People's Commissars announced a new policy toward religious institutions. Church-run schools were prohibited, as was any support for the church on the part of the state. Churches were barred from owning property and from requesting donations from their members. All citizens practicing Catholicism lost their civil rights.[5]

The final blow came in late 1919, when Lenin's government prohibited teaching the Catholic religion to children, not only in schools but also at home. From then on, communication between the Vatican and the Soviet Union ceased.

In response to these anti-religious measures, the Vatican and Pope Benedict XV had vacillated between acceptance and resistance. At first, the then-pope and his secretary of state decided to wait and see whether the revolutionary government might retract its harsh measures against Catholics. At the same time, however, Benedict XV decided to assign Michel d'Herbigny, as a senior member of the Holy Alliance and an expert in Russian affairs, to begin knitting his clandestine web to stretch throughout the Soviet Union. These actions were to be "unknown" to the supreme pontiff, who was to receive communications about this operation only when his approval was necessary for a particular religious appointment, as was the case with Eugène Neveu.[6]

As his last papal decision before his death, on January 22, 1922, Benedict XV signed his approval of a plan to send a mission to Russia.[7] The Holy Alliance took the reins of this operation, sending a North American Jesuit, Father Edmund Walsh, and thirty other priests to various parts of the country to distribute tons of clothes and food to the hungry populace. While these spies were gathering information about the Catholic communities for use in future deployments, Vatican diplomats carried out secret contacts with Lenin—first by way of Rome, through ambassadors, then through Berlin, between Secretary of State Gasparri and the Soviet leader.[8]

Despite the Vatican's giving an interest-free loan of more than ten million dollars to the Soviets, Lenin delayed making any concessions to the Catholics. The Soviet Union signed a resumption of diplomatic relations and economic cooperation with Germany, its old enemy, before it did so with the Vatican. The Church's reaction was not long in coming.

In the spring of 1923, three Catholic prelates and twelve priests were arrested by the secret police and accused of counterrevolutionary and anti-Soviet activities. Archbishop Jan Cieplak was sentenced to life imprisonment and forced labor, later commuted to ten years in prison. His vicar-general Konstanty Budkiewicz, a Holy Alliance agent, was sentenced to death and executed by a shot in the back of the head in one of the Lubyanka dungeons on the night of March 31, 1923.[9]

Thereafter, churches and seminaries and schools were shuttered, while priests were arrested, executed, or condemned to exile. In 1924, on Lenin's death, the aged Archbishop Zerr, of Tiraspol, was the only Catholic bishop both alive and at liberty within the Soviet Union. Some currents within the Church pressured Pope Pius XI to openly denounce Moscow's anti-Catholic policies and mobilize world Catholic public opinion against the danger of communism. After a brief speech to his cardinals to that effect, and on the advice of his Russian affairs expert Michel d'Herbigny, the supreme pontiff, in December 1924, instructed his nuncio in Berlin, Monsignor Eugenio Pacelli, to continue secret talks with Moscow.

On the Soviet side, Foreign Minister Georgy Chicherin led the pragmatic faction in Moscow that felt some kind of coexistence with the papacy was necessary. Pacelli, however, was determined to push for an accord that included official recognition of the Church by the Soviet state. The future Pius XII was determined to pressure Chicherin and even to threaten him with an economic embargo of the Soviet Union by all Catholic nations if Moscow would not accept an explicit recognition of Catholics' rights. Of course, the negotiations broke down.

A range of historians has argued that Pacelli did not want to reach any agreement with "a country of heretics and savages," as he himself put it, and therefore demanded the impossible from Chicherin. The ensuing rupture—sought and found—provoked the torture and execution of hundreds of priests and believers in the fearful Soviet gulags for their defense of the faith.[10] It was clear that Pope Pius XI should have left the negotiations in the hands of Monsignor Michel d'Herbigny, but Pacelli managed to push him aside. Catholicism paid a high price.

D'Herbigny had joined the Jesuit order at the age of seventeen and rapidly become interested in Russian culture and history during his studies in Paris. He was an erudite man but also a man of action. While writing discourses in Cyrillic about Russian philosophy, he took part in the Holy Alliance's programs to spread Catholicism to the farthest reaches of the Soviet Union. When his reputation reached Rome, he was called to the Vatican. By 1922, he was directing the new Pontifical Institute of Eastern Studies and serving as expert consultant to the Congregation for the Eastern Churches, the papal department responsible for ecclesiastical affairs in Russia and other Slavic countries.[11]

The fact is that until d'Herbigny joined the Holy Alliance, the Vatican had been very poorly informed about events in Russia, both in the tsarist period and in the ensuing communist one. Without a nuncio or apostolic delegate in Moscow, the Vatican relied on journalists with connections to the Holy See, who reported on political or religious developments.

Only the Jesuit Edmund Walsh, head of the papal aid mission, sent an occasional report to the Vatican by way of the German embassy in Moscow including such information as troop movements. But the communist government limited Walsh's activities, so the reports reaching the papal spy service tended more toward the flights of fancy of particular diplomats or rumors about what a certain Soviet bureaucrat said to a secretary who was the friend of a military attaché—things of little importance, in fact.

Walsh was replaced by Father Eduard Gehrmann, who continued providing cover for the Holy Alliance in Moscow. In April of 1924, for example, agents reported that Archbishop Cieplak had been released and deported. The priest went immediately to Rome to report to Pope Pius XI. By early 1925, safe refuges for Catholics were few and far between. The Vatican had to create its own network of informers inside the Soviet Union.[12]

In late 1925, suddenly, Michel d'Herbigny received an invitation from the Russian Orthodox Church to visit the country—an action evidently approved by the government in Moscow. His visa read, "vacation and study visit." D'Herbigny traveled to Moscow attired in his black cassock and white collar. Once there, he met with Western diplomats, Orthodox prelates, and with one of the most influential members of the Soviet government, Anatoly Lunacharsky, Commissar of Education and Culture. When Monsignor d'Herbigny returned to Rome, he carried under his arm an incalculable quantity of firsthand information. The problem was that fewer and fewer priests wanted to travel to Russia to take clandestine charge of the parishes scattered throughout the country. A rumor about three priests arrested by the OGPU in a small village of Siberia had reached many seminaries. After being questioned and tortured, the rumor said, the priests were tied to a stake and burned alive. This event never actually happened. It was a story that spread by word of mouth without anyone being able to say where it had originated. Still, many young priests believed it and refused to go to Russia.

While Soviet-Vatican relations were hurtling down their path, Pius XI decided to take action in response to the collapse of Church structures in Russia. He would give Russian bishops papal authorization to ordain priests, officiate at baptisms and weddings, and give last rites. Under this authorization, only bishops could exercise administrative authority in local church affairs. The problem, according to Michel d'Herbigny, was that this power conferred on the bishops by Pius XI would place them in a situation of maximum danger, because the Soviet secret police would need only to arrest the bishops in order to dismantle the religious networks they created. In 1924, in fact, the pope had decided to create an underground network of priests sent from Rome to spread the Catholic religion, but finally he was convinced to abandon this plan because its chances of success were so low, so attempts to achieve the same result through conversations with the Moscow regime resumed.[13] The problem with the clandestine plan was that the papal counselors who could lead it were under strict OGPU surveillance. Those who could possibly survive carrying out clandestine missions in Russia were not bishops but simple priests who knew how to blend into the populace without raising suspicion.

One of these was Father Eugène Neveu, who had first come to Russia in 1907 to lead the French and Belgian congregation in the city of Makeyevka. Neveu held this post until the 1917 revolution, when most foreigners returned to their home countries. Nothing more was heard from him until the Holy Alliance in the Vatican received a simple message from a far-off point in the Soviet Union in 1922, in which Neveu requested a good pair of pants and a world map.[14]

Neveu was brave, ethical, and firmly committed to his superior Monsignor d'Herbigny and the authority of the pope. At the same time, Pius XI knew that Neveu was a man of action, a perfect agent of the Holy Alliance. He would be much more useful in Moscow or St. Petersburg than in Washington or Brussels.

On February 11, 1926, Pius XI called d'Herbigny to his private chambers and gave him the order to carry out a secret mission inside the Soviet Union. The French Jesuit listened in silence to the supreme pontiff's instructions. His orders were to establish a clandestine Catholic hierarchy in Russia. The first step was to be his consecration of Father Eugène Neveu as bishop. As a good Jesuit, d'Herbigny accepted the pope's orders without hesitation.

One day in late March, Michel d'Herbigny left for France, so as to request a visa to Moscow from the Soviet embassy in Paris. From Paris he traveled by train to Berlin, where he met with the nuncio, Monsignor Pacelli. The French foreign minister had meanwhile issued instructions to his Moscow embassy to locate Eugène Neveu and summon him to the Soviet capital to await orders.[15]

D'Herbigny got his first chance to talk with Neveu on April 1, 1926. While the papal envoy and Holy Alliance agent began the secret operations ordered by the pope, he also made telephone calls and had meetings in public places to throw Soviet intelligence off the track. One of Monsignor d'Herbigny's protectors was the German ambassador, Count Ulrich von Borckdorff-Rantzau. The German diplomat provided cover to mislead the Soviet police so that d'Herbigny could finally meet with Neveu in the church of St. Louis-des-Français on April 21.

When the Holy Alliance agent returned to his hotel and found the order to report to the police for interrogation about this mission in Russia, he knew for the first time that there had to be a mole within his organization. He decided to tell no one, however, because this could provoke a panic within the members of the organization now beginning to call itself the underground.

In a second phase of his trip, d'Herbigny traveled openly with Neveu to Karlov, Odessa, Kiev, and Leningrad. For several days, d'Herbigny and Neveu met with priests and seminarians, while they also consecrated other bishops such as Father Boleskas Sloskans of Leningrad and Father Alexander Frison of Odessa. On May 10, d'Herbigny once again met in the church of St. Louis-des-Français with Madame Ott and Lieutenant Bergera, to consecrate Sloskans and Frison as the second and third secret bishops by order of Pope Pius XI.[16]

In truth, d'Herbigny was a novice in secret missions, and his actions in Bolshevik Russia had not gone unnoticed by the secret police. Within a few days, the OGPU had identified all the members of the underground, as well as their supporters and their meeting places, starting with the church of St. Louis-des-Français itself. Because d'Herbigny, Neveu, Sloskans, and Frison were not disturbed or interrogated at first, the pope's emissary did not understand that the entire network had been exposed. What the men serving Felix Edmundovich Dzerzhinsky (the all-powerful OGPU chief) did was to begin detaining the lowest-ranking members of the network. Many priests were arrested and sent to special camps to serve sentences of forced labor. While Michel d'Herbigny went on expanding his network for the Holy Alliance, the Soviet secret service went about dismantling it by way of the weakest links, the priests.[17]

At the end of August, the supreme pontiff's envoy traveled from the tourist-attraction city of Gorky to Leningrad, the former imperial capital. Behind the closed doors of the church of Notre Dame de France, Monsignor Michel d'Herbigny consecrated the fourth secret Russian bishop, Father Antoni Malecki, who had recently been freed after serving a five-year forced labor sentence for "crimes against the Revolution."

Without his knowing it, OGPU agents were following d'Herbigny's every step, but they had orders not to act until they had overwhelming evidence that would allow the Soviet Union to remove Michel d'Herbigny from the scene with a single stroke of the pen and without offending Catholic countries allied to the Vatican. Finally, the police decided they had enough proof in their hands. The Holy Alliance agent's visa was due to expire on September 4, 1926. On August 28, he went to a police station to request an extension and a permit to enter the Ukraine.

The authorities extended his visa until September 12 and told him they would study his request to go to the Ukraine. Three days later, four OGPU agents came to his hotel and informed him he had been declared persona non grata. They returned his passport and escorted him to a train to the Finnish frontier and from there in the direction of the Vatican to inform Pius XI himself.

Neveu was waiting for d'Herbigny in the capital, but he never arrived, so the priest decided to return to the church of St. Louis-des-Français to perform morning Mass. Suddenly, halfway through the ceremony, the sanctuary's doors flew open. A man in worker's attire approached the bishop and gave him a bundle containing money and clothing. "This is from the Holy Alliance," the man said. "May God protect you in your labors from this moment on." Then the man turned around and disappeared as he had come. Thus Neveu learned that he and the underground were alone, unprotected by the pope and the Holy Alliance, relying only on God.[18]

Soviet authorities now began systematically dismantling the Catholic hierarchy in Russia, bit by bit. This increased persecution gave the Vatican and the Holy Alliance a sense of the policy being imposed by the new leader, Josef Stalin, who after Lenin's death had become the strongman of the Soviet Union.

Stalin believed that Moscow's strategic position, owing to its military and economic potential, allowed it to confront the capitalist world. To him, one of the leading representatives of that world was the Catholic Church and its Vatican. To Marxist-Leninists, "the pope was a conspirator and his priests helped to spread conspiracy throughout the world. The Vatican was an ally of the anti-communist powers who wanted to destroy the Russian way of life." Stalin's goal was to spread communist ideas throughout the world. Perhaps that was why, during Pius XI's papacy, the Vatican signed treaties with Fascist Italy in 1929 and Nazi Germany in 1933, two of the most anti-Soviet governments.[19] In any case, to the Soviet leader, the Russian Catholics were potentially subversive, and the OGPU had already supplied clear reports about the intention of the pope's secret service to create an underground network of Catholic priests.

On October 15, 1926, weeks after the expulsion of Michel d'Herbigny, the Council of Ministers adopted a resolution that barred any foreigner from preaching any type of religion. Monsignor Vincent Ilyin, the secret apostolic administrator in Karkhov, was arrested for carrying foreign newspapers under his arm. A few months later, Monsignor Sloskans, who in November 1926 had made his status in the Catholic Church public, was arrested on espionage charges and sent to a forced-labor camp near the Arctic Circle. A week later Bishop Teofilus Matulionis was arrested and sent to the Arctic as well. In February 1929, Bishops Malecki and Frison were arrested, and all Catholic churches were blown up with dynamite by Stalin's express order.[20]

All in all, at the time of Lenin's death, there were an estimated two hundred Catholic priests in the Soviet Union. By 1936, this number had been reduced to fifty. By 1937, there were only ten. A year later, only two remained.[21]

In 1931, the debacle of agricultural collectivization brought increased hunger that required Moscow to radically change its policy toward the West and, therefore, toward the Catholic sector and the Vatican. Catholic rites were once again permitted, and priests such as Bishop Frison were freed, if only temporarily. Once the economic crisis had passed, religious services were banned again, and the clergy arrested and returned to labor camps. In 1937, the Holy Alliance reported to Pope Pius XI that Bishop Alexander Frison of Sebastopol had been executed by a shot to the back of the head in his labor camp cell. He weighed only eighty-five pounds when he died.[22]

Bishops and priests were kidnapped on the street, pushed into black cars, and taken to illegal detention centers, where they were tortured and executed. The cardinal secretary of state occasionally received reports from Moscow by way of the German and French embassies to the Holy See. After late 1926 or early 1927, the Holy Alliance's and the pope's only connection in the Soviet Union was Bishop Eugène Neveu. Because the bishop had been born in France, he could act more freely in Moscow without being arrested, in contrast to what happened to his colleagues born in Russia. Every two weeks, on the dot, Michel d'Herbigny received a report from Neveu, each more disheartening than the last.

The Jesuit labeled all information about Russia as "extremely confidential," while d'Herbigny and the Holy Alliance termed it "highly sensitive." Another of Eugène Neveu's missions was to save antique religious books and icons from destruction. For years, Soviet authorities had devoted themselves to indiscriminately burning religious objects and didactic material, including books. Monsignor Michel d'Herbigny decided to launch the so-called Operation Librorum.

When the Holy Alliance agent in the Soviet capital got word of the operation, he decided to take it on. At first it was a solitary task on a small scale, but within a few weeks, it became a large operation. Eugène Neveu bought seventeenth- and eighteenth-century books for a few rubles. Some others, from the eighteenth century, were donated by their owners to save them from the bonfire. Priests throughout Russia began to send all sorts of religious objects to Moscow, such as thirteenth- and fourteenth-century icons, sixteenth-century images of the Virgin, and occasional fifteenth-century crucifixes adorned with precious stones. When Operation Librorum was done, two years later, the Holy Alliance agents directed by Monsignor Neveu had saved something like a thousand incunabula, nearly two thousand icons, and almost three thousand religious objects such as chalices, crucifixes, and sacred images. The entire collection was given to the Pontifical Institute of Eastern Studies for later cataloguing. It was sent directly to Rome by diplomatic pouch, through the Italian embassy in Moscow.[23]

In the late 1920s, Soviet intelligence concluded there was an underground network run by a Catholic prelate (Neveu) under the orders of a superior in the Vatican (d'Herbigny). Stalin's spies also asserted that the church of St. Louis-des-Français was the headquarters of clandestine operations against the Soviet state. The Holy Alliance lost Monsignor Eugène Neveu in 1936 when he decided to leave the Soviet Union for medical treatment on the French coast. When he tried to return to Moscow, the Soviet embassy in Paris denied one visa request after another, until he finally gave up his efforts to resume operations in Stalin's Russia.

At the end of 1929, Pope Pius XI ordered the creation of a special unit within the Holy Alliance called *Russicum.* This new Vatican intelligence division grew out of the so-called Vatican Special Office, also known as the Commission for Russia. Leadership of the *Russicum* remained in the hands of Bishop Michel d'Herbigny.

The bishop decided to keep the Commission for Russia alive as a kind of institute in which future members of the *Russicum* could be trained before leaving for the Soviet Union. D'Herbigny and the supreme pontiff approved a program of studies that emphasized complete spoken and written fluency in the Russian language, as well as knowledge of Russian history, culture, and gastronomy. The future agents' reading matter consisted only of Russian literature and Russian newspapers. Small groups of students discussed current news, again only in Russian.[24] In a final phase of preparation, two members of the Polish army trained the "recruits" in parachute tactics so they could be dropped from airplanes into different parts of the Soviet Union.

In that same year, 1929, on the 11th of February, another event made newspaper headlines throughout the world and affected the operations of the Holy Alliance in Russia. The Vatican and Italy signed the Lateran Pacts, a series of agreements that settled the so-called Roman question, demonstrating to many countries and their foreign ministries a new level of understanding and communication between Pius XI and Benito Mussolini.[25] A long and complicated series of negotiations to regularize the Vatican's situation once and for all had begun back in 1926. The new concordat finally signed in 1929 allowed the creation of the tiny Vatican state, as specified in Article 26: "The existence of the Vatican city-state under the sovereignty of the Roman Pontiff is recognized." The territory was very small, only forty-four hectares, but from then on, independent action by the popes became easier. In the concordat, Pius XI won two fundamental safeguards from the Fascist regime: the right to religious instruction in public schools, and recognition (in Article 34) of the civil authority of the marriage sacrament as performed under canon law.

For his part, Benito Mussolini, although evidently an agnostic, was conscious of the Italian nation's Catholicism and knew he had to resolve the Vatican question sooner or later. The financial agreement—which was to say, the indemnity that Italy now paid the pope to compensate for its occupation and annexation of papal territories in 1870—first stipulated two billion lire, but Mussolini decided to reduce that.[26] In the end, the sum to be paid as indemnity was fixed at eighty-five million lire a year. A measure that the pope and his secretary of state Gasparri had to carry out, for their part, was to convince the politicians of Catholic parties such as the Partito Popolare to exit the political arena, as would occur in Germany later after the signing of a concordat between Hitler and Pius XI.

Pressures applied by the Holy Alliance to Luigi Sturzo, Partito Popolare leader, led him to opt for self-exile in Switzerland and complete withdrawal from politics. Thus the Vatican repaid Mussolini for what it had won in the Lateran Pacts, while Pope Pius XI himself encouraged priests throughout Italy to support the Fascists, characterizing Benito Mussolini as "a man sent to us by Providence."[27]

The text of the Lateran Pacts was drafted and negotiated by Francesco Pacelli, brother of Eugenio, the future Pius XII. It specified all possible attempts by Catholic groups at intervention in politics and thus would later be used as the basis for drafting the concordat with Hitler's Reich. Clearly, the future supreme pontiff felt an aversion to political Catholicism and felt that the political Catholic sectors could serve as bargaining chips in the Vatican's negotiations first in Italy and years later in Germany.

In November 1929, the pope decided to relieve Cardinal Pietro Gasparri, now nearly eighty, of his duties. In his place, Pius XI named his protégé of nearly a quarter century, Monsignor Eugenio Pacelli. By December, Pacelli was wearing a cardinal's purple. On February 7, 1930, he took up all the powers of a cardinal secretary of state, the most powerful position in the Catholic Church after that of the pope. He was then fifty-four years old.

With Pacelli in charge of the Vatican's foreign policy, Pius XI decided it was time once again to publicly denounce religious persecution inside the Soviet Union. The Holy Father condemned the Bolsheviks' "vicious attacks" while reproaching European governments for their seeming impassiveness in the face of such actions. Curiously, this exhortation was addressed not only to Catholic authorities but to Protestant ones throughout Europe—though not to very much effect.

Soviet periodicals characterized the pope as "a representative of the autocracy seeking to strangle the Soviet Union." They called priests, monks, and nuns "a gang of agitators" and the Vatican espionage service "a tool for destabilizing the ideals of the Revolution and the communist system of life."

Apparently, the Soviet secret services had no reliable source inside the Vatican during the 1920s. The few who had been operating there were discovered by the *Sodalitium Pianum*. In the next decade, however, this situation changed completely.

Cells set up by Stalin's regime began to infiltrate the structure of the Roman curia most efficiently. In Great Britain, France, and the United States, Soviet espionage tended to recruit local agents or Communist Party members, but the Vatican was different. One of the OGPU's most active agents in the Holy See was a man very close to Michel d'Herbigny.

Alexander Deubner was born in St. Petersburg on October 11, 1899. His father, a tsarist official secretly converted to Catholicism, decided to send Alexander to Belgium to be educated by the Assumptionist Fathers, a religious order much interested in Russia.

In 1921, Deubner was sent to a seminary in Turkey to prepare for missionary work. After five years of study, he found himself penniless, so he decided to appeal to his father's friend Archbishop Andreas Sheptyckyi in Warsaw. The prelate assigned Alexander Deubner to be the new parish priest of a congregation of Russian expatriates in the French city of Nice. There he converted to the Orthodox faith, but toward the end of 1928, he decided to renounce this apostasy and return to the bosom of Rome.[28]

Archbishop Sheptyckyi once again intervened in his favor, this time getting Michel d'Herbigny himself to tap Deubner for a position as an assistant in the new department of the Holy Alliance, the *Russicum*. The new researcher impressed d'Herbigny so much that the head of the *Russicum* invited Alexander Deubner to join him in writing a monograph about Russian Orthodox bishops. Deubner rose rapidly in the ranks of the Vatican espionage service, becoming d'Herbigny's most important aide. In the summer of 1932, the *Russicum* assigned him a delicate mission in Poland to do with Church affairs there. This would be the beginning of Deubner's end, and the first step toward Michel d'Herbigny's fall.

For some time, d'Herbigny had been convinced that, in spite of the Bolshevik dictatorship, Russia would someday experience a Catholic conversion. This could happen, however, only if the Vatican were ready to adapt its customs and religious practices to Russian culture, except for what pertained to Catholic dogma itself. The *Russicum* chief decided to send a report to Pope Pius XI and to his secretary of state Pacelli. The cover was marked with the seal "Russified," which meant the document was classified as "extremely sensitive." The text was, in fact, quite controversial, not only for traditionalists opposed to any change in Church rites, but also for those who sought liberalization of Church structures (something not well regarded by the Vatican apparatus).[29]

Many Russian Catholics were of Polish origin and had gone through a transformation from the most recalcitrant Catholicism to the most obedient communism. In the eyes of Stalin's regime, the Polish Catholics were a target to combat rather than convert. Michel d'Herbigny and *Russicum* were very interested in carrying out operations in Poland, creating an underground network of priests and bishops as they had done in the Soviet Union.

During his visit to Poland, Alexander Deubner attracted the attention of the secret services, who were curious not only about his relations with d'Herbigny but also his connections with Moscow. Deubner's father had been arrested by the Bolsheviks just after the Revolution and the fall of the tsar and sent to a prison in Siberia. His mother, who was French, lived in the Russian capital with an uncle of the future Holy Alliance agent, in an apartment within the Kremlin complex. Deubner's uncle was a friend of the famous German communist activist Clara Zetkin. When the *Russicum* agent passed through Berlin, he met with Zetkin. She introduced him to contacts in Germany, including several Soviet diplomats in Berlin who were, in fact, OGPU agents. The police also detected several encounters between Zetkin and the young priest in a small apartment, though they did not specify whether the purpose was sexual relations or exchanging information in a more confidential setting.

At the end of 1932, after being expelled from Poland for acts of espionage, Alexander Deubner returned to Rome in the midst of an uproar.

Diplomats and important members of the curia were spreading a rumor that secret and compromising documents about the *Russicum*'s Eastern European operations had been stolen from the supreme pontiff's desk. The press, as had been foreseen, snatched up this succulent anecdote. Deubner's name became notorious.[30]

Finally, the highest levels of the Holy Alliance demanded that d'Herbigny explain this leak in the heart of the *Russicum.* He could not do so. In an attempt to uncover the truth, agents of the *Sodalitium Pianum* summoned Alexander Deubner, but Deubner had disappeared. His desperate flight was interpreted by many as a confession of guilt. Major European dailies printed headlines such as "Soviet Spy Deubner Flees Vatican," "D'Herbigny's Secretary an OGPU Agent," and "To Moscow with Stolen Documents."[31]

It fell to Eduard Gehrmann, former director of the pontifical aid mission to Russia and advisor on Russian affairs to the nuncio in Berlin, to open the Pandora's box and extract a confession from Alexander Deubner. The fugitive *Russicum* agent confessed that he'd had sexual relations with the communist Clara Zetkin during his trip to Berlin and Warsaw. Gehrmann later learned that Deubner had turned very sensitive *Russicum* and Holy Alliance material over to Zetkin during their encounters, which she had passed on to Soviet agents in Germany. Names, dates, cities, and operations of the Vatican spy services thus came into the hands of the feared OGPU.

As a first step, it was decided to keep Deubner in isolation in a Jesuit residence in Berlin. But three days later, he managed to escape through a window, after which he disappeared from the face of the earth. In February 1933, according to the story put out by the Nazi apparatus, a communist set fire to the Reichstag, the German parliament. Adolf Hitler and his National Socialist Party, on the verge of seizing power, saw their chance to unleash their shock troops against the German Communist Party. The following days saw lynching of communist leaders, newspapers set on fire, and party offices attacked and destroyed. This was the moment in which Father Deubner rapidly exited Berlin.

Apparently, according to an agent of the Holy Alliance, the Nazis were hunting for Deubner because of his presumed relationship with the popular Communist Party member Clara Zetkin. The former *Russicum* agent had gotten involved in an argument with some of Zetkin's neighbors, one of whom was a Nazi leader in the neighborhood.[32] When he tried to cross into Austria disguised as a farmer, he was arrested by German border guards, jailed for two months, and released in late May after having been investigated for possible Soviet espionage connections. Then he dropped out of sight again until he turned up in Belgrade, where he appealed for help from Bishop Franz Grivec, an expert in Russian affairs.

At this point, Deubner called a press conference in which he denied all charges of espionage. Grivec advised him to return to Rome to answer to Pope Pius XI, Secretary of State Pacelli, and the Holy Alliance.

The Vatican counterespionage apparatus had in the meantime put out word in a variety of newspapers that Father Alexander Deubner had been only a temporary member of the *Russicum* with no access to important documents. By the time Deubner reached Rome in July 1933, Monsignor Michel d'Herbigny had been "sent" to a monastery to reflect on his actions and pray for forgiveness. D'Herbigny thought that the Holy Father would soon call him back to Rome to resume his espionage tasks. Alexander Deubner thought he could have recourse to the protection of his former chief, without knowing that d'Herbigny, one of the best papal secret agents, had been exiled from the Vatican on Pius XI's orders.

Michel d'Herbigny had made too many enemies among Roman celebrities and, worse, among high-ranking members of the curia. By 1933, the ranks of the *Russicum*'s enemies had dangerously increased. One of these was Vladimir Ledochowski, the Jesuit superior-general.

What happened next is surrounded by secrecy. All documents dealing with the case remain in the darkest corners of the Vatican Secret Archives. On September 29, 1933, Pius XI placed before d'Herbigny a large pile of photographs of priests confined in Soviet forced-labor camps, who had earlier been recruited by Monsignor Eugène Neveu's underground. Without further preamble, the supreme pontiff told d'Herbigny that Father Ledochowski had decided, on his superior's recommendation, to send him to a Belgian clinic for a rest cure.

On October 2, Michel d'Herbigny vacated his office under the observation of two Holy Alliance agents. That afternoon, alone, he left Rome forever.[33]

In late November, two Vatican counterespionage agents visited d'Herbigny along with Superior-General Ledochowski. One of them pulled from his pocket a document bearing the pope's wax seal. D'Herbigny opened it carefully. In the text, the supreme pontiff informed his former spy that it would be "appropriate" for him to resign from all his responsibilities and positions in the Roman curia. As required by the Jesuit order's strict code of obedience to the pontiff, d'Herbigny signed the document without the slightest protest.

Monsignor Michel d'Herbigny remained completely incommunicado inside a Jesuit residence until his death in 1957. The leaders of the order barred him from writing or speaking publicly about his activities in the *Russicum*.[34]

Meanwhile, thanks to help from priests who had served in the *Russicum* under d'Herbigny's orders, Father Alexander Deubner took refuge in a poorhouse, but he left it two months later. Italian espionage agents found him living in rented quarters in central Rome. He explained that he'd gotten a job in the library of the Pontifical Institute of Eastern Studies. His friends believed this story, but the Italian secret service did not. In September, their surveillance revealed that Father Alexander Deubner made frequent visits to the Soviet embassy. Arrested again, the former spy said his visits were part of his work in the Institute of Oriental Studies. The police discovered that Deubner did not really work in the Institute's library, but made use only of its reading room, and that he was living in his rented apartment without any known source of income. The Holy Alliance informed its Italian colleagues that Deubner had sought a visa to return to Russia but that Soviet authorities, knowing of his connections with d'Herbigny and the *Russicum,* had denied the request while offering him a salary in return for what he knew. Finally, one day, Alexander Deubner was arrested by the Italian secret services with orders for his deportation. Italy asked the Soviet embassy whether they would accept him, but they refused.

Deubner was useful to the Soviets within the Vatican, not outside it. In late 1934, the former papal spy was escorted to the French border. From France he made his way to Moscow, where he hoped to be decorated by Stalin for his services to the communist regime. His dreams did not come true. As soon as he set foot on Soviet soil, OGPU agents arrested him and sent him to a Siberian prison camp. There, one cold night whose date is unknown, he was executed by agents of the communist secret police. An official note sent to the Vatican explained that "Father Alexander Deubner had been murdered by bandits who attacked the work camp in order to rob and kill the prisoners." The secretary of state demanded no further explanations. The Deubner Affair was closed, its records buried in the basements of the Vatican Secret Archives.[35]

Between 1932 and 1939, Italian intelligence services concentrated their efforts on the Vatican, especially on those sectors of the Roman curia that were visibly opposed to Fascist policies.

Italian espionage also devoted itself to monitoring the Vatican's foreign relations with such countries as Spain, France, Germany, and Yugoslavia. Benito Mussolini's Italy wanted to be prepared for the great tragedy that was evidently approaching. No loose ends should be left hanging on the day that soldiers began marching across borders amidst smoke and blood.

The war years were coming, years of death and destruction. After sixteen years of peace, the Horseman of the Apocalypse rode again. The only language commanding attention was the sound of cannon fire.

14

RISE OF THE TERROR (1934–1940)

Thus sayeth the Lord: Woe to the city, rebellious and polluted, to the tyrannical city!
I will remove from your midst the proud braggarts, and you shall no longer exalt
yourself.

—Zephaniah 3:1 and 3:11

The Nazis' rise to power provoked a strong reaction among the upper reaches of the Catholic hierarchy in Germany. The new regime responded to growing protests from the bishops by trying to pacify them in order to gain time to entrench the Nazi party in all organizations and mechanisms of power, including the Church.

Shortly after Adolf Hitler was named chancellor on January 29, 1933, Vice-Chancellor Franz von Papen began secret meetings with Eugenio Pacelli. Pope Pius XI did not learn of these meetings until two years later, when he received a report from the Holy Alliance classified as "top secret."[1]

In these talks, which were first informal and then secret, von Papen and Pacelli crafted the major points that would make up the famous concordat signed by Berlin and the Vatican on July 20, 1933. That agreement committed the Reich to allowing free and public practice of the Catholic religion, recognized the Church's independence, guaranteed it the right to freely appoint its religious officials, and authorized the Vatican to create theology majors in all German universities. But each of these clauses came with conditions. The state could veto bishops' nominations for political reasons. Once appointed, bishops had to swear loyalty to the Reich and the Fuehrer.

The Holy Alliance learned that Pacelli, at the last minute, had decided to include in the concordat a stipulation that no clergyman could belong to any political party or organization. Franz von Papen accepted this point without understanding why Monsignor Eugenio Pacelli so ardently desired it.[2]

A variety of historians and researchers have characterized the signing of this concordat as an acceptance and, in part, a degree of support for Hitler's Nazi regime by the Holy See. Really, it was more of a concession on the part of Pacelli—the future Pius XII—than of Pius XI. To the former Vatican secretary of state, Cardinal Pietro Gasparri, failing to negotiate a concordat with Hitler meant abandoning the Catholics of Germany to persecution. Also, when the document was signed in 1933, the Nazi government had not yet instituted its policy of terror nor the barbarities that soon began.

Pius XI condemned Nazism and its leaders in his encyclical *Mit brennender Sorge,* dated March 14, 1937. As had Mussolini in Italy, Hitler wanted some kind of religious recognition of his regime to increase his international prestige, and there was no better way to do this than by signing a concordat with the Holy See. By early 1939, the situation was very different. Nazi atrocities began to extend beyond the German border. Pius XI then prepared a new text, which he planned to read in the presence of all the Italian and German bishops on the tenth anniversary of the signing of the Lateran Pacts. Because of the supreme pontiff's untimely death the day before that anniversary, his plan was not fulfilled. The document was not made public until Pope John XXIII's accession to the Throne of St. Peter in 1958, almost twenty years later.[3]

In the original text, titled *Nella Luce,* Pius XI highlighted the incompatibility of Fascist ideology and the doctrine of Jesus Christ. Things in Germany were no better. Respected Holy Alliance agents working in the Berlin nunciature began sending the Vatican reports of a Reich department devoted to "purifying" the Aryan race.[4] The Vatican spy service decided to send two expert agents, the priests Gunther Hessner and León Brendt, to Berlin to investigate.

Hessner and Brendt managed to penetrate the mysterious *Rasse-Heirat Institut* (Racial Marriage Institute), Hessner as a steward and Brendt as a cook. Gunther Hessner had been born in Bavaria to a family loyal to Kaiser Wilhelm II, conservative, nationalist, and therefore followers of the new Reich. Brendt came from a mixed family and had been brought up in an ideologically liberal home, logically opposed to Hitler.

The first report on the *Rasse-Heirat Institut* arrived in Rome in 1937, signed by Father León Brendt. The eight-page text gave detailed explanations of women classified as Aryan having sexual relations with leading members of the Nazi Party and SS and SA units. The women were treated as guinea pigs, always accompanied and observed, even during sexual acts with an "Aryan" member of the SS. A Nazi party nurse was always present.[5]

Another report from León Brendt told how some of these women had agreed to be artificially inseminated. The Vatican immediately responded, sending fifty-five protest notes through its nunciature, none of them explicitly referring to the *Rasse-Heirat Institut.* The Vatican in no way wanted to put its infiltrated agents in danger.

But alarm mounted in the hallways of the Vatican when the first report from Father Gunther Hessner arrived. Through a chambermaid of the *Rasse-Heirat Institut,* the Holy Alliance discovered that various hospitals and clinics under Nazi control were carrying out sterilizations and killings of people labeled mentally deficient under the racial laws passed by the Nazi party.[6] Hessner decided to send this report first to three of the most anti-Nazi members of the hierarchy—Cardinal Clement August von Galen, Cardinal Konrad von Preysing, and the Archbishop of Munich, Monsignor Michael von Faulhaber. The latter sent Father Hessner's report on to the Vatican. With all this material in hand, Pope Pius XI ordered the publication of his encyclical *Mit brennender Sorge,* which was secretly read in some German Catholic churches on Palm Sunday of 1937.

Hitler's reaction was not long in coming. Over the next few weeks, Nazi authorities acting through the SS and the Gestapo jailed more than a thousand Catholics, including journalists, priests, friars, seminarians, monks, and leaders of Catholic youth organizations. Early in 1938, 304 of them were deported to the Dachau concentration camp.[7]

Father Gunther Hessner continued to serve the Holy Alliance in various parts of Germany, and he informed the Vatican about the Jewish Holocaust until 1941, when the Gestapo arrested him and sent him to the concentration camp at Mauthausen. When camp guards found him giving last rites to an old Polish prisoner in his barracks, he was hanged. The SS arrested Father León Brendt in April 1940 for helping Jews escape to Switzerland by way of a secret network that he had organized without the authorization of the Holy Alliance. According to some reports, he assembled this network with the support of Cardinal August von Galen.

In response to what he had learned of Nazi measures, Pope Pius XI decided to seclude himself in his residence at Castel Gandolfo so as to avoid receiving

THE ENTITY

Adolf Hitler during Hitler's visit to Rome on May 3 to 9 of 1938. The Holy Father also ordered all Vatican museums closed and requested that *L'Osservatore Romano* not publish a word about the German chancellor's visit.

Meanwhile, in the heart of the Vatican, *Sodalitium Pianum* agents were hunting for spies. Since the late 1920s, the Italian secret services had been infiltrating moles into papal departments. The most important of these was Monsignor Enrico Pucci, a well-connected figure in the realms of the press and papal administration.

Although his position was never formalized, Monsignor Pucci served as an unofficial Vatican spokesman. He wrote and edited a small bulletin that reported on official Vatican events and on papal affairs affecting the city-state. He also freelanced for newspapers throughout Italy. Journalists accredited in the Holy See came to Monsignor Pucci for information about Cardinal So-and-so or about a bishop who had made such-and-such an unofficial statement. Pucci knew everything. Nothing happened within the Vatican's palaces without his being aware of it. From the doings of monks to members of the Swiss Guard, from cardinals to librarians, Enrico Pucci could be counted on to know.

Monsignor Pucci was also Mussolini's best spy inside the Vatican from the time of his recruitment in late 1927 by the Fascist police chief Arturo Bocchini. By the mid-'30s, the Holy Alliance started to get reports about a mole inside the Vatican. Pucci, who reported to Italian authorities as "Agent 99," passed on all varieties of information. His best operation came in 1932, when he succeeded in getting hold of a manuscript copy of Cardinal Bonaventura Cerretti's memoirs. His Eminence recounted in great detail the negotiations and secret conversations with Prime Minister Orlando that resulted in the 1929 Lateran Pacts, settling the "Roman question" about the Vatican's status.[8]

Holy Alliance agents informed the counterespionage service *Sodalitium Pianum* that the presence of a mole had been detected. The S.P.'s agents began trying to identify him.

As a tactic, the S.P. circulated a false document signed by the cardinal secretary of state, Pietro Gasparri. This report stated that a certain Roberto Gianille had been passing information about Italy and the Vatican to Britain's embassy in the Holy See. Of course, Roberto Gianille did not exist. He was merely invented for the purpose.

The S.P. agents succeeded in passing off the report as a real one, and it came into the hands of Monsignor Enrico Pucci. Very quickly, Bocchini ordered that Roberto Gianille be found and arrested for high treason. Neither the Italians nor Pucci knew that Gianille was an invention of the Vatican counterespionage to try and identify the spy. The mole fell in the trap.

Removed from all his official and unofficial functions in the papal administration, Enrico Pucci continued serving the Fascist regime until Mussolini's fall. Pucci's exposure brought the collapse of his network, which had consisted of Stanislao Caterini, Giovanni Fazio, and Virgilio Scattolini, all mid-level Vatican officials.[9]

Caterini, who was employed by the secretariat of state, had been recruited in late 1929. Until his exposure, he was one of Monsignor Enrico Pucci's best sources of information, since he worked in the *Reparto Crittografico,* the Holy Alliance unit in charge of the codes used by the nunciatures in secret correspondence. All communications to and from the Vatican passed through Caterini, who directly informed Monsignor Pucci about the most sensitive matters. For betraying his superiors, he was forced to resign and expelled from the Vatican.

The second member of the so-called Pucci Network was Giovanni Fazio, a Vatican police official. His position gave him access to the dossiers of all religious and lay personnel of the Vatican state. Once caught by the Holy Alliance, Fazio was relieved of his post and dishonorably discharged from the papal security force. He continued to work for Italian intelligence until 1942, when he was found hanged in his own home. Rumors at the time called the hanging an execution and attributed it to the long arm of the Black Order, the underground organization of friar-assassins founded in the seventeenth century by the powerful Vatican espionage chief Olimpia Maidalchini on the orders of Pope Innocent X.[10]

The third member of the Pucci Network to fall was Virgilio Scattolini, a journalist who served as assistant to Monsignor Mario Boehn, the editor-in-chief of *L'Osservatore Romano.* Scattolini had been recruited by the Italian secret services and put under Enrico Pucci's orders in early 1930. Scattolini's task was to infiltrate anti-Fascist journalistic circles and pass the names of their members to Pucci, who in turn informed Mussolini's security forces. Virgilio Scattolini resigned his post after being exposed by papal counterespionage. He continued his journalistic career, writing for a variety of Italian news media.[11]

Evidently, the Italian spy services had not reckoned with the powers of the Holy Alliance and papal counterespionage. The Germans were not about to make the same mistake. After the signing of the concordat, the

Reich's security services decided to strike as hard as possible at the bases of German Catholicism. In February of 1933, Adolf Hitler stated that the Catholic churches made up an integral part of German life. Only a month later, the chancellor declared, "I vow to completely eradicate Christianity from Germany. You are either Christian or German. You cannot be both."[12] The first blow fell on the Catholic lay organizations, which the Nazi regime accused of being the nexus of subversive activities against the Party, the Fuehrer, and the German people. All Catholic newspapers and publishers were closed, gatherings of Catholic youth were prohibited, and religious ceremonies were restricted.

Hitler had given his security and spy services direct orders to keep close watch on German bishops, their communications with the Holy See, the flow of their finances, and the activities of their espionage services. He conferred this task on the *Sicherheitsdienst* (SD), the Nazi Party's espionage service. SD leader Reinhard Heydrich was a true psychopath famous for his cruelty. He was also quite intelligent.

Heydrich was convinced that the pope and his spies inside Germany were a source of continual plots against the Reich and therefore had to be destroyed. Reinhard Heydrich planned to "strangle" the Catholic Church using all the tools at his disposal, including the intelligence services. In late 1933 and early 1934, the SD set up a small unit in Munich designed to keep track of Catholic organizations and their leaders. Its first director was Dr. Wilhelm August Patin, a former agent of the Holy Alliance.[13]

Patin had been a priest and had specialized in theology. For years he had acted as a free Holy Alliance agent in Germany, until Hitler came to power. Years later, it was discovered that Patin was a cousin of Heinrich Himmler, the all-powerful *Reichsführer.*

Patin's unit consisted of only five agents, whose work was mostly routine. His mistake was to complain to his cousin Himmler, going over the head of his immediate superior, Reinhard Heydrich, which cost him his job. His replacement, Martin Wolff, was one of Heydrich's trusted lieutenants, but Wolff occupied the post for only a few months because Heydrich soon named him to run the SD's anti-communist unit. Wolff then offered the anti-Catholic post to his second-in-command, Albert Hartl, who became one the Holy Alliance's fiercest enemies. *Obersturmbannführer* and a former Catholic priest, Albert Hartl was an apostate who now abjured all priests and monks.

He had begun working for the SD in early 1933 as a paid informant while studying at the seminary of Freising. There he met Father Josef Rossberger and became his best friend.

Within a few months, Hartl learned that Rossberger ran an anti-Nazi propaganda network within the seminary, and that he sometimes helped papal espionage agents carry out their operations in the heart of Nazi Germany. Albert Hartl decided to denounce his best friend to the SD.

The next day, while on his way to a meeting of his network, Father Josef Rossberger was arrested in the street and taken to a secret detention center where he was tortured for seven straight days. His betrayer asked to observe the sessions.

Albert Hartl's testimony in the trial of Father Rossberger made a deep impression on the Catholics of Bavaria. No one had believed that the Reich's security apparatus was capable of penetrating the doors of a seminary.

After the trial, Hartl became a protégé of Heydrich, who had begun a brilliant career that took him to the top ranks of Adolf Hitler's security services. The thirty-year-old seminarian knew how to take advantage of his mentor's ascent. Heydrich offered him a post in the SD and Hartl accepted. He left the priesthood and embraced the SD with all the fervor of a convert.[14]

His first tasks were collecting information on Nazi Party members suspected of close contact with the Church or the Holy Alliance, preparing reports on the history of the Inquisition to be used in the party's anti-Catholic press campaigns, and writing an extensive study of Jesuit history and organization, because the Reich security forces admired the religious order for its asceticism, discipline, and goals.

He spent a good deal of time on this work but gradually began to leave it behind. He then returned to it when Reinhard Heydrich appointed him Director of Church Affairs for the SD, a unit also called *Amt II*.[15]

From his office, Albert Hartl controlled all operations against the Catholic Church in Germany. Now that Heydrich had been named supreme head of the *Geheime Staatspolizei,* or Gestapo, Hartl's ambitions were clear. He wanted very much for the *Amt II* to stand out from the rest of the SD's operational units so as to later be absorbed, with all its staff, into the Gestapo. Up till then, the Department of Church Affairs of the Gestapo had been a small office made up of ten agents who processed unimportant anonymous accusations for which they paid out small sums of money. Those arrested by the

Gestapo, among them several Holy Alliance agents, were prosecuted only on moral charges. Albert Hartl wanted to escape from mundane bureaucratic police work and make his unit an important department of the Gestapo's giant assembly of acronyms. He decided to include investigation of Catholic political organizations in *Amt II*'s tasks. Heydrich, he knew, had a deep distrust of them.[16] Hartl's agents thus set about shadowing Catholic bishops, priests, diocesan administrators, politicians, editors, and journalists.

Between 1939 and 1941, Albert Hartl became the principal scourge of the German Catholic Church, leader of the Nazis' own Inquisition against the Vatican, and ferocious hunter of the pope's spies. The small SD Church Affairs unit became an important organization whose members were trained in a school outside Berlin.[17]

Pius XI's health had been declining since the previous November, and he barely had the strength for the 1938 Christmas celebrations. On Vatican Radio, his voice was noticeably weak. He spent most of the first months of 1939 in bed under the care of his personal physician.

On February 4, he got up early to conduct Mass, but a cardiac crisis sent him back to bed. Five days later, renal insufficiency deepened the crisis. He died peacefully on February 10 at 5:30 A.M.

The election of the next supreme pontiff was one of the most politicized in papal history. The Vatican became the first battlefield of the approaching world crisis. Bets on a successor were placed in all the foreign ministries of Europe and America. London, Washington, and Paris wanted a new pontiff who would continue the line of Pius XI, in opposition to the policies of Hitler and Mussolini. Rome and Berlin wanted a more pro-German pope.

The day of Pius XI's death, French foreign minister Georges Bonnet suggested to the British ambassador in Paris, Sir Eric Phipps, that France and Great Britain should cooperate in ensuring the election of a cardinal whose sympathies were clearly democratic and anti-dictatorial. The French minister had an individual in mind, Pius XI's secretary of state, Cardinal Eugenio Pacelli.[18]

Britain's representative in the Vatican, D'Arcy Osborne, assured the Foreign Office that Pacelli stood a good chance of being elected. The francophone cardinals met with the French ambassador to the Holy See, François Charles-Roux, and told him they would be voting for Pacelli. The only dissenter was Cardinal Tisserant, who preferred Cardinal Maglione, former nuncio in Paris with much more anti-Fascist and anti-Nazi ideas than Eugenio Pacelli's.

Germany and Italy were equally active. The Italian ambassador to the Vatican, Bonifacio Pignatti, met with his German opposite number, Diego von Bergen, to discuss their preferences. Both of them likewise favored Eugenio Pacelli, but von Bergen told Pignatti that the Fuehrer had not discarded the idea of supporting Maurilio Fossati of Turin or Elia dalla Costa of Florence.[19]

For Adolf Hitler, Pacelli was the ideal candidate, at the top of his list of preferences. He was a well-known Germanophile, had been an important nuncio in Germany for twelve years, spoke fluent German, and during his time as Vatican secretary of state, he had surrounded himself with an important coterie of Germans.

Ambassador von Bergen was not the only German observer in the Vatican with an interest in the conclave. The *Amt II* was also present. On Pius XI's death, the Third Reich's espionage services had managed to infiltrate an agent into the Holy See. Taras Borodajkewycz was from Vienna, born to Ukrainian parents. He had studied theology and claimed to have excellent contacts within the Roman curia. *Obersturmbannführer* Albert Hartl's department decided to send him to the Vatican.

Unfortunately, Borodajkewycz's contacts were not as good as he believed. Against expectations, his reports to Berlin were not satisfactory. The German spy alleged that one of the strongest candidates to succeed Pope Pius XI was Cardinal Ildefonso Schuster, the pro-Fascist archbishop of Milan. In fact, Schuster did not win a single vote in the conclave.[20]

Meanwhile, several cardinals and bishops had alerted Vatican counter-espionage to the presence of a German agent. The S.P. was determined to eliminate any interference by foreign agents seeking to manipulate the votes of cardinals empowered to elect the next supreme pontiff. But they didn't count on Albert Hartl and his *Amt II*'s ability to bring a pro-German pope to the Throne of St. Peter. To achieve this goal, the SD launched the so-called Operation *Eitles Gold* (Operation Pure Gold). Taras Borodajkewycz was to lead the operation.

The SD's agent in the Vatican had convinced Hartl that with three million marks in gold ingots, the Reich could buy the election. Borodajkewycz assured Hartl and Josef Roth, director of the Catholic section of the Department of Religious Affairs for the Reich, that with this sum of money it would be possible to convince several cardinals to shift their votes to the two German favorites, cardinals Maurilio Fossati and Elia dalla Costa. A wave of optimism swept through the headquarters of the *Amt II* and the Department of Religious Affairs of the Reich in Berlin.

The next morning, the head of *Amt II* was ordered to appear, alongside Josef Roth, for an audience with the Fuehrer. Roth spoke first, explaining to the Nazi leader that if the Third Reich would supply the three million marks in gold ingots, perhaps they could "buy" the election of the new pope. Hartl was much more cautious than his colleague. Intelligently, he preferred to keep more in the background and not appear too optimistic in Hitler's eyes. After all, if Operation *Eitles Gold* did not turn out as hoped, the responsibility would then fall on Josef Roth and his Department of Religious Affairs of the Reich.[21]

Hitler approved the plan and ordered the Reichsbank to turn the three million marks in gold over to Himmler's subordinates. The gold was sent to Rome by special train. While the valuable cargo was on its way to the Eternal City, the Holy Alliance received word of it. A report from the Berlin nunciature informed papal espionage in Rome that a cargo of gold had been shipped to Italy for the purpose of bribing high Church officials and possibly even cardinals who would be asked to change their votes during the conclave.

Taras Borodajkewycz, Hartl's spy in the Vatican, had contacted a priest who claimed to work in the secretariat of state as a messenger between the members of the College of Cardinals. This priest told Borodajkewycz that he would take charge of sounding out Their Eminences. The German agent told his contact that Hitler and Himmler had personally approved a plan to give him three million marks in gold ingots from the Reichsbank. His idea was to keep some of the shipment for himself and turn the rest over to the cardinals who would vote for Germany's favorites.[22]

Borodajkewycz's priestly contact assured him that with this quantity of money, they could live luxuriously somewhere in Switzerland. The German spy feared only the long arm of the SS, for he did not believe that Heinrich Himmler would simply sit on his hands after learning that one of his agents had made off with three million German marks that belonged to the Reich.

On March 1, 1939, at six in the morning, the conclave began with sixty-two cardinals assembled in the Sistine Chapel. On the first ballot, Pacelli received twenty-eight votes, followed by Cardinal dalla Costa and Cardinal Maglione. The necessary majority was not reached, and the vote was repeated.

In this second round, Cardinal Maglione won more votes, a total of thirty-five, which provoked another *fumata nera,* the plume of black smoke signaling an inconclusive vote. At 5:25 P.M. on March 2, Cardinal Eugenio Pacelli won the papacy on the third ballot with forty-eight votes. This was the shortest conclave in three hundred years. Pacelli chose the name Pius XII in deference to his predecessors.[23]

The news surprised the foreign ministry in Berlin, as it did the SS. Heinrich Himmler summoned Josef Roth and Albert Hartl and ordered them to get the shipment of gold back from the SD's agent in Rome, Taras Borodajkewycz. The problem was that for some days, the SD spy had failed to communicate with Berlin. The gold did not appear.

Borodajkewycz's last contact had come on February 27, three days before the papal election. That morning he had met with the priest from the secretariat of state in an apartment in Rome's Trastevere district. After that, he vanished.

The Italian police found the SD spy's body hanging by the neck from the roof of a small temple in one of the Eternal City's parks. The Reich's gold disappeared. Two versions of the story circulated for a long time. One said the German agent Taras Borodajkewycz had been executed by members of the SS sent to Rome by Heinrich Himmler and that the gold had been returned to the Reichsbank's vaults.[24] The other widely repeated version, which grew nearly to the stature of a legend, was that Borodajkewycz's priestly contact was really an agent of the Holy Alliance. This clergyman, allegedly, belonged to a secret society within the papal espionage service known as the *Assassini,* the heirs of the Black Order created by Olimpia Maidalchini in the seventeenth century.

An *Abwehr* report asserted that the SD agent Taras Borodajkewycz could have been executed by a papal agent named Niccolo Estorzi, with whom he had been in contact. The German military spy report claimed that Estorzi was a tall, handsome, dark-skinned man of about thirty with long black hair. Born in Venice, Estorzi had studied in a Roman seminary and, thanks to his knowledge of several languages, spent some months working for the *Sodalitium Pianum.* Soon afterwards, he joined the Holy Alliance, where he carried out special Vatican missions abroad.

Il Duce's secret service had kept Borodajkewycz under close surveillance and even observed his meetings with the Holy Alliance agent. The last Italian espionage report is dated February 26, 1939. It claims that "Taras Borodajkewycz spent the entire day visiting foundries on the outskirts of Rome along with a tall, handsome, dark-complexioned man." Evidently the German agent needed to erase any vestige of the Reichsbank symbol on the ingots, which led him to seek a foundry where he could recast the three million marks into new gold ingots.

Estorzi, it seems, could have made off with the gold after killing Taras Borodajkewycz. From Rome, the valuable cargo may have gone to the island of Murano, across from Venice, home for centuries to famous glass factories. In its ovens, the metal could have been recast into smaller ingots and from there taken to deposit in a Swiss bank, where it would rest under the Vatican seal displaying the papal tiara and two crossed keys, symbolizing those given by Christ to the Apostle Peter.

The truth is that the three million German marks in gold ingots disappeared from the face of the earth without leaving the smallest trace. Even today, the gold employed in Operation *Eitles Gold* remains one of the great mysterious treasures that vanished during the Second World War.[25]

Four days after his election as pope, Pacelli decided to summon the four German-speaking cardinals, Their Eminences Bertram, Schulte, Faulhaber, and Innitzer. During the meeting, Pius XII brusquely informed them that he would continue personally directing the Catholic Church's German affairs. At the end, he showed them a draft of a letter he was sending to Hitler the next day.

While Pius XI had planned to issue a strong protest against Adolf Hitler and the Third Reich regime, Pius XII wanted to moderate that position. His letter said:

> To the illustrious Herr Adolf Hitler, Fuehrer and Chancellor of the German Reich! Here at the beginning of Our Pontificate, We wish to assure you that We remain devoted to the spiritual welfare of the German people entrusted to your leadership. . . . Now that the responsibilities of Our pastoral function have increased Our opportunities, how much more ardently do We pray to reach that goal. May the prosperity of the German people and their progress in every domain come, with God's help, to fruition![26]

Pius XII's explicit support for Hitler and his regime was confirmed when the supreme pontiff ordered Archbishop Orsenigo, his nuncio in Berlin, to open a gala reception on the occasion of the Fuehrer's fiftieth birthday. From that year on, and throughout the years of the worldwide conflict, Adolf Hitler received an annual greeting from Cardinal Bertram of Berlin. The text was always the same:

Warmest congratulations to the Fuehrer in the name of the bishops and the dioceses in Germany. Fervent prayers which the Catholics of Germany are sending to heaven on their altars.[27]

At the same time as Pope Pius XII's birthday wishes reached Adolf Hitler, Hartl and his assistants at SD headquarters were analyzing and processing each bit of incoming data about people and organizations related to German Catholicism, including the Holy Alliance branch inside the Reich. In May 1939, Albert Hartl met with Josef Roth, former priest and theology professor who now directed the Catholic section of the Department of Religious Affairs of the Reich. Roth's job was to maintain frequent contact with the country's German bishops and lay Catholic leaders. His department controlled funds coming from outside the country for bishops and for priests traveling to the Vatican. Roth thus gathered a network of informers with whom he could discuss the results of their meetings in the Holy See. During one of those meetings, a priest told Josef Roth and Albert Hartl that the Vatican, through its espionage service the Holy Alliance, had a spy who came and went in and out of the Reich's territories carrying funds and bringing messages from high Church figures back to the Holy See. This agent was known as *The Messenger*.[28]

Hartl assigned several *Amt II* SD agents to uncover the Holy Alliance's Messenger. All the priests he had interviewed spoke of this figure as if they had met him, but none had actually seen his face. No one could recognize him.

The Messenger spoke fluent German and thus managed to cross easily into the Reich. He was, in fact, none other than Niccolo Estorzi, the member of the *Assassini* who supposedly had eliminated the SD's agent in the Vatican during Operation *Eitles Gold*.

Admiral Wilhelm Canaris, for his part, had chosen a new head for the German military intelligence unit in Rome. His name was Josef Müller. When he stepped off his train onto Italian soil in the Central Station, newspaper headlines were announcing the entry of German troops into Poland. It was September 1, 1939, the day the Second World War began.

The so-called White Plan, meticulously prepared by Hitler and his generals since the previous April, was put into effect on the anticipated day, as the Wehrmacht invaded Poland and the Luftwaffe bombarded its cities and strafed its civilian population. After having conquered Austria and Czechoslovakia without firing a shot, Germany now overwhelmed Poland, which disappeared from the European map.[29]

From that day on, Pope Pius XII ordered the heads of the Holy Alliance and the counterespionage unit *Sodalitium Pianum* to take measures affecting their communications with agents abroad and especially those operating in sensitive or war-torn zones.

Until 1939, the Vatican had used a code known as "Red." It consisted of twelve thousand numerical groups, printed in a codebook with twenty-five lines per page. To heighten security, the Holy Alliance had established that the numerical groups should be converted to letters that would replace the page numbers by way of a diphthong drawn from a pair of tables to be used alternately on even and odd dates. The Vatican's most secret messages—that is, all those sent by the supreme pontiff or those affecting the papal espionage services—were referred to as "Yellow" or "Green."

"Yellow" was a code of thirteen thousand numerical groups used through diphthong tables that represented page numbers and randomized mixed alphabets to represent line numbers. These tables and alphabets rotated every day. The "Green" code, still used today, is one of the Vatican's most closely guarded secrets, but indications are that it involves five-digit numerical codes assigned via short additive tables, each of which contains more than a hundred five-digit additive groups. Neither the "Yellow" nor the "Green" code was a mechanical one, which made them very difficult for the Italian and German intelligence services to break.[30] Out of almost eight thousand Vatican messages sent, the Italian *Servizio Informazione Militare* (SIM) succeeded in deciphering only about four hundred. Apparently, help in this effort came from the SIM's infiltration unit, the *Sezione Prelevamento,* which had agents inside the papal police and the secretariat of state.

News of Poland's tribulations had barely begun. While its thirty-five million inhabitants, most of them Catholics, faced the German blitzkrieg, Pope Pius XII remained silent. He ordered his secretary of state and the Vatican Radio (directed by the Jesuit superior-general Vladimir Ledochowski) to reduce radio broadcasts in German and temper their criticisms of the Reich about the invasion. The Polish ambassador to the Holy See hoped desperately for a public papal protest against Hitler's policies. When the Vatican did not respond, he petitioned Pius XII to grant an audience to the prominent cardinal August Hlond. The meeting lasted two and a half hours, but the result was the same. The supreme pontiff refused to speak in Poland's defense.[31]

Reports on the German war machine signed by The Messenger continued rolling in to the Vatican from various parts of Germany. Thus the Holy Alliance became a real information source for other secret services, both those of the Allies and those of the Axis powers.

Josef Müller, the Abwehr agent, was a familiar figure in Rome, thanks to his many visits to the Eternal City. At the military intelligence headquarters at number 74 Tirpitz Ufer Strasse in Berlin, on the other hand, he was a mysterious, obscure character. Nobody knew where he had come from, which perhaps made him more dangerous in the eyes of his superiors. Curiously, something similar occurred within the Vatican hierarchy with respect to the Holy Alliance agent, the priest Niccolo Estorzi. What no one knew was that Müller and Father Estorzi were friends. Müller, a prestigious Munich lawyer, devout Catholic, and fervent anti-Nazi, had been assigned by Admiral Canaris to contact Pius XII by way of the Holy Alliance. To avoid raising suspicions, Canaris made his emissary head of the Abwehr station in Rome.[32]

Before leaving Berlin, Müller met with Niccolo Estorzi to explain the dangerous mission on which Canaris was sending him to the Eternal City. The papal spy prepared the way for the German agent who had collaborated with the Holy Alliance in earlier times. The Messenger sent a long message in "Green" code to Cardinal Luigi Maglione, who had become secretary of state. These pages were filled with facts about Josef Müller and "Operation *Amtlich Vatikanische*" (Vatican Sources).[33]

Müller, like his Abwehr assistants Colonel Hans Oster and Major Hans Dohnanyi, belonged to the circle of important anti-Nazis led by the retired general Ludwig Beck. Müller first met with the exiled Monsignor Ludwig Kaas (former leader of the *Zentrum* and now archpriest of the Basilica of St. Peter) and with Monsignor Johannes Schönhöffer (a member of the Congregation de Propaganda Fide). The meeting took place in the Dreher beer hall, much frequented by the German community in Rome.

Müller told Kaas and Schönhöffer that he needed to speak with the supreme pontiff in private to give him an important message from high dignitaries of his country and that he had strict orders not to speak with anyone other than the pope himself.

Kaas told the Abwehr agent that he would have to speak first with a German Jesuit and professor of ecclesiastical history named Robert Leiber.

What few people knew was that this Jesuit was a sort of "special affairs" assistant to Pius XII. In Leiber, the Holy Father had a perfect assistant for intelligence matters, and many members of the curia claimed the Jesuit was, in fact, the head of the Holy Alliance. In any case, Father Robert Leiber was well-acquainted with the deepest secrets of the papacy.[34]

During the meeting that ensued between Müller and Leiber, the German told the pope's assistant that a wide circle of high-ranking German officials opposed to Hitler's war policy wanted Pope Pius XII to sound out London about a possible negotiated peace, including a change of government in Berlin.

Leiber, through his agent Father Niccolo Estorzi, knew that the disorganized anti-Nazi resistance could never pull off a coup d'etat against Hitler and his men. What Müller's superiors wanted was for London and Paris not to take advantage of any coup or coup attempt to make military advances against Germany.

Josef Müller's relationship with the Holy Alliance dated from when German bishops and cardinals had discovered that their correspondence was being intercepted by the Gestapo. Thus Müller had become the secret courier between Germany and the Vatican, and vice versa. It was also Müller who helped set up the cover for Father Niccolo Estorzi, The Messenger, in Berlin.

After a brief stay in Munich, Müller was called to Rome through Father Estorzi. When Müller reached Italian soil, Leiber told the Abwehr agent that Pius XII had decided that the German opposition's voice ought to be heard in London. This papal decision launched Josef Müller on a true clandestine mission that encompassed several months and many trips between Berlin and Rome.

Really, Müller succeeded not in talking directly with the supreme pontiff but only in communicating with him through Father Robert Leiber. Müller and Leiber met at first in the Jesuit priest's rooms in the Gregorian University, but for security reasons, the meeting place then changed to a Jesuit church on the outskirts of Rome.[35]

At last, in the spring of 1940, Leiber told Josef Müller that Pius XII had decided to receive him in his private rooms in the Vatican's Apostolic Palace. The meeting would also be attended by Sir D'Arcy Osborne, the British ambassador to the Holy See.

The German repeated his whole story to the pope and Osborne, including the organization of the Operation *Amtlich Vatikanische*. When the Foreign Office was informed, the British government displayed skepticism about the credibility and the declared motives of the conspirators. Winston Churchill did not believe that they had sufficient support within either the military or the civilian population to successfully stage a coup against Adolf Hitler. Time proved him right, when Wehrmacht units conquered France and Holland.

To demonstrate the conspirators' good faith, Josef Müller traveled to Rome at full speed to inform Pius XII that Hitler was preparing to launch a military campaign against France by way of Dutch and Belgian soil. The pope in turn ordered his nunciatures in Brussels and The Hague alerted and insisted they should put the governments of these nations on alert as well.

Leiber secretly informed the Belgian ambassador to the Holy See, Adrien Nieuwenhuys, who sent a cable to Brussels. For his part, Pius XII held a private audience with the crown prince of Italy, Umberto, and his wife, Princess Marie-Jose. The pope underlined the danger threatening Holland and the urgent need for Princess Marie to inform her brother, King Leopold. All these contacts took place between May 2 and May 4, 1940. On the 8th, however, both the Belgian and Dutch governments responded skeptically to the warnings and more so when they learned the source of the information was an Abwehr spy working for the Holy Alliance. That was their mistake. On May 10, the first German panzer units crossed the border on their way to France, blazing through Holland and Belgium in a trail of blood and fire.

The slight attention the Belgians and Dutch paid to the papal warning annoyed Pius XII and led him to order the Holy Alliance to set up secret relations with the British intelligence services and the Resistance in occupied France. By collaborating in secret negotiations with foreign governments and passing German and Italian military information to Allied countries, Pius XII put the Vatican's traditional neutrality in grave danger. The pope ordered his advisor and spy Father Robert Leiber to destroy any papers, including both documents and notes, that bore on the relations between the Vatican state and the Allies or the German resistance.

Inside the Vatican, only three more men knew about those contacts: Luigi Maglione, the cardinal secretary of state, and his two trusted lieutenants Monsignor Domenico Tardini and Monsignor Giovanni Montini. All three carried the secret to their tombs.

The pope ordered his loyal spy and advisor to write up a list of people who could have had some kind of contact with Operation *Amtlich Vatikanische*. On the list appeared Monsignor Johannes Schönhöffer, Josef Müller's friend; Monsignor Paul Maria Krieg, chaplain of the Swiss Guard and Schönhöffer's confessor; Ivo Zeiger, a Jesuit at the Germano-Hungarian College of Rome;

Augustine Mayer, a Benedictine monk and professor at the College of San Anselmo; Father Vincent McCormick, the American rector of the Gregorian University and Robert Leiber's immediate superior; and the superior-general of the Jesuits, Father Vladimir Ledochowski. Pius XII ordered the six clergymen, under pain of excommunication, never to make public any aspect of Operation *Amtlich Vatikanische.* To the rest of the world, even today, none of this ever happened. Thus was forged another legend in the long history of the Holy Alliance.

15

THE END OF THE

THOUSAND-YEAR REICH (1940–1945)

Thou therefore gird up thy loins, and arise, and speak to them all that I command thee. Be not afraid at their presence: for I will make thee not to fear their countenance. For behold I have made thee this day a fortified city, and a pillar of iron, and a wall of brass, over all the land, to the kings of Judah, to the princes thereof, and to the priests, and to the people of the land. And they shall fight against thee, and shall not prevail.

—Jeremiah 1:17–19

Herbert Keller was a dangerous man, ambitious and totally lacking in scruples. A Benedictine monk, he had belonged to a long-established abbey in Beuron, but just before the war his superior had ordered him exiled to a desert monastery in Palestine.

On his return to Germany, Keller had become a sporadic informant for the Abwehr and the SD, the Nazi party's intelligence service. The monk passed on to the Nazis any bits of intelligence he gathered as he traveled through France, Germany, and Switzerland in search of old books and manuscripts for the abbey's library. When Hitler and his armies flattened Poland, Herbert Keller found work more in accord with his ambitions, so he left monastic life.[1]

His career in the world of espionage was always motivated more by money than by loyalty. His first mission for the Abwehr took him to Switzerland, where he made contact with important figures in the anti-Nazi resistance.

Amidst women, brandy, and good cigars, some of these informants let slip the news that certain Abwehr and Wehrmacht officials were conspiring to depose Hitler and that an Abwehr agent named Müller was in contact with the Vatican and its espionage service, the Holy Alliance, through a priest known as The Messenger. Herbert Keller learned that Müller and The Messenger had been trying to negotiate a peace with the Allies that would take hold once they had managed to topple Hitler.

Keller already knew Müller. They had become bitter enemies when the Munich lawyer had helped the Benedictines investigate the matter that led to Keller's exile. Hoping to find more evidence against the Holy Alliance collaborator, Herbert Keller set off for Rome. Within a few days, he knew all the details of the conspiracy and of Josef Müller's mission and his important role in the plot.

Keller returned to Germany with his report. On reaching Berlin, the monk hurried to the headquarters of the Abwehr and the SD. His report was deemed so important that it landed on the desk of Reinhard Heydrich, now head of the *Reichsicherheitshauptamt* (RSHA), the Head Office of Reich Security.[2] The former Benedictine's precision impressed Heydrich, so the powerful RSHA chief summoned Herbert Keller to meet face-to-face. After expressing his hatred of the pope, whom he accused of being the worst conspirator against the Reich, Heydrich told Keller that Josef Müller had been under surveillance since 1936.

Reinhard Heydrich was convinced that Müller was a secret agent in Vatican service, and now that he had in hand a report on the operation called *Amtlich Vatikanische,* he was sure of it.[3] The first inkling of impending disaster for the plotters leaked out through Arthur Nebe, head of the RSHA's criminal police. Nebe made a copy of Herbert Keller's report and sent it to Admiral Wilhelm Canaris, who was in charge of the Abwehr. Canaris took quick action to try to protect as many of the plotters as possible.[4]

Canaris was an enigmatic figure motivated by his loyalty to Germany and by his hatred for the Nazi party and its leaders. Those twin motives led him to aid and protect anti-Nazi currents. To mitigate the danger he saw coming, Canaris asked Müller for an urgent report in which he would claim to have discovered a Vatican plot to make peace with the Allies. As the chief conspirators, Müller should name generals Werner von Fritsch and Walter von Reichenau. Canaris knew that von Fritsch had died in the Polish campaign and thus could not be interrogated, while von Reichenau was a well-known and fervent follower of Hitler and the Third Reich. Neither of the two had ever had anything to do with anti-Nazi circles, but Heydrich would surely be seeking some guilty party who could state that Müller was a spy for Pius XII and his Holy Alliance.

Canaris had been much more skillful than Reinhard Heydrich. When the false report reached the Fuehrer, Hitler insisted that Walter von Reichenau was one of his most loyal generals and it was impossible for his "most loyal son" to have conspired with the Vatican against the Reich. Finally, Hitler called the accusation against Werner von Fritsch and Walter von Reichenau "garbage." The Abwehr chief thus managed to divert suspicion from the Vatican and Josef Müller, at least for a while.[5]

In the summer of 1940, German intelligence once again picked up the trail of Operation *Amtlich Vatikanische*. In May, Adrien Nieuwenhuys, Belgium's ambassador to the Holy See, telegraphed his ministry in Brussels about Pope Pius XII's warning of the impending Wehrmacht offensive on the Western Front. His coded telegram was intercepted by the *Forschungsamt* (Research Office), one of the Third Reich's code-breaking services.

The decoded message reached the Fuehrer, who ordered the Abwehr to carry out an in-depth operation and expose the traitors. Reinhard Heydrich, who still had Father Herbert Keller's report fresh in his mind, was kept at arm's length from this operation because of his report about Werner von Fritsch and Walter von Reichenau. Canaris had maneuvered the SD into being the agency that passed Müller's false report to Adolf Hitler.

To run the new investigation ordered by the Fuehrer, Wilhelm Canaris chose none other than Josef Müller. The German spy returned to Rome to inform the "alleged" head of the Holy Alliance, the German Jesuit Father Robert Leiber, that they needed to invent a story that would convince Adolf Hitler, something that could credibly end with Ambassador Nieuwenhuys's message to Brussels about the German threat. Leiber and Müller put their heads together and invented an operation called "*Wind Westlich*" (West Wind). The two spies' idea was to create an entire spy operation, but working backwards from the end to the beginning.

Leiber proposed that the leak should come from someone in the orbit of Italy's foreign affairs minister, Galeazzo Ciano. Of course, Ciano had been told of the impending Wehrmacht operation by his opposite number, Joachim von Ribbentrop.[6]

The next step was to explain that the information about the military operation had been leaked by someone unknown, close to Ciano, and come to the attention of Father Monnens, a Belgian Jesuit who in turn had passed it on to his country's ambassador in Rome, Adrien Nieuwenhuys. Robert Leiber knew that neither Nieuwenhuys nor Father Monnens was within the German security services' reach. Nieuwenhuys had diplomatic immunity, while Father Monnens was on a mission somewhere in the jungles of Central Africa. Müller and Leiber thought this version would calm the Nazi leaders, but they were wrong. Reinhard Heydrich was not inclined that way.

An Abwehr lieutenant colonel named Joachim Rohleder, a friend of Heydrich's, smelled a rat in the story. Rohleder studied the Belgian ambassador's intercepted and decoded telegram. In the text, Nieuwenhuys mentioned a German source who had left Berlin on April 29, 1940, arrived in Rome on May 1, and stayed in Rome until the 3rd. With these data, Heydrich's friend the Abwehr official decided to review the list of all German citizens who had left the country on that day. Among the names appeared Josef Müller's. He had entered Italy on April 29 and returned on May 4.

Rohleder then contacted the Abwehr station in Munich, to which Müller was attached, to ask whether he had gone to Rome on the indicated days. Josef Müller, the Holy Alliance collaborator, had covered his tracks by reporting Venice as his destination. He had made use of Italian Holy Alliance agents within the Border Guard who had stamped his passport to demonstrate his entry into the beautiful city of the north. But Rohleder remained convinced that Josef Müller's contacts with the papal espionage service were the key to this mystery, and he told Heydrich as much. For a while the investigation stalled, until the Abwehr station in Stockholm took an interest in a well-known Catholic journalist, Siegfried Ascher. Ascher had visited Rome for the first time in 1935. Shortly afterwards, he got a job as secretary to Father Friedrich Muckermann, a German Jesuit famous for his fierce anti-Nazi statements.[7]

Alongside Muckermann, Ascher found his way into all important sectors of the Vatican curia, amassing a long list of friends. In 1937, when the Jesuits assigned Muckermann to Vienna, Ascher went along. When Germany annexed Austria in the so-called Anschluss, Ascher had to escape to Holland and then to Switzerland, where he got a job as Vatican correspondent for the *Basler Nachrichten* newspaper. After the approval of the racial laws, Ascher had needed to change cities, because his hidden secret was that his first name was not really Siegfried but Gabriel. He had converted from Judaism not so many years before.

At the end of 1940, Ascher found a new and better source of income—Abwehr Lieutenant Colonel Joachim Rohleder. The German counterespionage official had not given up his investigation of Josef Müller. Armed with valuable anti-Nazi credentials from his work with Father Muckermann, Ascher began to penetrate the security barriers with which Pope Pius XII had surrounded the Holy Alliance after the *Amtlich Vatikanische* case.

In January 1941, Siegfried Ascher was ready to travel to Rome from Berlin after having gone through rigorous training in the Abwehr's school for agents.[8]

Ascher got the editor of the *Basler Nachrichten* to write him a letter of accreditation as correspondent in the Holy See. The Abwehr spy told his boss that he didn't need payment, because he would be paid directly by the Vatican. Of course, he was lying. At the end of April, Siegfried Ascher met in Berlin with Lieutenant Colonel Rohleder to get the necessary funds for his trip to Rome. Before leaving, he telephoned the Vatican's nuncio, Cardinal Cesare Orsenigo, asking him for a letter of introduction. The cardinal referred Ascher to an influential figure in the Vatican secretariat of state, Monsignor Giovanni Montini, the future Pope Paul VI. In the Holy See, within only one week, Siegfried Ascher was received by Montini, Father Leiber, and Monsignor Kaas. Thanks to his cover as a journalist specializing in Church affairs, nobody suspected him at first. But Father Robert Leiber could not believe that someone of Jewish origin could travel freely through Germany. Leiber contacted his agent Niccolo Estorzi, The Messenger, to find out all he could about Ascher.

Leiber also got a warning from the highest official of the Benedictine order that Ascher might have had contacts with Herbert Keller, the SD agent and former monk. Estorzi told Leiber that a Jew masquerading as a journalist had recently been trained at the Abwehr school, in the counterespionage division, and that perhaps he was Swedish in origin.

Leiber then called Siegfried Ascher, planning to ask him about his travel through Germany. The spy excused himself from meeting with Leiber, claiming work pressures made it impossible. Robert Leiber then told Montini that his Holy Alliance agent in Germany had asserted that Siegfried Ascher might be a dangerous Gestapo agent.[9]

The fact was that by late February 1941, Rohleder's agent had a more or less clear idea of Josef Müller's mission in the Vatican and of Pius XII's complicity in warning the Dutch and Belgian governments in the spring of 1940 about the possible German intervention that soon came to pass.

Siegfried Ascher's final report was absolutely conclusive, and Rohleder communicated this to Canaris. The Abwehr chief tried to downplay the report, saying that without more concrete proof, it would be impossible to arrest one of his agents most skilled in Vatican affairs. Admiral Wilhelm Canaris was not going to let Rohleder and Ascher capture Müller. Finally, the report, labeled "Müller, Josef," was hidden in the depths of the Reich's military intelligence archives.

In late 1942, the SS arrested Ascher on a street in Berlin. Someone had filed a report in the form of an accusation, conveniently demonstrating the German spy's Jewish origin. Ascher was turned over to the Gestapo without the Abwehr being informed. When Lieutenant Colonel Joachim Rohleder, head of counterespionage, learned of Ascher's arrest, it was too late. The journalist had died under interrogation. Various writers and historians have said that by this time, Canaris had fallen into disgrace in Hitler's eyes, and a chasm had opened between the Reich's security forces, the Abwehr and the SS. Perhaps for this reason, when Himmler's SS agents got the report demonstrating the Abwehr agent's Jewish origins, they preferred to turn him over to the Gestapo for interrogation.[10]

Other sources claim that during the months before Siegfried Ascher's arrest by the SS, The Messenger of the Holy Alliance had been traveling through Holland and Sweden gathering information about the journalist. In fact, it was Father Robert Leiber, head spy of Pius XII, who ordered Father Niccolo Estorzi to set up this way of getting rid of the dangerous Siegfried Ascher. Once again, the long arm of the Vatican's Holy Alliance had struck a decisive blow against one of its enemies.

Meanwhile, Josef Müller, thanks to protection from Colonel Hans Oster and Major Hans Dohnanyi, both members of the anti-Hitler network, was named head of the Abwehr station in the Vatican.

A new danger faced the Holy See with the arrival of another German spy. Paul Franken reached Rome in February 1943 to serve as a history professor in a German school on the Nomentana, though in fact he was a military spy.

His preferred contacts were Josef Müller, Monsignor Kaas, Krieg, Schönhöffer, Ivo Zeiger, and the head of papal spies, Robert Leiber. Because of his background as a Catholic student who had been involved in workers' movements before the war, Franken had been arrested by the Gestapo and sentenced to two years in prison for activities against the regime.[11] All this helped him to swim in the deep and dark waters of the Roman curia.

Jacob Kaiser, a former labor leader, recruited Franken for the Abwehr because of his knowledge of Vatican politics, and that was what caused him to be sent to the Holy See. Leiber once again got in contact with The Messenger, in search of information about Franken. Two weeks later, Estorzi sent his chief a coded message from an Austrian city. The message, coded in "Green," was deciphered. The Holy Alliance agent's text warned Leiber about Paul Franken's true intentions, though without many definitive statements. Pius XII's spy decided to keep the German "in quarantine."[12]

On July 25, 1943, the Holy Alliance's alarm bells rang again when King Victor Emmanuel II, supported by generals and Fascist leaders, decided to dismiss Mussolini and name Marshal Pietro Badoglio as his replacement. *Il Duce*'s dreams of creating a new Roman empire dissolved at the same rate as the Italian army. The Allies had invaded Sicily on July 10, with the goal of freeing the entire Italian peninsula from the German yoke. After Mussolini's fall, Hitler, anticipating the collapse of the Italian army, decided to send German troops to northern Italy. News reaching the Vatican from its agent Niccolo Estorzi gave clear indications that Wehrmacht units were assembling to prepare for an assault on Rome. The papal spy's warnings came true on September 8, when Badoglio officially announced the signing of an armistice with the Anglo-U.S. forces that had by now occupied the southern part of the country. Hitler and his generals gave the go-ahead for German occupation of the Eternal City.[13]

The German leader's intentions were unclear. Rumors spread through Rome that the Fuehrer was convinced that Pius XII and his spy services had helped bring down Mussolini. In any case, papal authorities did not have many illusions about the respect Hitler would show for Vatican neutrality or the figure of the supreme pontiff. According to reports that papal espionage had already gathered, in the spring of 1941, during a meeting between the Italian foreign affairs minister, Count Galeazzo Ciano, Hitler's foreign minister Joachim von Ribbentrop had suggested the possibility of expelling Pius XII from Rome, because "the new Europe has no room for the papacy. In the new Europe dominated by National Socialism, the Vatican will be reduced to a mere museum."[14] In spite of calming messages from the Italian government, the rumors grew ever more real toward the end of 1943, the Nazis' tenth year in power. By then, German paratroopers already controlled the perimeter of the Piazza di San Pietro under the apprehensive eyes of the Swiss Guard.

Anticipating an attack on Rome by the troops of the Third Reich, foreign embassies had destroyed documents classified as "secret" or "sensitive," as well as their cryptographic coding machines. The Swiss Guard's commander received word that the Holy Father did not want any bloodshed and that his troops were not to resist a German invasion of the Vatican if it came.[15]

The officer refused to accept such an order, and he had to be called personally before the pope to confirm it. In fact, Hitler's plans did not include capturing the Vatican or the supreme pontiff. Adolf Hitler found himself between pressures from two sides. Josef Goebbels, the Reich's sinister Minister of Propaganda, told the Fuehrer that an invasion of the Vatican would have a devastating effect on world public opinion. Joachim von Ribbentrop, the foreign minister, advised Hitler to take advantage of the opportunity to rid himself of such a nuisance as the pope.[16]

In May of 1944, Paul Franken returned to Germany just as the Allied armies threatened to take Rome from the Axis. In February, after a series of mistakes by the Abwehr and the desertion of several of its members, Hitler had signed a decree subordinating it to the RSHA, the Nazi organization that controlled all the police and intelligence forces of the Reich. Admiral Canaris was demoted to a lesser job in the war economy department, while the Gestapo grew ever more interested in the strange contacts between civilians and Abwehr personnel.

Their investigations led to the arrest of Colonel Hans Oster and Major Hans Dohnanyi, two of the most important anti-Nazi thinkers in the Abwehr. Both refused to talk about their contacts with the Vatican and the Holy Alliance, despite being tortured. Finally they were executed. Each man was shot in the back of the head and his body hung from a butcher's hook.

The next to face arrest and brutal interrogation was Josef Müller. The agent denied all charges and any role in anti-Nazi plots involving the Vatican. He was one of the few Abwehr members to escape death.

Paul Franken, for his part, resigned his post in the Wehrmacht's military intelligence, trying to avoid the attention of the Gestapo and the SS. He got a new job as a translator for Italian workers in Germany. He managed to survive the Nazi regime and the war.[17]

In those years, everyone in the Vatican, and especially the Roman curia, was in favor of one side or the other. The Vatican secretary of state, Cardinal Maglione, and his top aides, Monsignors Montini and Tardini, had given orders to all high-ranking members of the curia not to talk or maintain any kind of contact with members of the German embassy to the Holy See.

Soon, however, the Holy Alliance reported nearly daily contacts by Bishop Alois Hudal,[18] the pro-Nazi rector of the German religious schools in Rome, with high members of the Third Reich's diplomatic staff. In a few years, Hudal would become one of the key figures in the "Odessa"[19] organization, created by former SS members to help war criminals escape to South America along the so-called Vatican Ratline. Little by little, the tide of war turned against the Axis. The remnants of Germany's glorious Sixth Army surrendered to the Red Army at Stalingrad; in Africa, Marshal Erwin Rommel's powerful Afrika Korps surrendered along with Italian units to the Anglo-U.S. forces, leaving the Mediterranean coast open to the landing in Sicily. U.S. bombers tirelessly pummeled the Nazi war industries, while the British reduced entire cities to ashes, as in the case of Dresden, bombed on Tuesday, February 14, 1945, in revenge for the Nazi bombardments of London.

Ernst von Weizsäcker, who had replaced Diego von Bergen as head of the German embassy in the Holy See, wanted papal mediation to end the war, but this was merely a dream. Now he needed to convince Pope Pius XII to negotiate a European peace that would avoid a total German defeat with the concomitant "Sovietization" of the whole continent or of Eastern Europe at the least. There were two spies left in the diplomatic legation, Harold Friedrich Leith-Jasper, whose cover position was press attaché, and Carl von Clemm-Hohenberg, an obscure intelligence officer assigned as commercial attaché. In the fall of 1942, Leith-Jasper informed Berlin of repeated trips by Myron Taylor, President Roosevelt's representative to the Vatican. Curiously, despite the U.S. being at war with Italy, Taylor could enter and leave Rome without problems. This report reached Heinrich Himmler in Berlin. The powerful SS chief ordered Carl von Clemm-Hohenberg to "liquidate" Myron Taylor during one of his trips. The order went through the German foreign affairs ministry, in a special dispatch.

At the same time, another dispatch arrived at Holy Alliance headquarters in the Vatican, informing them of the possible assassination of an Allied diplomat. Father Robert Leiber reported the information gathered by his agent, Father Niccolo Estorzi, to the supreme pontiff.

The Holy Alliance also alerted U.S. and British secret services to the threat, adding the contents of another dispatch from the same source, which said that three Gestapo agents had been sent to Rome to carry out the attempt. Leiber knew he had to save the American representative. On the morning of January 22, 1943, the three Nazi agents reached Italy by train and were aided by Italian agents. They moved into a small apartment from which they planned to run the operation.

For weeks, they watched Myron Taylor's every move. Finally, at the end of February, they decided it was time to strike. Their plan was to follow the American diplomat's car and machine-gun it at a propitious moment. The day before the attempt, one of the Gestapo agents disappeared without a trace, but his two partners decided to go ahead.

On a highway leading out of Rome, the two Nazi agents saw their target parked by the side of the road. They opened their windows and started shooting at the car and its single passenger, and then they fled.

After the shooting, they returned to the train station and disappeared. Once in Berlin, they reported to Himmler to tell him of their successful operation. That was a mistake. The man they had killed in the diplomat's car was the vanished Nazi agent. Someone had kidnapped him, drugged him, and put him in the car. Myron Taylor continued his special missions between Washington and the Vatican for President Roosevelt, without ever knowing that the papal spy service had saved his life.

It was Harold Friedrich Leith-Jasper who informed Himmler that a German secret agent had seen Myron Taylor entering the Vatican alive, to the surprise of the much-feared SS chief.

The Reich's intelligence operations aimed at the Vatican and the Holy Alliance multiplied in the last years of the war. In June 1941, Walter Schellenberg, a young and fanatical officer, had taken control of *Amt VI,* the RSHA division in control of foreign espionage. From then on, *Amt VI* was in ultimate charge of intelligence operations in the Vatican.

With the creation of the RSHA, Albert Hartl's intelligence section for Church affairs was transferred to the Gestapo, the secret police. Hartl, the SD specialist, was not much liked by the Gestapo commanders, mainly because he defended his own freedom of action, preferring to do his work without indiscreet observation by colleagues.[20]

Hartl was also accused of hiding important information and knowledge from his opposite numbers in other security departments. This charge reached the ears of the Heinrich Müller, head of the Gestapo, who viewed Hartl's methods with hostility. He decided to open an investigation to gather evidence that would allow him to charge Hartl with high treason. A week later, Müller concluded that Hartl, the former priest, was in fact a Jesuit and a double agent serving the Holy Alliance from inside the German secret services.

Adding to his troubles, Hartl had made himself famous in Berlin's nightlife scene for his sexual conquests. His indiscretions with female RSHA personnel had brought him serious sanctions, but he was not inclined to sacrifice his personal life for the Fuehrer's cause.

During a trip from Vienna to Berlin, Albert Hartl tried to seduce a sixteen-year-old girl who turned out to be the daughter of a high SS officer. Heinrich Müller then decided to demote Hartl and assign him to the Jewish extermination squads on the Russian front. When Reinhard Heydrich learned this, he issued a counterorder. In memory of past services rendered, Albert Hartl was sent as an RSHA field officer to Kiev, with the task of controlling public opinion in the occupied Ukraine. The man who had created one of the Nazis' most effective units for use against the Vatican and the Holy Alliance never again ran an espionage operation. From then on, Third Reich intelligence services responded to the "Heydrich Directive."

In 1941, Heydrich had attended a conference at Gestapo headquarters, at which the most important topics had been espionage operations against the Catholic Church, which included the "Vatican International Policy and Our Intelligence Operations" and "Intelligence Operations in the Conflict with the Political Catholicism within the Reich." Heydrich had spoken to those present about the need to improve espionage against the papacy through counterespionage operations to detect agents of the Holy Alliance and the *Sodalitium Pianum* in Germany and the occupied countries.[21]

The so-called Heydrich Directive ordered all the Reich's espionage and security forces to double their efforts to penetrate Vatican security. The first measure implementing the Directive was the dispatch of RSHA agents to all German embassies to collect information on Vatican connections in each country. This was Reinhard Heydrich's idea, and he convinced Joachim von Ribbentrop, the foreign minister, to create "police attachés" in the foreign legations. The police attaché in Germany's Vatican embassy was Richard Haidlen, an unscrupulous man loyal to Heydrich.

In early 1942, Haidlen was replaced by Werner Picot, a policeman well-connected inside the RSHA and the foreign affairs ministry. Picot was also a loyal Heydrich man. Each day, the all-powerful head of the Central Security Department of the Reich was kept informed about the actions of foreign secret services, the Holy Alliance, and the Italian intelligence service by concise reports that Picot wrote personally. Little by little, Werner Picot became a fixture at social events in the palaces of the Holy See, where he was invited by pro-Fascist cardinals. When the RSHA officer was out of the embassy, Heydrich turned the security work over to Major Herbert Kappler, the police attaché at the German embassy to Italy.[22] Kappler was a violent man, a lover of torture. He was short and blond and had a face scarred from the duels of his youth.

Kappler's first agent inside the Vatican was the assistant to a professor at the Gregorian University, the Jesuit university in Rome. This man had volunteered his services after reading Hitler's political manifesto *Mein Kampf*. Kappler's spy used his position at the Gregorian to open professors' mail and listen to their conversations so as to personally inform Herbert Kappler later. Named monitor in charge of students, the spy was called to Berlin by Archbishop Michael von Faulhaber. The *Sodalitium Pianum* had informed Pius XII's spy Robert Leiber about a supposed German agent in the Gregorian University. On Leiber's insistence, the German spy was sent back to Berlin.

Another of the famous Nazi spies in the Vatican was Alfred von Kageneck, son of an aristocratic German Catholic family. Recruited by Kappler's assistant Helmut Loos in May 1940, Kageneck was sent to Rome because of his excellent relations with Father Leiber, a family friend. On each trip to Rome, the German spy gathered important information for his superiors in Berlin, but what no one knew until after the war was that Kageneck actually worked for the Holy Alliance's *Teutonicum,* the papal counterespionage division in charge of feeding disinformation to the Third Reich's security services.[23]

Both Kappler and Loos were convinced that at last they had managed to penetrate the hermetic papal spy services. Alfred von Kageneck had been recruited by the Holy Alliance in April of that same year and immediately assigned to the *Teutonicum* by Father Robert Leiber. During his first trip to Rome, Kageneck confessed his connections with the Nazis' *Amt VI* to the Jesuit, as well as the purpose of his visit. Leiber informed Pope Pius XII and the Jesuit superior-general. Both advised Leiber to continue his contacts with the double agent.

For each meeting, the Holy Alliance prepared a report with documents that would appear important and sensitive. The *Teutonicum* agent in turn passed them on to Helmut Loos at the German embassy in Rome.

In the following years, information came and went from the Vatican to Berlin and vice versa, always by way of Alfred von Kageneck. The double agent betrayed to the Holy Alliance the names of German spies recruited by *Amt VI* to infiltrate the Vatican. His reports brought down Charles Bewley, a former Irish diplomat who had been ambassador in Germany and the Vatican. They also brought the downfall of Werner von Schulenberg, a German ex-army officer who had retired to Rome in hope of becoming a writer. Schulenberg frequented the aristocratic and intellectual circles of the Eternal City on the pretext of strengthening German-Italian cultural relations. Both Bewley and Schulenberg worked for the German spy apparatus for money.[24]

Heydrich was determined to penetrate the halls of the Vatican one way or another. He suggested to various priests loyal to the Reich that they should lend their hands to the effort. One of the most effective was the director of the College of Santa Maria dell'Anima—or simply "Anima" for short—a religious center near the Piazza Navona. The director was Bishop Alois Hudal, whom the Holy Alliance called the "Black Bishop" because of his sympathies for the Nazi regime and Heinrich Himmler. At first Hudal had been declared persona non grata by the secretariat of state because of a *Sodalitium Pianum* report suggesting the Austrian was really an agent of the Third Reich's secret services.

Alois Hudal had important social relations with members of the powerful Roman curia, so he circulated easily in its carpeted salons. One day the Holy Alliance informed Robert Leiber that Hudal was writing a paper he planned to present to both Adolf Hitler and Pope Pius XII. The paper put forth a series of arguments in favor of reconciliation between the Catholic Church and the National Socialist regime. Leiber ordered his agents to make off with the document before it could become public. He gave that mission to Alfred von Kageneck, the Holy Alliance spy in the RSHA. Kageneck had been introduced to Hudal during a Holy Week celebration in 1941. It didn't take much for him to get a job at the Anima promoting German-Italian cultural relations.

When the original document was nearly complete, the manuscript disappeared from Hudal's safe. It was never found, but some sources allege that it found its way to Leiber and from him to the pope, who ordered it sent to the Vatican Secret Archive where it still rests today, long forgotten. Several writers and historians have claimed that the document clearly showed Pius XII's knowledge of the "Final Solution"[25] to the Jewish problem and the extermination of Orthodox Serbs by pro-Nazi Croatian dictator Ante Pavelic's Ustashe movement. The pope always refused to send a clear message of protest and condemnation of these atrocities.[26]

Pope Pius XII and the members of the papal espionage services had for years seen the Croats as the Catholic Church's outpost in the Balkans. When Hitler decided to invade the country on April 6, 1941, as part of his offensive against Greece, the Croatian Fascists declared independence. On the 12th, Adolf Hitler announced a plan that awarded "Aryan" status to an independent Croatia led by Ante Pavelic. Pavelic's group, the Ustashe,[27] had opposed the formation of a southern Slavic kingdom after the First World War.

Between 1941 and 1945, the Ustashe carried out a terror campaign based on the systematic killing of Orthodox Serbs, gypsies, Jews, and communists. Ante Pavelic's idea was to create a pure Catholic Croatia through forced conversion, deportation, and extermination. The massive torture and killing were so terrible that even some members of German army units sent reports to their superiors in Berlin denouncing the Ustashe excesses.

The historical legacy behind the formation of the so-called NDH (*Nezavisna Drzava Hrvatska,* or Independent State of Croatia) consisted of a combination of old loyalties to the papacy that dated back thirteen centuries and a flaming resentment of the Serbs and their Orthodox religion because of injustices committed in the past.[28] For the Catholic Croats, the Serbs were guilty of favoring the Orthodox religion, encouraging schisms among Catholics, and colonizing Catholic areas so as to make them majority Orthodox. From the start of Pavelic's government, Pius XII publicly supported Croatian Catholic nationalism. He stated during a pilgrimage of Croats to Rome in November 1939 that the Ustashe were "the great outpost of Christianity," using the same words that had been spoken by Leo X. "The hope of a better future seems to be smiling on you, a future in which the relations between Church and State in your country will be regulated in harmonious action to the advantage of both," said Pius XII to the group who had come to the Vatican under the leadership of Archbishop Alojzije Stepinac of Zagreb.[29]

On April 25, 1941, the new authorities decreed a ban on all printed materials in the Cyrillic alphabet. A month later they approved anti-Semitic laws. At the end of May, the first Jews of Zagreb were deported to extermination camps. The Holy Alliance began to send coded telegrams to Father Robert Leiber in the Vatican about massacres of civilians and of Orthodox priests. Mysteriously, the secretariat of state urged its agents deployed in the Independent State of Croatia to avoid any "brushes" with the authorities.

On July 14 of that same year, the Croatian minister of justice gathered the country's bishops to inform them that an important sector of the population, mostly of Orthodox religion, should not be included in the forced conversions so as "not to contaminate Catholicism in Holy Croatia." When Stepinac asked what to do with those people, the official replied, "The options for them are deportation or extermination."

On this premise the Ustashes, whom the pope had called the "great outpost of Christianity," set out on a wave of indiscriminate killing. Holy Alliance agents, despite the warnings coming from the Vatican, continued to document the atrocities.[30]

On April 28, 1941, an agent who signed his communications with the initials *L.T.* sent Father Leiber a report describing how "a band of Ustashe attacked six villages in the Bjelovar district and detained 250 men, including a schoolteacher and an Orthodox priest. The victims were made to dig a ditch and were bound with wire. Then they were pushed into the ditch and buried alive." Another report that came through an agent of the papal counterespionage unit *Sodalitium Pianum* and was dated May 11, 1941, said: "The Ustashe took 331 Serbs prisoner, including an Orthodox Serbian priest and his nine-year-old son. The victims were hacked to pieces with axes. The priest was forced to pray while his son was torn apart. Later they tortured him, pulling out his beard, gouging out his eyes, and skinning him alive."

After the massacre, about which the Vatican had been informed by its secret agents, Pavelic (who styled himself *Poglavnik,* the Croatian equivalent of the German Fuehrer) decided to visit Italy to sign a pact with Benito Mussolini. During this visit, Ante Pavelic had a secret meeting with Pius XII. The *Poglavnik*'s action of kissing the papal ring not only symbolized the Holy See's recognition of the Independent State of Croatia but also sealed the pope's silence about the past and future atrocities committed by the Ustashe mobs in the name of the Catholic religion.

In his book *Hitler's Pope: The Secret History of Pius XII,* writer John Cornwell states that almost 487,000 Orthodox Serbs and 27,000 gypsies were killed between 1941 and 1945. Some 30,000 to 45,000 Jews who made up the Jewish community of Yugoslavia died as well. Of these last, 20,000 to 22,000 perished in Ustashe concentration camps, while the rest were deported to the gas chambers.

The Archbishop of Zagreb, Alojzije Stepinac,[31] supported the fundamental principles of the new State of Croatia from the outset and pressured Pope

Pius XII to recognize Ante Pavelic as one of the principal bulwarks of the Catholic Church in Slavic Europe. To Stepinac, Pavelic was "a sincere Catholic," as the monsignor wrote in his diary. From the pulpit he asked his parishioners to offer their sincere prayers for the *Poglavnik,* while other priests, always Franciscans, actively participated in the massacres.[32]

A Holy Alliance agent reported to the Vatican:

> Many of them [Franciscan priests] go around armed and carry out their murderous actions with extraordinary zeal. A priest named Bozidar Bralow, known for always carrying a machine gun, was accused of dancing around the corpses of a hundred and eighty Serbs killed in Alipasin-Most, and another of haranguing the Ustashe mobs with crucifix in hand while they cut the throats of Serbian women.

That last vignette was also related by an Italian journalist who added in his report that the massacre had taken place in Banja Luka.

Another researcher, Jonathan Steinberg, had access to the document and photograph archives of the Italian ministry of foreign affairs, which contained images of the massacres and decoded reports from papal espionage agents informing their superiors of the extermination of whole Orthodox cities and towns. All his discoveries appear in his book *All or Nothing: The Axis and the Holocaust, 1941–1943.* The question posed by many people then and now is how and why the Catholic Church, Pope Pius XII, the Vatican, Catholic authorities in Croatia, and Catholic intelligence services did absolutely nothing to stop the massacres, or even simply to denounce them.

Steinberg unearthed a letter sent by the Primate Archbishop of Zagreb, Alojzije Stepinac, to the dictator Ante Pavelic in which the priest cited the favorable opinions of all the Croatian bishops toward forced conversions and affirmed that the bishop of Mostar, Monsignor Miscic, was very much in favor of using all means necessary to "save countless souls" in Croatia. Stepinac, after praising the religious conversion operations of the Croatian authorities, went on to say, "In the parish of Klepca, seven hundred schismatics from the neighboring villages were slaughtered." Many of those were executed in the Jasinovac concentration camp, one of the largest of the time.[33]

The majority of the bishops, the Holy See itself, the secretariat of state, and even Pope Pius XII took advantage of Yugoslavia's defeat by the Nazis to increase the power and reach of Catholicism in the Balkans. The Croatian bishops' inability to distance themselves from the regime, to denounce it, to excommunicate Ante Pavelic and his accomplices, stemmed from their desire to take advantage of the opportunities this "good occasion" offered for constructing a powerful Catholic base in the Balkans.

The writer and investigator John Cornwell also gained access to documents in the Vatican Secret Archives, including a report from the Congregation for the Eastern Churches that indicated that the Vatican knew about the forced conversions as of July 1941. Cornwell also found a Holy Alliance document that described the deportation of nearly six thousand Jews to a barren island without food or water. "All attempts to come to their assistance had been forbidden by the Croat authorities," the report of the papal espionage service said. There is no record of any Vatican response or initiative on this subject.

Father Cherubino Seguic, Ante Pavelic's special representative, came to Rome to rebut what he called "rumors spread by communists and Jews and members of the Vatican secret service." On March 6, 1942, the French cardinal Eugène Tisserant—a Balkan expert, member of the Masonic Grand Orient Lodge, and confidant of Pope Pius XII—had a secret meeting with Nicola Rusinovic, who was the semiofficial Vatican representative of Pavelic's regime. Tisserant told Rusinovic:

> I know for a fact that it is the Franciscans themselves, for example Father Simic of Knin, who have taken part in attacks against the Orthodox populations so as to destroy the Orthodox Church. In the same way you destroyed the Orthodox Church in Banja Luka. I know for sure that the Franciscans have acted abominably, and this pains me. Such acts should not be committed by educated, cultured, civilized people, let alone by priests."[34]

The truth is that Pope Pius XII never ceased to look benevolently on Ante Pavelic's regime. For example, in July 1941, the supreme pontiff received a hundred Croatian security agents led by the Zagreb police chief, who after the war would be accused of "crimes against humanity" and of having personally executed six women and their nine children in front of witnesses. On February 6, 1942, Pope Pius XII held an audience with a small group belonging to the Ustashe Youth, whom he reminded that they were "the defenders of Christianity." Later he told a Pavelic regime official that "in spite of everything, no one wants to acknowledge the one, real, and principal enemy of Europe; no true, communal, military crusade against Bolshevism has been initiated."

With respect to Russia, the Vatican's Holy Alliance espionage service began a new operation during World War II. When Hitler unleashed his "Operation Barbarossa" on June 22, 1941, Pope Pius XII saw a chance to penetrate into the heart of the Bolshevik enemy by means of evangelization. He summoned Cardinal Tisserant and his spy chief Father Robert Leiber. The supreme pontiff ordered them to craft a plan that would allow the dispatch of Catholic missionaries in the wake of the Wehrmacht as the German armies marched toward Moscow, "liberating" the territories of the Soviet Union. Cardinal Tisserant, working with Leiber, prepared a true espionage operation that would become known as the Tisserant Plan.

Hitler, however, had other ideas. He declared that "Christianity is the hardest blow that ever hit humanity. Bolshevism is just the bastard son of Christianity; both are the monsters engendered by the Jews." Franz von Papen, in his testimony at the Nuremberg Trials beginning on October 12, 1945, stated:

> The reevangelization of the Soviet Union was a Vatican operation, whether carried out through its missionary department or its secret services.[35]

The Tisserant Plan was personally directed by Cardinal Eugène Tisserant, not by Robert Leiber, even though its main operatives were Holy Alliance agents. Inside the Soviet Union, it was led by Niccolo Estorzi, The Messenger.

The cardinal's activities in Eastern Europe had already been noticed in 1940. Alfred Rosenberg, Nazi leader and fervent anti-Catholic, prohibited the entry of priests into "liberated" areas of the Soviet Union. But it fell to Reinhard Heydrich, head of the Office of Reich Security, to hunt down the Holy Alliance and Vatican agents in Russia. On July 2, 1941, Heydrich circulated a document titled "New Tactics in Vatican Russia Work" among high-ranking Nazis. In this document, the powerful RSHA chief explained that the Vatican and its espionage services had conceived an operation known as the Tisserant Plan to smuggle Catholic priests into areas under Wehrmacht control. The essence of the plan designed by the Holy Alliance was to recruit chaplains, aided by Spanish and Italian priests, to accompany the units fighting on the eastern front.

These priests, under Estorzi's leadership, would go to work gathering information that would allow the introduction of Catholicism, under the protection of the German advance. Heydrich's report went on to explain:

> It is necessary to prevent Catholicism from becoming the real beneficiary of the war in this new situation that is developing in the Russian area con-quered by German blood. The pope's agents are taking advantage of the situation, and this must be stopped.[36]

An order dated September 6 required unit commanders to inform the army high command of any "sign of the activation of Vatican operations and those of its intelligence services in Russia." In fact, the Tisserant Plan was not really a new operation designed at this time, but dated back to the papacy of Pius XI.

Niccolo Estorzi set about interviewing the candidates for implementing the Tisserant Plan one by one. The abbeys of Grotta Ferrara in Italy, Cheve-togne in Belgium, and Velehrad in Moravia became the staging areas. There flocked the Holy Alliance agents seeking to take part in the Tisserant Plan, to participate in one of the most important operations in the history of the papal intelligence service.

Some traveled eastward in the guise of merchants, with folded crucifixes inside their fountain pens. Others pretended to be stable boys, blending in with the rear guard of the German advance. Once they reached areas that they deemed appropriate for holding clandestine Masses, the pope's spies left the German columns and continued on their own. Many were welcomed by the local residents, while others were executed by communist partisans or ar-rested and sent to Siberian labor camps. According to unofficial sources, an estimated 217 members of the *Russicum,* belonging to the Holy Alliance, died in the implementation of the Tisserant Plan.

Niccolo Estorzi, the head of operations for the plan, remained inside Russia until February 1943, when he rejoined the German troops in their disorderly re-treat in the face of the Red Army's advance. On January 31, General von Paulus had surrendered at Stalingrad. Of the 330,000 men who made up the German Sixth Army, only 91,000 survived. Many died in POW camps in Siberia.

The German surrender at Stalingrad was the beginning of the end of the "Thousand-Year Reich" of which Adolf Hitler had dreamed. Meanwhile, af-ter the failure of the Tisserant Plan, Pope Pius XII said in his encyclical *Ec-clesiae decus* of April 23, 1944:

The chief object of Our constant desires and prayers is that ... the day will dawn at last when there shall be one flock and one fold, all obedient with one mind to Jesus Christ and to His Vicar on earth ... Christ's faithful ones should labour together in heart and endeavour for union in the one Church of Jesus Christ, so that they may present a common, serried, united, and unyielding front to the daily growing attacks of the enemies of religion.

Nonetheless, historians John Cornwell, Carlo Falconi, Jonathan Steinberg, and Harold Deutsch all agree that Pope Pius XII's ambition to evangelize Eastern Europe does not explain his silence in the face of the extermination of six million Jews in the so-called Final Solution.[37] This historic silence about the killing of millions of Jews—silence from the Vatican in general and Pope Pius XII in particular—provoked a statement by the British ambassador to the Holy See, Sir D'Arcy Osborne:

A policy of silence in regard to such offenses against the conscience of the world must necessarily involve a renunciation of moral leadership and a consequent atrophy of the influence and authority of the Vatican; and it is upon the maintenance and assertion of such authority that must depend any prospect of a papal contribution to the reestablishment of world peace.[38]

On April 19, 1945, Soviet troops reached the gates of Berlin, the heart of the Reich. On the 30th, in a dark and dank underground bunker of the Third Reich's chancellery, the man who had been lord and master of Europe took his own life. Adolf Hitler had just turned fifty-six. Three days before, on April 27, *Il Duce* Benito Mussolini had also died, his body hung upside down in the Piazza Loreto of Milan.

As to the World War II activities of the Vatican and its espionage services, the Holy Alliance and the *Sodalitium Pianum,* a statement made by Cardinal Eugène Tisserant, head of the Congregation for the Eastern Churches, is worth quoting. In a letter to Cardinal Emmanuel Suhard in May of 1940, he wrote: "I fear that history will reproach the Holy See for having practiced a policy of selfish convenience and little else." Even near the beginning of the Second World War, this statement shows, the Vatican feared that its policy of "hidden" neutrality might be "judged" and "condemned" by history, as indeed it has been.

The End of the Thousand-Year Reich

Of the Thousand-Year Reich, only ruin, death, and destruction remained twelve years after Adolf Hitler's ascent to power. Those who died during the Second World War totaled more than fifty-five million people, both civilians and soldiers. Six years and one day after Hitler's attack on Poland, the guns fell silent. The new task was to save what survived in the ruins. Meanwhile, the killers, the executors of the Fuehrer's policies, began to flee from international justice by way of what became known as the Vatican Ratline and an organization called Odessa. The communist empire began to extend its tentacles through Eastern Europe. A new war loomed over the world: the Cold War.

16

"ODESSA" AND THE
"VATICAN RATLINE" (1946–1958)

On every side the wicked strut about; the shameless are extolled by all.
—Psalms 11:9

During the war, the Collegio di San Girolamo degli Illirici at 132 Via Tomacelli in Rome provided a home for Croatian priests who came to the Vatican to carry out various tasks. After the end of the war, the San Girolamo seminary and monastery became a safe house for Ustashe being pursued as war criminals. The Holy Alliance provided routes, false identities, and passports to facilitate their flight. The main leader of San Girolamo was Father Krunoslav Draganovic.

An ex-professor at a Croatian seminary, described by U.S. intelligence services as dictator Ante Pavelic's alter ego, Draganovic arrived in Rome in late 1943 on the pretext of working for the Red Cross. The Vatican espionage services asserted that he was really there to coordinate operations in Croatia with Italian Fascist groups. At the end of the war, he became the major figure in what has since been dubbed the Vatican Ratline. San Girolamo served as a center for organizing the departures of those trying to flee from Europe, especially to Argentina. These operations soon progressed to helping Nazi war criminals avoid arrest. Among them were Josef Mengele, the Auschwitz doctor; Klaus Barbie, the "butcher of Lyon," that French city's former Gestapo chief; Ante Pavelic, the Croatian dictator; SS captain Erich Priebke; SS general Hans Fischböck; and the famous Adolf Eichmann.

Some writers and historians say they have not found sufficient proof to assert that the Vatican or Pope Pius XII was aware of the Odessa organization's operations, but there is significant evidence that at least some important Holy Alliance agents were indeed involved in the Ratline.

For example, Franz Stangl, commandant of the Treblinka concentration camp, got a new identity, false papers, and a Roman refuge from Bishop Alois Hudal and members of the Holy Alliance. Klaus Barbie, too, was helped by Vatican agents.[1]

In return for this aid, the Vatican and various institutions received sizable sums of money, much of which had earlier been extorted from rich Jews in exchange for exempting them from being deported to death camps. One of these cases involved SS division general Hans Fischböck. Along with Eichmann and SS captain Erich Rajakowitsch, he had held important positions in Austria after its annexation and later in Holland. Holy Alliance reports and those of U.S. secret services showed that both Fischböck and Rajakowitsch had made true fortunes at the expense of Dutch Jewish millionaire families in return for leaving them off the SS deportation lists. Some of this money went into Eichmann's pockets, some into Fischböck's, and some into Rajakowitsch's, but the lion's share went into bank accounts in Argentina by way of Swiss banks, especially the Union Bank of Switzerland in Zurich.[2]

With some of this money and help from Odessa, the three former SS men succeeded in escaping to Argentina. The British secret service MI6 discovered that part of their escape was financed by two Swiss citizens—Arthur Widerkehr, a hard-hearted lawyer who had acquired nearly two million Swiss francs in Jewish ransom operations, and Walter Büchi, a young man who had shown great skill at turning his "clients" in to the Gestapo once they had paid their ransom money.[3] British reports showed that Büchi had "important contacts with the Roman curia and with certain elements close to the papal secret services."

Walter Büchi had maintained ties with agents of the *Teutonicum,* the German affairs division of papal espionage, as well as carried out special missions for the Holy Alliance. While Büchi acted as a "free agent" of the Vatican espionage apparatus, he also served as Swiss liaison for the SS's Monetary Unit, run by General Hans Fischböck. One of Büchi's most lucrative deals was his acting as go-between to ensure the safety of Jewish banker Hans Kroch. When persecution of the Jewish community in Berlin began, the financier managed to escape to Holland.

Kroch got in contact with Walter Büchi to arrange a ransom for his entire family. The Swiss businessman called Adolf Eichmann personally to request safe-conduct passes, but Kroch's wife had already been arrested by the Gestapo and deported to the Ravensbrück concentration camp. The lawyer Arthur Wiederkehr then advised Kroch to flee to Switzerland with his daughters, and from there to Argentina. Once in South America, Kroch sent Büchi and Wiederkehr a list of Jewish millionaires who would be willing to pay sizable fortunes for their families' freedom. This collection of names became known as the "Kroch List." From then on, Büchi and Wiederkehr in Switzerland worked with Eichmann and Hans Fischböck in Germany to extort large sums of money in gold and Swiss francs, which they deposited in numbered bank accounts and later sent on to accounts in Argentine banks.[4] Years afterwards, this money would finance important war criminals' escapes to South America, especially to Argentina, Bolivia, and Brazil, along the Vatican Ratline.

Nazi leaders began to design their escape plans two months before the end of the Second World War. When he saw that all was lost, Heinrich Himmler decided to create "Operation *Aussenweg*" (Road Out). At its head he put a thirty-four-year-old Argentine-born SS captain named Carlos Fuldner, who over the five years between 1945 and 1950 became the point man for war criminals escaping Allied postwar justice. Spain, Portugal, Morocco, Austria, and Italy became safe havens along the pathway for fugitives traveling with false documents and identities—created most often by the Vatican secret services. Many Holy Alliance agents served as guides and protectors of these war criminals until the escapees reached destinations where they would be beyond the reach of international justice.[5]

Carlos Fuldner set out on a counterclockwise circuit of European capitals, including Madrid and Rome. In Rome, he forged a relationship with Father Krunoslav Draganovic, the Church official in charge of San Girolamo. Draganovic assured Himmler's emissary that "his organization" was ready to provide assistance and refuge to high Nazi officials who decided to flee to South America. He even assured Fuldner that they could depend on the protection and support of the Vatican through the Holy Alliance, the papal secret service.

Fuldner had been born in Buenos Aires on December 16, 1910, to a family of German immigrants. In 1922, his father decided to return to Germany to settle in the city of Kassel. Early in 1932, Carlos Fuldner was admitted to an elite unit of the SS. He was twenty-one years old and stood just over five feet nine.

After the war, Carlos Fuldner took refuge in Madrid, where he established his new base of action. In the Spanish capital, the former SS captain kept up good relations with important members of the social and artistic world such as Gonzalo Serrano Fernández de Villavicencio, Viscount of Uzqueta; the journalist Victor de la Serna; and the Domingún brothers, famous matadors. To keep his meetings secret, Fuldner held them in the private rooms of the Horcher restaurant on Calle Alfonso XII, which had been opened in 1943 by Otto Horcher.[6] Here, Fuldner made his first contact with the Argentine archbishop Monsignor Antonio Caggiano, soon to be named a cardinal by Pope Pius XII. Caggiano came escorted by two men who said they belonged to the Holy Alliance. The name of one is unknown. They other was Stefan Guisan.

Stefan Guisan was a Franciscan priest born near the Swiss city of Berne. In the seminary where he studied, Stefan met a Croatian priest who introduced him to Draganovic. In 1944, Father Stefan Guisan began to work with the papal secret service, the Holy Alliance. After the Normandy landing in June of that year, he became the Vatican secret services' liaison in San Girolamo, under Krunoslav Draganovic's orders.

The agent whose name is unknown was the Holy Alliance liaison to the Pontifical Commission of Assistance (PCA) in the Villa San Francisco. The PCA, led by Pietro Luigi Martin, was the Vatican department in charge of issuing identity documents to refugees. After the Nazi defeat, it was assigned to provide false documents to a large number of Nazi fugitives. Nearly thirty priests worked in the PCA falsifying the seals of international organizations that aided refugees. These priests came from several different orders, but the majority were Franciscans. Father Guisan acted as a liaison linking various organizations in the Vatican city-state to help the war criminals escape. This aid ranged from simply hiding the fugitives to providing false documents, funding their travel costs, and providing a list of contacts to use on each leg of the escape route.[7]

Apparently there are documents demonstrating that Draganovic was not the ultimate head of the so-called Operation Monastery. A report from a U.S. spy agency suggests that the visible head of the Vatican Ratline was really Cardinal Eugène Tisserant. William Gowen, a member of U.S. military counterintelligence in Italy, wrote in a 1946 report:

Tisserant has told me that he firmly believes there is now a fifty-fifty chance Russia will provoke war this year. The Cardinal feels the Russians are in a favorable position to overrun Western Europe . . . which opportunity Russia realizes might not occur again.[8]

Monsignor Caggiano and Father Stefan Guisan met with Cardinal Tisserant in the Vatican to let him know that "the government of the Argentine Republic was willing to receive French persons, whose political attitude during the recent war would expose them, should they return to France, to harsh measures and private revenge." Tisserant was so anti-communist that he felt communists did not deserve Christian burial. Likewise, he felt it was necessary to set up a group of Nazi anti-communist experts in South America who could be utilized if war against the Soviet Union broke out. From then on, the Argentine embassy in Rome began to receive a rash of visa requests from French nationals.

On the orders of Antonio Caggiano, now a cardinal, French war criminals and collaborationists such as Marcel Boucher, Fernand de Menou, Robert Pincemin, and Émile Dewoitine received special visas to enter Argentina. The four carried sequentially numbered passports issued by the Red Cross of Rome and certificates of recommendation from the Vatican. Curiously, all four had found refuge in San Girolamo, the institution controlled by Krunoslav Draganovic and "penetrated" by the Holy Alliance and the *Sodalitium Pianum*.

Meanwhile, high-level negotiations were pursuing a secret agreement between Pope Pius XII and Argentina's president Juan Domingo Perón. Cardinal Giovanni Battista Montini, the future Pope Paul VI, told the Argentine ambassador in Italy that Pius XII wanted to find the best way to arrange emigration to Argentina "not only by Italians." The supreme pontiff wanted the "technicians of the Holy See [that is, members of its secret service] to be in contact with the Argentine technicians [members of Odessa] to make a plan of action." The Argentine diplomat understood that Pope Pius XII's interest extended to those detained in Allied prison camps in Italy, which meant high-ranking Nazis. After learning of this desire from Cardinal Montini, the Argentine contacted his foreign relations ministry in Buenos Aires for instructions.[9]

The men assigned to serve as links between the Nazis and the Vatican—which is to say, between Fuldner and Father Krunoslav Draganovic—were

Reinhard Kops from the German side and Gino Monti de Valsassina from the Holy Alliance.

Monti de Valsassina was an Italian nobleman of Croat origin who had fought in the Luftwaffe and then joined Himmler's secret services after being wounded in combat. In April 1945, he was captured by the English and held in a special prison camp for Nazis who might have something to contribute in the postwar period, whether that was merely information about Nazi fugitives or technical and scientific advice about materials and processes developed under Hitler's regime. Count Monti had made contact with the Holy Alliance late in 1944 while on a family visit to Milan. There he met and established close ties to several members of the curia. Monti was a fervent Catholic, after all.

One of these contacts, a clergyman close to Pope Pius XII's spy Robert Leiber, brought Monti into the Vatican secret service. In late 1945, Monti managed to escape from the prison camp and—according to information gathered by U.S. intelligence—took refuge in a Vatican institution, possibly San Girolamo.

Under the protection of Draganovic's men, Gino Monti de Valsassina reached Argentina by way of the port of Genoa, thanks to the help of Father Karlo Petranovic.[10]

Monti landed in Argentina on January 4, 1947, carrying a "stateless person" certificate issued by the Vatican. Seven months later, Perón sent him to Spain to recruit Germans with important technical expertise. The beneficiaries of his aid ranged from out-and-out Nazi war criminals such as Luftwaffe general Eckart Krahmer to German espionage agents like Reinhard Spitzy. In the summer of 1947, Monti returned to the Vatican through Italy to act as the Holy Alliance liaison in San Girolamo.

The German liaison in San Girolamo, Reinhard Kops, used the cover name Hans Raschenbach and a passport arranged by the Holy Alliance. Born in the German city of Hamburg on September 29, 1914, Kops ran Jewish deportation and extermination actions in Albania during the Second World War, according to an investigation by the Simon Wiesenthal Center, and performed similar duties in occupied France and Bulgaria. After Adolf Hitler's fall, Kops was detained by the British army but escaped from detention camp and made his way to Rome. Around this time, the German began to work for the Vatican's Secretariat for German Refugees, a papal department the Holy Alliance used as cover. In this post, always under the umbrella of the papal secret services, Kops facilitated war criminals' escapes, especially to South America and Australia, until he decided in 1948 to make that trip himself. He wanted to get as far as possible from Europe as the demands for apprehension of escaped Nazis increased.

According to a report of the Commission for the Clarification of Nazi Activities in Argentina (CEANA), during the war Reinhard Kops/Juan Maler had belonged to the Third Reich's counterespionage apparatus and, after the Nazi defeat and his subsequent flight to Rome, he became a "special aide" to the pro-Nazi bishop Alois Hudal and served as a Holy Alliance contact for the fleeing Nazis who reached the refuge of San Girolamo.

In Buenos Aires, Reinhard Kops (now using the name Juan Maler[11]) became an ardent far-right intellectual. He was the South American administrator of Odessa until the early 1950s and of the international neo-Nazi movement from the turn of the 1970s on. Kops fled to Argentina either through Genoa with the aid of Father Karlo Petranovic and Father Ivan Bucko,[12] two of Draganovic's most reliable Vatican Ratline operatives, or by way of Morocco with the help of an agent named Marguerite d'Andurain.

The mysterious and beautiful Marguerite d'Andurain had first made contact with SS Captain Carlos Fuldner and Reinhard Kops through Draganovic. Earlier, she had been connected with certain Holy Alliance operations in Berlin during the war and with Robert Leiber's Messenger, Niccolo Estorzi.

The daughter of a French judge, Marguerite had married Viscount Pierre d'Andurain when she was only seventeen. In 1918, the couple traveled to Lebanon, where they set themselves up as pearl dealers. Marga, as her friends called her, learned to speak Arabic fluently. For a time she was the proprietress of the Grand Hotel of Palmyra in the Syrian desert, later renamed Queen Zenobia Hotel in honor of the Bedouin queen.

Between 1918 and 1925, Marguerite d'Andurain entered the espionage world by way of the *Deuxième Bureau*, the French secret service. She had a romance with the famous British intelligence agent Colonel Sinclair, who soon afterwards was found dead in Damascus. Although his death was at first considered a suicide, French and English secret services suspected that d'Andurain and the Kaiser's secret service were involved. The truth never came out.

In 1925, Marguerite d'Andurain divorced her husband and married a Wahabi sheik named Suleyman. Some reports say she poisoned her new husband and inherited a sizable amount of land and money. Soon afterwards, she returned to Palmyra, where she remarried Viscount Pierre d'Andurain in 1937. Two months after the wedding, the viscount died from seventeen stab wounds. The murderer or murderers were never discovered.[13]

The widow then began a life of luxury, traveling between Nice and Cairo, always in the company of young men. During the German occupation of France, Marguerite d'Andurain carried out several spy operations for the Nazis, specifically for Reinhard Heydrich's Central Office for Reich Security. At the same time, she made contact with Vatican secret services, thanks to her good relations with the Vatican nuncio in Paris and with Austrian bishop Alois Hudal, one of the key figures in Odessa.[14]

In fact, there is no conclusive documentary evidence about d'Andurain's possible collaboration with the Holy Alliance, but there is for her collaboration with Hudal. After the war, the Austrian priest asked d'Andurain to join the Vatican Ratline network. At first she refused, but then her lover of the moment died from poisoning. The next day, Marguerite d'Andurain disappeared from the face of the earth, only to reappear months later on Morocco's northern coast.

As the owner of a luxury yacht called the *Djeilan,* d'Andurain frequently crossed the Straits of Gibraltar between the Rock and the city of Tangier.[15] It is said that in such mysterious crossings, the spy helped important Nazi figures escape through Morocco—such as Franz Stangl, commandant of the Treblinka concentration camp; Adolf Eichmann, chief architect of the Final Solution; Erich Priebke, a Gestapo chief in Italy who was responsible for the massacre at the Ardeatine caves; and Reinhard Kops, who directed the deportation and extermination of Albanian Jews during the war and then developed ties to the Holy Alliance.

D'Andurain was only a minor piece, really, in the great machine that the Vatican and Odessa had assembled to help Nazi war criminals escape along the two routes of the so-called Vatican Ratline. One path ran Switzerland–San Girolamo–Genoa–South America. The other was Switzerland–France–Spain–Gibraltar–Morocco–South America. In the latter, Marguerite d'Andurain's mission was to get the fugitives across the strait to Morocco, where they could then board freighters for ports in Argentina, Uruguay, Brazil, Peru, or Chile.

On the night of November 5, 1948, d'Andurain's lifeless body was found floating in the bay of Tangier. The British secret service station in Gibraltar investigated and then proposed an explanation for her murder. She could have been assassinated by members of Odessa so as to close the mouth of a woman who knew too much about the whereabouts of such important Nazi figures as Eichmann, Kops, Priebke, Mengele, and Fischböck.[16] Other sources questioned by the British and Americans insisted that d'Andurain had been involved with a certain Poncini, a tall, dark, and handsome man with whom she had been sleeping. They had been seen together at parties and in casinos. Pursuing this possibility, the British investigated one Hans Abel, a former member of the Reich secret services, as the presumed author of the murder or "execution" of the forty-seven-year-old spy.

A second possibility favored by the U.S. intelligence services, was that the killer could have been a member of the Israeli secret service. This version is also put forward by the researcher Richard Deacon in his book *The Israeli Secret Service,* about the history of Israeli espionage.

According to Deacon, the Americans knew that an Israeli agent stationed in Tangier had uncovered the whole plot that helped Nazi war criminals involved in killing Jews during the war escape with the aid of Pope Pius XII's Vatican. The Israelis had found their evidence in Tétouan, in Spanish Morocco, by way of a Spaniard who had provided safe houses on the Spanish side of the strait where fleeing Nazis waited until Marguerite d'Andurain could bring them across on her yacht *Djeilan.* This Spaniard told the Israelis that d'Andurain was part of the Odessa organization and was helping Nazi war criminals get to South America. When this information was passed on to Tel Aviv, it provoked an order for the Odessa collaborator's liquidation.

In late October of 1948, according to this account, three Israelis arrived by freighter in a Moroccan port and then took up lodgings in a small Tangier hotel. The afternoon of November 4, one of the Israeli agents spotted the *Djeilan* entering the harbor with Marguerite d'Andurain at the wheel.

That same night, the woman and the three Israeli agents all disappeared. Her corpse was found floating in the harbor the next night. The U.S. secret services suspected that the Odessa agent's assassination could have been carried out by their Israeli counterparts.

The third scenario to explain d'Andurain's murder came from the French secret services, who were also keeping tabs on her. According to French spies, Marguerite d'Andurain had been seen with a "tall, dark, handsome" man, a description that matched Father Niccolo Estorzi, the Holy Alliance agent known as The Messenger. A few weeks earlier, Estorzi had been seen in the nunciature in Madrid, where he apparently got instructions from his superiors.

Attracted as d'Andurain was to men, Estorzi didn't have much trouble getting in touch with her. The night before her death, the spy was seen in a crowded Tangier restaurant with a man whose description matched the Holy Alliance agent. The next morning, Estorzi disappeared and d'Andurain's corpse was found floating in the harbor with evidence of a sharp blow to the head.

The French secret service report revealed that the woman could have been "executed" by an agent of a mysterious organization or sect known as the *Assassini,* closely linked to the Vatican secret services. According to the *Deuxième Bureau,* d'Andurain was killed because she knew too much about Operation Monastery, organized by the Holy Alliance in conjunction with James Angleton, head of the OSS (Office of Strategic Services, forerunner of the CIA) in Italy, which allowed many Nazi war criminals to escape to South America.[17]

Whoever the killer was—whether from the U.S., Israel, or the Vatican secret service—Marguerite d'Andurain's death will continue to be one of the great mysteries swirling around the Holy Alliance. Years later, the names and whereabouts of Adolf Eichmann, Reinhard Kops, and Erich Priebke would become chips to be exchanged as part of a new collaboration between the Vatican secret services and their "Israeli friend," the Mossad.[18]

Another famous case involving the Holy Alliance as part of Operation Monastery was the escape of Carl Vaernet, also known as the "Danish Mengele." In the 1930s, Vaernet claimed to have developed a treatment based on what he called "inversion of hormonal polarity." His theories were publicized in Nazi Party newspapers because Heinrich Himmler saw in them a "final solution" to the homosexual question.[19] After Hitler's rise to power, Vaernet was recruited into the SS medical corps, founded by Josef Mengele.

In 1943, Carl Peter Jensen, alias Carl Vaernet, signed a contract with the RSHA, transferring exclusive patent rights in his discoveries to an entity of the SS, the Deutsche Heilmittel, in return for financing, laboratory supplies, and homosexual prisoners from concentration camps who could be used as human guinea pigs.[20] From January 1944 on, Himmler put the homosexual population of Buchenwald at Vaernet's disposal. Carl Vaernet experimented on fifteen prisoners, in whom he implanted an "artificial masculine sex gland." This was a metal tube that released testosterone into the groin for a certain period of time. Of the fifteen prisoners, only two survived, while the other thirteen died from infections.[21]

Already in late 1943, a Holy Alliance agent in occupied Copenhagen had reported to the Holy See about a possible experiment that could wipe out "the cruel disease of homosexuality" from the earth. This Vatican secret service report made reference to Dr. Carl Peter Jensen. At the end of the war, British forces in Denmark imprisoned Vaernet. On May 29, 1945, the Allied commander told the Danish Medical Association that Carl Vaernet would be tried as a "war criminal." At the end of that year, the British turned him over to the Danish court system, but he managed to escape just before his trial. The case of the doctor who succeeded in eliminating the "cruel disease of homosexuality" had reached the ears of Cardinal Eugène Tisserant, who apparently ordered his secret services to help the "efficient" scientist.

It seems that the former SS doctor took refuge in Stockholm, either in the Argentine embassy or in the Vatican nunciature. From Sweden, with the help of Odessa, he went to Argentina. Although Argentine authorities denied any knowledge of Carl Vaernet's arrival, a document says otherwise. The journalist Uki Goñi, in his book *The Real Odessa: Smuggling the Nazis to Perón's Argentina,* shows that file number 11692 was opened in his name, with an addendum numbered 3480 that contained his request for Argentine nationality.[22]

Another figure involved in rescuing Nazis was a Swiss army colonel, Henri Guisan. His father, General Guisan, had been accused of Nazi sympathies during the war, and his cousin Father Stefan Guisan was the priest and Vatican secret agent who accompanied Cardinal Antonio Caggiano to meet with ex–SS captain Carlos Fuldner in Madrid.

During the Second World War, Henri Guisan had formed ties with Waffen SS Captain Wilhelm Eggen, a German official whose responsibilities included buying wood in Switzerland. As a director of the Extroc lumber company, Guisan acquired the concession to supply wood products for the Dachau and Oranienburg concentration camps until 1944.[23] Guisan introduced Eggen to Roger Masson, head of the Swiss espionage service. Some sources, though, assert that Stefan Guisan, not Henri, organized this meeting in Wolfsburg Castle. It is unclear whether Stefan or Henri participated on the Holy Alliance's initiative or his own. One way or another, in 1949 and

1950, Guisan (either Henri or Stefan) made contact with the secret services of several countries including Argentina on behalf of scientists who had specialized in missile development and had worked with Werner von Braun, who had served the Nazis during the war and then became one of the fathers of NASA in the U.S.

(Henri or Stefan) Guisan offered nothing less than the plans for the V-3, successor to the famous V-2 missiles that Hitler launched against London. Perón, however, was not inclined to pay for such an expensive arms project. The information was passed on to the Vatican secret services, who found in South Africa a government more ready to pay for the escape of several scientists trapped in the Russian-occupied zone of Germany. At the end of this year, the "Croatian Gold" operation was about to fall into the hands of Pope Pius XII's secret services, who naturally did not want it to slip away.

Investigations carried out by Allied military intelligence services after the war revealed that the booty accumulated by Ustashe leaders totaled some eighty million dollars (at 1945 value) in gold coins, nearly five hundred kilograms in gold ingots, several million dollars more in cut diamonds and a considerable quantity in currency, primarily Swiss francs and U.S. dollars. When these leaders fled, their "Ustashe treasure" was loaded onto two trucks headed for Austria, accompanied by two former agents of Ante Pavelic's security force and by three priests, possibly agents of the Holy Alliance.[24] A sizable portion of this treasure went to the British to pay for the release of high Croatian officials such as the *Poglavnik* himself, Ante Pavelic, and his former foreign minister, Stjepan Peric.

After subtracting the British share of the booty, some 350 kilos of gold and eleven hundred carats of diamonds remained. According to one version of the story, nearly fifty kilos of gold ingots were separated out, placed in two boxes, and sent to Rome. This cargo traveled under the watchful eye of Father Krunoslav Draganovic and two Vatican secret agents. The rest was buried in a secret site on the Austrian border, but greed trumped the patriotic spirit of the escaped Croats. When Pavelic ordered General Ante Moskov and former economy minister Lavro Ustic to dig up the treasure and put it safely into a Swiss bank, they found the place where it had been buried, but the contents had disappeared.

A report from the U.S. Army Counter-Intelligence Corps (CIC) based in Rome stated:

British Lieutenant Colonel Johnson was placed in charge of two lorries laden with the supposed property of the Catholic Church in the British Zone of Austria. These two lorries, accompanied by a number of priests and the British officer, then entered Italy and went to an unknown destination.[25]

Another document, authored by U.S. agent Emerson Bigelow of the SSU (an espionage unit belonging to the War Department) and sent to the U.S. Treasury Department, explained:

Pavelic has removed a total of 350 million Swiss francs from Croatia, largely in gold coins. These funds were plundered from Serbs and Jews to support the Ustashe organization in exile. . . . The balance of some 200 million Swiss francs ended up in the Vatican vaults through the intervention of a priest named Draganovic and two other priests, who might belong to the secret services of the Holy See.

Other reports from U.S. intelligence and the U.S. Treasury Department claimed that part of the Ustashe treasure in Vatican hands was diverted to twenty-one accounts in four Swiss banks. This operation was run by the Slovenian bishop Gregory Rozman, a fervent anti-Semite and war criminal protected by Pope Pius XII and the Holy Alliance after the war.[26] The postwar Tito government in Yugoslavia repeatedly requested Gregory Rozman's extradition, but resistance from Great Britain, the United States, and of course the Vatican prevented him from being returned and tried. For the Americans and British, turning a high Catholic Church official over to a communist government was unthinkable. The Vatican also had no interest in turning over a high official who knew so much about *non sancta* operations of the papal administration at the close of the Second World War.[27]

Rozman, accompanied by three Holy Alliance agents, went to Rome to take charge of the "black funds" the Vatican had amassed to finance Operation Monastery. "Many escapees from the Afragola POW camp have gone into hiding at San Girolamo. This is the organizational center for spiriting German and Croat criminals to third countries," a U.S. intelligence report stated. "Draganovic's sponsorship of these Croat Quislings definitely links him up with the plan of the Vatican to shield these ex-Ustashe nationalists until such time as they are able to procure for them the proper documents to enable them to go to South America. The Vatican, undoubtedly banking on the strong anti-Communist feelings of these men, is endeavoring to infiltrate them into South America in any way possible to counteract the spread of the Red doctrine," explained the agent in charge of investigating the Ustashe activity in San Girolamo.

Since May of 1946, Ante Pavelic, the most important war criminal to flee along the Vatican Ratline, had been sheltered in the Collegio Pio Pontificio at Number 3 Via Gioacchino Belli in the Roman district of Prati. From there he was moved to a small house in the Castel Gandolfo complex, the popes' summer residence, where he met almost weekly with Cardinal Montini, the future Pope Paul VI. In December 1946, Pavelic moved to San Girolamo. He was about to be sent to Argentina through the port of Genoa, escorted by Father Ivan Bucko and Father Karlo Petranovic, but this plan was interrupted by the arrival of two U.S. agents. The *Poglavnik* had to be sequestered in the monastery of Santa Sabina to avoid arrest.

In April 1947, a U.S. agent infiltrated into San Girolamo reported that Pavelic's trail had gone cold. In August of that year, there were rumors that the heads of British and U.S. intelligence in Rome had met secretly with Cardinal Montini. During this meeting, Pius XII's envoy told the spy chiefs that "in the eyes of the Vatican, not of the supreme pontiff, Ante Pavelic is a militant Catholic, a man who erred, but who erred fighting for Catholicism. It is for this reason that he is in contact with the Vatican. His crimes of the past cannot be forgotten, but he can only be tried by Croats representing an independent Croatian government." To the Vatican, Pope Pius XII, and the Holy Alliance, Ante Pavelic was responsible for the deaths of nearly fifty thousand people, but Stalin was responsible for the deaths of millions of people in the Ukraine, Belorussia, Poland, and the Baltic, and Marshal Tito in Yugoslavia was his agent.

Finally, on October 11, 1948, the Ustashe leader proceeded to Genoa and boarded the ship *Sestriere,* where he lodged in a first-class cabin. He carried Red Cross passport number 74369 in the name of Pal Aranyos, a Hungarian engineer. In a 1950 report, the CIA claimed that two Vatican secret service agents accompanied Pavelic on the ship and stayed with him for the next two years, acting as his bodyguards.

The Vatican Ratline required one of the largest secret operations of all time. There is no conclusive proof that the Ratline or Operation Monastery was organized or planned by the Holy Alliance as a single, unitary operation. There is, however, conclusive evidence that the important members of the

Roman curia and agents of the Vatican secret services participated in innumerable escapes by war criminals to countries where they were out of the reach of international justice.[28]

Two prelates working with Alois Hudal in Rome, the Monsignors Heinemann and Karl Bayer, also helped Nazi war criminals escape. Heinemann, not very well regarded by the Germans, was assigned to tend to the needs of Nazi officials who had taken refuge in Hudal's church, Santa Maria dell'Anima. Karl Bayer, unlike Heinemann, was much appreciated by the Nazi fugitives. Interviewed years later by the writer Gitta Sereny for her book *Into That Darkness: An Examination of Conscience,* Monsignor Bayer remembered how he and Hudal had helped the Nazis with Vatican support: "The pope [Pius XII] did provide money for this; in driblets sometimes, but it did come."[29]

The opening of Red Cross archives from the postwar period has finally settled the controversy as to whether or not Nazi and Croat war criminals had Vatican assistance in their flight from justice to South America, Australia, South Africa, and Canada. The answer is quite clear. Cardinals Montini, Tisserant, and Caggiano designed the escape routes; bishops and archbishops such as Hudal, Siri, and Barrère did the paperwork to create false documents and identities for the murderers; priests like Draganovic, Heinemann, Dömöter, Bucko, Petranovic, and many others signed the applications for Red Cross passports for criminals like Josef Mengele, Erich Priebke, Adolf Eichmann, Hans Fischböck, Ante Pavelic, and Klaus Barbie. Was Pope Pius XII aware of Operation Monastery and the Vatican Ratline? Did the Vatican secret services, the Holy Alliance and the *Sodalitium Pianum,* participate in the escape plans of the war criminals?

According to figures from the Argentine immigration service, an estimated five thousand Croats reached the country in the postwar years, of whom two thousand came from Hamburg, two thousand from Munich, and nearly a thousand more from Italy, specifically from the Vatican.

In a Foreign Office report now declassified, the British specialist on South American affairs Victor Perowne wrote:

As regards the activities of the Catholic clergy in maintaining Yugoslav refugees and assisting their emigration to South America, it depends on one's point of view whether one regards them as humanitarian or as politically sinister. There are a number of minor fascist leaders, I believe, in sanctuary at San Paolo fuori le Mura, and it is not impossible that some

Yugoslav war criminals may have taken refuge at San Girolamo, there would be nothing very unusual about that. It is unlikely the Vatican approves the political, as opposed to the religious, activities of Father Draganovic & Company, so far as they can be disentangled. For this is a situation where it is almost impossible to disentangle religion from politics.

A Foreign Office colleague replied:

While we cannot condemn the charitable attitude of the Catholic Church toward sinful individuals, we feel, however, that there has been much evidence to show that the Vatican has permitted the encouragement both covert and overt, of the Ustashe.[30]

There is only one report that bears on the Holy Alliance's position with respect to Operation Monastery, the Vatican Ratline, and Father Krunoslav Draganovic. According to a CIA report dated July 24, 1952, Cardinal Pietro Fumasoni-Biondi, head of the Holy Alliance, was well informed about the operations of Father Draganovic and the goings-on at San Girolamo. Fumasoni-Biondi was most upset with the "Brotherhood," the aid organization led by Draganovic. In 1952, in spite of the Holy Alliance chief's express prohibition of granting any more visas to Germans and Croats, Father Krunoslav Draganovic continued to help war criminals.

During all the years of Operation Monastery, Cardinal Pietro Fumasoni-Biondi was informed of everything about the Vatican Ratline, thanks to the Franciscan priest Dominic Mandic, a Vatican counterespionage agent. Mandic worked in the San Girolamo print shop, where the false documents for war criminals protected by Draganovic were prepared. But the situation changed considerably on October 6, 1958, when Pope Pius XII suffered a cerebral thrombosis while at Castel Gandolfo. That night, he received last rites. The supreme pontiff, who knew more secrets of the Catholic Church than most, many of them of his own creation, died October 9 at midnight after several days of death throes. He was eighty-two years old. His mortal remains were buried in the chapel of the Madonna della Bocciata in the Vatican Grottos. Krunoslav Draganovic's glory days ended soon afterwards.

In October 1958, the CIA learned that the priest had been summarily expelled from San Girolamo by "express order of the Vatican Secretariat of State" and had been barred from taking anything with him when he left.

Five Holy Alliance agents carried out the order. They were led by a priest named Niccolo Estorzi, The Messenger, following strict orders of Cardinal Pietro Fumasoni-Biondi, the head of the Holy Alliance.

Once having lost his power within the Vatican, by 1962 Krunoslav Draganovic fell out of favor with Western spy services such as the CIA and MI6, for "security reasons." The CIA report stated that Draganovic, "alias Bloody Draganovic, alias Dr. Fabiano, alias Dynamo, is not amenable to control, too knowledgeable of unit personnel and activity, demands outrageous monetary tribute and U.S. support of Croat organizations as partial payment for cooperation." Repudiated by the U.S. and the Vatican, in 1967, Draganovic decided to cross the border back into Yugoslavia, where he devoted himself to issuing statements in favor of Tito. There are some indications he may have been kidnapped by Yugoslav agents.

Krunoslav Draganovic died in July 1983, in abject poverty. He took with him to the tomb one of the biggest secrets about the Vatican state—the "dangerous" relations between Nazi and Croat war criminals and the Holy See's secret services, as well as the ins and outs of Operation Monastery and its role in the so-called Vatican Ratline.

The arrival of a new pope brought some true fresh air or, as then–CIA director Allen Dulles said, "The election of a new pope will bring a fresh breeze into the ossified Vatican palaces, which will help to dilute the air of decay surrounding the previous papal administration."

Perhaps this prediction would prove true. October 25, 1958, brought the opening of a new conclave, which resulted in the election of Cardinal Angelo Giuseppe Roncalli. The newly elected supreme pontiff, seventy-seven years old, adopted the name John XXIII. A brief era of optimism dawned within the Vatican. For the Holy Alliance, this meant some years of tranquillity under a papacy more concerned about questions of the soul and the spirit than those of politics and earthly matters.

17

NEW ALLIANCES (1958–1976)

Then he veers like the wind and is gone, this culprit who makes his own strength his god!

—Habakkuk 1:11

During the four years, seven months, and six days that John XXIII governed the Church of Rome, the Holy Alliance experienced a period of inactivity. The pope was more interested in granting an audience to Soviet leader Nikita Khrushchev's daughter Raisa or preparing for the revolutionary Second Vatican Council than in worrying about more earthly and political affairs on the other side of the Iron Curtain.

The Holy Alliance devoted itself to placing agents in the countries of Eastern Europe, given the growing power of communism and full fury of the Cold War. The *Sodalitium Pianum,* for its part, carried out intense surveillance of figures in the Roman curia and their respective departments who would be in charge of launching Vatican II.

When Cardinal Pietro Fumasoni-Biondi, who had been in charge of the Vatican secret service since the papacy of Pius XII, died on July 12, 1960, the supreme pontiff John XXIII decided not to appoint a substitute. The pope was in favor of "opening the Vatican's doors to the world." This implied the end of secret operations by its intelligence services.

In late 1962, John XXIII himself suffered a severe hemorrhage, the first sign of a serious disease. On May 17, 1963, the Holy Father's ills grew worse, confining him to his bed. Toward the end of the month, his condition improved, but then one night peritonitis set in. On June 3, John XXIII died, leaving the Throne of St. Peter vacant. The conclave had to meet again, for the sixth time so far in the twentieth century, to elect a successor.[1]

A few days before retiring into the conclave, a group of cardinals led by Giacomo Lercaro of Bologna met in the Villa Grottaferrata, owned by Umberto Ortolani. There, protected by the night and by Holy Alliance agents charged with guarding Their Eminences until the meeting in which they would elect the new pope, this group considered which cardinal to support. Their choice was Giovanni Battista Montini, Archbishop of Milan, who had already been told about the meeting in the house of the famous Freemason.[2]

The conclave began on the afternoon of July 19, 1963. Two days later, on the fifth ballot, Cardinal Giovanni Battista Montini, sixty-five years old, was elected pope. He received his crown nine days later, having taken the name Paul VI. The new pope's first decision was to reciprocate the Mason Ortolani's hospitality by conferring on him the status of a "Gentleman of His Holiness."

The man who had helped Krunoslav Draganovic to create the so-called Vatican Ratline, who had been one of the highest officials of the Roman curia to be implicated in Operation Monastery, which aided the flight of Nazi and Croat war criminals after the Second World War, was now the supreme pontiff.[3] The Vatican secret services, the Holy Alliance and the *Sodalitium Pianum,* would be reborn from their ashes, once again operating at full steam. Paul VI put this difficult task in the hands of a simple priest. His name was Pasquale Macchi. He had met Cardinal Montini when the latter was first assigned to lead the archbishopric of Milan. Macchi became not only his private secretary but also his best source of information. Now that he had been chosen as pope, Paul VI turned one of the most powerful information apparatuses on earth over to Macchi. The Holy Alliance was only a few years shy of completing its fourth century in operation since its creation by order of the inquisitor general Cardinal Miguel Ghislieri, soon to become Pope Pius V.

Some evidence points to Pasquale Macchi as the ultimate chief of the Vatican state's espionage services, while other reports suggest that perhaps he never rose to the height of directing the Holy Alliance but was only a buffer connecting and separating the supreme pontiff and a cardinal who truly ran the espionage services. In any case, Paul VI's papacy of just over fifteen years became one of the most fruitful for the Holy Alliance's operations.

Names such as Michele Sindona, Roberto Calvi, Paul Marcinkus, Carlos the Jackal, Black September, Golda Meir, and Mossad indicate some of the people and organizations that occupied the Holy See's espionage agents during this time. The enemy was not only outside the Vatican's walls but also inside; Freemasonry is one example.

One of the most spectacular Vatican counterespionage operations carried out by the *Sodalitium Pianum* took place during the first years of Paul VI's papacy. Evidently, Moscow and the KGB had a heightened interest in the Vatican state, and therefore Soviet intelligence determined to place a mole in the highest ranks of the Roman curia, alongside the supreme pontiff himself.

Alighiero Tondi had studied in a Jesuit seminary and, thanks to his efficiency, had become Monsignor Montini's secretary and aide. When Montini assumed the papacy in Rome, he brought young Tondi with him from Milan.[4]

In fact, however, the Jesuit was an undercover agent for the KGB within the Vatican, perhaps one of the most active. When he graduated from seminary in 1936, Tondi began working in Catholic publishing houses, where he first formed ties with communist groups. He was even selected by the Italian Communist Party to study at Lenin University in Moscow. There Soviet intelligence recruited him to operate inside the Vatican.

Tondi began work as a Soviet agent in 1944, betraying the *Russicum* priests sent to the Soviet Union as undercover evangelists. The Holy Alliance later calculated that Alighiero Tondi betrayed some 250 members of the *Russicum,* many of whom ended their lives in Soviet gulags or were executed on charges of having spied against the USSR.[5]

In 1967, a *Sodalitium Pianum* agent reported that Tondi had been seen in a Roman café with a "supposed" KGB agent posted to the Soviet embassy in Rome. From then on, without Pope Paul VI's knowledge, Father Alighiero Tondi was placed under counterintelligence surveillance. The Holy Alliance wanted to know how far Tondi had penetrated Vatican security. Finally, one night in 1968, the counterespionage agency got word that His Holiness's secretary had requested some documents from the Vatican Secret Archives. Immediately, Cardinal Eugène Tisserant, head of the Archives, was told to stall Tondi until Holy Alliance agents could get there. The file requested by Alighiero Tondi included communications between Paul VI and his nunciatures and legations in Eastern Europe, on the other side of the Iron Curtain. If Tondi had gained access to these communications, the cover and safety of Holy Alliance agents in Hungary, Poland, Czechoslovakia, and Romania would have been jeopardized.

Tondi told the counterespionage agents that the pope himself had requested these files. He said that since he was following a papal order, he would answer only to Paul VI. The Jesuit was taken to an office, where he remained under the guard of two Vatican security agents overnight. The first call went out to the cardinal secretary of state, Amleto Giovanni Cicognani. The head of the Holy Alliance told the cardinal that the pope's secretary had been arrested on suspicion of spying for the Soviet Union inside the Vatican. Cicognani immediately informed the supreme pontiff, counseling him to turn Tondi over to the Italian police for prosecution. But the papal espionage service urged Paul VI to expel Tondi from the Vatican without explanation, on the condition that he never return.

That same night, wearing only the clothes on his back, Alighiero Tondi, Pope Paul VI's secretary and a KGB agent in the Vatican for the past twenty-four years, was taken to the Vatican-Italian line by a group of Swiss Guards. From there he set out for Russia, where he became an advisor on Church affairs to the Soviet leader Leonid Brezhnev.[6]

It was not only the Soviets who infiltrated the Vatican, however. The Masons had their spies as well. Since late 1968, Vatican counterintelligence had been investigating various members of the curia in search of possible Masonic "infiltrations." The investigation went on until early 1971, when one day the head of the *Sodalitium Pianum* was called before the pope. Paul VI wanted to hear the details of this operation. The S.P. head offered the supreme pontiff a thick dossier with names, dates, and places demonstrating all the links between Freemasonry and various Vatican departments.[7]

The Masons within the curia knew that they needed to be close to the heartbeat of history, as the writer Cesare Pavese said, and they followed the simple dictum "Believe as little as possible without becoming a heretic, so that you can obey as little as possible without becoming a rebel."

The report prepared by papal counterespionage exposed the tentacles of the Masonic octopus that had spread through the palaces of the Vatican. Many years had passed and many popes come and gone between the time Clement XII (July 12, 1730–February 8, 1740) had issued a bull excommunicating all Masons and an October 19, 1974, article in the magazine *Civiltà Cattolica* in which the Jesuit priest Giovanni Caprile tried to put Catholics affiliated with Freemasonry at ease. In truth, since Montini's accession to the Throne of St. Peter, Masons had begun appearing everywhere in the Vatican's halls. The most important was the banker Michele Sindona, whom the pope named as his financial advisor. A few years later, Paul VI would entrust the power of the IOR[8] to four Masons: Sindona, Roberto Calvi, Licio Gelli, and Umberto Ortolani.

The pope himself told the counterespionage chief to close the investigation of Freemasonry in the Vatican. He ordered the report deposited in the Secret Archive.

Years later, in 1987, journalist Pier Carpi put forward the claim that many cardinals and bishops belonged to the Masonic lodge Propaganda 2 or P2,[9] which he called the *Loggia Ecclesia,* closely tied to the United Lodge of England and its grand master Michael, Duke of Kent. Another press report[10] revealed that "Masonry has divided the Vatican into eight sections, in which four Scottish Rite lodges are active. Their members, high officials of the small Vatican state, belong to the rite as individuals and are apparently unknown to each other, even by the signal of three taps with the thumb." Be this as it may, since Paul VI ordered the SP's investigation closed in 1971, there has been no further probing of the issue within the Vatican's walls.[11]

The *Sodalitium Pianum*'s list of Masons included such illustrious cardinals as Augustín Bea, secretary of state during the papacies of John XXIII and Paul VI; Sebastiano Baggio, prefect of the Sacred Congregation of Bishops; Agostino Casaroli, secretary of state during the papacy of John Paul II; Achille Lienart, Archbishop of Lille; Pasquale Macchi, Pope Paul VI's private secretary; Salvatore Pappalardo, Archbishop of Palermo; Michele Pelligrino, Archbishop of Turin; Ugo Poletti, vicar of the diocese of Rome; and Jean Villot, Pope Paul VI's secretary of state.[12]

The famous dossier on Freemasonry's tentacles inside the Vatican prepared by the counterespionage agents remained "buried" in the Vatican Secret Archives.

In early January 1974, the supreme pontiff ordered the heads of the Holy Alliance and *Sodalitium Pianum* to meet with him in his private dining room. The three men met for about three and a half hours. No one else knew what was said or how, but during this meeting Paul VI asked his intelligence directors to put in motion what became known as "Operation *Nessun Dorma*" (Let no one sleep).

The goal of this operation was to assemble a broad report revealing the needs and deficiencies of all Vatican departments and detailing accusations of corrupt behavior by Vatican officials. Although the investigation itself was assigned to the Holy Alliance, the task of writing the final report fell to Archbishop Édouard Gagnon and Monsignor Istvan Mester, the head of the Congregation for the Clergy.[13]

For months, Holy Alliance agents walked kilometer after kilometer of Vatican hallways, questioning and interrogating all the officials of the many papal departments. In a few weeks, the pope's spies had hundreds of accusations of irregularities and crimes committed by bishops and cardinals. Finally, Monsignor Gagnon, as president of the commission, spent three months organizing all the material the Holy Alliance had collected. The voluminous report exposing hidden activities within the curia bore the title *Nessun Dorma,* the same as the Holy Alliance operation. Holy Alliance and S.P. agents kept watch over it every night. Still, other forces were determined to keep the report from ever reaching Paul VI.

Once he had finished writing the report, Monsignor Gagnon requested an audience with the supreme pontiff through the secretariat of state. Gagnon wanted to personally inform Paul VI of what the Holy Alliance agents had found. Weeks went by, and he got no response. Finally the secretariat replied that, given the sensitive nature of the matter, the dossier should be handed over to the Congregation for the Clergy, directed by Cardinal John Joseph Wright. There it would remain in the custody of Monsignor Istvan Mester until Gagnon was summoned before the pope.

The dossier was ensconced in a chest with iron locks inside one of the rooms of the *Congregatio pro Clerici.* On the morning of June 2, 1974, Monsignor Mester opened the door to this room and found books scattered on the floor, papers in disarray, and boxes opened. He immediately called Monsignor Édouard Gagnon, who in turn called the heads of the Holy Alliance and the *Sodalitium Pianum.* When they arrived, they found Mester on his knees in front of the chest in which the dossier *Nessun Dorma* had been placed on the afternoon of May 30. The locks had been ripped off. The report of the completed investigation was gone. The counterespionage service concluded that the thieves must have had keys to the quarters of the Congregation for the Clergy, because none of the door locks had been forced. Sometime during Saturday, May 31, and Sunday, June 1, the unknown intruders had carried out the theft.

When Pope Paul VI learned of this assault, the supreme pontiff ordered everyone connected to the case, including the espionage agents involved in the investigation, to put themselves under the rule of "Pontifical Secrecy."[14]

Monsignor Gagnon informed the secretariat of state that he was ready to write a new report. Mysteriously, he was ordered (still under "Pontifical Secrecy") to turn his notes over to the secretariat and suspend any further work on the matter until he received new orders. Investigation of the robbery was turned over to Camillo Cibin, head of the *Corpo di Vigilanza* (the Vatican police force). The secret services, who had gathered the information in *Nessun Dorma,* were incomprehensibly left out.

Cibin was to inform only the secretariat of state, without filing written reports on any part of his investigation. The pope ordered the entire affair to be kept an absolute secret, but rumors about the theft of a secret dossier had already begun circulating outside as well as inside the Vatican.

On Tuesday, June 3, the press began to report that "thieves had broken into a secured room somewhere inside the Vatican, and there is speculation that a report prepared on the orders of the pope himself has disappeared." Dr. Federico Alessandrini, the Vatican spokesman, could not escape from journalists' repeated questions. Finally, even the Holy See's official paper, *L'Osservatore Romano,* reported the theft: "It is a case of true and shameful robbery. Unknown thieves entered the office of a prelate and stole files from a solid chest with a double lock. This is a true scandal," the article said.

In the following days, fourteen members of the curia who had spoken with Holy Alliance agents and given them information on corruption in various departments were expelled from the Vatican. Five more were sent to Africa on an "evangelical mission."

Although Monsignor Gagnon was not told to write a new report, the clergyman secretly put together a replacement for the stolen one. When he had finished, he again requested an audience with Pope Paul VI. Again his request was rejected. Then he asked the secretariat of state to forward the report to the pontiff, but the dossier did not get there. Someone in the secretariat told the pope that the *Nessun Dorma* report could not be found. Rumors of conspiracy all pointed to Cardinal Jean Villot, ex–secretary of state and former cardinal-chamberlain of the Apostolic Chamber, who was known in the Vatican as the "vice-pope."

Finally, Monsignor Édouard Gagnon asked permission to retire, leaving the Holy See for his home country of Canada. In 1983, John Paul II recalled him to Rome, raising him to the rank of cardinal on May 25, 1985.

Nothing more was heard about Operation *Nessun Dorma* in the halls of the Vatican. No future pope ever again assigned the Holy Alliance and the

Sodalitium Pianum any similar investigation. But the Vatican secret services continued to run in high gear during Paul VI's papacy, fighting new enemies. One of these was Black September.

The Holy Alliance's "Operation Jerusalem" and the Mossad's[15] "Operation Diamond" showed that the two espionage services were working together. This collaboration would bear fruit in a few years when the Mossad, at war with Black September over the killing of Israeli athletes at the 1972 Olympic Games in Munich, exposed an operation to kidnap or assassinate Pope Paul VI.

In late autumn of 1972, Israeli prime minister Golda Meir received a secret message from Pope Paul VI. He said he would like her to come for a brief personal audience. On December 11, Meir met with her cabinet and with Mossad's *memuneh*[16] Zvi Zamir to ask their advice about the meeting with the supreme pontiff and the security measures it would require.

Meir made it clear that she "did not want to go to Canossa," a popular Israeli expression alluding to the Italian castle where in 1077 Henry IV of the Holy Roman Empire had humiliated himself by presenting himself before Pope Gregory VII as a penitent. Meir was too proud for that.

Zamir (through the Holy Alliance) and the Israeli foreign ministry (through the Vatican secretariat of state) knew that January 15, 1973, was the date selected for the meeting. Cardinal Jean Villot said the encounter would last thirty-five minutes, followed by an exchange of gifts. The meeting between Paul VI and Golda Meir would not follow a specific agenda, which was to say that any subject could be brought up by either side. For security reasons, surveillance and control would be in the hands of Mossad, directed by Zamir, and the Holy Alliance. Under no circumstances would there be any public announcement of the meeting between the two high officials, either before or after the event.[17]

According to the plan, Meir would fly to Paris to attend a conference of the Socialist International on January 13 and 14. From there, an unmarked plane rented by El Al airline would take her to Rome. The aides accompanying Meir would not know their final destination until the flight was in the air. After meeting the pope, Meir would travel to the Ivory Coast to meet for two days with President Félix Houhouiet-Boigny, and from there she would return to Israel.

Zamir decided to get to Rome a week earlier so as to prepare the security measures and create a channel connecting him to the Holy Alliance agents.

The *memuneh* saw the Eternal City as a possible staging area for an Arab terrorist attack. Since Black September's assault on the Israeli delegation to the Munich Olympics the year before, the Italian capital had become a meeting ground for terrorists of all factions in search of information and arms traffickers in search of clients.

The liaisons connecting Mossad and the Holy Alliance were Mark Hessner on the Israeli side and Father Carlo Jacobini on the Holy Alliance side. Hessner was joined by Shai Kauly, the case officer of the Mossad station in Milan. In a secret meeting, Zvi Zamir briefed Jacobini, Kauly, and Hessner on all the details of Golda Meir's trip to meet with Pope Paul VI. Clearly, none of this information could be allowed to leak out if they wanted to avoid a possible assassination attempt against the Israeli leader.

A day later, the Vatican counterespionage, the *Sodalitium Pianum,* informed Jacobini that someone, possibly a priest attached to the secretariat of state, had passed information about Meir to a contact in Rome known to have relations with Arab extremists.

The Holy Alliance agent alerted Zamir, who called Golda Meir personally to try to convince her it might be wiser to cancel the visit with Paul VI. Knowing the prime minister as he did, he was aware that a mere threat would not set her back in her attempt to win Vatican recognition of Israel, even if she had to risk an assassination attempt by Arab terrorists. Meir's only response to Zamir was, *"Memuneh,* your work is to prevent this. Israel cannot be stopped by a threat."

The Vatican assigned an additional *Sodalitium Pianum* counterespionage expert to provide security for the meeting. This was Father Angelo Casoni. It was he, in fact, who had discovered that word of Golda Meir's clandestine trip to meet with Pope Paul VI in the Vatican could have reached the ears of Abú Yúsuf. The Holy Alliance's Carlo Jacobini and the Mossad's Zvi Zamir knew that sooner or later some terrorist group would put in an appearance. In fact, Yúsuf had sent a message to Ali Hassan Salameh, alias the *Red Prince,* the top leader of the Palestinian terrorist group Black September and the brains behind the operation against the Israeli athletes in Munich. The text of this message said: "Let's get the one who is spilling our blood all over Europe."[18] The method and exact site of the attempt on Meir would depend on Salameh. While the assassination of Golda Meir would be a master stroke in the Red Prince's fight against the Israelis, for Yúsuf it would be a spectacular way to show the world that Black September remained a powerful terrorist group that had to be taken into account. Assassinating the Israeli leader in the Vatican would put his group in the top headlines of every communications medium.[19]

On January 10, five days before the meeting, *memuneh* Zvi Zamir and *katsa* Mark Hessner and Shai Kauly stepped into a black car to be driven through the streets of Rome to the Vatican. The Swiss Guards at the gate stood at attention as the car passed through into the administrative area of the Holy See. When the passengers emerged, they were met by Father Carlo Jacobini. From his report on Jacobini, Zamir knew that the priest had studied in the United States and that he had taken several courses on intelligence work at Langley, the CIA headquarters in Virginia. The Holy Alliance agent spoke six languages fluently. In the Vatican, he was regarded as a true "noble" because of his family ties to Cardinal Dominico Maria Jacobini, Cardinal Ludovico Jacobini (who had been secretary of state to Pope Leo XIII), and Cardinal Angelo Jacobini. Without a doubt, Zvi Zamir knew that young Carlo was a very useful contact in the mazes of the Vatican, especially since the Holy Alliance's loss of confidence in the CIA.

Nothing is known about the content of this secret meeting between Mossad and the Holy Alliance inside the Vatican, but Zamir surely departed satisfied with what he heard. Crossing the Piazza San Pietro, the *memuneh* told his driver they were going to the airport so he could catch a flight to Tel Aviv.

The "Institute," as the Israeli intelligence service was known, was now well aware that Ali Hassan Salameh had been informed about Golda Meir's impending trip to Rome. Thanks to the work of Father Angelo Casoni, they knew they had to be ready for an attack.

The terrorist groups had a special relationship with the KGB. They received political indoctrination in Moscow, as well as training in assassination techniques and in the use of explosives, which they later placed in shopping centers and crowded airport terminals.

Both Mossad and the Holy Alliance knew they could not count on the KGB to detect any Black September attempt on the life of Golda Meir. If they wanted to stop it, they could depend only on their own efforts, working against the clock.

The Soviets were not about to reveal that Hassan Salameh's men had Russian-built missiles hidden in an industrial building in a Yugoslav port. The plan was to ship the missiles in a fishing boat from Dubrovnik to Bari on the Italian Adriatic. From there, they would go to Rome by truck in time to arrive before Golda Meir. Zvi Zamir and Father Carlo Jacobini continued to work side by side to discover when and how the attack would come, but now they could only wait.

The anti-Israeli attack began on December 28, 1972, when Black September commandos attacked the Israeli embassy in Bangkok. Salameh wanted to divert Mossad's attention from Rome, and an attack on the far-off Jewish diplomatic legation was the way.

Angelo Casoni, of the Vatican counterespionage, said that one of his sources had reported that Black September's attack on Israel's embassy in Thailand was only a feint to distract public opinion. Jacobini didn't believe him, but Zamir did.[20] Mossad knew that Israeli commandos could free the hostages there, and Golda Meir was not going to allow the Thais to shoot their way into the embassy. At last, after hours of negotiations, the attackers were granted safe conduct to leave the country en route to Cairo. Carlo Jacobini advised continued readiness for a possible strike against Israeli policy that would come on Vatican soil.

Very early on January 14, one day before the planned meeting between Paul VI and Golda Meir, a Vatican counterespionage agent reported to Angelo Casoni that an informer had told him about rumors of a Palestinian guerrilla operation in Ostia or Bari. At the same time, a *sayan*[21] told the Mossad station at the Israeli embassy in Italy about a conversation in which a man with an evident Arabic accent told another man with the same accent to expect a shipment of candles.

At the same time, too, the Mossad station in London reported to Zvi Zamir that one of their informers had indicated that Black September's objective was "one of your own." The Mossad chief was sure that the shipment of candles had to be missiles, yet he also knew that neither Golda Meir nor Paul VI would ever cancel their meeting.

Zamir called Hessner and Kauly while requesting a meeting with Fathers Jacobini and Casoni. The Vatican secret services had to be kept informed at every step of the operation, for they surely had better sources in Rome than the Israelis did.

Ali Hassan Salameh, alias Abú Hassan, alias the Red Prince, was well-educated, energetic, and cruel. It was said that he had killed his stepbrother with a shot in the eye when he found the stepbrother passing information to

Al Fatah, the PLO faction led by Yasser Arafat.[22] Salameh was married to a Lebanese beauty, Georgina Rizak, who had been Miss Universe of 1971.

According to Mossad, the Red Prince was behind the attempt to assassinate Golda Meir, but the Holy Alliance doubted that the Palestinian terrorist could be in Rome without their knowing it.

The day slated for the meeting, January 15, dawned cold and rainy. Mossad, the Holy Alliance, and the *digos* (the Italian anti-terrorist unit) were on a state of full alert. Father Carlo Jacobini was sure that Black September would not allow Meir to leave Rome alive, and he so informed Pope Paul VI. Zamir and Jacobini knew that if the plan were a missile attack, the place to carry it out would be near the airport, when the plane was either landing or taking off. Both Mossad and the Holy Alliance deployed their agents in the airport and its vicinity to watch for any suspicious activity.[23]

The first alert came just a few hours before Golda Meir's planned arrival. A *Sodalitium Pianum* agent watching the vicinity of the airport warned Father Angelo Casoni that he had seen a station wagon near a runway and had approached it and asked whether the occupants needed any help. The men inside had nervously answered that they'd already called a tow truck. Casoni radioed this to Zamir and Hessner, who set out for the spot. When they arrived, they found a Fiat station wagon. Armed, they asked the driver to step out of the vehicle and identify himself. A prudent distance away, Carlo Jacobini of the papal secret services was watching.

At that moment, the vehicle's back gate opened and a fusillade of shots rang out. The Mossad agents escaped unharmed, but they left two terrorists gravely wounded, while the driver fled on foot. The Israeli agents caught him and put him into a car, apparently one with Vatican license plates. Hessner sat in the driver's seat, Jacobini alongside, and Zamir in back with the terrorist. The *memuneh* of Mossad beat the Palestinian's head with his pistol butt, demanding to know where the other missiles were. With the silhouette of the plane approaching in the distance, the agents saw another station wagon, this time a white one, with a roof that had been modified. Several tubes stuck out, pointing skyward.

Hessner floored the accelerator and rammed the car from the side, making it roll over. Inside, two members of Black September were trapped, crushed under the weight of the missiles. Zamir told Father Jacobini to turn away so he could execute the terrorists, but before he could shoot, the Holy

Alliance agent told the Mossad chief that if he killed them, there would be no alternative but to tell the supreme pontiff, which would place Israel in a difficult position.

Zamir preferred not to further complicate the already difficult relations between Israel and the Vatican, so he turned the terrorists over to the Italian *digo.*

Golda Meir had her meeting with Pope Paul VI. Though he informed her the time was not right to establish relations, he did commit himself to visiting the Holy Land. On leaving the Vatican, Golda Meir told Zvi Zamir that "the Vatican clock runs on different time than the rest of the world," which may, in fact, be the case.

From then on, Mossad and the Holy Alliance maintained close relations, which continued on into the papacy of John Paul II. Fathers Carlo Jacobini and Angelo Casoni, of the Vatican espionage and counterespionage services, continued to serve as liaisons with Israeli secret services in the following years, even after Jacobini ceased to belong to the Holy Alliance. The terrorists whom the Italians had arrested were set free and sent to Libya. Months later, most of them were executed by a unit of the *kidon,*[24] the Mossad assassins. As to the identity of the person in the secretariat of state who could have informed the Black September terrorists about Meir's secret trip, the *Sodalitium Pianum's* suspicions pointed to Father Idi Ayad. What Mossad didn't know then, and possibly never knew, was that Ayad was not only a member of the Holy Alliance but also an unofficial liaison between Pope Paul VI and the leadership of the PLO.[25]

Meanwhile, in an office lost somewhere amidst the kilometers of Vatican hallways, a man placed a seal upon a folder labeled "Operation Jerusalem" and ordered it to be interred in the Vatican Secret Archives, a division of the Vatican Library. To the world at large, the operation charged with saving Golda Meir's life had never existed. But Mossad would never forget that Israel's prime minister still drew breath thanks to the Holy Alliance.

Three years later, Mossad repaid the favor. The occasion came in April of 1976.

On December 25, 1971, the terrorist Carlos the Jackal had carried out an operation against OPEC delegates meeting in Vienna. From then on, he was in open confrontation with the Palestinian groups who had previously been aiding him. In their eyes, Carlos was simply a mercenary who had acquired a good deal of money to "spend on bourgeois comforts." Carlos and his associates had pocketed nearly twenty million dollars out of the ransom the Saudis paid to free their OPEC representative Sheik Ahmed Zaki Yamami.[26]

Wadi Haddad, leader of the Popular Front for the Liberation of Palestine (PFLP), demanded a share of this money from Carlos, but the Jackal refused. Haddad, a dyed-in-the-wool guerrilla, was not pleased by the attention Carlos had attracted, since to him the Jackal was merely "a bad actor who wants to be a movie star." After the action against OPEC in Vienna, Carlos and his confederates moved to Algeria and then to Yemen, where they were given a heroes' welcome, complete with a band. Carlos the Jackal's legend continued to grow.

One morning in late March of 1976, the telephone in an administrative department of the Vatican rang. A priest picked up the phone to hear a speaker identify himself as Yitzhak Hofi, the new *memuneh* who had replaced Zvi Zamir at the helm of Mossad two years before. Hofi told the priest that he needed a meeting in a safe location.

That same afternoon, the priest made his way on foot to a downtown Rome hotel. When he identified himself, two crew-cut men led the clergyman to a guest room, where Yitzhak Hofi awaited him, seated in a chair. The new arrival also took a seat. The Israeli spy chief told him the moment had come to repay the Holy Alliance for the favor of having helped to save Golda Meir's life in January 1973.

Father Carlo Jacobini said although he no longer worked for the Holy Alliance, perhaps he could connect the Israelis with someone in the papal espionage service. Hofi rejected that offer, saying his orders from his predecessor Zvi Zamir were to work only with Jacobini. Before he could hear the information Mossad had to give him, Jacobini responded, he had to get a specific order from the Vatican. Hofi repeated that he could deal only with Jacobini, or with Angelo Casoni of the papal counterespionage.

Yitzhak Hofi shifted in his chair and told Jacobini that a Mossad station had unearthed a plan by an Arab terrorist group to kidnap or assassinate Pope Paul VI. After some beating around the bush, the Israeli explained that his *katsas* were sure the author of the attack was Carlos the Jackal. Jacobini's blood ran cold. He knew from Holy Alliance reports that Carlos rarely failed in his objectives, and even if he didn't succeed, he always left a trail of blood and death.

In fact, Hofi's information did not come from a Mossad station, but rather from a political attaché in the U.S. embassy in Tehran, John D. Stempel. This diplomat had reported to the CIA that during a meeting with the second secretary of the Soviet embassy in Iran, Guennady Kazankin, the latter had told him the KGB had discovered a possible plan to kidnap or assassinate Pope Paul VI, which might involve several members of the Baader-Meinhof Gang, who had collaborated with Carlos the Jackal in the OPEC kidnapping in Vienna. Hofi finished his briefing of Carlo Jacobini by promising the Holy Alliance all possible help from Mossad in frustrating this plan.[27]

When the meeting ended, the priest took a taxi to the Vatican. Hofi's words echoed in his brain, and he needed to share them with someone. When he passed through the Vatican gate, he directed his steps toward the offices housing the papal secret services. He said he urgently needed to speak with his friend Father Angelo Casoni. In the two hours they spent together, Jacobini told Casoni what the Mossad *memuneh* had told him.

Carlos's idea revolved around two possible plans. One was to take control of the Basilica of St. Peter by storming it with arms in hand while the pontiff was conducting Mass. The other was to have sharpshooters fire at Paul VI when he emerged onto his balcony facing the plaza to welcome the faithful on Sunday. The first idea was the subject of several weeks of study, given the successful use of this tactic in the kidnapping of the OPEC representatives in Vienna. The Jackal doubted that his group would meet much resistance from the Swiss Guard, armed as they were with lances and halberds.

The second option had the support of Wilfred Böse, a German anarchist and friend of Carlos the Jackal and of Gabrielle Kroche-Tiedemann, a twenty-three-year-old terrorist who had taken part in the Vienna operation alongside Carlos the year before. Böse thought it would be simple enough to get hold of a large-caliber rifle with a telescopic sight and use it against an "immobile objective dressed in white." The plan appealed to Kroche-Tiedemann because killing the supreme pontiff of Rome in the act of blessing the faithful gathered in the Piazza San Pietro, in full view of television cameras from around the world, would bring Carlos the Jackal the greatest publicity any terrorist had ever gathered.

The Holy Alliance worked against the clock, in collaboration with Mossad, to prevent the looming debacle. Jacobini needed to know more, so he called Hofi personally. The *memuneh* promised to send copies of the dossiers on the men and women who had accompanied Carlos in all his actions. The next day, a pile of folders covered with seals appeared on the desk of Father Angelo Casoni of the papal counterespionage. Black-and-white photographs of corpses paraded before his eyes, as did faces captured from a distance by the camera of one or another spy.

Shortly afterwards, Jacobini and Casoni received another Mossad message to the effect that Wilfred Böse and Gabrielle Kroche-Tiedemann had been spotted in Bahrain and Carlos Ramírez in Yemen. At that moment, however, neither the two Vatican agents nor Yitzhak Hofi knew that the Jackal's organization had decided to change its target. Kidnapping or killing Paul VI no longer interested Carlos Ramírez. On a whim, he had decided instead to skyjack an Air France jet, Flight AF139 en route from Tel Aviv to Paris with a stop in Athens.

This plane would become world famous on July 4, 1976, when, in a lightning operation at the Ugandan airport of Entebbe, a squad of Israeli commandos and Mossad *kidon* members stormed the jetliner and freed the hostage passengers. In the gunfight that broke out on the airport runways and terminal, Wilfred Böse and Gabrielle Kroche-Tiedemann died from Israeli fire, as did five other terrorists.

A few days after Operation Entebbe, Father Carlo Jacobini received a mysterious phone call in the Vatican. Hofi, on the other end of the line, told him about the dead terrorists and assured him that the "crisis involving Paul VI" had ended. On January 22, 1979, the Mossad finally located Ali Hassan Salameh, alias the Red Prince, the top leader of Black September, in Beirut. A remote-control bomb placed by the *katsa* Erika Chambers of the *kidon,* the operative arm of the *Metsada,* killed Salameh. It also killed four of his bodyguards, several passers-by, and Susan Wareham, a secretary at the British embassy in Lebanon.

Some rumors had it that Salameh had been tracked down in the Lebanese capital thanks to the work of the Vatican secret services by way of a CIA leak that a Holy Alliance or *Sodalitium Pianum* agent passed on to the Mossad *memuneh,* Yitzhak Hofi. That agent could well have been Carlo Jacobini or Angelo Casoni. But, like everything in the Vatican and its intelligence services, "whatever isn't sacred, is secret."

Paul Casimir Marcinkus, Michele Sindona, and Roberto Calvi would become the main actors in one of the greatest scandals in the history of the Holy See. The Vatican Bank collapse was about to surprise the world. The ensuing investigations of financial organizations and courts in the United States and Italy, as well as books by writers in several countries, would show that although the Holy Alliance was not directly and officially involved in the dark doings of the IOR under Monsignor Paul Marcinkus, some of its agents did take part in certain specific operations. For many of them, defending "Vatican, Inc." was a question of loyalty to the supreme pontiff.

18

"VATICAN, INC." AND

GOD'S BUSINESS (1976–1978)

For such false apostles are deceitful workmen, who masquerade as apostles of Christ. And no wonder, for even Satan masquerades as an angel of light. So it is not strange that his ministers also masquerade as ministers of righteousness; their end shall be according to their works.
—II Corinthians, 11:13–15

Along with the Vatican espionage services, the *Istituto per le Opere di Religione* (IOR), commonly known as the "Vatican Bank,"[1] is one of the papal departments most shrouded in secrecy. Entering the Vatican through St. Anne's Gate and passing to the right of Bernini's columns, with St. Anne's Church on one's right and the Swiss Guard barracks on the left, one can find the building that houses the IOR. The tower was built on the orders of Pope Nicholas V almost 650 years ago as part of the defense system of the Holy See. Today only a small group of Swiss Guards stand watch over its marble entrance and the hermetically sealed bronze doors that may be opened only by select members of the curia.

The Vatican Bank has given rise to endless scandals and been involved in multimillion-dollar losses, bankruptcies, arms sales to warring nations, dummy companies in fiscal paradises, financing of coups d'etat, laundering of Mafia money, and mysterious "suicides." The IOR has broken hundreds of international finance laws without any of its directors having been charged before any earthly court. Since its founding, the IOR has never been an official department of the Vatican city-state. It exists as an entity, but without any clear ties to ecclesiastical affairs or other departments of the Holy See. Its oversight and control lies only in the hands of the supreme pontiff.[2]

Unlike other international financial institutions, the Vatican Bank is not audited by any internal or external agency, nor is there a written record of its operations. For example, in 1996, Cardinal Edmund Szoka, the internal auditor of the Holy See, told several investigators that he had no authority over the Vatican Bank and added that he was completely ignorant of its actions and workings.

In 1990, the Vatican state declared a deficit of $78 million, while the Vatican Bank in that same year unofficially "declared" earnings in excess of $10 billion.[3]

In 1967, Pope Paul VI created a general accounting office called the Prefecture of Economic Affairs of the Holy See. The supreme pontiff named his friend Cardinal Egidio Vagnozzi as director, but Vagnozzi resigned a few months later. Apparently he learned of the strange relations between the pope and the so-called Mafia banker Michele Sindona. Curiously, Vagnozzi was barred from talking about the Prefecture or anything related to it, under the famous "Pontifical Secret" rules.

Every week, the erstwhile director had discovered, million of dollars of unknown origin were deposited without explanation in the vaults of the Vatican Bank. As rapidly as it came in, the money flowed out the back door toward numbered Swiss bank accounts and toward companies belonging to the Sindona Group. That money could be used to finance riots and coups, like the coup of April 1967 in Greece.

The Propaganda 2 lodge, closely linked to the Vatican and its secret services, had centered its attention on the next Greek election. The likely winner was leftist leader Andreas Papandreu, a political enemy of King Constantine II, the monarch who was also head of the armed forces. Polls showed Papandreu with a lead, but the army feared he would turn the country over to the communists. Colonel Papadopoulos insisted that the fallout would be civil war.[4]

Toward the end of that year, Continental Bank of Illinois, which belonged to Sindona, transferred four million dollars to the Banca Privata Finanziaria, within the Vatican orbit. When the money arrived, Sindona himself assigned a Holy Alliance agent to take charge of the funds and turn them over to Colonel Papadopoulos in person. The money was to be deposited in a checking account in the name Helleniki Tecniki, a real estate firm controlled by the Greek army and guaranteed by the National Bank of Greece.

The Holy Alliance, together with Michele Sindona, Licio Gelli, and Propaganda 2, decided to finance a coup to keep the left out of power. Researchers disagree as to whether the Vatican secret services were merely an instrument wielded by Gelli and Sindona or whether the Holy Alliance in fact designed "Operation Tatoi"[5] and Gelli and Sindona were simply its sources of funds.

In either case, on April 21, 1967, a group of colonels did stage a coup and impose martial law. They suspended the constitution and severely repressed democratic movements and especially unions and communist organizations. Socialist leader Andreas Papandreu was sentenced to nine years in prison.

That December, King Constantine tried to topple the junta, but he failed. He and his family had to go into exile in Rome. The officers appointed General Zoitakis as president and Papadopoulos as prime minister. The "colonels' regime," as it became known, continued to get aid from the United States, from the Masonic lodge Propaganda 2, and from wealthy Greek businessmen like Aristotle Onassis and Stavros Niarchos.[6]

This success in Greece spurred Michele Sindona to finance extreme right-wing groups. In this effort he made use of Vatican funds that passed through a structure he created within the IOR. He also made use of free agents of the Holy Alliance. A few years later, the mysterious Paul Casimir Marcinkus arrived on the scene, apparently attached to the Vatican secret services as well.

Born in the environs of Chicago in 1922, he attended seminary in the U.S. and then enrolled in Rome's Gregorian University to study canon law. In 1952, Marcinkus joined the secretariat of state and was posted to the nunciatures in Canada and Bolivia. Finally, he became head of security for Pope Paul VI. During his time in the secretariat of state, Marcinkus formed close ties with the Vatican secret services in general and with important individuals in the Holy Alliance in particular, who would provide valuable aid in the coming years. One of these, who would be implicated in the future Banco Ambrosiano scandal, was the Polish Jesuit Kazimierz Przydatek.

In 1969, Pope Paul VI made Marcinkus a bishop. The next morning he was likewise "consecrated" as secretary of the Vatican Bank. Two years later, Paul VI unexpectedly rewarded Paul Marcinkus's loyalty by naming him as the top director of the IOR, which launched his meteoric financial career.

His inner circle consisted of Michele Sindona, Roberto Calvi, Umberto Ortolani, and Licio Gelli, all linked to the Gambino Mafia family, the Masonic lodge Propaganda 2, and the Vatican financial structure.

Marcinkus used the Holy Alliance as his own intelligence source. One report by the Vatican secret service, now in the possession of Paul Marcinkus, showed that Sindona had funded (possibly with Vatican money) a holding company in Liechtenstein called Fasco AG, through which he had acquired a Milanese bank, the Banca Privata Finanziaria (BPF). The report did not specify that some of the earnings from this acquisition financed construction of the Casa della Madonnina. Then-cardinal Montini, Archbishop of Milan, needed money, and Sindona provided it. In all, two and a half million dollars entered the archbishopric's coffers to pay for the religious institution.

Marcinkus learned years later that these funds did not actually come from the acquisition of the BPF, but from laundering the dirty money of the Sicilian Mafia, especially international heroin profits. In any case, from then on, by way of Cardinal Montini, Sindona acquired an impressive list of clients whom he advised on taxes, investments, and also tax evasion.

Little by little, the business dealings of the Vatican Bank and its "advisors" grew more and more risky, putting various financial institutions into dire straits and finally compromising the economic systems of the Vatican and of Italy. A CIA report on Michele Sindona from those years that fell into the hands of the Holy Alliance detailed the extensive relations of Paul VI's banker with the Gambino family in the U.S. and the Inzerillo and Spatola families in Sicily. This twenty-page dossier explained Carlo Gambino's connection with the Colombo, Bonanno, Lucchese, and Genovese families, all deeply involved in the processing, traffic, and sale of heroin, cocaine, and marijuana. The report said that Sindona was in charge of hiding drug, prostitution, bank fraud, pornography, and loan-sharking profits in secret bank accounts in Switzerland, Liechtenstein, and Beirut. Michele Sindona, in short, served as financial advisor not just to Pope Paul VI and the Vatican but also to Mafia families.[7] Apparently Marcinkus ordered this CIA report on the banker destroyed. Years later, the IOR head reminded Sindona about it, shortly before his fall.

Meanwhile, the health of the great protector of such dark Vatican financial dealings began to decline. In 1968, at the age of seventy-one, Paul VI underwent a prostate operation. In 1978, he was much affected by two events that marked the last few months of his life: the kidnapping and execution of Christian Democratic Party leader Aldo Moro by the Red Brigades and the passage of an abortion law in Italy.

On Saturday, August 5, the pope had his dinner, prayed the rosary in his private chapel, signed several documents apparently related to the Vatican Bank, and then went to bed. The next morning, August 6, he was unable to conduct Mass. In the afternoon, his health grew worse, and Vatican doctors diagnosed a serious pulmonary edema. Treatment soon proved useless, and he died.

Immediately, the machinery of the Vatican began moving toward the election of a new pope. Factions and conspiracies swirled around the convocation of the new conclave to choose a successor to the late Paul VI.[8]

In the Vatican Bank, personnel of various departments set about burning documents to avoid a possible investigation at the hands of a more liberal pope. Figures like Marcinkus, Gelli, Calvi, and Sindona would not find it easy to explain many of the financial dealings they had undertaken in the names of the Vatican, the pope, and God.

On August 10, Cardinal Albino Luciani, patriarch of Venice, arrived in Rome to take part in the conclave. Since his name was nowhere among the list of leading candidates, he rested quietly in his room, number sixty.

After only nine hours, 110 cardinals voted by acclamation for the person who would assume the papacy.[9]

In meetings held before the conclave, Cardinal Giovanni Benelli made a surprising statement to Cardinal Luciani, Polish primate Cardinal Stefan Wyszynski, and Hungarian primate Cardinal Laszlo Lekai. He said that the next pope would find himself in difficult circumstances when he ascended the Throne of St. Peter because the Church's economic and financial situation was not good. Benelli told the three cardinals that the situation was "not only critical, but about to explode."

Cardinal-chamberlain Jean Villot, who was nearby, overhead Cardinal Benelli's warning and demanded silence. Then he hurried to call the Vatican's prefect of economic affairs, Cardinal Egidio Vagnozzi. He told Vagnozzi to enlist the Holy Alliance in preparing a report on the critical situation to which Cardinal Benelli was referring.

Vagnozzi knew where such an investigation could lead. He also knew, however, that it would never penetrate the dark secrets of IOR moneys managed by Monsignor Paul Marcinkus and the tentacles established under the protective mantle of Paul VI. Mysteriously, Cardinal Pietro Palazzini told the Holy Alliance and the counterespionage *Sodalitium Pianum* that they should lend all their aid to Vagnozzi, but the problem was that many Holy Alliance agents had carried out special tasks for Marcinkus, and they, of course, were well aware of what Benelli and Palazzini were doing.

Paul Marcinkus and Michele Sindona, meanwhile, had received encouraging words from Cardinal Villot about the nearly sure election of Cardinal Giuseppe Siri of Florence, a figure both majestic and conservative. Marcinkus knew that if Siri were elected, the IOR would not suffer any intrusive investigations. Cardinal Giuseppe Siri was not on good terms with Cardinals Benelli and Palazzini.

One of the staunchest supporters of an investigation of the IOR, on the other hand, was Cardinal Sergio Pignedoli. Months before the conclave, Pignedoli had been speaking to other cardinals—perhaps too openly—about the need to look into these millions of dollars coming out of the Vatican. Pignedoli had met secretly with Cardinals Benelli, Palazzini, and Vagnozzi and had voiced his concern about the constant rumors linking the IOR and certain operations carried out by Nicaraguan dictator Anastasio Somoza.

During the conclave, Cardinal Franjo Seper told Cardinal Luciani that dark forces inside the Vatican had managed to derail the "dangerous" Cardinal Pignedoli from the race for the papacy. The Yugoslavian prelate added that at dinner someone had spoken in a low voice, intended only for his neighbor at the table, about Sergio Pignedoli's sexual behavior among the youth and that "sometimes his apartment filled with sleeping bags when he couldn't find them any other lodging."[10]

The rumor was, in fact, a slander intended only to reduce Pignedoli's chances to zero, in which it succeeded. Seper said the cardinal who started the rumor had been expelled from the conclave, but the damage had already been done. Apparently, the rumormonger had served in the Vatican Bank for years until finally he had transferred to another post. The "dark forces," as Albino Luciani himself called them, had quickly eliminated a candidate who would bring problems for the IOR and Paul Marcinkus.

On Saturday, August 26, 1978, the first vote, seen as kind of a straw poll, showed a clear preference for Cardinal Giuseppe Siri. However, since he fell short of the necessary two-thirds majority, another vote followed. In this one, Luciani got fifty votes and Pignedoli got twenty.[11]

After a brief break, the members of the conclave returned to the Sistine

Chapel for two more votes in the afternoon. The first took place at four o'clock. Cardinal Bafile read out Cardinal Albino Luciani's name more than seventy-five times. Immediately afterwards, the powerful Cardinals Villot (for the episcopate, or bishops), Siri (for the presbyterate, or priesthood), and Felicio (for the diaconate, or lower orders) pressed Luciani to accept his destiny. When he said the words, "I accept," Cardinal Jean Villot asked, "What would you like to be called, Holy Father?" "John Paul," Luciani replied. "You will be John Paul I," Cardinal Felici responded, unaware of his faux pas. The pope who inaugurates a dynasty is never referred to by a number until a second supreme pontiff adopts that name. The new pope's following words were nearly a premonition. "Let me be John Paul the First, because the Second will come soon," the now-ex-cardinal Albino Luciani said.

While newspapers like *L'Osservatore Romano* splashed the election of the new pope, John Paul I, across their front pages, *The Economist* magazine headlined the strange operations carried out by financiers in the service of the Vatican Bank.

When he heard this news, Paul Marcinkus warned his partners in the IOR and Roberto Calvi, who was in Buenos Aires at the time. He told them to remember that the new pope was very different from Paul VI, and then he recommended that they should transfer all the international bank's promissory notes to a safer country like the Bahamas or Switzerland.

Meanwhile, rumors and speculations about the actions of high IOR officials swirled through the Vatican hallways. The officials denied ever having met with figures like Michele Sindona or Roberto Calvi. A few days after the appointment of Cardinal Bernardin Gantin as president of the Pontifical Council *Cor Unum,* the pope found in his office a copy of a report by the Italian securities and exchange commission, the UIC. Someone had decided to leave a first clue about the IOR's murky business dealings for John Paul I to find.[12]

The report, signed by external commerce minister Rinaldo Ossola, declared that the Vatican Bank was a nonresident financial institution; it was "foreign" and untouchable.[13]

Minister Ossola was disturbed by the abuses in money trafficking that had provoked a flight of currency from Italy, leaving the lira very weak. Ossola thought he knew who inside the Vatican or close to it was running this operation out of the IOR.

It is said that the new pope—when he was still only a cardinal—had asked several times for an explanation of the rumors about the financial state of the IOR. In response, Pope Paul VI had sent Paul Marcinkus to him with a repeated litany of questions. "Your Eminence, do you have something better to do today? You should do your job and let me do mine." That was how the Vatican finance chief responded to the Venetian patriarch.[14]

On reading the report, John Paul I held a secret meeting with Cardinal Benelli and Cardinal Felici. He asked them to explain everything they had discovered in the past few years about the Bank of Italy's investigation of the Banco Ambrosiano.

Over the course of several nights, Benelli told the supreme pontiff about the IOR's relations with Licio Gelli, Propaganda 2, Michele Sindona, and Roberto Calvi. Felici, for his part, detailed Calvi's other relations and his connections with the IOR and Paul Marcinkus. Apparently Benelli had been kept informed of each step in the investigation by a secret source, a "deep throat" in the Bank of Italy, while Monsignor Felici got his information from a source within the Holy Alliance.

It was this latter source who told Cardinal Benelli about the investigation of Roberto Calvi's empire, which was entering its most intense phase in September of 1978.[15] The Holy Alliance agent reporting to Benelli was a priest named Giovanni DaNicola whom the Alliance had infiltrated into Marcinkus's IOR. A graduate in economics and an expert in setting up financial services companies and companies' headquarters in tax havens, Father DaNicola had no trouble infiltrating the IOR. His services were in high demand given that the Vatican Bank owned companies in the Bahamas, the Cayman Islands, Luxembourg, Monaco, Geneva, and Liechtenstein. DaNicola had revealed to Cardinal Benelli that the Bank of Italy was investigating the Vatican's connections with Calvi's companies and that investigators had sufficient proof to begin pressing charges. Those under investigation included Paul Marcinkus, head of the IOR; Luigi Mennini, IOR secretary-inspector; and Pellegrino de Strobel, chief accountant of the Vatican Bank.

Not only Cardinal Benelli had access to this information. From inside the heart of the Bank of Italy, P2 lodge members kept Licio Gelli in Argentina informed, and he passed the news on to Roberto Calvi and Umberto Ortolani, a Mason and a "Gentleman of His Holiness," as he had been named by Pope Paul VI.[16] At the same time, members of P2 in the magistrate's office in Milan told Gelli that the investigation of the Banco Ambrosiano was over and that its voluminous report would be submitted to Judge Emilio Alessandrini.

The Holy Alliance report, according to Father DaNicola, included an article published in *Osservatore Politico* (OP) under the byline of a journalist named Mino Pecorelli. The article was called "The Great Vatican Lodge," and it named 121 members of the Vatican who belonged to a variety of Masonic lodges. Cardinals, bishops, prelates, and officials of the Holy See all appeared in the list. The final name, though, was Licio Gelli, grand master of Propaganda 2. Pecorelli, the Holy Alliance learned, was an active member of the lodge who had become disenchanted and was determined to air its dirty linen, even if he stained the reputation of the Vatican as well.

On September 12, Father Giovanni DaNicola formally and in person presented this list to the supreme pontiff. John Paul I read the names of Cardinal Jean Villot, the cardinal-vicar of Rome Monsignor Agostino Casaroli, Ugo Poletti, Cardinal Sebastiano Baggio, Bishop Paul Marcinkus, and Monsignor Donato de Bonis of the Vatican Bank.[17]

The pope asked Felici and Benelli if this list was correct. Both clergymen answered that a similar list had circulated in the *Sodalitium Pianum* as far back as 1976.

Roberto Calvi believed that Pope John Paul I wanted revenge for the financial assault his group had launched against the Banca Cattolica del Veneto. What Calvi's associates in the IOR did not know was that Calvi had managed to divert nearly four hundred million dollars and deposit them in secret accounts scattered around Latin America. Gelli told Calvi that, according to his sources, Pope John Paul I wanted to reform the Vatican's finances, which would expose the continual diversion of funds, the straw companies in financial paradises, the laundering of Mafia money, and much more.[18]

Licio Gelli told Roberto Calvi that the "problem" had to be resolved. Calvi never knew whether the head of Propaganda 2 meant the leak in the Banco Ambrosiano or Pope John Paul I.

On the morning of Sunday, September 17, after a light breakfast, the supreme pontiff sent for Father DaNicola to bring him the Holy Alliance report on the Vatican finance crisis, which was titled "IOR-Vatican Bank. Situation and legal case." It was categorized as "top secret" and "under Pontifical Secret."[19] The report, handwritten by an agent of the Holy Alliance, began by stating that "Pope John XXIII had left his successor some reserve funds derived from the Obolo di San Pietro and administered by the IOR. The total exceeded fifty billion lire." At the time the head of Special Administration was Gustavo Testa, and the head of the IOR was Monsignor Alberto Di Jorio.

"Paul VI had prepared a decree to unify all these departments, but mysteriously at the last minute it was not carried out," the report said. "I [the agent of the Holy Alliance who wrote the report] believe that the presence of Michele Sindona in our financial environs and his alliance with Licio Gelli had a lot to do with the withdrawal of the edict."

The papal espionage service's analysis also referred to "a sinister person called Umberto Ortolani, a Bolognese who is a close friend of Cardinal Giacomo Lercaro and Cardinal Joseph Frings."

The papal service with the best information on Ortolani was the *Sodalitium Pianum.* According to the S.P. report, Ortolani was a short, fat Bolognese who always wore a gold chain across his vest. He ran his operations from the showy villa of Grottaferrata, where he also periodically hosted Cardinals Lercaro and Frings. "Umberto Ortolani devotes himself to rescuing businesses in crisis, and once they have recovered, he dismembers them and sells the pieces to the highest bidders," the report said. A special appendix stipulated that Ortolani had joined the Order of Malta and later Licio Gelli's lodge P2.[20]

Since January of the previous year (1977), the Holy Alliance had known the contents of the so-called List of Five Hundred. At that time, Mario Barone, an old college friend of Michele Sindona, revealed the existence of the famous list containing the names of five hundred entrepreneurs, politicians, financiers, members of the curia, industrialists, and Mafiosi who had used Sindona's banks to smuggle enormous sums of capital out of Italy. Barone promised to turn the list over to authorities in return for immunity, but when he opened the safe deposit box in the Banca Privata that supposedly held the list, it was empty. No one knows how the papal espionage service had gotten a copy.[21]

By September 23, Pope John Paul I had almost all the pieces of the investigation of "Vatican, Inc." in his hands. That afternoon he met with the head of the Holy Alliance, and the papal spy chief told the supreme pontiff about another dark figure who moved in the Vatican financial circles, the Slovakian Monsignor Pavel Hnilica.[22] Some argue that he was the member of the curia who passed information from inside the IOR to Holy Alliance agents, but this has never been proved.

Another report that the Holy Alliance agent Father Giovanni DaNicola had given to John Paul I offered further information from his source inside the IOR. Apparently, inspectors from the Bank of Italy had begun to investigate the Ambrosiano after an anonymous tip (from Luigi Cavallo, a small-time Mafioso who was a friend of Michele Sindona) on November 21, 1977. The ultimate target was Roberto Calvi. Little by little, the financial investigators began to pick apart the threads of his many-sided operation.

Calvi had financial entities in Peru and Nicaragua, in Puerto Rico and the Cayman Islands, and in Canada, Belgium, and the United States, but the chinks in his armor were the Suprafin and Ultrafin companies. Neither Calvi nor Sindona wanted the truth about these companies to come out. Their only possible savior was Paul Marcinkus. When the Italian inspectors began to decipher the structure of these two companies and their transfers of funds, Carlo Oligati, the general administrator of the Ambrosiano, appeared on their doorstep to declare that the Suprafin was Vatican property and therefore "untouchable." Marcinkus had only to nod his head in agreement to scare off the Italian authorities.

The last day of John Paul I's life—September 28, 1978—was a normal workday for him. It began with a prayer in his private chapel, a frugal breakfast while he listened to the news on RAI, and a conversation with his secretaries John Magee and Diego Lorenzi.

At 9 A.M., his audiences began. John Paul I received Cardinal Bernardin Gantin and Father Riedmatten, both directors of social assistance work. About two in the afternoon, the supreme pontiff retired to eat lunch with a small group who tended to accompany him. That day the group at his table included Cardinal Jean Villot and Fathers Lorenzi and Magee. Afterwards, they took a long walk, lasting nearly an hour, through the Vatican grounds.

At 1 P.M., the pope turned to reviewing papers and personal letters he needed to answer. He was accompanied by two members of his escort and followed by two agents of the Holy Alliance. In late afternoon, he spent several hours with Villot, the cardinal secretary of state, on business of the Holy See. He spoke by telephone with Cardinals Giovanni Colombo, Archbishop of Milan, and with Benelli.

At 8 P.M., he retired to pray the rosary accompanied by two nuns and his two secretaries. Then he had a dinner of fish soup, green beans, cheese, and fruit. About nine, as was his habit, he sat down in front of the television to watch the news. Then he went into his bedroom and asked Sister Vincenza to bring a tray with a glass of water for his night table. At nine-thirty, John Paul I closed his bedroom door, uttering what would be his last words.[23]

Before going to sleep, John Paul I's custom was to read in bed for a while, by the light of a small lamp placed on his night table. The Holy Alliance agents who guarded the pope had been called off by order of an unidentified superior, as the agent Father Giovanni DaNicola would tell Cardinal Benelli the next morning.

The supreme pontiff died of either "natural causes" or "assassination" between 9:30 P.M. on September 28 and 4:30 A.M. on the 29th.[24]

There are two differing stories about who first saw his corpse. The official Vatican version is that the first person to enter the room of the dead pontiff was his secretary John Magee.[25] The unofficial and true version was that the nun Sister Vincenza Taffarell went into the pope's room when he failed to respond to her calling him, and so she found John Paul's corpse.

At 5:40 A.M., as she did every morning, Sister Vincenza knocked on the door to wake the Holy Father. Then she nervously called out to him, but still got no response. When she went into the room, she found the bedside lamp lit and John Paul I's body immobile. He was dead. She quickly left the room, and the well-greased Vatican machinery went into motion. The nun informed Father John Magee. Magee informed the cardinal secretary of state, Jean Villot, and the dean of the Sacred College of Cardinals, Cardinal Carlo Confalonieri. Villot informed the pope's doctor, Renato Buzzonetti. Inside the bedroom, confusion reigned. The papal doctor certified the death as having occurred about 11:30 P.M., September 28, by an acute heart attack. At seven-thirty in the morning, the news agency ANSA reported the supreme pontiff's passing.

A commission of cardinals led by Cardinal Silvio Oddi and Cardinal Antonio Samore was created to investigate the death of John Paul I. Their finding was "natural death by heart attack," yet many questions still remained unanswered when Pope John Paul II ordered the dossier of the investigation classified as a "Pontifical Secret." Like many others, this report rests in some corner of the Vatican Secret Archives.

Why was it said that the pope had heart trouble when his lifelong physician, Dr. Antonio da Ros, denied this? If, as the pope's secretary John Magee reported, the pope grimaced in pain several times during his last day and felt pressure in his chest, why was Dr. da Ros not consulted? Why was it said that the pope took only vitamins, when in truth, by prescription of Dr. Buzzonetti, he had received injections to stimulate his adrenal gland? Why was it not reported that John Paul I had been prescribed injections to counter his low blood pressure? Why was the thermos of coffee that Sister Vincenzo brought the pope every day intact when the pontiff's corpse was discovered, only to disappear shortly afterwards without a trace? Who called off the Holy Alliance agents who had been guarding the pope, and why? Why, when Swiss Guard officer Hans Roggan informed Paul Marcinkus of the supreme pontiff's death, did Marcinkus (by Roggan's own testimony) not show any surprise? Why was it said that no autopsy had been performed on the pope's corpse, when in fact there were three? Why were none of the autopsy results made public? Why was the Holy Alliance ordered not to open any investigation? These are only some of the questions that remain unanswered.[26]

Father Giovanni DaNicola, who kept the supreme pontiff informed about how Paul Marcinkus and his friends had siphoned money through the IOR, knew that after the death of John Paul I, his own days were numbered. The spy requested Cardinal Benelli's protection, but for one reason or another, this protection did not have the desired effect. Benelli arranged for the Holy See, through the secretariat of state, to transfer DaNicola to the nunciature in Canada. The confirmation for the spy's transfer never came through.

Four days after John Paul I's death, while the world was still recovering from its surprise, the Holy Alliance spy turned up hanged in a secluded Roman park often used by transvestites and prostitutes in search of customers. Although Italian police ruled his death a suicide and closed the case, no one investigated the unusual marks on DaNicola's arms and body that made it look as if he'd been fighting. The autopsy showed that Giovanni DaNicola had a broken neck, apparently caused by a strong blow and not by the weight of his body falling with a noose around his neck. Without a doubt, the man who knew the most about the secrets of the IOR and Paul Marcinkus had been murdered. No one asked questions, not even the espionage and counterespionage chiefs of the Vatican state.

John Paul I's mysterious death brought a new conclave to elect his successor. On October 14, 1978, at 4:30 P.M., 110 cardinals began their deliberations. In the Sistine Chapel, the cardinals listened in silence as the strict rules of the conclave were read aloud. On the eve of the first day of voting, Cardinal Wojtyla was calm.[27]

The next day, Sunday, October 15, the voting began, pitting Cardinal Giuseppe Siri against Cardinal Benelli. Each got thirty votes.[28] On the second ballot, each of the two lost some support, but by the afternoon, Cardinal Ugo Poletti, president of the Italian Bishops Conference, had thirty votes. On the fourth ballot, Cardinals Felici and Wojtyla made their appearance.

Wojtyla garnered five votes. In spite of the silence reigning over the monkish rooms surrounding the Sistine Chapel where the members of conclave were lodged, a great battle for control of the Catholic Church was under way.

Although Siri's backers did not retreat, with each new vote, new contestants' names came and went without any decision being reached. On the night of October 15, Cardinal Franz König discussed with French, German, Spanish, and North American cardinals their possible support for the Polish cardinal, Wojtyla. On Monday the 16th, there were two more votes in the morning. Siri continued to lose ground to other cardinals such as Giovanni Colombo, Ugo Poletti, and Johannes Willebrands.[29]

On the next ballot, the total in favor of Cardinal Karol Wojtyla grew. That same afternoon, Wojtyla met in his room with the primate cardinal of Poland, Wyszynski. The latter told him that if elected, he should accept. Two ballots later, Karol Wojtyla listened to the repetition of his name. Out of 108 cardinals voting, 99 had voted for him.

This had never happened before, and it bordered on the unimaginable: a pope from a country of Eastern Europe, a nation behind the Iron Curtain. After speaking his words of acceptance and announcing the name he would adopt as supreme pontiff, the new pope was escorted to the anteroom known as the *camera lacriminatoria,* the room where the new supreme pontiff dons the white habit.

Immediately afterwards, with firm steps, John Paul II stepped onto the balcony to confer his blessing *Urbi et Orbi* on the faithful and the world. Moments later, the pope invited members of the conclave who were still there to dine with him. The anxiety surrounding the ascension of a new pope subsided with his first appointments. To direct the Holy Alliance and the *Sodalitium Pianum,* John Paul II named Monsignor Luigi Poggi, born sixty-one years earlier in the Italian city of Piacenza, who had been apostolic delegate in Poland since 1975. Without doubt, Poggi offered what the Holy Alliance would need in the years when the first breaches in the Iron Curtain began to appear. New times were coming, and they would require active espionage services. This was to be one of the most political papacies in the history of the Roman Catholic Church. Furthermore, the repercussions of the IOR's financial dealings had by no means come to an end.

If Cardinal Benelli had been elected pope, then surely Cardinal Jean Villot would have been replaced. Marcinkus, Mennini, and De Strobel would have been dismissed and perhaps put on trial. But none of this occurred. The

Polish Cardinal Karol Wojtyla was elected, and everything continued the same despite the change.

All the information about the financial scandal gathered by Cardinal Benelli, the Holy Alliance, the *Sodalitium Pianum,* and Cardinal Felici was placed at John Paul II's disposal. He was also given evidence about members of Masonic orders among the curia, but everything went on as before. Cardinal Jean Villot was confirmed at the helm of the secretariat of state; Paul Casimir Marcinkus, aided by Mennini and De Strobel, continued to chart the course of the IOR and to cover up the illegal activities of the Banco Ambrosiano. Calvi, Gelli, and Ortolani stayed free to devote themselves to systematic robbery with the support of the IOR. Sindona, for his part, remained at liberty in the United States, far from the Italian courts. As the character Prince Lampedusa in the famous novel *The Leopard,* put it, "Everything has to change so that everything can go on the same."

Ten years after its founding by Licio Gelli, the Propaganda 2 lodge continued operating, manipulating the politics of several countries and supporting coups d'etat like that of the Argentine officers.

Between 1979 and 1982, five cardinals tied to the investigation of the IOR and Banco Ambrosiano mysteriously died. They were in good health, with an average age of sixty-nine: Jean Villot, at seventy-three; Sergio Pinedale, at seventy; Egidio Vagnozzi, at seventy-four; Pericle Felici, at seventy; and Giovanni Benelli, at sixty-one.

Several writers have dug into the mysterious death of John Paul I. These include the researcher David Yallop for his book *In God's Name: An Investigation into the Murder of Pope John Paul I,* and the historian John Cornwell for his work *A Thief in the Night: Life and Death in the Vatican.* While Yallop claims that John Paul's death was the result of a plot organized by the P2 lodge and the financial circles around the IOR, Cornwell holds that, although the pope's death could have been natural, he does not reject the possibility of a financial sector conspiracy that "conveniently needed" the pope's death in order to continue its murky operations.

Be that as it may, John Paul I's death remains one of the biggest and best-kept secrets in the history of the Vatican state. The Holy Alliance and *Sodalitium Pianum* interventions in this affair were only such as to allow them to bear witness, and were nearly accidental. On the ascension of John Paul II to the Throne of St. Peter, Holy Alliance agents took on a much more active role in clandestine operations, such as the sale of arms to Argentina during the Malvinas/Falklands war against Margaret Thatcher's Britain or the illegal financing of Lech Walesa's Solidarity union with funds diverted from the IOR. And one way or another, there were still accounts waiting to be settled with many of the leading figures in the financial scandals involving the Vatican. The Holy Alliance would take an active part in these. The time of the assassins was coming.

19

TIME OF THE ASSASSINS (1979–1982)

All the day they twist my words; their every thought is of evil against me; they hide together in ambush, watching my every step.

—Psalms 55:6–7

Colonel Ryszard Kuklinski threw open the door to General Wojciech Jaruzelski's office to announce that Karol Wojtyla had just been named supreme pontiff. At the age of fifty-seven, the defense minister of the Popular Republic of Poland received that piece of news as something neither better nor worse than most. He didn't realize that the selection of a Pole as the new pope would bring him more than one headache in times to come.

Meanwhile, the loose ends of the IOR scandal continued to hang over the Vatican, and the sinister hand of Licio Gelli moved to gather them up. In January 1979, Mario Sarcinelli persuaded Roberto Calvi to appear before the Bank of Italy's special commission. There, "God's banker" was questioned about his relations with Suprafin, the connections between Marcinkus's IOR and the Banco Ambrosiano, and specifically about the bank's branch in Nassau. One of the investigators asked Calvi to name the stockholders of the Ambrosiano. "God's banker" refused.

Another obstacle was the lawyer and journalist Carmine "Mino" Pecorelli. In his publication *OP,* Pecorelli had broken quite a few scandals of the 1960s. He drew on a wide range of sources, many of them with Mafia connections. As time went by, *OP* became a valuable information source not only for politicians but also for financiers, lawyers, and prosecutors.[1]

Pecorelli had access to privileged sources of information thanks to his close contacts with members of the Italian and papal secret services and, of course, with important members of the Propaganda 2 lodge. He was a member of P2 thanks to his relationship with Licio Gelli.

The grand master himself had asked his powerful lodge brothers to supply papers and documents to *OP* in order to expose anyone who secretly opposed either the lodge itself or its interests. In mid-1977, Pecorelli decided to launch an investigation into one of the most important series of thefts in the history of Italian business. The affair had to do with the adulteration and fraudulent sale of diesel fuel for trucks and fuel oil used in central heating. The profits, according to Pecorelli's data, totaled nearly $9.5 billion. The journalist continued digging into this dangerous scandal until he found that the IOR and Monsignor Marcinkus were involved. Through a free agent of the Holy Alliance, apparently the Polish Jesuit Kazimierz Przydatek, the Vatican Bank diverted dirty money from this fraudulent business to its foreign accounts, especially those in Nassau and Switzerland. One day in August 1977, the fuel scandal disappeared from *OP.* Pecorelli had been pressured to forget about the affair by Senator Claudio Vitalote of the Christian Democratic Party, Judge Carlo Testi, and General Donato Lo Prete of the Guardia di Finanza, the Italian financial police. There was also talk of a mysterious visit that Przydatek paid to the journalist. After Pecorelli's assassination the following year, one source claimed that the Polish Jesuit and Vatican spy Kazimierz Przydatek was a free agent following Monsignor Marcinkus's orders.

In early 1978, Mino Pecorelli returned to publishing articles about Masonic infiltration in the Vatican, especially in its three major power centers: diplomacy, finance, and the secret services.[2] In one article, the journalist published a list with the names of the most important Masons in the Vatican, including the powerful cardinal Jean Villot. Licio Gelli knew that if this list reached the pope, it could place him in serious jeopardy. For Paul Marcinkus and Roberto Calvi, the same was true—or worse.

Once Pope John Paul I was dead, Gelli decided to negotiate directly with Pecorelli. Apparently the journalist set a price of about three million dollars for his silence. Gelli refused to pay that much.

The first article then appeared in *OP,* casting Licio Gelli in a very poor light. The story charged that the P2 lodge's grand master had spied for the KGB, then for the CIA, and finally for the Vatican's Holy Alliance.[3]

A few days after the appearance of this first installment in the five-part series planned by *OP,* Licio Gelli decided to invite Mino Pecorelli to dinner to talk things over. Przydatek was seen in the area of Pecorelli's house that night, although he was never questioned about this by the Italian police.

Pecorelli spent the next day—the day he was supposed to dine with Gelli—working in his office. An hour before the time set for them to eat together, Mino Pecorelli left the building and walked toward his parked car. Two men approached and shot the journalist three times in the mouth. Pecorelli had fallen victim to a Mafia brand of justice, the *sasso in bocca,* which meant that a traitor would never talk again.[4] To this day, no one has been arrested for his murder.

On March 29, 1979, someone did order the arrest of the Bank of Italy officials investigating the connections between the Banco Ambrosiano and Marcinkus's IOR. Mario Sarcinelli and Paolo Baffi were jailed on accusation of suppressing information about the investigation.[5]

Although Sarcinelli, the Bank of Italy's chief investigator, was released, the judge refused to allow him to return to the bank or, therefore, to continue his work on the Banco Ambrosiano case.[6]

Another figure who tried to carry out an independent probe of Sindona's relationship with the Vatican Bank was the lawyer Giorgio Ambrosoli. As the court-appointed liquidator of Sindona's empire after its 1974 crash, he was in a position to uncover the operations the Mafia banker had carried out in collaboration with the Vatican Bank.

His investigation had allowed him to identify almost ninety-seven high officials in the administration, in politics, in finance, and in the Vatican who were linked to foreign bank accounts, especially in London, Switzerland, and the United States. On this list appeared the names of trusted advisors to Paul VI and now to John Paul II, such as Máximo Spada and Luigi Mennini.[7]

Ambrosoli found irrefutable evidence of the Vatican Bank's complicity in Michele Sindona's illegal activities. In May 1979, the lawyer calculated that the collapse of Sindona's empire had resulted in losses totaling nearly 757 billion lire.

Giorgio Ambrosoli's collaborators in this investigation included Boris Giuliano, police superintendent in Palermo, and Lieutenant Colonel Antonio Varisco, head of security for Rome. Giulano had begun investigating Sindona when by chance, in the pocket of a murdered Mafioso, he found two checks that linked the Mafia banker with a transfer of heroin trade profits to a bank account in the Caribbean. Varisco, for his part, was conducting a probe into the roots of P2. Ambrosoli discovered how the Banca Cattolica del Veneto had changed hands and how a Holy Alliance agent in an eastern bloc country (possibly Kazimierz Przydatek) had carried two suitcases filled with nine and a half million dollars in commissions for Roberto Calvi, Paul Marcinkus, and Cardinal John Cody.[8]

On June 11, 1979, Ambrosoli was assassinated in the doorway of his home by William Arico, a professional killer. Witnesses told police how some days before the killing of the prominent lawyer, a tall man with light brown hair had been seen in the area taking notes on something. Przydatek, the papal espionage agent who worked for Marcinkus, matched that description.

On June 13, two men machine-gunned Lieutenant Colonel Antonio Varisco while his car was stopped at a traffic light. On July 20, as he did every morning, Boris Giuliano walked into the Lux Bar in Palermo for a cup of coffee. When he headed for the counter to pay his bill, a man approached from behind and fired a fatal shot into his neck. Before leaving the establishment, the killer left a white carnation on the corpse. Years later, an investigation found that the white carnation had been used by the Roman Inquisition during the years when Cardinal and Inquisitor-General Miguel Ghislieri[9] spread terror through the Eternal City. Anonymous accusers left white carnations to indicate the houses of those whom the Holy Office should arrest and torture.

Although Ambrosoli's murder cut short his investigation, the voluminous dossier served as incriminating evidence in the trial of Michele Sindona that opened in New York. Both Roberto Calvi and Paul Marcinkus continued to deny having received any commission for the sale of the Banca Cattolica del Veneto. Sindona's trial for the collapse of the Franklin Bank began in early February 1979.

High members of the Roman curia such as Paul Marcinkus and illustrious cardinals such as Giuseppe Caprio and Sergio Guerri were ready to speak in Sindona's favor, but a few hours before their depositions were to be taken in the U.S. embassy in Rome, Cardinal Agostino Casaroli, seemingly on the order of John Paul II, ordered Marcinkus, Caprio, and Guerri to "keep their mouths closed." Later the Vatican, through the secretariat of state, issued a communiqué that stated:

They may create a very conflictual and prejudicial precedent. There has been too much publicity. It gives us much pain that the government of the United States does not diplomatically recognize the Vatican, because the Vatican is a legal state.[10]

Casaroli surely saved the Vatican state from a scandal, without knowing he had disobeyed an express order by John Paul II, who had authorized Marcinkus, Caprio, and Guerri to speak out in favor of Sindona. The loyal Casaroli would not know this until years later.[11]

Finally, on March 23, 1980, Michele Sindona, the Mafia's banker, was found guilty of ninety-five charges, including fraud, conspiracy, perjury, falsification of bank documents, and unauthorized appropriation of funds deposited in his banks. Sindona was jailed in the Metropolitan Correction Center in Manhattan while awaiting sentencing. While Sindona languished in his cell, clad in an orange jumpsuit instead of his customary fifteen-hundred-dollar suits, Roberto Calvi and Paul Marcinkus continued their lucrative business deals. One of the companies that brought the most profit to the Vatican was Bellatrix, headquartered in Panama.

Though founded in 1976 by Calvi with IOR money, Bellatrix's operations were all controlled and directed by Marcinkus himself (as representative of IOR), Licio Gelli, the Freemason Umberto Ortolani, and Bruno Tassan Din, the executive director and financial strategist of the powerful Rizzoli publishing group.[12]

Through Bellatrix, millions of dollars a day were transferred from numbered accounts. Money laundered from drug trafficking or fraudulent financial operations entered on one side. It exited on the other side into the hands of corrupt South American politicians. To oversee Bellatrix, Marcinkus assigned three members of the Holy Alliance who reported directly to him, over the head of their immediate boss, Monsignor Luigi Poggi.

Vatican espionage knew that in September 1976, Calvi had opened a Managua branch of the Grupo Ambrosiano subsidiary Banco Comercial. Although its official function was to facilitate commercial transactions between Central American countries, its unofficial role—with the approval of Paul Marcinkus—was to divert funds from fraudulent businesses into Nassau bank accounts.

Clearly, Luigi Poggi and the Holy Alliance found it advisable to close their eyes to the fraudulent operations that Marcinkus organized through the IOR. The profits, after all, could always be used to finance covert operations for the good of the Church and in defense of the faith.

It was, in fact, Licio Gelli who introduced Calvi to Anastasio Somoza. In return for making Nicaragua a safe haven for the Vatican's "B" money and for a Nicaraguan passport that Calvi would carry until the day of his death, the IOR paid large sums of money to the dictator, always transmitted in suitcases carried by one or another agent of the Holy Alliance.[13]

In mid-1978, the Sandinistas managed to topple the dictator and take power in that country. The new regime's first measure was to nationalize every foreign bank except the Grupo Ambrosiano's Banco Comercial. Just in case, as in the entire history of the Vatican foreign policy, Paul Marcinkus's IOR had given millions of dollars to the *comandantes* of the Sandinista National Liberation Front (Spanish initials FSLN) to buy arms in countries such as Spain, France, and Belgium.

Banco Ambrosiano shares illegally sold and hidden in shell companies created by the IOR in Panama were out of the reach of the Bank of Italy's inspectors, but Calvi was not entirely comfortable with the arrival of the Sandinistas, so he decided to move the business from Nicaragua to Peru. Therefore, on October 1, 1979, he founded the Banco Ambrosiano Andino. Only Bellatrix's operations were moved to Lima. The rest of the companies continued to proliferate in Luxembourg. Altogether, nineteen financial corporations operated from that European city, all of them property of the IOR, as is demonstrated by the certification issued by the Vatican Bank itself and signed by Paul Marcinkus.

As the year 1979 drew to a close, the economic losses of the IOR reached $200 million, and those for the following year were predicted to be $280 million. According to Cardinal Sergio Guerri, who served as chief administrator of the Vatican city-state, Pope John Paul II told him personally that if things continued the way they were going, he was sure the Vatican state would be completely ruined by the end of 1985. But at the same time a report of the Bank for International Settlements had become public, which indicated that between 1978 and 1979 the IOR had deposited between $0.9 billion and $1.3 billion in foreign banks. The total sum deposited inside and outside the Vatican for those years would have been about $2.5 billion. John Paul II knew this fact, but he did not mention it in his meetings with Cardinals Felici and Benelli.[14]

In the early 1980s, as Poland's foreign debt grew and the country faced a winter without coal, the government once again froze wages and raised the prices of basic goods, so no one was surprised when strikes broke out across the land. While the pope worked with his spy chief Monsignor Luigi Poggi in Castel Gandolfo, a broad-shouldered, striking electrician with an enormous mustache climbed atop a bulldozer in the Lenin shipyard. His name was Lech Walesa. For months, the shipyard workers had refused to join the strikes.[15]

The Polish economy was in free fall, millions of workers clearly discontented, and the strikes that had begun as small spontaneous actions had now spread through more than fifty large state enterprises.

Although the police had killed forty-five shipyard workers since 1970, no one wanted a new confrontation. But that day, while Gdansk shipyard director Klemens Giech promised wage increases to those who would resume working, Lech Walesa atop the bulldozer shouted to the assembled crowd that Giech was a liar.[16]

In fact, what had begun as isolated strikes soon became true "counter-revolutionary political insurrections," as Leonid Brezhnev put it. On August 16, when some workers were on the point of going back on the job in return for a fifteen-hundred-zloty wage increase and a promised monument in honor of the victims of December 1970, Walesa counterattacked. Emboldened, he presented a list of sixteen demands. When these were about to be accepted, he added twenty-one more, including government acceptance of a free trade union. That same day, 180 more factories joined the strike in support of Walesa's demands.

Meanwhile, in the Vatican, John Paul II was receiving handsomely bound reports written by Holy Alliance agents and passed on to him by Monsignor Luigi Poggi in the presence of Cardinal Agostino Casaroli. Poggi had ordered the Polish Jesuit and agent Kazimierz Przydatek to form a group of Polish priests to infiltrate the strikers and unionists. From then on Przydatek made himself Walesa's shadow and the Vatican's best informant on the Polish situation.

According to the pope, Walesa had been "sent by God, by Providence," and Poggi needed a full-time contact close to the union leader. Every night, the Holy Alliance agent assembled firsthand information he had gathered from talking with everyone from workers to priests. One of his best sources was Father Henryk Jankowski, priest at the Church of St. Brigida, Lech

Walesa's parish in Gdansk. John Paul II liked hearing how a handful of ship-yard workers had climbed the high barbed-wire fences to hang huge pictures of the pope, to the astonishment of the police guarding the facility. From his earlier work with Paul Marcinkus, Przydatek knew what the Vatican wanted to hear, and he was happy to provide it. Kazimierz Przydatek even invented the "fact" that the workers had disobeyed an order to stop and, after climb-ing the fence, had torn down pictures of Polish government leaders to replace them with those of John Paul II. This was a lie, of course, but the supreme pontiff was very pleased with the story.

Solidarity, the union newly created by Lech Walesa, was the Holy Al-liance's next target.

Faced with the danger that the union could become one more refuge for moderate communists, the pope ordered Poggi to assign his agents to infil-trate Solidarity and maneuver its leaders into accepting a much more open organization, one that clearly included Catholic leaders and intellectuals.

Przydatek persuaded Walesa to bring Tadeusz Mazowiecki, editor of the Catholic newspaper *Wiez,* and Catholic historian Bronislaw Geremek into the Solidarity leadership. From this moment on, the strike movement fell under the control of the Church. Within a few days, the Holy Alliance in-formed Poggi that Cardinal Primate Wyszynski was writing a homily oppos-ing the strike, which the Warsaw government would report on the state television network. Poggi reported this to Casaroli, but the diplomatic ex-pert knew that he couldn't say anything to the pope about his friend and for-mer protector.

Cardinal Wyszynki began that day speaking about the mistakes commit-ted by all sides. No one (referring to the strikers) should point a finger at his neighbor (the Polish communist government). "We all make mistakes and commit sins," said the cardinal from the pulpit of Czestochova. The most important part of his speech was his reference to the strikers' demands: "You cannot demand everything at once. It is better to have a program. Nobody should put the country in danger."

The speech fell like a bomb. The strikers took it as a clear message from the Church to retract their demands for an independent union; Catholic in-tellectuals protested but maintained public silence; Walesa paid no attention to the elderly cardinal; and John Paul II spent three days muttering between his teeth in the hallways of Castel Gandolfo, "Oh! That old man . . . that old man!"[17]

On August 31, 1980, the famous Gdansk Accords were signed. The accords accepted the first independent trade union behind the Iron Curtain. With political support from the Vatican and Pope John Paul II and with financing through the Holy Alliance, Solidarity began to spread through the length and breadth of Poland. A few days later, Edward Gierek fell from power, replaced by Stanislaw Kania.

On October 29, 1980, the Soviet Politburo met in a secret special session. Andropov, Gorbachev, Kirilenko, Chernenko, Rusakov, and the rest discussed the Polish situation. "I think, and the events themselves demonstrate, that the Polish leaders don't fully understand the gravity of the situation they face," said Yuri Andropov, head of the KGB. "Unless martial law is imposed, things can get worse. Our northern forces are prepared and ready to fight," declared Ustinov. But the most radical position belonged to Andrei Gromyko, the foreign minister, who insisted, "We must not lose Poland. The Soviet Union lost six hundred thousand soldiers freeing it from the Nazi yoke. We cannot allow a counterrevolution now." His audience remained silent.

No one wanted a new revolt like the Hungarian one of 1956 or a Prague Spring like that of 1968. Really, by early 1980, no Soviet leader wanted to see Russian tanks roll into Warsaw to repress a counterrevolution.

Two days after that meeting, thanks to a Holy Alliance infiltrator in the Polish defense ministry, John Paul II and Agostino Casaroli knew exactly what messages Warsaw was getting from Moscow. Their agent was Colonel Ryszard Kuklinski, an aide to General Wojciech Jaruzelski.

On January 20, 1981, Ronald Reagan became President of the United States. Several weeks before his swearing-in, however, strategic contacts had already been initiated between Washington and Vatican City, between Ronald Reagan and Pope John Paul II, and between the CIA's William Casey and the Holy Alliance's Monsignor Luigi Poggi.

Since late 1980, U.S.-Vatican discussion of the Polish situation had been carried out by Zbigniew Brzezinski, President Carter's national security advisor, and Cardinal Josef Tomko, Vatican propaganda chief and former head of the counterespionage service *Sodalitium Pianum.* Tomko had been in charge of the S.P. until John Paul II named Monsignor Luigi Poggi to run both Vatican intelligence services under a joint command, as they have remained organized to this day.

With authorization from Jimmy Carter and John Paul II, Tomko and

Brzezinski designed "Operation Open Book," a plan to inundate the Eastern European countries as well as Soviet areas like the Ukraine and the Baltic states with anticommunist books. This operation was to be coordinated by the CIA and the Holy Alliance through priests working in those areas.

While John Paul II aided Operation Open Book, Carter did nothing but raise objections. For eleven years, Colonel Kuklinski had been providing very valuable information to the Vatican secret services. As events pointed to a greater and greater likelihood that Soviet armed forces might enter Poland, the Holy Alliance decided to share the information coming from the Polish general staff officer with the CIA.

As the new U.S. administration got under way, the Vatican had two new key contacts in Washington with respect to Polish affairs: national security advisor Richard Allen and CIA director William Casey. Reports from Kuklinski, the Holy Alliance, and the Vatican were of great value from the point of view of strategic analysis. Zbigniew Brzezinski also maintained his role as a link between the White House and Poggi's Holy Alliance.

Ronald Reagan's view of the Catholic Church and the Vatican was quite different from those of previous administrations, including that of John F. Kennedy, the only Catholic president of the United States. Reagan was the son of an Irish Catholic worker, and that background had left its mark. Catholic voters had formed one of his major electoral blocs, and he felt comfortable in the presence of Catholics. For Reagan and his advisors, the Church was the perfect counterweight to communism. Like John Paul II, the U.S. president regarded Marxism, Leninism, and communism as evils to be eradicated from the earth.

It was clear by now that Moscow saw Solidarity as an unprecedented threat, an "infection" that was spreading within the monolithic communist system. If it infected the Baltic states, it could eventually dismember the Soviet bloc.

John Paul II and his main Vatican advisors were convinced that if Solidarity won in Poland, the shock wave would spread through the Ukraine, the Balkans, Latvia, Lithuania, Estonia, and perhaps Czechoslovakia as well. Reagan understood that if this were so, it could mean the end of the Cold War and the triumph of capitalism over communism.[18]

During a meeting attended by President Reagan, William Casey, and presidential advisor William Clark, the latter said, "We can't be going into the country and overthrowing the government in the name of the people. All we can do is use Solidarity as a weapon to accomplish that." That was when Reagan decided Solidarity would get financial aid from the United States. Casey didn't know where those funds would come from, but deep inside the Vatican this issue had already been resolved.

The liaison for the new joint operations of the CIA and the Holy Alliance in Poland was Jan Nowak, head of the Polish-U.S. Congress. His role was to keep up a constant flow of information between Warsaw and the Vatican and from the Vatican to Washington. Nowak also took on the task of fundraising and dispatching money to Poland to finance underground media, printing presses, photocopiers, and the like.[19]

Another figure who took a leading role in "Operation Poland" was the pope's apostolic delegate in Washington, Archbishop Pio Laghi. Casey and Clark liked to visit Laghi at his residence. While they drank cappuccinos, they talked about the political situation in Central America or about birth control, but especially about Poland. Ronald Reagan needed to know about all facets of the intelligence operation mounted by the Holy Alliance in Poland. Cardinal John Krol of Philadelphia also made his appearance on the Polish scene.

Allen, Casey, and Ronald Reagan himself began to meet with Krol, who took to entering the White House by the back door. More than any other churchman, Cardinal Krol kept the White House informed about Solidarity's situation, needs, and relations with the Polish bishops.[20] Although Krol often interfered with operations and communications undertaken by the Holy Alliance under Monsignor Luigi Poggi, for the Vatican and John Paul II, the Philadelphia archbishop's relationship with President Ronald Reagan was something to take advantage of. Ronald Reagan's men called John Krol "The Pope's Buddy." In the spring of 1981, relations between the White House and the Vatican were very fluid, especially in regard to Poland and Central America. William Casey, Vernon Walters, William Clark, and Zbigniew Brzezinski, on the U.S. side, and Monsignor Luigi Poggi and Cardinals Pio Laghi, John Krol, and Agostino Casaroli on the Vatican side became a sort of shock force whose only responsibility was to support the Solidarity union in its struggle against the communist government in Warsaw.

With each trip to Rome to meet secretly with John Paul II, Reagan's special ambassador Vernon Walters sent back more and more abundant reports. Walters spoke with the pope about Poland, Central America, terrorism, Chile, Chinese military power, Argentina, liberation theology—or Leonid Brezhnev's health, Pakistan's nuclear ambitions, the Ukraine, or the situation in the Near East. In sum, John Paul II and Vernon Walters established geostrategic contact.

In return, the Holy Alliance received CIA reports based on intercepted telephone conversations of Nicaraguan and Salvadoran priests and bishops, which revealed their support for liberation theology and their active participation in opposition to the forces backed by the U.S. On William Casey's orders, Oliver North and other members of the National Security Council made secret payments to upper-class Central American priests who were loyal to the pope and the Holy Alliance. There is no document to prove that Pope John Paul II or any other high Vatican official approved these payments, but there are indications that Luigi Poggi must have known.

On April 23, 1981, William Casey arrived in Rome. The purpose of his trip was to try to maintain CIA and Holy Alliance support for Solidarity. The Agency's director knew that the Polish situation was more an evolutionary process than a revolutionary one and that removing Poland from the Soviet orbit was essential. John Paul II and Casaroli spoke with the Soviet ambassador in Rome on three different occasions, and Casey was kept informed about what was said.

Jaruzelski feared a true disaster that would culminate in Red Army troops entering Warsaw and crushing the men of Solidarity. He had asked for Wyszynski's help in convincing Walesa to call off the general strike.

When Walesa and the rest of the leaders refused, the cardinal went down on his knees before the union leader. He held Walesa by the pants leg and said he wouldn't let go until Walesa agreed to end the strike.

The emotional blackmail worked. Walesa ordered an end to the strike, which allowed General Jaruzelski to tell Moscow that he had the situation under control. On February 9, 1981, Jaruzelski became prime minister of the Popular Republic of Poland in place of Josef Pinkowski in a coup d'etat.[21] Jaruzelski, as Poggi told the pope, was seen as a hard-liner opposed to any liberalization of public life. Doubtless he would become the main enemy of Solidarity, and of the Holy Alliance's operations in Poland.

While meeting with the pope, William Casey spoke of Central America, the possible extension of communism throughout that region, and Cuba's training of Nicaraguan and Sandinista combatants. Casey told John Paul II that "the Russians, the Cubans, the Bulgarians, and the North Koreans are involved." He also gave John Paul II a binder containing a report labeled

"Top Secret." The pope didn't open it, but passed it on to Monsignor Poggi, who was seated by his side, always present when the supreme pontiff met with the head of the CIA.

The report had been supplied to the CIA by the Italian espionage service. When Lech Walesa had come to Rome in January to see the pope, according to this report, he had also met with Luigi Scricciollo of the Italian Confederation of Labor. The Italian counterespionage said in the report that Scricciollo was really a Bulgarian secret service agent. To the Italians, this meant that Solidarity's plans could have been exposed, or that Lech Walesa might be the target of an assassination attempt.

On May 13, 1981, nothing suggested a tragedy about to unfold. John Paul II lunched with several guests. Around five, the pope left for the Apostolic Palace to conduct his weekly general audience in the Piazza di San Pietro. The ceremony began on time. Thousands of people crowded into the circle formed by Bernini's columns, 264 columns crowned with 162 statues of saints. A young Turk had reached the plaza half an hour earlier.

A fenced-off passageway indicated the route the open "Popemobile" would travel. John Paul II had refused an escort. He reached the vehicle and mounted the platform. Close behind him came Camillo Cibin, head of Vatican security, two agents in blue suits, two Holy Alliance agents, and ahead of them four members of the Swiss Guard. Poggi had summoned Cibin months before to warn him that a French intelligence report suggested there could be a plot by a Warsaw Pact country's secret service to kill the supreme pontiff, so Cibin's men needed to be on the alert.[22]

At 5:18 P.M., just after the pope had been holding a child in his arms, the first shot rang out through the Piazza di San Pietro. With his hands grasping the railing of the "Popemobile," John Paul II began to wobble. The bullet from Mehmet Ali Agca's gun had pierced his stomach and produced serious wounds in his small intestine and colon. John Paul II knew he must be wounded because of the unbearable pain in his stomach. Without blinking, he tried vainly to stop the flow of blood with his hands, as it bubbled out through the small hole pierced by the bullet.

Only a few seconds had gone by when the attacker fired again. This time the ball hit the pope's right hand. Agca's third shot hit the pope higher up, in the arm. The driver looked back, not understanding what had happened. Cibin was now holding the pope's head, which had slumped down onto the seat leaving a large pool of blood underneath.

Cibin shouted to his agents who, arms in hand, were searching for the shooter who had disappeared into the crowd. Agca ran with his weapon in hand, a Browning 9 mm automatic. He was getting away when he felt someone striking blows to his legs, making him fall. It was an Italian police agent who had been taking a walk in the plaza and so became the one to make the arrest.

While Mehmet Ali Agca was on the ground, several papal agents kicked and beat him before he was dragged to a police van. Meanwhile, the "Popemobile" rushed at full speed toward the Bronze Gate to transfer the pope to an ambulance. Amidst shouts and cries, the vehicle made its way to the Clinica Gemelli di Roma, the closest hospital to the Vatican.[23]

On the ninth-floor surgical unit, the Clinica's staff cut away Pope John Paul II's white cassock, exposing a gold medal and a cross, both bathed in blood. Curiously, the medal had been bent by the impact of one of the bullets. Apparently the medal kept the projectile from reaching the pope's chest. It diverted the trajectory of the bullet to the pope's right hand, where it injured his index finger.

When he recovered after six hours of life-or-death surgery, John Paul II believed he'd been saved by the Virgin of Fatima. During his long months of recuperation, the desire to know who had ordered his assassination became an obsession for John Paul II. He read all the Holy Alliance reports that came his way from the CIA, the German BND, the Israeli Mossad, the Austrian secret service, and the Turkish one. None answered his question. Nor did he learn anything when Mehmet Ali Agca was brought before a Roman court the last week of July 1981 and sentenced to life imprisonment.[24]

According to writer Gordon Thomas in his book *Gideon's Spies: The Secret History of the Mossad,* it was Monsignor Luigi Poggi, head of the Holy Alliance, who finally provided the answer. For months, the papal spy had been working closely with Yitzhak Hofi, the *memuneh* of Mossad. Poggi held secret meetings in Vienna, Warsaw, Paris, and Sofia. In November 1983, Monsignor Luigi Poggi returned from a meeting in Vienna with the answer to John Paul II's question, Who had ordered him killed?

Poggi's driver waited several hours in the airport for the plane from the Austrian capital to arrive. When he and his passenger reached the Gate of the Bells, the car's Vatican seal gained it entry, but even so the Swiss Guard stopped it to identify the passenger. On seeing who it was, the soldiers snapped to attention and paid their respects to the head of the Holy Alliance.

The archbishop was clothed in a long black coat with a scarf covering his entire face, but his large frame was still evident. While he warmed up, recovering from the chilly air, he continued to reflect on his secret meeting in the Jewish quarter of Vienna. In a rather dilapidated apartment, Poggi had listened attentively to a *katsa* named Eli, who answered the question John Paul II had so constantly posed.

A butler accompanied Poggi as far as the pope's study. Books and military reports were piled on the shelves. The papal espionage chief knew that the assassination attempt had troubled the pope both physically and mentally. After a quick greeting, Poggi sat with his hands on his knees and in a low voice began to recount the story he had heard in Austria. News had flowed regularly into the Mossad headquarters in Tel Aviv after that fateful May 13, 1981. Because all the intelligence services were carrying out their own investigations, Hofi could keep Mossad out of the affair.

The Israeli investigation really began in 1982 by order of Yitzhak Hofi's replacement, Nahum Admoni. The American view was that Ali Agca had pulled the trigger on the orders of the KGB, for fear that John Paul II and his intelligence services' clear support for Solidarity could light the fuse of Polish nationalism. This same view is argued by the writer Claire Sterling in her book *The Time of the Assassins*.[25] To the Israelis, however, the conspiracy had been woven in Tehran on the orders of Ayatollah Khomeini. Assassinating the pope was the first step in a *jihad* against the West. Russian journalist Eduard Kovaliov advances this thesis in his book *Atentado en la plaza de San Pedro*. Fearing that Agca might fail, the Iranian secret services had planned to present the Turk as a lone fanatic.[26]

Poggi told the pope Agca's story as contained in a Holy Alliance report, which he handed to the supreme pontiff in a red folder: "Mehmet Ali Agca was born in the village of Yesiltepe in eastern Turkey. At the age of nineteen he joined the Gray Wolves, a pro-Iranian terrorist group financed by Tehran. In February 1979, Agca assassinated the editor of a newspaper famous for its pro-Western positions. A few days later, the newspaper received a list supposedly written by Agca that referred to John Paul II as the commander of the Crusades and threatened to kill him if he [the pope] set foot on Islamic soil."

The pope interrupted Poggi's story only for brief pauses to drink water and ask specific questions. Agca moved on to Libya, the papal spy continued, and then in February 1981 to Bulgaria to meet with secret service agents of that country. Furious that the KGB had tried to implicate the CIA in the attempt to assassinate the pope, William Casey had then ordered the invention of a "Bulgarian connection." According to this version, the KGB had ordered the Bulgarians to orchestrate a conspiracy to liquidate the pope for his policy toward Poland and Solidarity.

On December 23, 1983, Pope John Paul II had the opportunity to directly ask Mehmet Ali Agca the question that had been ricocheting through his brain for the past two years. In Rome's Rebibbia prison, the pope walked unaccompanied to cell number T4. Ali Agca knelt and kissed the Fisherman's ring in a sign of respect.

The two men sat down, and with their heads nearly touching, Acga began to speak, almost whispering in the pope's ear. As he listened to what Agca said, his face grew graver and graver. At last, John Paul II had the answer to his question.

Later, the pope's spy, Monsignor Poggi, would explain: "Ali Agca knows about things up to a certain level, that's all. Beyond that, he doesn't know anything. If this was a conspiracy, it was put together by professionals, and professionals leave no trails. One never finds a trace."

Since May 13, 1981, dozens of books and articles have been written to explain who tried to kill Pope John Paul II that afternoon in the Piazza di San Pietro. The writers have put forward hundreds of alleged conspirators and dozens of political motives. Some accuse the Iranians of *jihad;* some accuse the Soviets because of papal policies in Poland; some accuse the CIA because of Mehmet Ali Agca's connection with an ex-agent in Libya; some accuse the Bulgarians as KGB puppets. But more that twenty years after the shooting in the Piazza di San Pietro, no one knows for sure who was behind Mehmet Ali Agca's trigger—not even the Holy Alliance.

A few years after the supreme pontiff's December 23 meeting with Ali Agca in Rebibbia prison, it came out that he had ordered Monsignor Luigi Poggi and by extension the Holy Alliance and the *Sodalitium Pianum* to halt any and all investigations related to the assassination attempt. On receipt of this "Pontifical Order," the papal spy acted in purest Vatican style, which is to say, he shrouded everything relating to May 13, 1981, in a veil of deepest secrecy. On December 24, 1983, while the Vatican prepared for Christmas, two Holy Alliance agents flanked by four members of the Swiss Guard transferred all pertinent documents in hermetically sealed cases bearing the pontifical emblem. They took the cases to the Vatican Secret Archives, where they rest to this day.

Meanwhile, the loose ends that had remained hanging from the IOR–Banco Ambrosiano–Calvi–Marcinkus case were about to be neatly tied up. On June 13, 1980, a United States court sentenced Mafia banker Michele Sindona to twenty-one years in prison. He still had more to say, however, until he was murdered in 1986. There was more to say, in general, during the Polish years.

20

THE POLISH YEARS (1982–2005)

For, lo, the wicked have bent their bow; they have fit their arrow to the string to shoot from the shadows at the upright of heart.

—Psalms 11:2

The 1980s were exhausting times for the Holy Alliance because of the operations it carried out on foreign soil. The majority of its operatives were on assignment in Poland, with a smaller group in Central America. In these years, Monsignor Luigi Poggi asked the supreme pontiff to be relieved of "such an elevated responsibility," but John Paul II was unwilling to lose his spy chief at such a crucial moment. As many as eight times, he rejected Poggi's request.

In Poland, things were going from bad to worse, verging on disaster. On November 4, 1981, Jaruzelski proposed to Walesa and the Polish cardinal primate Josef Glemp the creation of a "Front of National Accord" to negotiate an end to the chaos reigning in the country. Walesa refused, because Jaruzelski's only goal was to smother Solidarity under the weight of the numerous official unions.

The Holy Alliance then reported to Pope John Paul (still convalescing), Cardinal Casaroli, and Monsignor Poggi about a letter of protest that Brezhnev had written to Jaruzelski. The letter had been seen by papal spy and Jaruzelski aide Colonel Ryszard Kuklinski, who went by the code name *Gull.* In closing, the Soviet leader told General Jaruzelski, "I warn you that if Solidarity and the Church are given important roles in the exercise of power, destruction of socialism will be the result." More than an analysis, this was surely a premonition.[1]

On the morning of November 30, Ronald Reagan's special envoy Vernon Walters met with the supreme pontiff. The U.S. diplomat brought the pope a series of photos taken from spy satellites. The black-and-white images showed the shipyard and docks of Gdansk—and, less than forty kilometers away, several columns of Soviet-made tanks approaching the facilities. The pope knew what this meant even better than Walters did.

Gull had reported through his Holy Alliance contact that General Jaruzelski and the Polish general staff were readying a military operation to impose martial law. However, Gull didn't known when or how this would happen, and after that message all contact ceased. In the morning, Kuklinski attended a meeting in the office of the chief adjutant of the Polish army, who was in charge of planning the legal details of applying martial law. In a large room overflowing with maps and photographs, the general told Kuklinski that he didn't know how it had happened, but the Vatican and the U.S. had learned of their plans.[2]

In fact, Kuklinski himself had passed on the information. During the meeting he stayed calm, but he knew he was under suspicion when he found himself shadowed by secret service agents as he left the Polish general staff headquarters. Gull was now in their sights. He clearly needed help to escape.

Apparently, someone inside the Vatican had informed the KGB that a Holy Alliance agent, perhaps an officer close to the circles of power, was passing information to the U.S. and Vatican secret services. The KGB had in turn told their Polish opposite numbers.

Colonel Ryszard Kuklinski, code name Gull, hurried home to his family. Within a few days, he managed to contact his Vatican liaison and report that he and his family needed a secure escape route. Monsignor Luigi Poggi set the machinery of papal espionage in motion to devise a safe passage for his spy.

Thanks to contacts with the Canadian curia and to the fact that Kuklinski was in the habit of passing that country's diplomatic building in Warsaw every morning, the Holy Alliance prepared the escape plan. The date was set for the following Friday, a festival day throughout Poland.

In the morning, closely watched, Kuklinski and his family got into their car, casually dressed and carrying picnic baskets as if heading for the countryside. In fact, the baskets held all the family members' documents. When they neared the avenue facing the main door of the Canadian embassy, the vehicle speeded up. It turned sharply to the left while a truck driven by the agent Kazimierz Przydatek, heavily laden with metal pipes, blocked the passage of the black sedans that followed closely behind Kuklinski. The ex-agent's car sped into the courtyard of the diplomatic legation, whose large gates closed behind it. Colonel Ryszard Kuklinski, Gull, the Holy Alliance's best spy in Poland, left that life behind. The long of arm of Luigi Poggi in collaboration with the CIA had managed to bring him and his family to safety.[3] On December 12, General Wojciech Jaruzelski imposed martial law.

While the halls of the Vatican shook with the alarming news from the supreme pontiff's native land, in the depths of the IOR, Paul Marcinkus was preparing one of the most fruitful operations that the Vatican Bank had ever been involved in. His instrument would be the famous company Bellatrix.

For this undertaking, Marcinkus selected a team of three Holy Alliance agents led by Father Kazimierz Przydatek, who had returned from Warsaw after rescuing Kuklinski and his family. In late 1981, he turned his attention to "Operation Flying Fish."

Since March 24, 1976, when a junta of high ranking army officers led by General Jorge Videla overthrew President Isabel Martínez de Perón and assumed power in Argentina, relations between Buenos Aires and the Holy See had grown closer. In fact, many of the commanders who made up part of the "triumvirate," such as Admiral Emilio Eduardo Massera, had important connections with Licio Gelli's P2 lodge.

Thanks to the latter, via cover provided by free agents of the Holy Alliance, Roberto Calvi channeled millions of the Argentine junta's dollars through the Bellatrix company, a Vatican property, to buy French-made Exocet missiles. The code name of this secret operation, Flying Fish, came from the common name of the fish *Exocoetus,* which skimmed the surface of the waves just like the Exocet.[4] While the Argentine military tried to get as many missiles as possible, making use of Calvi and the Vatican secret services in their efforts, Prime Minister Thatcher and Britain's MI6 spy service tried by all possible means to prevent them. "The Argentineans had only a limited number of the devastating French Exocet missiles. They made desperate attempts to increase their arsenal. . . . We for our part were equally desperate to interdict this supply," wrote Margaret Thatcher herself years later in her memoir, *The Downing Street Years.*[5]

Thatcher ordered British intelligence to spare no effort to detect and prevent any Argentine effort to acquire Exocet missiles or any other armaments.

In 1981, Argentina had contracted with the French government to buy four-teen Super-Éntendards and fourteen Exocets. By April 2, 1982, they had re-ceived only five aircraft and five missiles.

What the British prime minister did not know at the time, however, was that those seeking missiles in the black market were not the Argentineans, but a conspiracy orchestrated by the Propaganda 2 lodge, financed by the Vatican and carried out by free agents of the Holy Alliance.

As can be inferred from an MI6 report, the Argentine military junta man-aged to acquire as many as six Exocet missiles by unknown means. The result of Operation Flying Fish would become clear when on May 4, 1982, two Super-Éntendards took off from Rio Grande naval air base, each armed with one Exocet. Then they descended into the dead zone of the enemy radar where they could fly undetected by the British. Each pilot caught sight of one large target and three medium ones, locked his Exocet onto the biggest objective, and launched the missile from a distance of some fifty kilometers. The destroyer HMS *Sheffield* suffered a mortal blow.[6]

At the end of the conflict, the missiles provided by the Vatican's men had hit the British destroyers HMS *Sheffield* and HMS *Glamorgan* and the con-tainer ship SS *Atlantic Conveyor,* causing fifty-five deaths and more than a hundred wounded.

At the end of Operation Flying Fish, the financial firm belonging to the Holy See had succeeded in channeling more than $700 million, of which $11 million ended up in the Vatican state's account "B." According to a later investigation, Cardinal Luigi Poggi, chief of the Holy Alliance, with the connivance of Monsignor Paul Casimir Marcinkus, head of the IOR, Cardi-nal Agostino Casaroli at the head of Vatican diplomacy, and with the author-ization of the supreme pontiff John Paul II, used these funds to finance the Polish trade union Solidarity. But a dark hand had decided to eliminate the loose ends still hanging from the Banco Ambrosiano scandal. Roberto Calvi, known to some as "God's banker," was the first to be secured.

Since May 31, 1982, Calvi had been complaining to a group of cardinals, including Pietro Palazzini, prefect of the Congregation for Beatification. Calvi told them in threatening tones that if the Banco Ambrosiano fell, the Vatican Bank would fall with it. For years, Roberto Calvi had been demand-ing that Marcinkus solve the joint problem of an enormous debt accumu-lated in the transatlantic companies belonging to the web created by the IOR and the Banco Ambrosiano. But once more this attempt failed. Calvi then threatened IOR director Luigi Mennini. He said he would tell Italian financial authorities everything he knew about the Vatican Bank.[7]

On Monday, June 7, Roberto Calvi presented the dramatic situation facing the Banco Ambrosiano to its administrative council: He asserted that if the Vatican Bank did not make good on its letters of credit, the Ambrosiano would have to declare bankruptcy instead. The next day, the banker received a strange visit from one Alvaro Giardili, who according to the police might have been connected to both the Mafia and the Vatican's Holy Alliance. Giardili told Roberto Calvi that his wife and children were in mortal danger. Apparently Giardili also had ties to a man named Vincenzo Casillo, a Mafia executioner who had done various jobs for Marcinkus and the Vatican espionage services. Casillo would later be identified by the Roman prosecutor's office as one of the immediate killers of Roberto Calvi. He himself would be murdered on January 23, 1983.[8]

Roberto Calvi's complaints were becoming more and more dangerous not only to the IOR but also to the Holy Alliance's operations in Poland. "God's banker" openly complained that Paul Marcinkus, to avoid being investigated by order of the pope or by the *Sodalitium Pianum* under the command of Monsignor Luigi Poggi, had on his own authority withdrawn a hundred million dollars for transmittal to Lech Walesa's Solidarity union.[9]

On Monday, June 14, at 11 A.M., Monsignor Paul Casimir Marcinkus submitted his resignation as a member of the board of directors of the Banco Ambrosiano Overseas Limited (BAOL) headquartered in Nassau. Through this bank, the IOR withdrew uncontrolled funds worth close to a billion dollars to plug up the hole in the Banco Ambrosiano.

On Tuesday, June 15, Roberto Calvi arrived in London and registered in room 881 of the Chelsea Cloisters hotel. The Cloisters was a respectable enough hotel for an ordinary business traveler, but not for the president of one of the most important and powerful Catholic banks of Europe. By this point, Calvi distrusted everyone. On Wednesday, June 16, he told his wife, Clara, over the telephone that he was in fear of "the black men [Holy Alliance agents] around Paul Marcinkus. They always know how to find me."

On Thursday, June 17, Calvi kept up the desperate phone calls to his family, urging them to leave Switzerland for the safety of the United States.

At 5 P.M., Calvi was fired from the management of the Banco Ambrosiano. When he heard this, "God's banker" knew he was done for and had only a few hours left to live. Around 10 P.M., according to documents from the Roman prosecutor's office, two Italian-speaking men—they might have been Holy Alliance agents or they might have been Mafia assassins—picked up Roberto Calvi at his hotel. All three left by the rear door, out of view of the receptionist, and got into a black limousine. The next day Roberto Calvi was found hanging by the neck under the London bridge called Blackfriars.

Three autopsies were performed on Calvi's body. All found that he died at 2 A.M. on June 18, 1982. The famous forensic specialist Antonio Fornari claimed in his report that, without a doubt, Calvi was murdered. If he had committed suicide, Calvi would have had to descend a steep, wet stairway, then jump nearly a meter to reach the platform under the bridge, all this in water above his knees because of the high tide and while bearing the weight of nearly five kilograms of stones that were found in the pockets of his jacket and pants. In addition, once having reached the platform, he would have had to keep going seven meters farther on to reach the end where he was found hanging. There was no doubt that Roberto Calvi had been assassinated.[10] What Calvi died without knowing was what had happened in Milan a few hours earlier.

That same June 18, two men identifying themselves as "sent by the Vatican" came to Banco Ambrosiano headquarters to turn over a series of documents from the IOR. They rode the elegant elevator up to the fourth floor of the imposing building. At the end of the hallway was the former office of the powerful Roberto Calvi, still alive in London. The two men reached a small office connected to Calvi's. There they found Graziella Corrocher, the loyal secretary of "God's banker" and one of those best acquainted with the secrets of her formerly all-powerful boss. Minutes later, she flew out the window, a "suicide."[11] A note found by the police held her boss, Roberto Calvi, responsible for everything that had happened in the Banco Ambrosiano. There was no mention of her family, her life, or her friends—just an opportune accusation against her boss.

In the month of September, Liceo Gelli was charged with espionage, political conspiracy, criminal association, and fraud. At first he was able to avoid arrest, but on September 13 the grand master of the P2 lodge, the man everyone called *il Burattinaio* (the puppeteer), was arrested in Geneva while trying to withdraw fifty million dollars from a bank account into a suitcase.

A month later, October 2, 1982, Giuseppe Dellacha, a high executive of the bank, also "committed suicide" by jumping from a sixth-floor office window in the same Banco Ambrosiano building in Milan. Apparently Dellacha was the "special messenger" between Roberto Calvi and Monsignor Paul Marcinkus. Dellacha's "sensitive" work consisted of carrying messages that were better off not being committed to writing anywhere in the Vatican Bank. Because Giuseppe Dellacha knew too much, he, too, had to die.

Little by little, the loose ends were being tied off by a mysterious hand. Clara Calvi, Roberto's widow, charged that "the Vatican killed my husband to hide the bankruptcy of the Vatican Bank." Since Michele Sindona's fall, Roberto Calvi had taken over Sindona's old functions of laundering Mafia money, dealing arms, helping important figures divert money to fiscal paradises under the radar of Italian authorities, and financing dictatorial regimes in Nicaragua, Uruguay, Argentina, and Paraguay.

In October 1982, John Paul II appointed a special commission to investigate the role played by the Vatican, the IOR, and the papal secret services in the Banco Ambrosiano irregularities. Investigations of the Calvi case, the bank's failure, and its connections to the IOR followed one after another until 1989. On March 22, 1986, Michele Sindona was poisoned in Italy's Voghera prison, where he was being held pending his extradition to the United States. Cyanide had been placed in his coffee. The Mafia's former banker died in his cell without anyone coming to his aid, only two days after a jury had sentenced him to life imprisonment and he had declared that if no one helped him, he would "decide to tell all he knew about the relations between the Mafia and the Vatican and the role played by papal departments like the IOR or the secret services." On February 20, 1987, the Milan investigative magistrate Antonio Pizza ordered the arrest and jailing of Monsignor Paul Casimir Marcinkus, Luigi Mennini, and Pellegrino de Strobel, the three highest IOR officials. Until that moment, John Paul II had kept them at their posts, perhaps because they knew too much and it was better not to stir up the turbid waters of Vatican finances. All around San Pietro and at every Vatican City gate, police waited to slap handcuffs on the upper tier of Vatican Bank officials and the president of the Vatican state administration, because Marcinkus presided over not only the IOR but also the Vatican's governing council.

Monsignor Marcinkus, in fact, had been within arm's reach of a cardinal's purple when the scandal blew up, requiring John Paul II to keep him inside the Vatican to prevent his arrest by Italian authorities and subsequent deportation to the United States. Today, he lives in retirement in Sun City, Arizona, shielded by his Vatican diplomatic passport, which renders him untouchable by U.S. authorities.

Thanks to the pressures applied by John Paul II, a high Italian court suspended the arrest order and granted the Vatican bankers immunity as "directors of a foreign bank."

The Vatican Bank had to pay out more than 240 million dollars to discharge its responsibilities to Banco Ambrosiano creditors. In the criminal trials related to the Ambrosiano's failure, which ended in 1998, those receiving the heaviest sentences were the leaders of Propaganda 2. Licio Gelli got eighteen years in prison, and Umberto Ortolani nineteen.

In 1988, the Roberto Calvi murder trial opened. When it concluded in 1993, three men were convicted of complicity: Monsignor Pavel Hnilica—an important agent of the Holy Alliance and trusted member of the pope's inner circle—Flavio Carboni, and Giulio Lena. This concluded the investigation of Vatican, Inc., and finally tied up its loose ends. But a new case of financial corruption was about to explode in the heart of the Vatican state.

Leopold Ledl was an ex-butcher who had been involved in several shady Vatican business deals and carried out some strange operations for the Holy Alliance. The former papal secret agent had served as intermediary between the Vatican and the Mafia for an operation involving falsified stock certificates and bonds. When the affair came to light, Ledl became not only its organizer but also its victim.

The scheme, apparently, involved Ledl acquiring phony stock worth a billion dollars for someone in the Vatican. The ex-spy's job was to serve as intermediary between the Vatican and the U.S. Mafia in the production and then sale of forged shares of Boeing, Chrysler, General Motors, and ITT. The Vatican side of the operation was run by Monsignor Marcinkus in person. At times, Cardinals Tisserant and Benelli would attend the meetings with Ledl.[12]

Finally, Monsignor Pavel Hnilica warned Marcinkus about the danger of trying to pass so many falsified stock certificates through the financial markets. This could only bring a confrontation with the U.S. Treasury Department, Hnilica pointed out, and he reminded Marcinkus of his U.S. citizenship. "If Reagan wants to, he can request the supreme pontiff to agree to your extradition," the dark agent of the Holy Alliance pointed out to Paul Marcinkus. Marcinkus, still the chief of the IOR, did not want to risk committing a federal crime in the eyes of his native land, knowing how his countrymen would repay such a transgression.

In May of 1992, Licio Gelli, held under house arrest, received word of the sentence imposed for his part in the Banco Ambrosiano's collapse. Six years after filing an appeal, the former grand master of the P2 lodge found his original sentence ratified. On Wednesday, May 20, 1998, Gelli fled from his home in full view of watching policemen. Nearly four months later, on September 10, he was rearrested on the Costa Azul, apparently thanks to a leak from the Vatican secret service to the French counterespionage service DST.[13]

When the Freemason and P2 member Umberto Ortolani had been questioned in 1990, meanwhile, he revealed another operation of the Vatican secret services. They had spent several months trying to recover compromising photographs of John Paul II.

One day in April 1981, Licio Gelli had shown an Italian Socialist Party member some photos of Pope John Paul II stark naked in the Castel Gandolfo swimming pool. Gelli assumed that if such photos could be taken with a telephoto lens, it would be equally simple to shoot the supreme pontiff with a rifle equipped with a telescopic sight.[14]

Poggi decided to put Holy Alliance agents to work recovering or "ransoming" the missing negatives. The Holy Alliance chief dubbed this mission "Operation Image."

The papal spy director knew that the largest packet of these was already in the possession of the Rizzoli publishing empire, by way of Licio Gelli and then Christian Democratic politician Giulio Andreotti. These photos were personally turned in to the supreme pontiff in Monsignor Poggi's presence.[15]

Immediately, the Vatican espionage chief summoned two priests who belonged to the *Sodalitium Pianum.* As always, Poggi's orders were brief and to the point. His agents had to find the missing negatives for two reasons: First, to avoid their publication and a subsequent scandal. Second, and even more important, to find out how the photographers had managed to snap the photos without being detected by the pontifical security services. Somehow, ordinary photographers had managed to foil the rings of security surrounding the pope.

The agents went to work making the rounds of Roman photo labs that developed film for professionals. By the end of the week, the S.P. found a man trying to sell what he said were very compromising images, though he wouldn't say what they showed.

The man in question was a lab worker in a firm famous for its rapid developing services for photographers employed by celebrity gossip magazines.

This man lived in a small apartment on the outskirts of Rome. One day, on returning home from work, he found his apartment in complete disarray, with boxes emptied onto the floor, the mattress sliced open, and armchairs stripped of their upholstery. Somebody had been searching for something, and the man knew what.

When he went into his small bathroom, he saw that the intruders had found what they were looking for. One of the lead pipes had been cut, and the plastic cylinder holding the negatives had been removed. Poggi's men had done their job well. Operation Image had never existed. Later, Monsignor Luigi Poggi would destroy all the material.

The *Sodalitium Pianum* discovered that a Holy Alliance agent and priest named Lorenzo Zorza had been involved. This agent had been connected in some way to the Banco Ambrosiano bankruptcy and had participated in an operation with Francesco Pazienza, an ex-agent of the Italian military intelligence agency SISMI. Zorza was also investigated for his suspected relations with Mafia groups involved in drug and art smuggling.

As in many previous such situations, when the Italian authorities requested that the Holy See turn over Lorenzo Zorza, the Vatican secretary of state refused. He argued that the subject was an official of a foreign country and therefore not subject to Italian law. Months late, the Holy Alliance agent was conveniently dispatched to an African nunciature, but the intrigues did not end there. A new conspiracy would shake one of the best regarded and most popular Vatican organizations, the Swiss Guard.

On Monday, May 4, 1998, a little past 9 P.M., three blood-soaked bodies were found in an apartment within the Swiss Guard barracks. All three had been shot. Their corpses had been found by a nun whose identity was concealed by the Holy Alliance. The first to arrive after the discovery were Vatican spokesman Joaquín Navarro-Valls, *"sostituto,"* or second-in-command, in the secretariat of state Cardinal Giovanni Battista Re, and a secretariat of state advisor, Pedro López Quintana.

A half hour later, the crime scene was teeming with high officials of the curia, Holy Alliance and counterespionage agents, and Swiss Guard members in civilian clothes.[16]

Forty-five minutes after that, three high officials of the Vatican *Vigilanza* arrived: Inspector-General Camillo Cibin, Chief Superintendent Raoul Bonarelli, and another superintendent. Cibin's first survey of the room revealed that someone had removed four glasses. Possibly this had been done by agents of the Holy Alliance, who had mysteriously been the first to arrive at the scene of the crime.[17] An official of the Vatican city-state then appeared to take Polaroid photos of the victims: Swiss Guard commander Alois Estermann; his Venezuelan wife, Gladys Meza Romero; and a Swiss Guard corporal named Cedric Tornay. Bonarelli pointed out to Cibin that several large drawers of Estermann's desk were open. Without a doubt, someone had been searching the officer's desk and files.

Not far away, Cardinal Luigi Poggi,[18] who only two months before had been allowed to give up his responsibilities at the head of the papal secret services, reported the tragedy to Pope John Paul II. Outside St. Anne's Gate, where a Swiss Guard unit was on duty, a crowd of press and curious onlookers began to gather. Rumors were spreading fast.

The three corpses were removed to a mortuary, laid on the floor, and covered with a sheet. Members of the *Corpo della Vigilanza* and the Holy Alliance tidied up the apartment, locked the door, and secured it with a papal seal, which barred entry by anyone or anything, under pain of excommunication.

Only a few hours before the murders, Alois Estermann had been named commander of the Swiss Guard by the pope himself. Born in the town of Gunzwill in the Swiss canton of Lucerne, he had been subcommander of the Guard since 1989. He was forty-four years old when he died.

Estermann's official promotion ceremony had been scheduled for May 6, two days after the murder. His wife, Gladys Meza, worked in the Venezuelan embassy to the Holy See. The third victim, Corporal Cedric Tornay, was twenty-three years old and had been born in Saint-Maurice in the Swiss canton of Valais. He had joined the papal army on January 1, 1994.[19]

Navarro-Valls, the Vatican spokesman, tried too quickly to issue an explanation of the events. His reconstruction would later be revealed to bear little resemblance to what had actually occurred. According to Navarro-Valls, "the bodies were found by a neighbor.[20] Estermann, Meza, and Tornay had all been shot to death, and the weapon used was found under the corporal's body." According to the spokesman, "In a fit of madness, the corporal used his service pistol to kill his commander and his commander's wife. The Vatican is certain that this is what occurred." No one asked any further questions of the spokesman.

On the night of May 5, three SISMI agents met with a former member of the Swiss Guard. In truth, neither the Italian intelligence service nor the

Italian police believed the story the Vatican had put out. Three different hypotheses circulated in the press: One, that Estermann was involved in a homosexual relationship with Tornay. Two, that Tornay was involved with Estermann's wife. Three, that some much deeper and more obscure conspiracy lay behind the crime.

The Vatican officially proffered the theory that Tornay had serious conflicts with Estermann, who had denied him a promotion and a decoration, but Italian intelligence did not give this notion much credence. According to Joaquín Navarro-Valls, Tornay in his attack of madness had fired his service weapon five times. One bullet remained in its chamber, two killed Estermann, and another was found in the ceiling. This was not the only such incident to have occurred inside the Swiss Guard.[21]

Questions continued flowing up and down the Vatican hallways. If Tornay fired five shots, why were only four shell casings recovered? Why was Estermann's apartment door open when the supposed nun who discovered the bodies arrived?

Another question asked by investigators was how, if Tornay used his Sig Sauer 75 service pistol with a nine-bullet clip, he could fall forward onto it after firing his suicide shot. The Sig Sauer 75 was a powerful weapon, and the expected result would be for him to fall backwards from the impact of the bullet. There was also speculation as to why the Swiss Guard had gone without a commander for months on end, and then when one was named, he died within a few hours. Questions mounted, but the Vatican preferred not to respond.

On May 6, when asked by journalists, Italian interior minister Giorgio Napolitana stated that Italian authorities had not received any request for aid in the investigation of the Swiss Guard case.[22] The Vatican agency that had rapidly opened and then concluded the investigation was the *Corpo della Vigilanza*. During the funeral ceremony for the victims, at which the three caskets lay side by side, the supreme pontiff stated that Alois Estermann "was a person of great faith and deep devotion to his duty. For eighteen years he offered loyal and valuable service, for which I personally thank him."

But questions about the crime were not buried with the bodies. Why, for example, was the apartment door open if the three bodies were found in the office at the back? Why did the supposed neighbor who found the bodies say that she heard "several muffled noises in the apartment, which alarmed her"? The neighbor should have heard five loud shots from Tornay's gun. The woman told a journalist that she heard five clipped shots, "as if fired with a silencer." This issue got further complicated when four important cardinals, Silvio Oddi, Darío Castrillón, Roger Etchegaray, and Carlo Maria Martini, told Pope John Paul II that they did not trust the official version of the events. A theory that casts the affair in a darker light is advanced by writer John Follain in his book *City of Secrets: The Truth behind the Murders at the Vatican.* Follain charges that control of the Swiss Guard was contested between followers of Opus Dei, who wanted to make it an elite body for anti-terrorist work, and the Masons within the curia, who wanted to do away with it except as a symbolic presence and tourist attraction in contrast to the *Corpo della Vigilanza.*[23]

On May 7, 1998, the *Berliner Kurier* newspaper published a story linking Commander Alois Estermann to the Stasi, the East German intelligence service. The article contained quite a few explicit facts and details. The newspaper also asserted that Alois Estermann, while still a Swiss Guard captain, had worked in undercover operations for the Vatican secret service, the Holy Alliance. For instance, he made several trips to Warsaw and Gdansk when radical factions of Solidarity favored militarizing the union for a possible armed defense of the strikers after General Jaruzelski's December 12, 1981, imposition of martial law. Estermann coordinated acquisition of black market arms with IOR money and maintained training camps in Austria and Germany for the future Solidarity fighters.[24]

Markus Wolf, the powerful Stasi chief for thirty-three years, asserted that the code name *Werder* hid an agent who was actually a member of the papal army. According to Stasi files declassified after the fall of the Berlin Wall, Werder became an informer in early 1980, the year that Alois Estermann joined the Swiss Guard.[25]

This report of Alois Estermann's connection with East German secret services provoked indignation in the Vatican and the Holy Alliance.[26] Later, Markus Wolf himself, in an interview with a Polish newspaper, confirmed that Alois Estermann had been a Stasi agent: "We felt very proud in 1979 when we succeeded in recruiting Estermann as an agent. That man had unlimited access to the Holy See and with him, we did too. When we initiated contacts with him, his great desire was to join the Papal Guard. When the Vatican granted this, his value as an informer grew tremendously."[27]

Estermann's liaison inside the Vatican for communicating with the Stasi was a Dominican friar named Karl Brammer, code-named *Licht Blick* (Ray of Hope). Brammer was expelled from the Vatican in the late 1980s after the

Sodalitium Pianum agents caught him gathering secret information from the files of the Vatican Scientific Commission. The papal agents caught Brammer passing the information to an Italian journalist.

A month after the murders, Tornay's mother made a number of statements to the Italian weekly *Panorama*.[28] She claimed to have spoken with her son the morning of the crime and not found him to be at all depressed. At one point in the *Panorama* interview, Tornay's mother mentioned a certain "Father Yvan" as her son's spiritual counselor, with whom he had planned to meet that afternoon to speak about a possible job in a Swiss bank as a security officer.

This "Father Yvan" or "Father Ivano" was in fact Yvan Bertorello, a Frenchman between the ages of thirty-five and forty who circulated freely through the Vatican hallways, clad always in a cassock. Bertorello was a Holy Alliance agent who had participated in special operations of the papal espionage service. It was said that he had military training, acquired either in the French army or in the Swiss one.

Later, Cedric Tornay's mother told a Vatican judge that she herself had known Yvan, but she was informed afterwards, according to a *Corpo della Vigilanza* report, that the Vatican had no knowledge of a priest named Yvan or Ivano or anything of that ilk.

In truth, Yvan Bertorello, of French-Italian origin, was an agent of either the Holy Alliance or the *Sodalitium Pianum* who had been sent on diplomatic and spy missions to Africa and Bosnia. Bertorello's boss, Monsignor Pedro López Quintana, assigned him the mission of spying on the Swiss Guard in search of its connections to Opus Dei.[29]

López Quintana, born in the Spanish city of Barbastro on July 27, 1953, had belonged to the Holy See's diplomatic corps and the Disciplinary Commission of the Curia until 1987, when he was named one of His Holiness's prelates of honor and sent to the nunciature in New Delhi. In 1992, he was recalled to the Vatican and assigned to the secretariat of state as an advisor on general affairs. Within the Vatican, it was rumored that Monsignor Pedro López Quintana had taken over control of Vatican counterespionage after Luigi Poggi's resignation on March 7, 1998.

A French secret service source told writer David Yallop that the murders of May 4 involved a conspiracy in which three members were directly involved: Alois Estermann himself, Gladys Estermann, and the Vatican spy Yvan Bertorello.

In March of 1999, new Swiss Guard commander Pius Segmüller was ordered to create a special unit within his corps, the "Security Committee," with the approval of the Pontifical Commission for the Vatican City-State. This new committee's mission was to coordinate activities related to the safety of the Holy See and the supreme pontiff, and to prevent criminal activities within the Vatican.

In fact, the "Security Committee" was a sort of secret service free of the influence of the Holy Alliance and the *Sodalitium Pianum.* It operated under the control of Monsignor Giovanni Danzi, secretary-general of the Vatican government.

Danzi was, according to Vatican sources, an unscrupulous man wielding great power within the Pontifical Commission for the Vatican City-State. From his luxurious residence, Danzi managed the "Security Committee" with an iron hand. The investigation that was carried out suggests the possibility that on the night of May 4, a fourth person may have been inside the Estermanns' apartment along with Cedric Tornay.[30]

What is sure, however, is that any fourth person who may have been inside the Estermann apartment was only a witness. All the bullets were shown to have been fired from Tornay's service pistol, and powder traces were found on his hand and trigger finger. The fourth person may also have remained hidden somewhere inside the apartment until the first authorities arrived and then escaped by leaving with them. The first to arrive are said to have been four Holy Alliance agents, the same ones who removed the drinking glasses from atop Alois Estermann's desk.

Later it was found that Cedric Tornay had been under surveillance for months—by the Holy Alliance, the *Sodalitium Pianum,* or the "Security Committee." The young Swiss Guard corporal had been seduced by an Italian young woman named Manuela, whom he met in a cafeteria near the Vatican where Swiss Guards tended to gather. They said Manuela told a Vatican bishop about Tornay's every move, which makes it impossible for the young man to have entered Alois Estermann's house without being seen.[31]

Also, in spite of the Vatican's fine words recognizing the pain suffered by Cedric Tornay's mother, Muguette Baudat, a member of the Holy Alliance devoted his time to pressuring Baudat and her lawyers.

Since that night in 1998, many conspiracy theories have been advanced. One holds that the Holy Alliance "executed" Alois Estermann because he knew too much about its covert operations. Another says Tornay loved him and felt rejected because a different young Guard member had replaced him in Estermann's bed. A third sees Estermann as having been killed for his close ties to Opus Dei or to the Masonic clan of the Vatican lodge. A fourth alleges that Estermann could have been killed for his former relations with an espionage service behind the Iron Curtain. And there are many more. Tornay's friends in the Swiss Guard and his family insist that he was neither crazy nor taking drugs and that he must have been involved in some kind of situation outside his control and over his head that led finally to his death.

Vatican authorities never undertook any independent police or judicial investigation of what happened on the night of Monday, May 4, 1998. Neither the Holy Alliance nor the *Sodalitium Pianum* nor the "Security Committee" nor the *Corpo della Vigilanza* carried out a serious investigation. With the approval of the supreme pontiff John Paul II, Secretary of State Angelo Sodano decided to seal all the documentation related to the tragic night on which three people lost their lives within the Vatican walls and to bury it in the Secret Archives.

No one can ever know the truth about the killing of Swiss Guard commander Alois Estermann, his wife, Gladys Meza, and Lance-Corporal Cedric Tornay. The Holy Alliance spy Yvan Bertorello, who probably knew the most, simply disappeared. He was never seen again in the conspiratorial hallways of the Vatican state.

In the book *In God's Name: An Investigation into the Murder of Pope John Paul I,* writer David Yallop rendered a harsh judgment of Pope John Paul II:

We have a pope who publicly berates Nicaraguan priests for their involvement in politics and simultaneously gives his blessing for large quantities of dollars to be made available, secretly and illegally, to Solidarity in Poland. It is a papacy of double standards: one for the pope and another for the rest of mankind. The papacy of John Paul II has been a triumph for the wheeler-dealers, for the corrupt, for the international thieves such as Calvi, Gelli, and Sindona. While His Holiness has maintained a very highly publicized image, not unlike some endless rock'n'roll tour, the men backstage are ensuring that it is business as usual. It is to be regretted that the severely moralizing speeches of His Holiness cannot, apparently, be heard backstage.

Be that as it may, there can be no doubt that during John Paul II's long papacy, the Vatican sold arms and financed dictatorships and coups d'etat.

Further, the financial and bank collapses provoked "suicides," and the Vatican ordered its spy services to carry out covert operations.

Today, in the opening years of the twenty-first century, no one hears of Vatican secret services like the Holy Alliance. In the world of contemporary espionage, the papal secret service (both espionage and counterespionage) is dubbed The Entity. Whatever it is called, its guiding principles are the same as they were when Pope Pius V created the body in the year of our Lord 1566. Defense of the faith, defense of the Catholic religion, defense of the interests of the Vatican state, and complete obedience to His Holiness continue to be the four great pillars that will carry it into the far reaches of future history. As long as the Catholic Church continues to spread its faith to the ends of the earth, The Entity will continue to pursue any enemy that may appear in the path of the supreme pontiff or his policies. Meanwhile, to this day, the Vatican state continues to deny that its espionage service exists.

Epilogue

THE YEARS TO COME: BENEDICT XVI

I have learned to confront every situation. I know how to be full and how to go hungry, how to live in abundance and how to be in need. I can do all these things thanks to Christ who strengthens me.
— Philippians 4:12–13

On the morning of April 1, 2005, the Vatican state's head of espionage and counterespionage was summoned by Cardinal Chamberlain Eduardo Martínez Somalo. Stepping into the cardinal chamberlain's office in the Apostolic Palace, he confronted the somber faces of Cardinal Joseph Ratzinger, prefect of the Congregation of the Doctrine of the Faith; Archbishops Leonardo Sandri and Giovanni Lajolo, head of Vatican internal and external affairs, respectively; Cardinal Angelo Sodano, the secretary of state; and Camillo Ruini, the vicar of Rome. The supreme pontiff's health had reached a critical stage. At the last moment, Cardinal Giovanni Battista Re, prefect of the Congregation for the Clergy, joined the group as well.

The archbishop in charge of espionage and counterespionage services knew that he'd been brought there to prepare the operation that would have to go into motion once His Holiness John Paul II had expired.

It would be his job to protect the pope's body once Dr. Renato Buzzonetti had certified the pontiff's passing. That would be the first mission of the papal counterespionage, the *Sodalitium Pianum*. The agents of the Holy Alliance and the *Sodalitium Pianum* would automatically put themselves at the disposal of the chamberlain. Operation *"Catenaccio,"* or "Lock," would begin once the supreme pontiff's death was certified.

On the morning of Saturday, April 2, Italian interior ministry delegate

Acquile Serra passed through the Vatican gates. A high Church official had called him to announce, "The Pope is dying. Be ready."

About 9 P.M. the Vatican spy chief received a new summons. When he entered the area adjoining the papal rooms in the Apostolic Palace, he found Colonel Pius Segmüller, Swiss Guard commander-in-chief Colonel Elmar Theodor Mader, Vatican police inspector-general Camillo Cibin, and sub-inspector Dominico Giani. The five men present would be responsible for the security of the Vatican state and of the 115 members of the Sacred College of Cardinals who would begin to meet on Monday, April 18, to name a new pontiff. Until that occurred, during the interregnum preceding the election of St. Peter's newest successor, the cardinals would constitute the highest authority of the Vatican state and the Catholic Church.

At 9:37 P.M., Dr. Renato Buzzonetti certified the passing of John Paul II: "I certify that His Holiness John Paul II, born in Wadowice on May 18, 1920, residing in Vatican City with Vatican citizenship, has died at 9:37 P.M. on April 2, 2005, in his rooms in the Vatican Apostolic Palace as a result of septic shock and irreversible cardiocirculatory collapse."

Only murmurs reached the room from outside. A great wave of silence engulfed the chambers of the Vatican. The five men knelt, each on his left knee, and crossed themselves. Camillo Cibin, who had covered John Paul II's bullet wound with his hand during the attempted assassination in the Piazza di San Pietro on May 13, 1981, led a brief prayer. The five men knew that from this moment on a well-oiled, centuries-old machine would begin to whir. They and their departments were important parts of the machine.

Segmüller and Mader were ordered to position their men around the Piazza di San Pietro as more and more of the faithful flowed into the Vatican, drawn by concern for the health of the pontiff. Cibin and Giani were ordered to assign their men to the highest-ranking cardinals and to take on special powers until the new pope should be elected. The head of the espionage services had the task of guarding the chamberlain, Martínez Somalo, and protecting the papal rooms until they could be sealed.

From the moment he heard of John Paul II's death, the Holy Alliance chief began to issue orders to his agents. The first was to escort Cardinal Martínez Somalo to the pontiff's office to destroy the Fisherman's lead seal and the one he wore on his finger. Thus no one could use the papal seals to sign documents that had not been approved before the supreme pontiff's demise.

On leaving the office, Martínez Somalo ordered the pope's rooms to be closed. The vicar of Rome, Cardinal Ruini, put in place the five seals of wax dripped over red ribbon. Two counterespionage agents and two members of the Swiss Guard would stand continuous guard to ensure that the seals were not disturbed until the new pope elected in the conclave should break them. St. Peter's successor would be the only person authorized to enter that room that had served as John Paul II's office for the past twenty-six years.

Next, Martínez Somalo told Cibin, Colonel Mader of the Swiss Guard, and the espionage chief to prepare for a meeting of the "Crisis Committee" made up of Italian and Roman civil authorities. Cibin, Mader, and the Holy Alliance head would be the Vatican's liaisons with Italian public safety forces. At 9:55 P.M. on April 2, just eighteen minutes after the pope's demise was certified, Archbishop Leonardo Sandri announced it to the world.

About 11:30 that same night, the cardinal chamberlain again called the archbishop who headed the Holy Alliance, this time to direct him to the rooms of Monsignor Stanislaw Dziwisz, who had been the late pope's secretary for more than forty years. Monsignor Dziwisz was the custodian of John Paul II's will, not to be read until a specified date. The espionage chief offered the Polish bishop a secure room in which to deposit the valuable document, but Dziwisz chose to keep it in his power, exactly as the Holy Father had ordered.

Although Rome was in a state of high tension, the noise of the crowd gathered in the Piazza di San Pietro could not be heard inside the Bronze Gate that led to the Apostolic Palace. Inside the palace, the only sounds were the footsteps of Swiss Guard patrols and the whispers of cardinals and high-ranking members of the curia. Clearly, after so many centuries of repeated ceremonies, the Catholic Church's heart continued to beat as regularly as a clock, marking the minutes of the ritual called *Sede Vacante.* The days went by in a sort of controlled panic. Cardinal Eduardo Martínez Somalo gave precise orders to the vicar of Rome, Cardinal Camillo Ruini, and to Cardinal Joseph Ratzinger, who as dean of the Sacred College of Cardinals had the responsibility to issue the official order convoking the conclave and to see to the needs of its members once they reached Rome.

The security and espionage services got their orders at the same time as Martínez Somalo, Ruini, and Ratzinger. About midnight on Thursday, April 7, the day before John Paul II's funeral, the Argentine archbishop Leonardo Sandri, *sostituto* to the secretariat of state, urgently informed the espionage chief that he had received a communication from Air Force One, the U.S. presidential aircraft. When the plane landed in Rome, the heads of the U.S. delegation would proceed to the Basilica of St. Peter to pray over the body of the pope. Within a few hours, in other words, one president and two ex-presidents of the United States would kneel before the corpse of John Paul II.

The head of the *Sodalitium Pianum,* following the orders of the archbishop who directed the espionage services of the Vatican state, got in contact with Italian authorities in Rome and with the U.S. Secret Service. The U.S. delegation—made up of President George W. Bush, his wife, his father, the ex-president George Bush, ex-president Bill Clinton, and Secretary of State Condoleezza Rice—reached the Vatican gates at approximately 1:35 A.M. Security inside the basilica was tight, but the U.S. Secret Service men were asked not to bring weapons inside. For a few minutes, the safety of the three North American chief executives was in the hands of the Swiss Guard, the *Corpo della Vigilanza,* and the Vatican counterespionage.

At that same time, an emergency meeting was under way in the cardinal chamberlain's office. Apparently those attending were studying the possibility that, after the funeral service attended by nearly two hundred heads of state, kings, and leaders of other religions, John Paul II's body would be taken by helicopter to the Basilica of St. John Lateran, the Roman cathedral, so that the people could pay their last respects to the late pope. Ratzinger agreed with this plan, but Ruini said the body's safety would be hard to assure outside the Vatican walls. Cibin, supported by the Holy Alliance chief, warned the assembled cardinals that to put together a mobile operation outside the Vatican would be very complicated, given the avalanche of faithful who would try to get inside St. John Lateran. "The Swiss Guard can control security in the Vatican, but outside is the responsibility of the Italian police," Cibin said.

Cardinal Martínez Somalo then decided to end the discussion, declaring he had come to a decision. Pope John Paul II would be buried after the funeral service without any kind of delay. Looking out the window overlooking the Piazza di San Pietro, the members of the Roman curia and their security forces could see long lines of the faithful stretching for kilometers into the distance, as far as the bridges over the Tiber. Each line moved at a rate of two hundred meters every three hours. It was going to be a long night for everyone.

On Friday, April 8, after an opening prayer, the final meeting between the security chiefs of the Vatican and Italian states took place. Like a general before a battle, Cardinal Chamberlain Eduardo Martínez Somalo, accompanied by Major Penitentiary James Francis Stafford, Vicar of Rome Camillo Ruini, and Vicar-General for Vatican City Angelo Comastri, had spread out a large map of the Vatican and another of the Piazza di San Pietro. The latter map was peppered with small flags of various colors representing presidents, prime ministers, kings, and religious leaders. Mayor Walter Beltroni of Rome and Italian civil defense chief Guido Bertolasso listened to Martínez Somalo's explanations. Every detail was planned like clockwork.

During the night, Holy Alliance and Vatican counterespionage agents had filtered through the crowd so as to take up the best positions before Cardinal Joseph Ratzinger began his homily. Farther off, members of the *Corpo della Vigilanza* of the Holy See, dressed in jackets and black ties, patrolled the outskirts. Headsets kept them in touch with the office of security coordination, directed by one representative of the Italian republic and another from the Holy See. On the surrounding rooftops, hundreds of photographers, television camera operators, and journalists from ninety countries representing more than three thousand communications media waited for the ceremony to begin. Among them mingled disguised Holy Alliance agents and elite sharpshooters from the police and the Italian army.

Since the early hours of the morning, nearly 600,000 people had gathered behind the barriers placed by Italian police around Bernini's columns. One member of Vatican security said that "never before in history have so many security forces from all over the world massed within so few square kilometers." The statement clearly referred to the bodyguards of nearly two hundred heads of state and government seated in front of the supreme pontiff's corpse. The Vatican security chiefs knew they were guarding the first funeral on a global scale.

The morning dawned cloudy with a strong wind blowing through the Piazza di San Pietro, raising the skirts of the cardinals' red robes. Everyone was on alert around the two hundred powerful figures assembled to pay their last respects to the late pope.

Inside the basilica, the private ceremony began. Cardinal Martínez Somalo, accompanied always by a member of the counterespionage and three agents of the Vatican police, conducted the rite of closing the casket, a simple cypress box. Archbishop Pietro Marini, master of liturgical ceremonies, read the *rogito*, a brief biography of the deceased, and then placed it inside the casket. Immediately after, the pope's secretary Dziwisz covered the corpse with a white cloth. None of them knew that the head of Vatican espionage and Camillo Cibin, inspector general of the Vatican police, had just received an alert from the Italian high command warning of a security violation.

An unmarked airplane was entering Vatican airspace. Apparently Italian flight controllers had not managed to contact the pilot. Through the minds of Cibin and the head of the Holy Alliance flashed images of an airplane exploding among dozens of monarchs, three princes of the blood, fifty-seven chiefs of state, seventeen heads of government, and twenty-some religious leaders. It was an explosion they could do absolutely nothing to prevent. There was no way to evacuate quickly enough. Dressed in strict mourning, the dignitaries were already in their seats waiting for the entrance of John Paul II's coffin and the beginning of Cardinal Joseph Ratzinger's homily.

Within seconds, five Italian Air Force fighter planes surrounded the unidentified aircraft and forced it to land at a military base. As it touched ground, police and members of the Italian and Vatican spy services found no trace of explosives or bombs. Apparently, the pilot had experienced communication problems. He had been headed for Ciampino airport to pick up the Macedonian delegation that had arrived for the papal funeral. The command center informed Cibin and the Holy Alliance chief about the incident while the supreme pontiff's rites continued.

When Cardinal Ratzinger, dean of the College of Cardinals, took up position to begin his homily, Cibin and the archbishop who headed the papal espionage service got word of a second alert. This time the incident pitted Italian agents against U.S. Secret Service men. Apparently, President Bush's bodyguards had tried to bring their weapons into an area controlled by the Italian secret services. The incident in which the Italian spy Nicola Calipari had been shot to death by U.S. marines in Iraq was clearly still giving rise to suspicion between the U.S. and Italian agents. Cibin ordered Bush's bodyguards expelled from the security perimeter controlled by the Italian secret services and those of the Holy See.

The clamor of the invited guests and the more than 350,000 people who had reached San Pietro dropped to a murmur when the coffin emerged, surrounded by 140 cardinals dressed in red, and was placed upon a red carpet. The Holy See's agents did not stop their scrutiny of the front rows of the faithful, those who stood closest to the area occupied by the dignitaries. Many carried placards with slogans like *"Santo Subito"* ("Immediate Sainthood") or "John Paul the Great," making it hard to keep a close watch throughout the crowd.

In the meeting held the day before the funeral, Camillo Cibin, Swiss Guard commander Elmar Theodor Mader, and the head of the Holy Alliance had proposed that the Italian police could deny entrance to parishioners with placards. Perhaps they could say that the signs took up too much room, so as not to offend those carrying them. Camillo Ruini, vicar of Rome, even advised putting up a sort of booth in which the mourners could leave their placards and then reclaim them once the ceremony was over. Finally Cardinals Martínez Somalo and Ratzinger rejected the proposal, saying it might offend the faithful who had waited for hours in the cold and wind in the hopes of being able to pay their respects to the late pope. This decision required the Holy See security forces to infiltrate counterespionage agents among the faithful.

After the homily, which was interrupted thirteen times by applause, the ceremony ended with communion, the prayer for the dead, and cries from the crowd of "Santo, Santo." The Vatican Choir sang the *Magnificat* accompanied by the pealing of bells. Once again the Holy Alliance agents and Vatican police began to move. The supreme pontiff's coffin would now be carried inside St. Peter's Cathedral for burial in its crypt.

The site had been secured by members of the police and the *Sodalitium Pianum*. The wooden coffin was encircled with red ribbons to which were applied the seals of the Apostolic Chamber, the Prefecture of the Papal Household, the Office of Papal Liturgical Celebrations, and Vatican Chapter. The cypress box was placed inside another of varnished elm, adorned with a crucifix and the late pope's coat of arms. A simple stone tablet bearing the Latin name, birth, and death dates of John Paul II was placed atop the crypt, completing the burial. The notary of the Chapter of the Basilica then drew up the official notice of interment and read it to those present, a small group presided over by the chamberlain and other officials of the "pontifical family" and including the late pope's secretaries, the nuns who cared for him, his personal physician, and Stanislas Dziwisz, his loyal secretary.

With this act and the last head of state's departure for the airport, Operation Lock came to an end. The Vatican security forces lowered their degree of alert. Now the time had come for the Holy See's espionage and counterespionage services—the Holy Alliance and the *Sodalitium Pianum*—to prepare for the conclave that would choose John Paul II's successor. "It is time for the *novemdiales* (the nine days of mourning), the conclave, and a new pope," Martínez Somalo told his security chiefs.

On Monday, April 11, after attending an early-morning Mass in memory of the late pope, the five men in charge of Vatican state security met at the Apostolic Palace with Cardinal Chamberlain Eduardo Martínez Somalo and Cardinal Joseph Ratzinger. After a brief greeting and prayer, Swiss Guard colonel Pius Segmüller; Swiss Guard commander-in-chief Colonel Elmar Theodor Mader, Vatican police inspector-general Camillo Cibin, subinspector Domenico Giani, and the head of Vatican espionage began a sort of debriefing on the recent events.

Cardinal Ratzinger took the floor to congratulate the five men. He asked them to continue their efforts in the upcoming period so important for the Holy See, the opening of the conclave.

These five men were the first to learn that the day chosen for the beginning of the conclave would be Monday, April 18. They had only seven days to organize all that needed to be done.

Agents of the *Sodalitium Pianum* were in charge of protecting the 115 cardinal-electors to avoid any influence by outside forces during the voting. They would also guard the interior of the Domus Sanctae Marthae, the residence where the cardinal-electors would live until the new supreme pontiff was elected. Every day they had to "sweep" each of the cardinals' rooms for hidden microphones or even radios and televisions. From the outset of the conclave, every communication device was strictly prohibited. Any cardinal who broke this rule would face immediate excommunication.

The espionage agents of the Holy Alliance were in charge of sweeping the Sistine Chapel every morning before the arrival of the cardinals. They would also monitor the door to be sure that none of the 115 cardinal-electors carried any electronic device, including cell phones, inside. The Vatican intelligence services would also set up and maintain an electronic barrier around the Sistine Chapel and the cardinals' lodgings at Sanctae Marthae so that even if a cardinal managed to get a mobile phone through the counterespionage controls, there would be no coverage available.

At the last minute, Cardinal Martínez Somalo informed the head of the Holy Alliance that his men would also be in charge of protecting the two clergymen chosen to orient the conclave in keynote speeches, or "meditations." The first of these was the Capuchin father Raniero Cantalamessa, seventy-one years old, official preacher to the papal household and an expert in spiritual exercises. The second was the Czech cardinal Tomas Spidlik, eighty-six, one of the leading experts in religion in Eastern Europe.

Meanwhile, the betting was on as to who would next occupy the Throne of St. Peter. The heads of the spy services wanted someone who would continue the policies of John Paul II. If possible, they wanted a member of the so-called Polish circle, the cardinals closest to the late pope. The archbishop who headed the Holy Alliance knew that, in contrast, there were three other candidates who were most likely to want to rein in the spy service. These were Cardinal Dionigi Tettamanzi, Archbishop of Milan and defender of anti-globalization youth; the Brazilian Claudio Hummes, Archbishop of São Paulo, a friend of President Lula and defender of the landless; and the Honduran Oscar Andrés Rodríguez Maradiaga, Archbishop of Tegucigalpa, who was said to have flirted with liberation theology. Memories of 1958 were still fresh: the conservative Cardinal Roncalli, elected pope on October 28, 1958, under the name of John XXIII, soon became one of the most progressive pontiffs in the history of the Catholic Church, convoking Vatican Council II. The secret services, both espionage and counterespionage, were consigned to complete inactivity for five years, until John XXIII's death on June 3, 1963.

Cardinal Montini, elected as Paul VI, had reactivated the Holy Alliance and the *Sodalitium Pianum,* which reached their crowning intensity of activity during the first decade of the papacy of John Paul II, between 1978 and 1988. Clearly, the election of a "progressive" to the Throne of St. Peter would be dangerous for the Holy Alliance.

Before April 18, the date the conclave began, the main favorites to succeed John Paul II were Cardinal Dionigi Tettamanzi and the German Joseph Ratzinger. On Saturday April 16, in a last meeting of cardinal-electors before the conclave, Ratzinger ordered "complete silence." Statements to communications media were prohibited. The cardinal therefore ordered Camillo Cibin and the head of the papal espionage to ensure that between that moment and the moment they were sequestered in Sanctae Marthae to prepare for the conclave, all 115 of the cardinal-electors, from fifty-two countries on five continents, were accompanied at all times.

The moment of truth had arrived for the 115 cardinals charged with choosing the 265th pontiff of the Catholic Church. Minutes after Archbishop Pietro Marini, master of ceremonies of the Vatican state, declaimed the famous words, *"extra omnes"* (everybody out), Cardinal Dean Joseph Ratzinger read aloud the vows by which every elector commits to observe the norms of the constitution *Universi Dominici Gregis* and the most absolute secrecy about everything concerning the election of the new pope.

The silver and bronze urns for the paper ballots—protected by two *Sodalitium Pianum* agents and two Swiss Guards—were in their places in front of the main altar. The two ovens were ready as well—the old one for burning the ballots and the more modern one that, with chemical aid, would produce the *fumata bianca* or the *fumata nera*. The cardinals' benches were ready, as was the table covered with purple cloth where those in charge of inspecting and counting the ballots would open the small sheets of paper, read the names aloud, and thread a thick needle through them before they were burned. The newspaper *L'Osservatore Romano*, official organ of the Holy See, already had prepared sixty possible front pages. At 5:30 in the afternoon of April 18, 2005, the conclave officially began. That evening, at 8:06 P.M. Vatican time, the first *fumata nera* appeared in the chimney above St. Peter's. No candidate had won the seventy-six-plus-one votes needed to be elected supreme pontiff.

On the morning of Tuesday, April 19, the members of the conclave met again. A select group of cardinals led the bloc favoring Cardinal Ratzinger: the Spaniard Julián Herranz, member of Opus Dei and Prefect for the Interpretation of Legislative Texts; the Colombian Darío Castrillón Hoyos; and another Colombian, Alfonso López Trujillo. All three belonged to the conservative wing of the curia.

A bit later, the Italian cardinals Angelo Scola and Camillo Ruini joined this group. Ruini had been one of Ratzinger's pupils. Austrian cardinal Christoph Schönborn, a personal friend of the so-called *Panzerkardinal*, also joined the group supporting Ratzinger's candidacy.

Ratzinger's victory began to look more and more likely. Clearly, the bloc led by Angelo Scola would oppose Tettamanzi, and vice versa. Cardinal Carlo Maria Martini, reform leader and promoter of Tettamanzi's candidacy, sent a signal to his group to end their support for the Archbishop of Milan. Joseph Ratzinger gained in numbers and unity. According to Vatican observer Orazio Petrosiello of the newspaper *Il Messagero*, on the conclave's first vote, on Monday afternoon, Martini won forty votes compared to Ratzinger's thirty-eight.

At 5:50 P.M. Vatican time, what looked like a *fumata bianca* puffed from the chimney, but the bells of St. Peter's did not ring. Confusion spread through the Piazza di San Pietro until, suddenly, the great bells of the basilica began to sound. The 115 cardinals had chosen St. Peter's 264th successor.

A few minutes earlier, after the fourth ballot of the conclave, German cardinal Joseph Aloysius Ratzinger had won the necessary majority to be elected the new supreme pontiff. In all, he won 107 votes out of 115 cast by the cardinal-electors.

Immediately afterwards, Cardinal Angelo Sodano asked Ratzinger, "Do you accept your canonical election as supreme pontiff?" The German answered in the affirmative. To the second question, "By what name would you like to be called?" Cardinal Ratzinger answered, "By the name of Benedict XVI."

The new Pope Benedict XVI prayed before the altar of the Sistine Chapel and later moved to the small chamber known as the *camera lacriminatoria,* the room of tears where he was alone with his feelings for a time. There, too, Benedict XVI was helped into the clothing befitting a supreme pontiff. Outfits of three different sizes had been crafted by the famous tailor Gammarelli.

As decreed by tradition, the cardinal proto-deacon, the Chilean Jorge Arturo Medina Estévez, fulfilled his responsibility of making the official announcement: *"Annuntio vobis gaudium magnum; habemus Papam: Eminentissimum ac Reverendissimum Dominum, Dominum Josephum Santae Romanae Ecclesiae Cardinalem Ratzinger qui sibi nomen imposuit Benedictum XVI."*

Simultaneously, Benedict XVI appeared on the balcony to issue his blessing *Urbi et Orbi.* While millions of eyes watched this scene, inside the Vatican the security services were told that a new pontiff had been chosen and a protection plan had to be organized around him.

That same night, Cardinal Eduardo Martínez Somalo met with Camillo Cibin, Colonel Elmar Theodor Mader of the Swiss Guard, and the archbishop in charge of the Holy Alliance. "You must be ready to be called before the Holy Father," Somalo told them. "Now is the time to pray after the election of our new supreme pontiff." The members of the police force and the Swiss Guard would continue their task of patrolling inside the Apostolic Palace, while the counterespionage agents, for this night at least, would protect the supreme pontiff. Pope Benedict XVI would dine in the residence of Sanctae Marthae with the 114 cardinals who had entered the conclave along with him, until his own lodgings in the Apostolic Palace were ready.

Late that night, Cibin was informed that the next day the pope wanted to visit his former office in the Congregation for the Doctrine of the Faith and also to spend a moment in his former Vatican residence to collect some belongings. Camillo Cibin, inspector-general of the Vatican police, telephoned subinspector Domenico Giani and told him to inform the Holy Alliance of the pontiff's wishes. Before the papal visit, Vatican espionage agents had to inspect the office and the private apartment to be sure that Pope Benedict XVI could not come to any harm.

On Wednesday, April 20, at 7 A.M., the cardinals still living in the Sanctae Marthae residence saw Pope Benedict XVI enter the dining room, just as he had for years, to breakfast with his colleagues. The only difference was that now he came dressed in immaculate white and escorted by three agents from the counterespionage and the police.

The bags under his eyes indicated the enormous burden he'd taken on the day before by accepting his selection as supreme pontiff. Cardinal Schönborn was the first to approach him and kiss the Fisherman's ring. Then the pope summoned Cardinal Sodano to tell him something in private.

After breakfast, Benedict XVI went to the Apostolic Palace along with Cardinal Eduardo Martínez Somalo and Cardinal Angelo Sodano. Once there, the Spanish cardinal instructed the Swiss Guard member and the two *Sodalitium Pianum* agents to move aside so he could break the seals on what had been, for twenty-six years, the door to the office of Pope John Paul II. With the pope himself as witness, Martínez Somalo proceeded to cut the red ribbons and break the five wax seals around the great door. Then Benedict XVI ordered a set of modifications that should be made before he occupied the office of his predecessor, who had died only eighteen days ago.

Immediately afterwards, the supreme pontiff confirmed the seventy-seven-year-old Cardinal Sodano's continuation in the position of Vatican secretary of state, where he had served John Paul II since 1990. The pope also confirmed Archbishop Giovanni Lajolo as head of foreign affairs and Leonardo Sandri as vice-secretary of state. Together, these three formed the triumvirate of power in the Roman curia. The new pope's first order to his secretary of state was to reconfirm all the heads of congregations, commissions, and security forces in their posts.

To complete the so-called German circle that would replace the old Polish circle, Benedict XVI added his private secretary, Father Georg Gaenswein, and a woman, Ingrid Stampa.

The former, according to Holy Alliance reports provided to the secretary of state, was a forty-nine-year-old priest, a theologian, blond, tall, and athletic in addition to being perceptive and effective in his work. "He can understand any complex question in less than ten seconds and give a clear and immediate answer," those who knew him declared.

The woman, fifty-five years old, had replaced her sister Maria as then-cardinal Ratzinger's aide for administrative tasks upon the sister's death in 1991. Stampa served as assistant, secretary, and even as cook if need be. Ingrid Stampa was intellectually gifted and had been a music professor in Hamburg before turning to theological research in Italy, along with translating for Catholic publishers and teaching activities. Like Pope Benedict XVI, she was a great lover of Mozart.

For the first year of his papacy, the well-oiled machinery of the Vatican whirred onward without interruption, but in February 2007, before the second year was out, a spy scandal shook the ancient foundations of the Holy See. A book titled *Polish Priests and the Communist Security Police,* by the priest and researcher Tadeusz Isakowicz-Zaleski, named thirty-nine Catholic clergy who had served as "informers" for the former Warsaw regime's intelligence service, *Sluzba Bezpieczenstwa* (SB).

Father Zaleski himself had been a Solidarity chaplain in the days when Lech Walesa headed the union. He based his book on declassified documents held by the Polish Institute of National Memory (INM). This independent public entity, whose charter had been approved by the Warsaw parliament in December 1998, sought to reestablish the historical truth about the period of Nazi oppression and the communist period in Poland, which together lasted from 1939 to 1989. Some of the names Zaleski found in the archives raised alarms within the Roman curia and its intelligence services—and for Pope Benedict XVI, a personal friend of many of those named.

One of the officials who had collaborated with the SB was Juliusz Paetz, Archbishop Emeritus of Poznan. According to the Holy Alliance, Paetz's inclusion in the list had the most impact within the Holy See because he had been one of the closest aides to the late Pope John Paul II.

Between 1978 and 1982, Juliusz Paetz had been assigned to the Apostolic Chamber in Rome. At the end of 1982 he had been sent back to Poland to become bishop of Lomza, a post he held until 2002, when he was forced to resign because the rector of the seminary forbade his entrance after various attempts by the bishop to sexually abuse seminarians. In the SB documents, Bishop Juliusz Paetz appeared under the code name "Fero." He began to spy for Poland's communist regime in early March 1978.

The opening of the INM files—which take up nearly ninety kilometers of shelves—also provided a useful information source for the papal spy services themselves. The first file on Karol Wojtyla is dated 1949, when he was twenty-nine years old. Those that follow are meticulously arranged by date from 1949 to 1989, the year the Polish communist regime fell, and they cover his rise from a young priest named Woltyla *(sic)* to a pope named John Paul II.

Over those forty years, the SB wove a perfect web around the supreme pontiff, made up of spies, collaborators, informers, and infiltrators who penetrated even his intimate inner circle in the Vatican. There is only one inexplicable gap in the SB's files on Wojtyla: the year 1981, when Mehmet Ali Agca shot at him in the Piazza di San Pietro.

"It is almost certain that they had nothing to do with that assassination attempt. It would have been too risky for them," explains historian Andrzej Friszke, who has worked for the past six years at the Institute of National Memory. Many documents relating to the Church were destroyed just before the fall of communism, while many others are still being declassified, to make them available to scholars and researchers and, of course, to the pope's envoys as well.

The Vatican secret services, for example, would like to determine the identities of the priests shielded behind the code names "Seneca," "Torano," and "Ares." Torano hid the priest Wladyslaw Kulczycki, recruited in 1948 as a Polish intelligence agent and serving until his death in 1967. Father Kulczycki had been interned in a Nazi concentration camp during the Second World War, so he knew what confinement in a communist work camp would mean. He also had a sin to wash away. During his time in the priesthood, agents of the SB had photographed him having homosexual relations.

In 1953, Department Number IV of the Polish security ministry, whose duty was to keep track of the Church's political activities, stated in a now-declassified report: "His evaluation is positive. He is the only one working in Cracow who can be trusted. He is a parishioner of St. Nicholas and a friend of Cardinal Stefan Wyszynski. Kulczycki shows a sincere dislike of the young priest Karol [Wojtyla] of Wadowice. The subject [Kulczycki] cannot explain how the latter has risen so rapidly in the ecclesiastic hierarchy."

Another famous SB spy was Tadeusz Nowak, a financial officer and administrator of the Catholic weekly *Tygodnik Powszechny*. Under the code name Ares he spied for the Polish secret service between 1955 and 1982. Jovial, sociable, and always ready with a joke, Nowak was one of the most active SB spies during his twenty-seven years as an informer. He reported directly to Josef Schiller, subdirector of Department IV, about various aspects of the Polish curia. His information ranged from how much money the Church possessed and how much it collected from the faithful to who was on the way up or down within the curia and even the reactions of various Church officials to the taxes the state imposed on the Church.

Nowak's file includes a photo of the priest alongside Wojtyla, receiving the "Pro Ecclesia et Pontifice" medal awarded by Pope Paul VI. This was the highest Vatican decoration conferred on a Polish clergyman since World War II. The ceremony was observed by another SB spy in the heart of the Polish Church, Waclaw Debski, code-named "Panther." Debski was a radical anticommunist who had been sentenced to life in prison. In 1965, after being released, he was recruited by Polish intelligence services and remained on the SB payroll for almost twenty years.

Debski informed on the Catholics who cooperated with the editors of *Tygodnik Powszechny,* in whose offices the Panther himself had authorized the SB to install hidden microphones. He even turned over the office keys so that agents could raid the archives in search of evidence against his comrades.

Once Karol Wojtyla was named cardinal, the regime saw him as an "open enemy" because of his attempt to lay the cornerstone of the church of Nowa Huta. As he grew more dangerous, the SB ordered all its agents and informers to concentrate on Cardinal Wojtyla. The SB distributed a form with the identifying numbers Kr08/141 588-591 and Kr08/141 592-594, on which its spies had to answer nine questions about Cardinal Karol Wojtyla's habits.

Another priest suspected of having collaborated with the communist secret services was Michael Jagosz, canon of the Basilica of St. Mary Major in Rome and head of the historical commission studying the possible beatification of John Paul II. "They tried to recruit me because of my closeness to John Paul II, but I never gave any type of information."

Historian Marek Lasota, author of the book *Wojtyla Denounced,* charges in one paragraph of his work: "Jagosz was recruited during the '70s. He began to collaborate with the Polish secret service but then cut off all communication when he arrived in Rome." A figure who does not come out so well in Lasota's book is Mieczyslaw Malinski, Wojtyla's fellow seminarian, personal friend, and first biographer. Under the code name "Delta," Malinksi reported to the SB about Wojtyla's personal affairs—what he ate, when he woke up, whom he talked with, and what he said about a given event that occurred on a given day.

The list of traitors went on, including SB informers infiltrated first into the Polish curia and then into the Vatican after Cardinal Karol Wojtyla's election as Pope John Paul II. New revelations mean more uncomfortable surprises for Cardinal Tarcisio Bertone, who on September 16, 2006, had replaced Cardinal Angelo Sodano as Vatican secretary of state. In the Apostolic Palace of the Holy See, the Polish scandal had become an explosive and established fact. The name of Archbishop Wielgus now appeared among those of secret service informers during the Polish communist regime.

Stanislaw Wojciech Wielgus, born April 23, 1939, in the Polish city of Wierzchowiska, was ordained in 1962. In 1999, Pope John Paul II named him Bishop of Plock, and he became Bishop of Warsaw seven years later. On January 5, 2007, he assumed this office, but indignation among the Poles and pressures placed on the Vatican led to Archbishop Wielgus's resignation the next day. He presented his resignation to the priest in charge of the Wawel cathedral, Janusz Bielansky. Bielansky himself resigned soon afterwards, for the same reason as Archbishop Wielgus.

Because he was a personal friend of Stanislaw Dziwisz (John Paul II's secretary and confidant, titular archbishop, and later Cardinal of Cracow under Benedict XVI), Wielgus had been able to join the Holy Father's inner circle. Thus he provided the SB a steady stream of firsthand information about Pope Wojtyla.

According to Vatican estimates, nearly 2,600 clergy had collaborated with the Polish SB in the late 1970s, or nearly 15 percent of all the priests in Poland.

The Wielgus spy case left the Holy Father in a difficult situation and his spy service in a worse one. Pope Benedict XVI wanted to get to the root of the problem, primarily because he had been kept poorly informed of the crisis as it was developing. On December 21, 2006, a report written by The Entity claimed that, before Stanislaw Wielgus had been named Archbishop of Warsaw, his entire past life had been studied and analyzed. Strangely, that was precisely the time when word of his collaboration with the communist espionage service was just beginning to come out. Trusting in this document, the pope and Bertone, his secretary of state, had placed their full trust in Wielgus and given him the mission of leading the important Warsaw diocese. After his dismissal in January 2007, many inside the Vatican began to wonder what the pope had really known about Wielgus's past. Had Wielgus told Pope Benedict XVI of his collaboration with the SB? Had The Entity done its duty of passing on what had been discovered about Archbishop Wielgus's past? Had some names on the list been kept hidden from the pope?

After the first mass media reports, Benedict XVI supported Wielgus, an intellectual like himself who had written several books. But when the pope learned the truth, he acted rapidly and efficiently, requiring Wielgus to present his "voluntary" resignation. "The Vatican pushed him [Wielgus] to take this step," according to Luigi Accattoli, the Vatican expert of the newspaper *Il Corriere della Sera*. Wielgus himself read an extremely brief statement: "In accordance with canon law, I have tendered to His Holiness my resignation as Metropolitan of Warsaw."

Immediately thereafter, hundreds of the faithful gathered in front of the cathedral to plead with the archbishop to stay in his post, but the Vatican's Warsaw nunciature replied that Wielgus's resignation had occurred at the Vatican's behest, in accord with the Church's law: Any high curia official who cannot carry out his ministry as required has the responsibility to resign.

Roman Graczyk, author of the book *On the Trail of the SB,* admits that studying several cases of clergy who became informers and spies for the Polish intelligence service, he feels a certain compassion. "Many of them were forced into it by circumstances, but Wielgus's case is different because he became an SB informer voluntarily, which is unpardonable," Graczyk says. Another "collaborationist" with the Polish communist regime and its feared intelligence services was Archbishop Henryk Nowacki, the apostolic nuncio in Slovakia.

Another surprise that confronted Pope Benedict XVI and his intelligence services was the presence of the Dominican father Konrad Stanislaw Hejmo on the list of informers who spied on the curia for Poland's communist intelligence services. Hejmo was a personal friend of Pope John Paul II, in charge of Polish priests' journeys to the Vatican.

In spite of his denials, Father Hejmo stood accused by a file totaling nearly seven hundred pages, divided according to his three code names: "Hejnal," "Fox," and "Dominik." The mammoth file included nearly twenty receipts signed in his own hand, showing sums of money received from Polish communist secret services as payment for his valuable services.

In 1974, when Hejmo edited the Catholic publication *In Marcia* in

Rome, his SB contact was a so-called Peter, possibly Waclaw Glowick, the Polish espionage agent assigned to Poland's embassy in the Italian capital. Hejmo admitted that as a theology student in Rome he had been in contact with a German citizen of Polish origin who may have been a member of the Stasi, the secret police of the former German Democratic Republic. Hejmo passed on to the communist spy services of Poland and East Germany reports he himself wrote at the behest of the Polish Church on the situation in the Vatican and on John Paul II's image in the Italian mass media.

The next spy scandal to involve the Vatican during Benedict XVI's papacy broke in April 2007 in the pages of the magazine *L'Espresso*. Apparently, in the spring of 2005, agents of the Italian military intelligence agency SISMI had foiled an operation orchestrated by Venezuelan spy services against the Holy See.

An unidentified source (said by some to be from Vatican intelligence) informed the SISMI that two beautiful Venezuelan women were about to arrive in Rome with the mission of luring a ranking Venezuelan prelate to a hotel and photographing him in clearly sexual poses. The prelate was known for his strong opposition to Venezuelan president Hugo Chávez. The two women, both Venezuelan agents, arrived in Rome and were followed by the SISMI. Both women were detained and deported back to Venezuela.

The blackmail target could have been Archbishop Jorge Urosa Savino, the same official who in December 2006—now as cardinal—wrote a letter to President Chávez in the name of the Venezuelan Conference of Bishops that called for amnesties, pardons, or speedy trials for the objects of political prosecutions.

Cardinal Urosa stated in this letter that it "went beyond the legal and the political, concentrating more on the humanitarian and religious." This offended Chávez, who in turn launched a ferocious attack on the Venezuelan Church. Cardinal Urosa reiterated that the Conference of Bishops' requests to the Venezuelan president had little to do with political interests. He repeated that Chávez "should govern in a way that respects minorities irrespective of ideology."

Meanwhile, the Vatican continued to open other fronts, including one in China. In 2000, under the papacy of John Paul II, the Holy See had decided to canonize two hundred martyrs killed during the Boxer Rebellion of 1899–1901. For John Paul II this was a way to pay homage to Chinese Catholicism, but to China's then-president, Jiang Zemin, it was one more affront from the far-off Vatican state. From the viewpoint of Chinese history, the priests tortured and assassinated by the so-called Boxers were little more than spies for foreign powers.

The death of John Paul II in 2005 did not bring any immediate Vatican-Beijing détente. China was one of the few countries not to send representatives to the papal funeral, because Taiwanese president Chen Shui-bian attended. In fact, the Taiwanese leader had not been invited by the Vatican, but the funeral was open to all heads of state and so his presence was inevitable.

Today, however, Benedict XVI's intelligence services are creating strong connections with the "Chinese Patriotic Catholic Association" supported by the communist government, which is in charge of appointing bishops. Eighty-five percent of the clergy who make up the Association are fully recognized by the Vatican, and no bishops are named by the Association without prior approval by the Holy See.

For Benedict XVI, for the secretariat of state, and for the papal intelligence service, the nearly fourteen million Chinese Catholics are very important. So is the state of near-clandestinity in which five to seven million of them live.

Other fronts opened by the Vatican in recent times have, curiously, included groups such as Amnesty International and the virtual encyclopedia Wikipedia. The secretariat of state ordered The Entity to monitor all Wikipedia entries dealing in any way with the Vatican, its departments, or the popes. In August of 2007, an Internet tool called the Wikipedia Scanner, which identifies organizations that modify pages of the virtual encyclopedia, revealed that someone in the Vatican was altering many entries. The British Broadcasting Corporation revealed that several Vatican computers had changed entries such as the biography of Gerry Adams, leader of Sinn Fein, the Republican Catholic organization in Northern Island and political arm of the IRA.

Vatican spokesman Federico Lombardi then declared, "These accusations are completely unserious and devoid of logic. It is absurd to even imagine that such an initiative could be considered." But, in fact, the BBC proceeded to show that organizations such as the U.S. CIA or National Security Administration and the Vatican, possibly by way of its intelligence services, had indeed changed various entries in the virtual encyclopedia Wikipedia.

The second polemic pitted the Vatican against Amnesty International. It began when Cardinal Renato Martino, president of the Council for Justice and Peace, publicly asked the faithful to stop supporting AI because of its new policy that backed abortion in certain cases.

Martino charged that AI had betrayed its own mission and "all of its faithful supporters throughout the years who have trusted AI for its integral mission of promoting and protecting human rights." This campaign against Amnesty International begun by the Council for Justice and Peace once again tarnished the Vatican's relations with nongovernmental organizations fighting inequality and human rights violations in the Third World.

From its Rome office, Amnesty International replied to Cardinal Martino that "the organization has never received any financial support from the Vatican or from departments of the Catholic Church," adding that AI's policy in respect to abortion "grew out of the campaign against violence against women." What Amnesty called for was guaranteed access to legal and safe abortion services for women whose pregnancies resulted from sexual violence or incest or brought serious risk to the women's life or health. The Vatican chose not to respond to this explanation but to continue its public attack on the human rights organization.

Between March 7, 1998 (when Luigi Poggi managed to finally leave his post as head of The Entity after his resignation was accepted by Pope John Paul II), and today, two new figures are known to have been appointed as heads of The Entity. Just four years before, on November 26, 1994, Poggi— universally known as the Pope's Spy, had been elevated to cardinal as compensation for his special services to the supreme pontiff.

With Luigi Poggi's departure as head of Vatican secret services, one of the greatest eras of the Holy Alliance came to an end. He was the man who knew the most about the Vatican's ties to Solidarity, the secrets of the attempted assassination of John Paul II, the Vatican's and Washington's murky operations in Poland, and the relations between Israel's Mossad and Ronald Reagan and William Casey's CIA. Now he had retired to his native city of Piacenza, in northern Italy.

Vatican rumors said Poggi's replacement was a Spanish priest named Pedro López Quintana, only forty-six years old. Born in the city of Barbastro, Pontevedra (Spain), on July 27, 1953, López Quintana in late 1999 took on responsibility for the papal intelligence services from his position as advisor to the secretariat of Vatican affairs of state. The Spanish prelate, ordained in 1980 by John Paul II, had become a trusted advisor to Cardinal Angelo Sodano, the secretary of state. Since his ordination as a priest, his advancement had been carefully protected and guided by the all-powerful bishops Leonardo Sandri and Antonio María Vegliò.[1]

On January 6, 2003, four years later, John Paul II consecrated Pedro López Quintana as a bishop for his "special services provided to the Catholic Church." Just a month after that, he was named papal nuncio to India and Nepal.

The name of the head of The Entity from February 2003 to December 2007 is unknown. What is known is that Cardinal Joseph Ratzinger, once elected as Pope Benedict XVI, named a new head of espionage and counter-espionage services as well as a new chief of the so-called Security Committee, which ensured the safety of the supreme pontiff on his travels.

The newest head of The Entity, whoever that may be, can expect that the German papacy of Benedict XVI will not be very different from the Polish years of John Paul II. He can expect years of glory but also years of enormous activity for the espionage services of the Vatican state. The communist enemies of Pope John Paul II have been replaced by others. Evangelical sects, more and more influential in Latin America, are costing the Church many Catholics. In China, the representatives of the Catholic Church continue to be persecuted by the government in Beijing. Elsewhere, there are Catholic theologians attempting to stray from the strict directives of the Vatican. In short, the world offers many enemies and many operations still to be carried out by agents of the Holy Alliance.

"I seem to feel his strong hand [that of John Paul II] gripping mine. I seem to see his smiling eyes and to hear his words, addressed at this moment particularly to me: 'Be not afraid!'" So declared Benedict XVI. Perhaps—and only perhaps—this is truly the philosophy that will shape the actions of the espionage and counterespionage services of the Vatican state, the Holy Alliance and the *Sodalitium Pianum,* in the years of Benedict XVI. *Alea jacta est!* The die is cast.

APPENDIX

List of Popes Since the Creation of the Holy Alliance

Pius V, St.	January 7, 1566–May 1, 1572
Gregory XIII	May 13, 1572–April 10, 1585
Sixtus V	April 24, 1585–August 27, 1590
Urban VII	September 15, 1590–September 27, 1590
Gregory XIV	December 5, 1590–October 15, 1591
Innocent IX	October 29, 1591–December 30, 1591
Clement VIII	January 30, 1592–March 5, 1605
Leo XI	April 11, 1605–April 27, 1605
Paul V	May 16, 1605–January 28, 1621
Gregory XV	February 6, 1621–July 8, 1623
Urban VIII	August 6, 1623–July 29, 1644
Innocent X	September 15, 1644–January 7, 1655
Alexander VII	April 7, 1655–May 22, 1667
Clement IX	June 20, 1667–December 9, 1669
Clement X	April 29, 1670–July 22, 1676
Innocent XI	September 21, 1676–August 12, 1689
Alexander VIII	October 6, 1689–February 1, 1691
Innocent XII	July 12, 1691–September 27, 1700
Clement XI	November 23, 1700–March 19, 1721
Innocent XIII	May 8, 1721–March 7, 1724
Benedict XIII	May 29, 1724–February 21, 1730
Clement XII	July 12, 1730–February 8, 1740
Benedict XIV	August 17, 1740–May 3, 1758

Clement XIII	July 6, 1758–February 2, 1769
Clement XIV	May 19, 1769–September 21, 1774
Pius VI	February 15, 1775–August 29, 1799
Pius VII	March 14, 1800–August 20, 1823
Leo XII	September 28, 1823–February 10, 1829
Pius VIII	March 31, 1829–November 30, 1830
Gregory XVI	February 2, 1831–June 1, 1846
Pius IX	June 16, 1846–February 7, 1878
Leo XIII	February 20, 1878–July 20, 1903
Pius X, St.	August 4, 1903–August 20, 1914
Benedict XV	September 3, 1914–January 22, 1922
Pius XI	February 6, 1922–February 10, 1939
Pius XII	March 2, 1939–October 9, 1958
John XXIII	October 28, 1958–June 3, 1963
Paul VI	June 21, 1963–August 6, 1978
John Paul I	August 26, 1978–September 29, 1978
John Paul II	October 16, 1978–April 2, 2005
Benedict XVI	April 19, 2005–

NOTES

1. Between the Reformation and a New Alliance (1566–1570)

1. Leonardo Gallois, *Historia General de la Inquisición,* Servicio de Reproducción de Libros, Barcelona, 1869.
2. Javier Paredes, Maximiliano Barrio, Domingo Ramos-Lissón, and Luis Suárez, *Diccionario de los Papas y Concilios,* Editorial Ariel, Barcelona, 1998.
3. In 1873, excavations in the cellars of the Inquisition's palace in Rome brought to light the remnants of clothes from many eras as well as remains of human hair and coins bearing the likeness of Pope Pius VII (March 14, 1800–August 20, 1823). These finds demonstrated that even during that later pontifical reign, the Inquisition's agents were still operating in Rome.
4. Walter Goetz, Paul Joachimsen, Erich Marcks, Wilhelm Mommsen, and Hans Heinrich, *La época de la revolución religiosa, la Reforma y la Contrareforma (1500–1660),* vol. V, Espasa Calpe, Madrid, 1975.
5. The black monks covered their faces to keep their identities secret. They reported only to the supreme pontiff. Over time they became the action arm of the Holy Alliance, a capacity in which they acted for several centuries.
6. Manuel Fernández Álvarez, *Felipe II y su tiempo,* Espasa Calpe, Madrid, 1998.
7. *Dictionary of Beliefs and Religions,* W. & R. Chambers Ltd., London, 1992.
8. Eric Frattini, *Secretos vaticanos,* EDAF, Madrid, 2003.
9. *Dictionary of Beliefs and Religions.*
10. Susan Doran, *Monarchy and Matrimony: The Courtships of Elizabeth I,* HarperCollins, New York, 1996.
11. John Elliott and Laurence Brockliss, *The World of the Favourite,* Yale University Press, New Haven (Connecticut), 1999.
12. Stefan Zweig, *Maria Stuart,* Williams Verlag AG, Zurich, 1976.
13. Alison Weir, *Mary, Queen of Scots and the Murder of Lord Darnley,* Random House Ltd., London, 2003.
14. Zweig, *Maria Stuart.*
15. Goetz et al, *La época de la revolución religiosa.*
16. Weir, *Mary, Queen of Scots and the Murder of Lord Darnley.*
17. Michel Duchain, *Elisabeth I d'Angleterre,* Editions Fayard, Paris, 1992; and Wallace MacCaffrey, *Queen Elizabeth and the Making of Policy, 1572–1588,* Princeton University Press, Princeton, 1981.
18. Weir, *Mary, Queen of Scots and the Murder of Lord Darnley.*
19. Robert Naunton, *Fragmenta Regalia or Observations on Queen Elizabeth, Her Times and Favourites,* Cerovski Publishers, Toronto, 1985.
20. Elliott and Brockliss, *The World of the Favourite.*
21. Zweig, *Maria Stuart.*
22. Elliott and Brockliss, *The World of the Favourite.*
23. Manuel Carbonero y Sol, *Fin funesto de los perseguidores y enemigos de la Iglesia, desde Herodes el Grande hasta nuestros días,* Librería y Tipografía Católica, Barcelona, 1878.

24. Zweig, *Maria Stuart.*
25. Ibid.
26. Naunton, *Fragmenta Regalia.*
27. Weir, *Mary, Queen of Scots and the Murder of Lord Darnley.*
28. Duchain, *Elisabeth I d'Angleterre.*
29. Malachai Martin, *The Jesuits: The Society of Jesus and the Betrayal of the Roman Catholic Church,* Simon & Schuster, New York, 1988.
30. Naunton, *Fragmenta Regalia.*
31. Zweig, *Maria Stuart.*
32. Duchain, *Elisabeth I d'Angleterre.*
33. Weir, *Mary, Queen of Scots and the Murder of Lord Darnley.*
34. Sir Banister Fletcher, *Historia de la arquitectura por el método comparado,* part I, vol. 1, Editorial Canosa, Barcelona, 1931.
35. Naunton, *Fragmenta Regalia.*
36. Weir, *Mary, Queen of Scots and the Murder of Lord Darnley.*
37. This legendary sect, the *ashishin,* is the source of the word *assassins.*
38. Edward Burman, *Assassins: Holy Killers of Islam,* HarperCollins Publishers, New York, 1987.
39. Both Marco Polo's writing about his 1273 visit to the castle of Alamut and Matteo Ricci's travel diary remained under Papal Guard and became part of the so-called *Index Liborum Prohibitorum* by order of Paul IV in 1557. Both texts were mysteriously recovered during the pontificate of Pius V.
40. Duchain, *Elisabeth I d'Angleterre.*
41. Fernández Álvarez, *Felipe II y su tiempo.*
42. Weir, *Mary, Queen of Scots and the Murder of Lord Darnley.*
43. Frattini, *Secretos vaticanos.*
44. Duchain, *Elisabeth I d'Angleterre.*

2. Dark Years (1570–1587)

1. Goetz et al, *La época de la revolución religiosa.*
2. *La Stampa a Firenze, 1471–1550: Omaggio a Roberto Ridolfi,* L. S. Olschki, Rome, 1984.
3. Duchain, *Elisabeth I d'Angleterre.*
4. Fernández Álvarez, *Felipe II y su tiempo.*
5. Goetz et al, *La época de la revolución religiosa.*
6. This letter is cited in Fernández Álvarez, *Felipe II y su tiempo.*
7. Neville Williams, *All the Queen's Men: Elizabeth I and Her Courtiers,* Cardinal, London, 1974.
8. Duchain, *Elisabeth I d'Angleterre.*; and MacCaffrey, *Queen Elizabeth and the Making of Policy.*
9. Jane Resh Thomas, *Behind the Mask: The Life of Queen Elizabeth I,* Houghton Mifflin, London, 1998.
10. Neville Williams, *A Tudor Tragedy: Thomas Howard, Fourth Duke of Norfolk,* Barrie & Jenkins, London, 1989.
11. Susan Doran, *Elizabeth I and Religion, 1558–1603,* Taylor & Francis Books Ltd., London, 1993.
12. Harry Kelsey, *Sir John Hawkins: Queen Elizabeth's Slave Trader,* Yale University Press, New Haven (Connecticut), 2003.
13. Ibid.
14. Duchain, *Elisabeth I d'Angleterre.*
15. N. Williams, *A Tudor Tragedy.*
16. Doran, *Elizabeth I and Religion.*
17. Roberto Ridolfi returned to Florence, where he continued to work as a banker and to finance operations of the Holy Alliance. Some sources insist that Ridolfi was assassinated by English agents in September of 1600, while others claim he died of disease in 1601. Both versions are unsubstantiated.
18. R. Po-chia Hsia, *The World of Catholic Renewal 1540–1770,* Cambridge University Press, Cambridge, 1998.
19. Paredes et al, *Diccionario de los Papas y Concilios.*
20. MacCaffrey, *Queen Elizabeth and the Making of Policy.*

21. Robert Fagle, *William of Orange and the Revolt of the Netherlands, 1572–84,* Ashgate Publishing Company, London, 2003.
22. Duchain, *Elisabeth I d'Angleterre.*
23. MacCaffrey, *Queen Elizabeth and the Making of Policy.*
24. Philippe Erlanger, *St. Bartholomew's Night: The Massacre of Saint Bartholomew,* Greenwood Publishing Group, New York, 1975.
25. Norman Sutherland, *The Massacre of St. Bartholomew and the European Conflict, 1559–1572,* Barnes & Noble, New York, 1996.
26. Duchain, *Elisabeth I d'Angleterre.*
27. Fagle, *William of Orange and the Revolt of the Netherlands.*
28. Martin, *The Jesuits.*
29. Nicholas Canny, *Making Ireland British, 1580–1650,* Oxford University Press, Oxford, 2001.
30. John O'Beirne, *A Short History of Ireland,* Cambridge University Press, Cambridge, 1995; and Canny, *Making Ireland British.*
31. The Irish Catholics considered Nicholas Sanders a martyr to the faith, and even today some churches of the Republic of Ireland celebrate him on the anniversary of his death.
32. Duchain, *Elisabeth I d'Angleterre.*
33. Antonia Pakenham, *King James VI of Scotland, I of England,* Random House, New York, 1975.
34. Esmé de Aubigny, Duke of Lennox, was a first cousin of Henry Darnley, supposed father of James VI, and thus a possible heir to the Scottish crown on the Stuart-Lennox side.
35. Duchain, *Elisabeth I d'Angleterre;* and Roy Strong, *Gloriana: The Portraits of Queen Elizabeth I,* Pimlico, London, 2003.
36. John Bossy, *Giordano Bruno and the Embassy Affair,* Yale University Press, New Haven (Connecticut), 2002.
37. Duchain, *Elisabeth I d'Angleterre.*
38. Bossy, *Giordano Bruno and the Embassy Affair.*
39. Six years after putting an end to the Throckmorton Plot, the Dominican and philosopher Giordano Bruno, born in Naples, was burned at the stake by the Inquisition. Bruno raised doubts about the dogma of the Trinity and therefore was burned in 1600 in the Campo dei Fiori in Rome.
40. Pakenham, *King James VI of Scotland.*
41. Martin, *The Jesuits.*
42. Fagle, *William of Orange and the Revolt of the Netherlands.*
43. The Jesuit priest Crichton was set free and expelled from England, with the order that if he should ever again be arrested on English soil, he would be executed on the spot. The Holy Alliance agent escaped the gallows because he was not an English subject and had been detained outside English territory. Crichton returned to Rome, where he lived until his death at the age of eighty-six.
44. Duchain, *Elisabeth I d'Angleterre.*
45. Geoffrey Parker, *Success Is Never Final: Empire, War, and Faith in Early Modern Europe,* Basic Books, London, 2002.
46. Martin, *The Jesuits.*
47. Parker, *Success Is Never Final;* and Pakenham, *King James VI of Scotland.*
48. Zweig, *Maria Stuart.*

3. Times of Action (1587–1605)

1. Duchain, *Elisabeth I d'Angleterre.*
2. Pakenham, *King James VI of Scotland.*
3. Neil Hanson, *The Confident Hope of a Miracle: The Real History of the Spanish Armada,* Doubleday, London, 2003.
4. Duchain, *Elisabeth I d'Angleterre.*
5. Colin Martin and Geoffrey Parker, *The Spanish Armada: Revised Edition,* Manchester University Press, Manchester, 2002.
6. Harry Kelsey, *Sir Francis Drake: The Queen's Pirate,* Yale University Press, New Haven (Connecticut), 2000.

7. Duchain, *Elisabeth I d'Angleterre*.

8. Kelsey, *Sir Francis Drake*.

9. Duchain, *Elisabeth I d'Angleterre*.

10. Hanson, *The Confident Hope of a Miracle*.

11. Garrett Mattingly, *The Defeat of the Spanish Armada*, Random House, London, 2000.

12. The Lancastrian dynasty ruled England in the fourteenth and fifteenth centuries.

13. Martin and Parker, *The Spanish Armada*.

14. Pakenham, *King James VI of Scotland*.

15. Cardinal Archduke Alberto, the Spanish viceroy in Portugal, in a report to Pope Sixtus V through an agent of the Holy Alliance.

16. Kelsey, *Sir Francis Drake;* and Michel Le Bris, *D'or, de rêves et de sang. L'épopée de la fliguste (1494–1588),* Hachette, Paris, 2001.

17. Le Bris, *D'or, de rêves et de sang*.

18. The so-called *legati a latere* are a sort of papal flying squad who carry out special diplomatic missions and, therefore, have diplomatic immunity. See Frattini, *Secretos vaticanos*.

19. Paredes et al, *Diccionario de los Papas y Concilios*.

20. Fernández Álvarez, *Felipe II y su tiempo*.

21. Burman, *Assassins: Holy Killers of Islam*.

22. Doran, *Elizabeth I and Religion, 1558–1603*.

23. This assassination attempt is summarized in Michel Duchain's *Elisabeth I d'Angleterre*. There is no further information.

24. Elliott and Brockliss, *The World of the Favourite;* and Naunton, *Fragmenta Regalia*.

25. Duchain, *Elisabeth I d'Angleterre*.

26. During the trial, emphasis was placed on Rodrigo López's Jewish origins, which unleashed a wave of anti-Semitism throughout England, until Queen Elizabeth intervened. It is said that William Shakespeare drew on the doctor's character to breathe life into the Jewish merchant Shylock in his play *The Merchant of Venice*.

27. Fernández Álvarez, *Felipe II y su tiempo*.

28. Duchain, *Elisabeth I d'Angleterre*.

29. Pakenham, *King James VI of Scotland*.

30. Zweig, *Maria Stuart*.

4. New Horizons (1605–1644)

1. See chapter 3.

2. Paredes et al, *Diccionario de los Papas y Concilios*.

3. David Buisseret, *Henry IV: King of France,* Unwin Hyman, Boston, 1990.

4. Burman, *Assassins: Holy Killers of Islam*.

5. Ibid.

6. The word *fida'i* means "self-sacrificed." An assassin willing to die in the name of the true faith, the Catholic one, accomplishing the objective assigned in a mission.

7. Burman, *Assassins: Holy Killers of Islam*.

8. Buisseret, *Henry IV: King of France*.

9. Edward Frederick Langley, *Henry of Navarre: Henry IV of France,* Hale Publishers, London, 1998.

10. Ibid.

11. Roland Mousnier, *The Assassination of Henry IV: The Tyrannicide Problem and the Consolidation of the French Absolute Monarchy in the Early Seventeenth Century,* Scribner Publisher, New York, 1973.

12. Buisseret, *Henry IV: King of France*.

13. Mousnier, *The Assassination of Henry IV*.

14. This group of assassins would reappear in later years, especially during the Napoleonic era. Some of its actions have been described in a variety of works, though its concrete involvement in the attacks and assassinations with which it has been linked have not been proved, nor has its existence. Its relation to the Holy Alliance has not been demonstrated either.

15. J.-F. Dubost, "Between *Mignons* and Principal Ministers: Concini, 1610–17," in Elliott and Brockliss, *The World of the Favourite.*
16. Sharon Jansen, *The Monstrous Regiment of Women: Female Rulers in Early Modern Europe,* Palgrave Macmillan, New York, 2002.
17. Lloyd Moote, *Louis XIII, the Just,* University of California Press, Los Angeles, 1991.
18. Dubost, in Elliott and Brockliss, *The World of the Favourite.*
19. Jansen, *The Monstrous Regiment of Women.*
20. "He manipulates his ministers as he pleases." (Bentivoglio, nuncio in France. Bibliothèque Nationale, Paris. Ms. Ital. 1770, fol. 237, 1/13/1617.)
21. Dubost, in Elliott and Brockliss, *The World of the Favourite.*
22. Moote, *Louis XIII, the Just.*
23. Joseph Bergin, *The Rise of Richelieu (Studies in Early Modern European History),* Manchester University Press, Manchester, 1997.
24. Dubost, in Elliott and Brockliss, *The World of the Favourite.*
25. Jansen, *The Monstrous Regiment of Women.*
26. Anthony Levi, *Cardinal Richelieu and the Making of France,* Carroll & Graf, New York, 2000; and Moote, *Louis XIII, the Just.*
27. Goetz et al, *La época de la revolución religiosa.*
28. Martin, *The Jesuits.*
29. Paredes et al, *Diccionario de los Papas y Concilios.*
30. Bergin, *The Rise of Richelieu.*
31. Hsia, *The World of Catholic Renewal.*
32. Levi, *Cardinal Richelieu and the Making of France.*
33. Ibid.
34. Henry B. Hill, *Political Testament of Cardinal Richelieu: The Significant Chapters and Supporting Selections,* University of Wisconsin Press, Wisconsin, 1964.
35. Richard Bonney, *The European Dynastic States 1494–1660,* Oxford University Press, Oxford, 1992; and *The Thirty Years' War 1618–1648,* Osprey Publishers Company, London, 2002.

5. *Era of Expansion (1644–1691)*

1. Alfio Cavoli, *La Papessa Olimpia,* Editoriale Scipioni, Milan, 1992.
2. Paredes et al, *Diccionario de los Papas y Concilios.*
3. Cavoli, *La Papessa Olimpia.*
4. William Beik, *Louis XIV and Absolutism: A Brief Study with Documents,* Palgrave Macmillan, London, 2000.
5. Bonney, *The European Dynastic States.*
6. In fact, the Black Order was not a counterespionage service in the modern sense, but rather a unit of assassins whose only duty was to do away with all the French agents working for Mazarin within the Vatican. The Vatican counterespionage service called the *Sodalitium Pianum* (Association of Pius), or S.P., was officially created in 1906 by order of Pope Pius X. See also Frattini, *Secretos vaticanos.*
7. Eric Jon Phelps, *Vatican Assassins: Wounded in the House of My Friends,* Halcyon Unified Services, London, 2000.
8. Cavoli, *La Papessa Olimpia.*
9. Goetz et al, *La época de la revolución religiosa.*
10. Wendy Gibson, *A Tragic Farce: The Fronde (1648–1653),* Intellect, New York, 1998.
11. Orest Ranum, *The Fronde: A French Revolution, 1648–1652 (Revolutions in the Modern World),* W. W. Norton & Company, London, 1993.
12. Carbonero y Sol, *Fin funesto de los perseguidores y enemigos de la Iglesia, desde Herodes el Grande hasta nuestros días,* Librería y Tipigrafía Católica, Barcelona, 1878.
13. Beik, *Louis XIV and Absolutism.*
14. Gibson, *A Tragic Farce.*

15. Cavoli, *La Papessa Olimpia.*
16. Robert A. Stradling, *Philip IV and the Government of Spain, 1621–1665,* Cambridge University Press, Cambridge, 1988.
17. Cavoli, *La Papessa Olimpia.*
18. Paredes et al, *Diccionario de los Papas y Concilios.*
19. Goetz et al, *La época de la revolución religiosa.*
20. Stradling, *Philip IV and the Government of Spain, 1621–1665.*
21. Carlo Castiglioni, *Storia dei Papi,* Editrice Torinese, Turin, 1939.
22. Paredes et al, *Diccionario de los Papas y Concilios.*
23. Castiglioni, *Storia dei Papi.*
24. The complete text of this secret papal bull is in the archives of the Vatican Library and was published by Carlo Castiglioni in his work *Storia dei Papi.*
25. Hsia, *The World of Catholic Renewal.*
26. Jaime Do Inso, *China,* Edições Europa, Lisbon, 1938.
27. Ibid.
28. Paredes et al, *Diccionario de los Papas y Concilios.*
29. Castiglioni, *Storia dei Papi.*
30. Ibid.
31. Beik, *Louis XIV and Absolutism.*
32. See chapter 1.
33. Paredes et al, *Diccionario de los Papas y Concilios.*
34. Castiglioni, *Storia dei Papi.*
35. Paredes et al, *Diccionario de los Papas y Concilios.*
36. The *régale* was the right assumed by the French crown over some dioceses since the Middle Ages, which consisted of administering their goods and collecting their rents (temporal *régale*) and appointing nominees to their benefices (spiritual *régale*). In 1673, Louis XIV extended this right to every diocese in France.
37. Paredes et al, *Diccionario de los Papas y Concilios.*
38. The *scriptors* were friars who had begun hand-copying manuscripts for the Vatican Library in 1431, during the papacy of Martin V (1417–1431). Even today the workers at the Vatican Library are called scriptors. See also Frattini, *Secretos vaticanos.*
39. Jeremy Black, *From Louis XIV to Napoleon: The Fate of a Great Power,* UCL Press, London, 1999.
40. Beik, *Louis XIV and Absolutism.*
41. Martin, *The Jesuits.*
42. Paredes et al, *Diccionario de los Papas y Concilios.*

6. Time of Intrigue (1691–1721)

1. See chapter 5.
2. Paredes et al, *Diccionario de los Papas y Concilios.*
3. Frans Ciappara, *The Roman Inquisition in Enlightened Malta,* Pubblikazzjonijiet Indipendenza, Malta, 2000.
4. The "four articles" can be found in the *Declaratio Cleri Gallicani* (Declaration of French clergy) approved in 1682 under the papacy of Innocent XI.
5. Carbonero y Sol, *Fin funesto . . .*
6. Ibid.
7. Heinrich Brueck, *History of the Catholic Church,* Benziger Brothers, Chicago, 1885.
8. José Calvo Poyato, *Carlos II el Hechizado y su época,* Editorial Planeta, Barcelona, 1991.
9. Adrienne Mayor, *Greek Fire, Poison Arrows & Scorpion Bombs: Biological and Chemical Warfare in the Ancient World,* Overlook Duckworth, London, 2003.
10. This story remains a legend, without documentary proof or bibliographical support. Therefore the "possible" assassination of Cardinal Paluzzo Paluzzi, head of the Holy Alliance from 1670 to 1698, by agents of Louis XIV employing the poison black hellebore, or "Nativity Rose," must be taken as just that.

11. Henry Arthur Kamen, *Philip V of Spain: The King Who Reigned Twice,* Yale University Press, New Haven (Connecticut), 2001.

12. Ricardo García Cárcel and Rosa María Alabrús, *España en 1700. ¿Austrias o Borbones?* Arlanza Ediciones, Madrid, 2001.

13. Calvo Poyato, *Carlos II el Hechizado y su época.*

14. John Lynch, *The Hispanic World in Crisis and Change, 1598–1700 (History of Spain),* Blackwell Publishers, London, 1992.

15. Pope Clement XI would later promote his nephew Annibale Albani to cardinal, in return for services rendered as head of the Holy Alliance during the War of Succession.

16. Paredes et al, *Diccionario de los Papas y Concilios.*

17. Henry Arthur Kamen, *The War of Succession in Spain, 1700–15,* Indiana University Press, Bloomington, 1969.

18. In the wars with France toward the end of the eighteenth century, Spain had lost the Franche-Compté, most of the northern Netherlands, and almost all its possessions in the Caribbean.

19. Kamen, *The War of Succession in Spain, 1700–15.*

20. Kamen, *Philip V of Spain.*

21. In 1709, Anne Stuart was proclaimed Queen of Great Britain, when the kingdoms of England and Scotland definitively joined.

22. Kamen, *The War of Succession in Spain.*

23. Henry Arthur Kamen, *Spain in the Later Seventeenth Century, 1665–1700,* Longman Group, London, 1983.

24. Kamen, *Philip V of Spain.*

25. Murray Williamson and Alvin Bernstein, *The Making of Strategy: Rulers, States, and War,* Cambridge University Press, Cambridge, 1996.

26. Oscar Browning, *Journal of Sir George Rooke, Admiral of the Fleet,* Navy Records Society, London (facsimile edition, 1897), 1998.

27. Cardinal Portocarrero (1635–1709) persuaded King Charles II to name Philip of Anjou heir to the throne after the death of the previous candidate, Joseph Ferdinand of Bavaria. He was regent of the realm along with the widowed queen, Maria Anna of Neuburg. When the Duke of Anjou became king (Philip V), he named Portocarrero prime minister, but in the later years of the War of the Spanish Succession, he went over to the Archduke Charles's side.

28. David Cordingly, *Under the Black Flag: The Romance and the Reality of Life among the Pirates,* Harvest Books, New York, 1997.

29. Williamson and Bernstein, *The Making of Strategy.*

30. Archivo General de Indias. Indiferente, legs. 2530, 2634.

31. Several historians have claimed that the Marquis of Louville, Philip V's tutor, was a double agent who spied for Louis XIV and for the Holy Alliance at the same time. This subject has been much debated. Letters signed by Louville and addressed to Fabrizio Paolucci, cardinal and secretary of state, have been found in the Vatican archives. They constituted important reports about the actions of Philip V and his court.

32. Roberto Fernández Díaz, *La España del siglo XVIII,* Anaya, Madrid, 1990.

33. Castiglioni, *Storia dei Papi.*

34. Paredes et al, *Diccionario de los Papas y Concilios.*

35. The breaking of relations between Philip V and Rome lasted until 1717. However, King Philip knew that Clement XI was acting under pressure, so he continued to accept the spiritual role of the papacy, while taking the position that the pope was a prisoner.

36. Kamen, *Philip V of Spain.*

7. Some Brief Reigns (1721–1775)

1. Castiglioni, *Storia dei Papi.*

2. Martin, *The Jesuits.*

3. Kamen, *Philip V of Spain.*

4. Fernández Díaz, *La España del siglo XVIII.*

5. Fieschi next surfaced in Rome in the service of Cardinal Annibale Albani, head of the Holy Alliance until his suspension in 1730. Some sources claim that Fieschi then retired to Florence, where he died in the epidemics of 1732–1740.

6. Kamen, *Philip V of Spain.*

7. Paredes et al, *Diccionario de los Papas y Concilios.*

8. Brueck, *History of the Catholic Church.*

9. The term "Trojan" is still used in the Vatican state espionage service to define those Holy Alliance agents who manage to penetrate organizations or states that are militant enemies of the Vatican or the pope. The first "Trojans" were used by Cardinal Albani, head of the Holy Alliance from 1701 to 1730, in 1726 during the investigation of Cardinal Coscia.

10. Frederic J. Baumgartner, *Behind Locked Doors: A History of the Papal Elections,* Palgrave Macmillan, New York, 2003.

11. Castiglioni, *Storia dei Papi.*

12. Paredes et al, *Diccionario de los Papas y Concilios.*

13. De Rosa, *Vicars of Christ: The Dark Side of the Papacy,* Poolbeg Press Ltd., Dublin, 2000.

14. Ibid.

15. Michael J. Walsh, *The Conclave: A Sometimes Secret and Occasionally Bloody History of Papal Elections,* Sheed and Ward, London, 2003.

16. Baumgartner, *Behind Locked Doors.*

17. Castiglioni, *Storia dei Papi.*

18. Pope Clement XII named Cardinal Annibale Albani to the post of Bishop of Sabina on July 24, 1730. There he remained until his death in October 1751, carrying with him the secrets he had unearthed during his almost thirty years as head of the Holy Alliance.

19. Walsh, *The Conclave.*

20. Castiglioni, *Storia dei Papi.*

21. Ibid.

22. Ibid.

23. Martin Short, *Inside the Brotherhood: Explosive Secrets of the Freemasons,* HarperCollins Publishers, New York, 1989.

24. Ibid.

25. Paredes et al, *Diccionario de los Papas y Concilios.*

26. Kamen, *Philip V of Spain.*

27. Philip V was the first king since the sixteenth century not to be buried in El Escorial.

28. Martin, *The Jesuits.*

29. Walsh, *The Conclave.*

30. Paredes et al, *Diccionario de los Papas y Concilios.*

31. Castiglioni, *Storia dei Papi.*

32. The Duke of Aveiro was quartered alive. The Marquis of Távora and his two sons were hanged. The Marchioness of Távora, the king's mistress and a participant in the plot, was beheaded.

33. Really, neither of these charges could ever be proved, not even in the documents related to the trial of "the Twelve" (as this affair was called), which are still extant today. Prime Minister Pombal and the prosecutor relied on mere rumors about the relations between some of the accused and a Holy Alliance agent named João Aristide, who had worked in Portugal under the orders of Cardinal Saldaña, Archbishop of Lisbon. Aristide was not a member of the Jesuit order, but rather a Dominican.

34. Paredes et al, *Diccionario de los Papas y Concilios.*

35. Walsh, *The Conclave.*

36. Martin, *The Jesuits.*

37. Paredes et al, *Diccionario de los Papas y Concilios.*

38. At the end of August 1775, Lorenzo Ricci sent an appeal for his freedom to Pope Pius VI. But while his demands were being considered by the supreme pontiff's advisors, death caught up with him, on November 24. The pope then ordered a sumptuous funeral in the church of St. John of the Florentines, near the Sant'Angelo castle. Ricci was later buried in the church of the Gesù, along with his predecessors in the Society.

39. Carbonero y Sol, *Fin funesto . . .*

Notes

8. The Rise and Fall of Eagles (1775–1823)

1. Walsh, *The Conclave*.
2. Thomas Carlyle, *The French Revolution: A History*, Modern Library, London, 2002.
3. Simon Schama, *Citizens: A Chronicle of the French Revolution*, Vintage, New York, 1990.
4. See chapter 4.
5. Douglas Liversidge, *The Day the Bastille Fell: July 14, 1789, the Beginning of the End of the French Monarchy*, Franklin Watts Inc., New York, 1972.
6. Cardinal Giovanni Battista Caprara led the Holy Alliance from July 18, 1790, until June 18, 1808, when he was replaced by Cardinal Bartolomeo Pacca, who served from July 18, 1808, until his death on April 19, 1844, at the age of eighty-seven.
7. T. C. Blanning, *The French Revolutionary Wars, 1787–1802 (Modern Wars)*, Edward Arnold Publisher, Oxford, 1996.
8. John Hardman, *Louis XVI*, Yale University Press, New Haven (Connecticut), 1994.
9. Ibid.
10. David Álvarez, *Spies in the Vatican. Espionage and Intrigue from Napoleon to the Holocaust*, University Press of Kansas, Lawrence, 2002.
11. Ibid.
12. Philippe Delorme, *L'Affaire Louis XVII*, Jules Tallandier, Paris, 2000.
13. Deborah Cadbury, *The Lost King of France: How DNA Solved the Mystery of the Murdered Son of Louis XVI and Marie Antoinette*, Griffin Trade Paperback, London, 2003.
14. Deborah Cadbury, *The Lost King of France: A True Story of Revolution, Revenge, and DNA*, St. Martin's Press, London, 2002.
15. Ibid.
16. Delorme, *L'Affaire Louis XVII*.
17. Álvarez, *Spies in the Vatican*.
18. An estimated two thousand priests were lynched during the Revolution. The Terror unleashed in 1794 accounted for 1,750 of these cases. The only other options were the gallows or the guillotine. Eight bishops were executed. In Orange alone, sixty-seven clergy were killed in a single day.
19. The adventure of the abbot and spy Salamon under orders of the papal espionage were collected in a book written by the Viscount of Richemont titled *Correspondance Secrète de l'Abbé de Salamon*, issued in 1898 by the publisher Plon, Nourrit et Cie, in Paris.
20. Robert Asprey, *The Rise of Napoleon Bonaparte*, Basic Books, London, 2001.
21. Max Gallo, *Napoléon*, Robert Laffont, Paris, 1997.
22. J. Balteau, *Dictionnaire de biographie française*, Letouzey et Ané, Paris, 1933.
23. This was the organization to which the priest Jean-François Ravaillac, assassin of King Henry IV of France, belonged. See chapter 4.
24. Asprey, *The Rise of Napoleon Bonaparte*.
25. J. G. G. Robinson, *Historical and Philosophical Memoirs of Pius the Sixth and of His Pontificate*, S. Hamilton, London, 1799.
26. Paredes et al, *Diccionario de los Papas y Concilios*.
27. Walsh, *The Conclave*.
28. Black, *From Louis XIV to Napoleon*.
29. Margaret O'Dwyer, *The Papacy in the Age of Napoleon and the Restoration: Pius VII, 1800–1823*, Rowman & Littlefield, London, 1986.
30. Nils Forssell, *Fouché, the Man Napoleon Feared*, AMS Press, New York, 1971.
31. Stefan Zweig, *Fouché*, Fischer, Frankfurt, 2000.
32. Gallo, *Napoléon*.
33. Robin Anderson, *Pope Pius VII (1800–1823): His Life, Times, and Struggle with Napoleon in the Aftermath of the French Revolution*, Tan Books & Publishers, New York, 2000.
34. Forssell, *Fouché*.
35. Gallo, *Napoléon*.
36. Black, *From Louis XIV to Napoleon*.
37. Eddy Bauer, *Espías. Enciclopedia del Espionaje*, 8 vols., Idees & Editions, Paris, 1971.

Notes

38. Ibid.

39. George Bruce, *Dictionary of Wars,* HarperCollins, London, 1995.

40. Asprey, *The Rise of Napoleon Bonaparte.*

41. When the Austrians occupied France in the wake of the "Hundred Days"—Napoleon's attempt to return to power in 1815—they arrested the spy. To escape execution, Karl Schulmeister spent his entire fortune on bribes and fled to Strasbourg. There, he lived in complete poverty until his death in 1820. He was buried in a common grave in the cemetery of Saint Urbain.

42. O'Dwyer, *The Papacy in the Age of Napoleon.*

43. Anderson, *Pope Pius VII.*

44. Ibid.

45. Zweig, *Fouché.*

46. David Howarth, *Waterloo: Great Battles: A Near Run Thing*, Phoenix Press, London, 2003.

47. David Hamilton-Williams, *The Fall of Napoleon: The Final Betrayal*, John Wiley & Sons, London, 1996.

48. Black, *From Louis XIV to Napoleon.*

49. Hamilton-Williams, *The Fall of Napoleon.*

9. An Era of Spies (1823–1878)

1. Paredes et al, *Diccionario de los Papas y Concilios.*

2. Baumgartner, *Behind Locked Doors.*

3. G. D. Painter, *Chateaubriand*, Random House, London, 1998.

4. Eric Frattini, *Mafia, S.A. 100 años de Cosa Nostra,* Espasa Calpe, Madrid, 2002.

5. Jean-Charles Pichón, *Histoire Universelle des Sectes et des Sociétés Secrètes,* Robert Laffont Éditions, Paris, 1969.

6. Frank J. Coppa, *The Modern Papacy since 1789,* Wesley Longman Ltd., Essex, 1998.

7. Castiglioni, *Storia dei Papi.*

8. Álvarez, *Spies in the Vatican.*

9. Paredes et al, *Diccionario de los Papas y Concilios.*

10. Walsh, *The Conclave.*

11. Álvarez, *Spies in the Vatican.*

12. Ibid.

13. Castiglioni, *Storia dei Papi.*

14. Paredes et al, *Diccionario de los Papas y Concilios.*

15. Baumgartner, *Behind Locked Doors.*

16. Raffaele De Cesare, *The Last Days of Papal Rome,* Zimmern Publisher, London, 1946.

17. David Baguley, *Napoleon III and His Regime: An Extravaganza,* Louisiana State University Press, Baton Rouge, 2000.

18. Cardinal Bartolomeo Pacca, head of papal espionage for nearly twenty-eight years, died on April 19, 1844, at the age of eighty-seven.

19. Denis Mack Smith, *Mazzini,* Yale University Press, New Haven (Connecticut), 1996.

20. Walsh, *The Conclave.*

21. Bauer, *Espías, Enciclopedia del Espionaje.*

22. Wilhelm Stieber, *The Chancellor's Spy: Memoirs of the Founder of Modern Espionage*, Grove Press, London, 1981.

23. Michael Morrogh, *The Unification of Italy,* Palgrave Macmillan, London, 2003.

24. Nicholas Doumanis, *Italy (Inventing the Nation),* Edward Arnold, London, 2001.

25. Coppa, *The Modern Papacy since 1789.*

26. Smith, *Mazzini.*

27. Morrogh, *The Unification of Italy.*

28. Jasper Ridley, *Garibaldi*, Phoenix Press, London, 2001.

29. Denis Mack Smith, *Cavour and Garibaldi 1860: A Study in Political Conflict,* Cambridge University Press, New York, 1985.

30. Doumanis, *Italy (Inventing the Nation).*

31. Coppa, *The Modern Papacy since 1789.*

32. Álvarez, *Spies in the Vatican.*
33. Ibid.
34. Stieber, *The Chancellor's Spy.*
35. Ibid.
36. Paolo Pinto, *Vittorio Emanuele II: Il re avventuriero,* Arnaldo Mondadori, Milan, 1995.
37. Iván Ballesteros, *La Guerra Civil Americana.* Essay published on the Internet.
38. Howard Means, *C.S.A.: Confederate States of America*, William Morrow Publisher, New York, 1998.
39. Herman Hattaway, *Jefferson Davis, Confederate President,* University Press of Kansas, Lawrence, 2002.
40. William Gienapp, *Abraham Lincoln and Civil War America: A Biography*, Oxford University Press, New York, 2002; and David Detzer, *Allegiance: Fort Sumter, Charleston, and the Beginning of the Civil War,* Harvest Books, Fort Washington, 2002.
41. Ridley, *Garibaldi.*
42. Álvarez, *Spies in the Vatican.*
43. David Álvarez, "The Papacy in the Diplomacy of the American Civil War," *Catholic Historical Review,* num. 69, Washington, D.C. (April 1983).
44. Coppa, *The Modern Papacy since 1789.*
45. Means, *C.S.A.: Confederate States of America.*
46. Randall Miller and Harry Stout, *Religion and the American Civil War*, Oxford University Press, New York, 1998.
47. Álvarez, *Spies in the Vatican.*
48. Frattini, *Mafia, S.A. 100 años de Cosa Nostra.*
49. Álvarez, *Spies in the Vatican.*
50. *Consular Relations between the United States and the Papal States: Instructions and Despatches* (American Catholic Historical Association, Washington, D.C., 1945).
51. Ridley, *Garibaldi.*
52. Morrogh, *The Unification of Italy.*
53. Pinto, *Vittorio Emanuele II: Il re avventuriero.*
54. Pope John Paul II would beatify Pius IX on September 3, 2000.
55. Frattini, *Secretos vaticanos.*

10. The League of the Impious (1878–1914)

1. Paredes et al, *Diccionario de los Papas y Concilios.*
2. Baumgartner, *Behind Locked Doors.*
3. Theodore S. Hamerow, *Otto von Bismarck: A Historical Assessment*, Heath Publisher, London, 1972.
4. David Álvarez, "The Professionalization of the Papal Diplomatic Service," *Catholic Historical Review,* num. 72, Washington, D.C. (April 1989).
5. *Zentrum* remained the largest German political party until 1903, when a grave internal crisis shook the political organization.
6. John L. Offner, *An Unwanted War: The Diplomacy of the United States and Spain over Cuba, 1895–1898,* University of North Carolina Press, Chapel Hill, 1992.
7. Elbridge S. Brooks, *The Story of Our War with Spain,* Ross & Perry, Inc., New York, 2001.
8. David F. Trask, *The War with Spain in 1898,* University of Nebraska Press, Lincoln, 1997.
9. Álvarez, *Spies in the Vatican.*
10. Luigi Bruti Liberati, *La Santa Sede e le origini dell'imperio americano: La guerra de 1898,* Edizioni Unicopli, Milan, 1984.
11. Letter of Archbishop John Ireland to Cardinal and Secretary of State Mariano Rampolla, April 1, 1898. John Ireland Papers, Archives of the Archdiocese of St. Paul, St. Paul, Minnesota.
12. Brooks, *The Story of Our War with Spain.*
13. Offner, *An Unwanted War.*
14. Álvarez, "The Professionalization of the Papal Diplomatic Service."
15. Letter of Monsignor Donato Sbarretti to Cardinal Mariano Rampolla, secretary of state, April 1, 1902. Posizione 975, fasc. 369. Archivio Storico della Sacra Congregazione degli Affari Ecclesiastici Straordinari, Vatican City.

16. William Howard Taft would be President of the United States from 1909 to 1913.
17. Paolo Enrico Coletta, *The Presidency of William Howard Taft*, University Press of Kansas, Lawrence (Kansas), 1973.
18. Ibid.
19. Álvarez, *Spies in the Vatican.*
20. Marcel Givierge, *Au Service du chifre: 18 ans de souvenirs, 1907–1925,* NAF 17573–17575, Bibliothéque Nationale de France (Paris, France).
21. Maurice Larkin, *Church and State after the Dreyfus Affair,* Harper & Row, New York, 1972.
22. Álvarez, *Spies in the Vatican.*
23. Eduardo Soderini, *Leo XIII, Italy, and France*, Burns & Oates, London, 1935.
24. Álvarez, "The Professionalization of the Papal Diplomatic Service."
25. The European countries were Austria, Bavaria, Belgium, France, Holland, Portugal, and Spain.
26. Bauer, *Espías. Enciclopedia del Espionaje.*
27. Álvarez, *Spies in the Vatican.*
28. Peter Hebblethwaite, *The Next Pope, a Behind the Scenes Look at How the Successor to John Paul II Will Be Elected and Where He Will Lead the Church,* HarperCollins Publishers, San Francisco, 2000.
29. John Cornwell, *Breaking Faith: The Pope, the People, and the Fate of Catholicism,* Viking Press, New York, 2001.
30. Álvarez, *Spies in the Vatican.*
31. Émile Poulat, *Catholicisme, démocratie et socialisme: Le mouvement catholique et Mgr Benigni de la naissance du socialisme à la victoire du fascisme*, Casterman, Paris, 1977.
32. Álvarez, *Spies in the Vatican.*
33. Lorenzo Bedeschi, "Un episodio di spionaggio antimodernista," *Nuova Rivista Storica,* num. 56, Milan (May–August 1972).
34. Álvarez, *Spies in the Vatican.*
35. John F. Pollard, *The Unknown Pope. Benedict XV (1914–1922) and the Pursuit of Peace*, Geoffrey Chapman Publishers, London, 1999.
36. Ibid.
37. In a pun on his double surname, Cardinal José de Calasanz Vives y Tutó was known within the Vatican as *Vives fa Tutto* (Vives does everything). When the Spanish cardinal went insane and had to be hospitalized in 1908, Mariano Rampolla replaced him in office until his own death on December 16, 1913. Cardinal Vives y Tutó died on September 7, 1913.
38. The College of Protonotaries Apostolic was an anachronistic institution which no longer had any powers or functions. New members of the College were generally elderly former high officials. When Benigni was named protonotary, however, he was only forty-eight years old. Since he came from such an important department as the secretariat of state, this transfer could only imply a bump in the road of his career.
39. Poulat, *Catholicisme, démocratie et socialism.*
40. Álvarez, *Spies in the Vatican.*
41. Bedeschi, "Un episodio di spionaggio antimodernista."
42. Umberto Benigni would end his days as an informer within the Vatican for Benito Mussolini's secret service.
43. Cornwell, *Breaking Faith.*

11. The Horseman of the Apocalypse (1914–1917)

1. Lavender Cassels, *The Archduke and the Assassin: Sarajevo, June 28th, 1914,* Scarborough House, London, 1985.
2. Ibid.
3. Edmond Paris, *The Vatican Against Europe,* The Wickliffe Press, New Zealand, 1989.
4. Pollard, *The Unknown Pope.*
5. Monsignor Umberto Benigni died in 1934, at the age of seventy-two. All the documents relating to his trajectory through the various departments of the Vatican were labeled "top secret" and deposited in the well-known Vatican Secret Archives, section "Separate Collections," within the

"Family and Individual Papers." The documents on "Benigni, Umberto," are among those of the Beni and Benincasa families. They have still not been declassified. See also Francis X. Blouin, ed., *Vatican Archives: An Inventory and Guide to Historical Documents of the Holy See,* Oxford University Press, Oxford, 1997.

6. Pollard, *The Unknown Pope.*
7. C. Falconi, *The Popes in the Twentieth Century,* Faber & Faber, London, 1960.
8. Martin Gilbert, *The First World War: A Complete History,* Henry Holt & Company, New York, 1996.
9. Álvarez, *Spies in the Vatican.*
10. Álvarez, "The Professionalization of the Papal Diplomatic Service."
11. Leslie Shane, *Cardinal Gasquet: A Memoir,* Burns & Oates, London, 1953.
12. Cowley, *The Great War.*
13. Pollard, *The Unknown Pope.*
14. Roger Chickering, *Imperial Germany and the Great War, 1914–1918,* Cambridge University Press, Cambridge, 1998.
15. Álvarez, *Spies in the Vatican.*
16. Klaus Epstein, *Matthias Erzberger and the Dilemma of German Democracy*, Princeton University Press, Princeton, 1959.
17. Pollard, *The Unknown Pope.*
18. William Renzi, *The Shadow of the Sword: Italy's Neutrality and Entrance into Great War, 1914–1915,* Peter Lang Publisher, New York, 1987.
19. Ibid.
20. Ibid.
21. Ibid.; and Alberto Monticone, *La Germania e la neutralitrà italiana, 1914–1915*, Il Mulino Editore, Bologna, 1971.
22. Politician and spy Matthias Erzberger was elected Reichstag deputy and then named imperial treasury minister and secretary of state. He coined a famous but ill-chosen phrase that would follow him all his life: "No one should worry about violating the rights of the peoples or the laws of hospitality." As president, Erzberger formed part of the German delegation that signed the armistice ending the First World War. In 1921, he was assassinated by a far-right group close to the National Socialist (Nazi) party, who accused him of having sold Germany to the Entente powers during the signing of the armistice.
23. In June 1916, fourteen months after its declaration against Austria, Italy declared war on Germany as well.
24. Álvarez, *Spies in the Vatican.*
25. Brian Inglis, *Roger Casement*, Penguin Books Ltd., London, 2003.
26. Reinhard R. Doerries, *Sir Roger Casement in Imperial Germany, 1914–1916*, Irish Academic Printed, Dublin, 2000.
27. Adrian Weale, *Patriot Traitors: Roger Casement, John Amery and the Real Meaning of Treason,* Penguin Books Ltd., London, 2001.
28. Bauer, *Espías. Enciclopedia del Espionaje.*
29. John O'Beirne Ranelagh, *A Short History of Ireland*, Cambridge University Press, Cambridge, 1995.
30. Doerries, *Sir Roger Casement in Imperial Germany.*
31. Bauer, *Espías. Enciclopedia del Espionaje.*
32. Doerries, *Sir Roger Casement in Imperial Germany.*
33. Brendan O'Brien, *The Long War. The IRA & Sinn Fein from Armed Struggle to Peace Talks*, The O'Brien Press, Dublin, 1993.
34. Weale, *Patriot Traitors.*
35. Álvarez, *Spies in the Vatican.*
36. Ibid.
37. Pollard, *The Unknown Pope.*
38. Álvarez, *Spies in the Vatican.*
39. After the war, Monsignor Rudolph Gerlach sent a letter to Pope Benedict XV in which he asked to be released from his priestly vows. The petition would be granted once Gerlach returned a series of

confidential documents that he had taken with him from the Vatican when he left for Switzerland. It was said that the documents demonstrated Vatican intervention against Italy, as well as permission from Benedict XV or his secretary of state Pietro Gasparri to carry out covert Holy Alliance operations in favor of the Central Powers. See Renzi, *The Shadow of the Sword*.

40. Álvarez, *Spies in the Vatican*.

12. Intriguing Toward Peace (1917–1922)

1. Pollard, *The Unknown Pope*.
2. This refers to the papal intelligence agents who are authorized by the pope to pass on certain pieces of information to other espionage services.
3. Álvarez, *Spies in the Vatican*.
4. Antonio Scotta, *La conciliazione ufficiosa: Diario del Barone Carlo Monti,* Libreria Editrice Vaticana, Vatican City, 1997.
5. Bauer, *Espías. Enciclopedia del Espionaje*.
6. Ibid.
7. Born in London on October 5, 1856, he was ordained as a priest of the Order of St. Benedict. Promoted to cardinal on May 25, 1914, he was named archivist of the Vatican Library by the pope and then head of the Vatican Secret Archives on May 9, 1919. Cardinal Gasquet died April 5, 1929.
8. Martin Conway, *Catholic Politics in Europe: 1918–1945*, Routledge, New York, 1997.
9. Pollard, *The Unknown Pope*.
10. Cardinal Luigi Maglione was the papal delegate in Switzerland until he was named papal nuncio in the same legation on September 1, 1920. On December 16, 1935, he was raised to cardinal by Pope Pius XI. On March 10, 1939, Pope Pius XII named him secretary of state, a position he held until his death on August 22, 1944.
11. Álvarez, *Spies in the Vatican*.
12. Marguerite Cunliffe-Owen, *Imperator et Rex: William II of Germany,* Fredonia Books, Amsterdam, 2002.
13. Cipher A. Deavours and Louis Kruh, *Selections from Cryptologia: History, People, and Technology*, Artech House, London, 1998.
14. David Kahn, *The Codebreakers: The Comprehensive History of Secret Communication from Ancient Times to the Internet,* Scribner Publisher, New York, 1996.
15. Álvarez, *Spies in the Vatican*.
16. Gilbert, *The First World War*.
17. Paris, *The Vatican Against Europe*.
18. See chapter 11.
19. Paris, *The Vatican Against Europe*.
20. Chickering, *Imperial Germany and the Great War*; Cornwell, *Breaking Faith*.
21. See chapter 10.
22. The *Sodalitium Pianum*, or S.P., would renew its counterespionage operations, independently of the Holy Alliance, in March of 1939, when Cardinal Eugenio Pacelli was elected supreme pontiff under the name of Pius XII.
23. Álvarez, "The Professionalization of the Papal Diplomatic Service."
24. David Stevenson, *Cataclysm: The First World War as Political Tragedy*, Basic Books, London, 2004.
25. John Cornwell, *Hitler's Pope. The Secret History of Pius XII*. Penguin Books, New York, 2002.
26. Klaus Scholder, *The Churches and the Third Reich*, John Bowden Publishers, London, 1989.
27. Cornwell, *Hitler's Pope*.
28. Ibid.
29. Papers of the Foreign Office, 371/43869/21. Public Record Office, Kew. See also Pierre Blet, *Pius XII and the Second World War*, Paulist Press, New Jersey, 1997.
30. Castiglioni, *Storia dei Papi*.

Notes

13. Era of the Dictators (1922–1934)

1. Paul Lesourd, *Entre Rome et Moscou: Le jésuite clandestin, Mgr Michel d'Herbigny*, P. Lethielleux, Paris, 1976; and Álvarez, *Spies in the Vatican*.
2. Cornwell, *Breaking Faith*.
3. Ulisse A. Floridi, *Moscow and the Vatican*, Ardis Publishers, London, 1983.
4. Malachai Martin, *The Keys of This Blood. Pope John Paul II versus Russia and the West for the Control of the New World Order*, Simon & Schuster, New York, 1990.
5. Donald Rayfield, *Stalin and the Hangmen*, Viking, London, 2004.
6. Richard Pipes, *Russia Under the Bolshevik Regime*, Vintage Press, New York, 1995.
7. Pollard, *The Unknown Pope*.
8. Álvarez, "The Professionalization of the Papal Diplomatic Service."
9. Andrea Riccardi, *Il Secolo del Martirio*, Arnaldo Mondadori Spa, Milan, 2000.
10. It is said that Eugenio Pacelli's anti-communism led him, as Pope Pius XII, to applaud Adolf Hitler's decision to conquer the Soviet Union during the so-called Operation Barbarossa of June 22, 1941.
11. León Tretjakewitsch, *Bishop Michel d'Herbigny SJ and Russia: A Pre-ecumenical Approach to Christian Unity,* Augustinus-Verlag, Berlin, 1990.
12. Álvarez, *Spies in the Vatican*.
13. Lesourd, *Entre Rome et Moscou*.
14. Tretjakevitsch, *Bishop Michel d'Herbigny SJ and Russia*.
15. Ibid.; and Pipes, *Russia Under the Bolshevik Regime*.
16. Lesourd, *Entre Rome et Moscou*.
17. Tretjakewitsch, *Bishop Michel d'Herbigny SJ and Russia*.
18. Lesourd, *Entre Rome et Moscou*.
19. Rayfield, *Stalin and the Hangmen*; and Floridi, *Moscow and the Vatican*.
20. Riccardi, *Il Secolo del Martirio*.
21. Eugene H. Van Dee, *Sleeping Dogs and Popsicles: The Vatican Versus the KGB,* Rowman & Littlefield, New York, 1996.
22. KGB files dealing with this period were opened after the fall of the Berlin Wall and communism. One such document cites the order for Monsignor Alexander Frison's execution and an order to incinerate his corpse so as to leave no trace. See also Van Dee, *Sleeping Dogs and Popsicles*.
23. Álvarez, *Spies in the Vatican*.
24. Lesourd, *Entre Rome et Moscou*.
25. Anthony Rhodes, *The Vatican in the Age of the Dictators, 1922–1945*, Henry Holt & Company, Inc., New York, 1974.
26. The concordat signed by Benito Mussolini and Pope Pius XI remained in force until February 18, 1984. See Frank J. Coppa, *Controversial Concordats: The Vatican's Relations with Napoleon, Mussolini, and Hitler*, Catholic University of America Press, Washington, D.C., 1999.
27. Cornwell, *Hitler's Pope*.
28. Álvarez, *Spies in the Vatican*; and Floridi, *Moscow and the Vatican*.
29. Tretjakewitsch, *Bishop Michel d'Herbigny SJ and Russia*.
30. Floridi, *Moscow and the Vatican*.
31. Álvarez, *Spies in the Vatican*.
32. Christopher Andrew and Vasili Mitrokhin, *The Sword and the Shield: The Mitrokhin Archive and the Secret History of the KGB,* Basic Books, London, 2000.
33. Tretjakewitsch, *Bishop Michel d'Herbigny SJ and Russia*.
34. Lesourd, *Entre Rome et Moscou*.
35. Floridi, *Moscow and the Vatican*.

14. Rise of the Terror (1934–1940)

1. Joseph E. Persico, *Nuremberg: Infamy on Trial,* Penguin Books, New York, 1994.
2. Paredes et al, *Diccionario de los Papas y Concilio*.
3. Thomas Cahill, *Pope John XXIII*, Viking Penguin, New York, 2002; and Georges Passelecq and

Notes

Bernard Suchecky, *Un silencio de la Iglesia frente al fascismo. La encíclica de Pío XI que Pío XII no publicó,* PPC Editorial, Madrid, 1995.

4. Robert Jay Lifton, *The Nazi Doctors: Medical Killing and the Psychology of Genocide,* Basic Books, New York, 2000.

5. George J. Annas, *The Nazi Doctors and the Nuremberg Code: Human Rights in Human Experimentation,* Oxford University Press, New York, 1995.

6. Robert N. Proctor, *Racial Hygiene: Medicine Under the Nazis,* Harvard University Press, Cambridge, 1989.

7. Riccardi, *Il Secolo del Martirio.*

8. Frank J. Coppa, *Mussolini and Hitler,* Catholic University of America Press, Washington, D.C., 1999.

9. Álvarez, *Spies in the Vatican.*

10. See chapter 5.

11. Carlo Fiorentino, *All'ombra di Pietro: La Chiesa Cattolica e lo spionaggio fascista in Vaticano, 1929– 1939,* Casa Editrice Le Lettere, Florence, 1999.

12. Martyn Housden, *Resistance and Conformity in the Third Reich,* Routledge, London, 1997.

13. George Browder, *Hitler's Enforcers: The Gestapo and the SS Security Service in the Nazi Revolution,* Oxford University Press, Oxford, 1996.

14. David Álvarez and Robert A. Graham, *Nothing Sacred: Nazi Espionage Against the Vatican, 1939– 1945,* Irish Academic Press, New York, 1998.

15. Browder, *Hitler's Enforcers.*

16. Álvarez, *Spies in the Vatican.*

17. Ibid.

18. Álvarez and Graham, *Nothing Sacred.*

19. Walsh, *The Conclave.*

20. Álvarez and Graham, *Nothing Sacred.*

21. Álvarez, *Spies in the Vatican.*

22. Walsh, *The Conclave.*

23. Cornwell, *Hitler's Pope.*

24. Kenneth D. Alford, *Great Treasure Stories of World War II,* Da Capo Press, New York, 2001.

25. Ibid.; and Kenneth D. Alford and Theodore P. Savas, *Nazi Millionnaires: The Allied Search for Hidden SS Gold,* Casemate Publishers, New York, 2002.

26. Cornwell, *Hitler's Pope.*

27. Klaus Scholder, *A Requiem for Hitler and Other New Perspectives on the German Church Struggle,* John Bowden Publishers, London, 1989.

28. Branco Bokun, *Spy in the Vatican 1941–1945,* Tom Stacey Ltd., New York, 1997.

29. *Gran crónica de la Segunda Guerra Mundial,* 3 vols., Reader's Digest, Madrid, 1965.

30. Simon Singh, *The Code Book: The Science of Secrecy from Ancient Egypt to Quantum Cryptography,* Anchor Publishers, New York, 2000.

31. Cornwell, *Hitler's Pope.*

32. Álvarez and Graham, *Nothing Sacred.*

33. Heinz Hohne, *Canaris: Hitler's Master Spy,* Rowman & Littlefield, London, 1999.

34. Blet, *Pius XII and the Second World War.*

35. Harold Deutsch, *The Conspiracy Against Hitler in the Twilight War,* University of Minnesota Press, Minneapolis, 1968.

15. The End of the Thousand-Year Reich (1940–1945)

1. Álvarez, *Spies in the Vatican.*

2. Fred Ramen, *Reinhard Heydrich: Hangman of the 3rd Reich,* Rosen Publishing Group, London, 2001.

3. See chapter 14.

4. Hohne, *Canaris: Hitler's Master Spy.*

5. Ibid.

6. Álvarez, *Spies in the Vatican.*

Notes

7. Lauran Paine, *German Military Intelligence in World War II: The Abwehr*, Stein & Day Publishers, Munich, 1984.

8. Álvarez and Graham, *Nothing Sacred*.

9. Deutsch, *The Conspiracy Against Hitler in the Twilight War*.

10. Admiral Wilhelm Canaris was head of the Abwehr from 1939 to 1943. In late 1942 he was about to fall into disgrace in Hitler's eyes and was under surveillance for his possible relationship with anti-Nazi circles. On July 23, 1944, he was arrested and interrogated on suspicion of having participated in the coup attempt against Hitler three days before. On April 9, 1945, he was executed in Flossenburg prison, accused of high treason. See also Hohne, *Canaris: Hitler's Master Spy*.

11. Álvarez, *Spies in the Vatican*.

12. Bokun, *Spy in the Vatican 1941–1945*.

13. Eugen Dollmann, *Roma Nazista, 1937–1943*, RCS Libri, Milan, 2002.

14. Michael Bloch, *Ribbentrop*, Omnibus, Berlin, 1998.

15. Blet, *Pius XII and the Second World War*.

16. Bloch, *Ribbentrop*.

17. According to Holy Alliance reports, Paul Franken lived in Bonn until 1963, when he moved to a small town outside Frankfurt. He died in 1971.

18. Alois Hudal, an Austrian bishop, became one of the Vatican's main instruments for organizing Nazi flight. Hudal collaborated on the escape of Franz Stangl, commander of the Treblinka concentration camp, through the so-called Vatican Ratline.

19. *Organisation der ehemaligen SS-Angehörigen* (Organization of ex-members of the SS).

20. Álvarez, *Spies in the Vatican*.

21. Ramen, *Reinhard Heydrich*.

22. Susan Zuccotti, *Under His Very Windows. The Vatican and the Holocaust in Italy*, Yale University Press, New Haven, 2002.

23. David Kahn, *Hitler's Spies: German Military Intelligence in World War II*, Da Capo Press, New York, 2000.

24. Álvarez and Graham, *Nothing Sacred*.

25. On January 20, 1942, Reinhard Heydrich presided over a meeting of fifteen high-ranking Nazis gathered in a villa on the shores of the Wannsee lake. In their unanimously approved report, they determined on the "Final Solution," the extermination of the European Jews. According to Adolf Eichmann, who attended this frightful summit, eleven million Jews had to be killed. The Holy Alliance informed the Vatican of the Wannsee meeting and its conclusions on February 9, just twenty days later. On March 18, 1942, the Vatican received the first report from papal espionage agents about massive killings and deportations of Jews in Slovakia, Croatia, Hungary, and occupied France.

26. Blouin, *Vatican Archives*.

27. From the verb *ustati*, "to rise up" or "rebel."

28. Cornwell, *Hitler's Pope*.

29. Carlo Falconi, *The Silence of Pius XII*, Faber, London, 1970.

30. In the early 1960s, the writer and researcher Carlo Falconi was able to assemble documents about the atrocities committed in Ante Pavelic's Croatia. Falconi was granted access to the archives of the Federal Republic of Yugoslavia and to the Vatican Secret Archives bearing on the position taken by the Church and the Vatican toward the massacres in Croatia. He found several Holy Alliance reports about specific massacres. The Vatican Archives relating to the *Nezavisna Drzava Hrvatska* were opened by order of John XXIII and then were closed once more at the request of Paul VI.

31. The Archbishop of Zagreb, Monsignor Alojzije Stepinac, provided Catholic support to the pro-Nazi government of Ante Pavelic; knew right from the start about the massacres and extermination of Serbs, Jews, and gypsies; and was one of the pillars of the effort to help Nazi and Croatian war criminals escape to South America after the Second World War. He was beatified by Pope John Paul II during his visit to Croatia, October 3, 1998.

32. Falconi, *The Silence of Pius XII*; and Cornwell, *Hitler's Pope*.

33. The author in person, along with the reporter Julio Fuentes of *El Mundo* newspaper, was a witness to the massive bombardment of the Croat town of Jasinovac by Serbian artillery in 1991. Serbian

authorities told the author that the bombardment was "a matter of honor and vengeance" against the Croats fifty years later.

34. Jonathan Steinberg, *All or Nothing: The Axis and the Holocaust, 1941–1943*, Routledge, London, 2002.

35. Richard Overy, *Interrogations: The Nazi Elite in Allied Hands, 1945*, Penguin Books, New York, 2002.

36. Falconi, *The Silence of Pius XII*.

37. The Vatican's espionage service, the Holy Alliance, had little to do with the tragic fate of millions of Jews throughout Europe. There are reports indicating that only a few Holy Alliance agents helped some dozens of Jewish families to hide or escape from Nazi-occupied areas, and they did so acting on their own authority. There is no documentary evidence or bibliography about official actions or operations carried out or organized by the Vatican espionage service to save the Jews from deportation and extermination. There is simply no evidence of such activities, which is why this book does not contain any summary of the issue of the Holy Alliance and the Final Solution.

38. Owen Chadwick, *Britain and the Vatican during the Second World War*, Cambridge University Press, Cambridge, 1987.

16. "Odessa" and the "Vatican Ratline" (1946–1958)

1. Mark Aarons and John Loftus, *Ratlines: The Vatican's Nazi Connection*, Arrow, New York, 1991.

2. Uki Goñi, *The Real Odessa: Smuggling the Nazis to Perón's Argentina*, Granta Books, London, 2002.

3. Ibid.

4. Report of the Independent Commission of Experts Switzerland (ICE), chapter 5, cases "Kroch, Hans; Hellinger, Bruno; Kooperberg, L.H."

5. Goñi, *The Real Odessa*.

6. Ibid.

7. Mark Aarons and John Loftus, *Unholy Trinity: The Vatican, the Nazis, and the Swiss Banks*, St. Martin's Griffin, New York, 1998.

8. Report by William Gowen from Vatican City, September 18, 1946. National Archives and Records Administration (NARA), RG 59/250/36/27, Box 4016, 761.00/9-1946.

9. The communication between Cardinal Giovanni Battista Montini, the future Pope Paul VI, and the Argentine ambassador in Rome was revealed in a "Secret Letter," number 144 from the diplomat in the Vatican to his minister of foreign affairs, Juan Bramuglia, dated June 13, 1946. The letter was published in the report of the Commission to Clarify Nazi Activities in Argentina (CEANA) in 1999.

10. Father Karlo Petranovic, a Holy Alliance agent, was accused of participation in massacres of Orthodox Serbs during the war. There are photographs of Father Petranovic giving last rites to Serbian corpses in a common grave in the city of Ogulin. Marshal Tito's communist government requested Father Karlo Petranovic's extradition from the Vatican. The extradition was never granted.

11. The German agent entered Argentina on September 4, 1948, on the steamship *Santa Cruz,* which had departed from Genoa and made a brief stop in a Moroccan port. His Argentine immigration file was numbered 180086-48. Later, thanks to a safe-conduct issued by the Vatican to Reinhard Kops, he received an identity card that named him Juan Maler. The former German spy told the Argentine authorities he was a "stateless person."

12. Father Ivan Bucko was accused of blessing the massacres of Jews and partisans by the much-feared Galicia Division, a unit of the Ukrainian SS, during the Nazi occupation of the Ukraine.

13. Richard Deacon, *The Israeli Secret Service*, Warner Books, New York, 1977.

14. Élise Nouel, *Carré d'as . . . aux femmes!: Lady Hester Stanhope, Aurélie Picard, Isabelle Eberhardt, Marga d'Andurain*, G. Le Prat, Paris, 1977.

15. Bauer, *Espías*.

16. Nouel, *Carré d'as . . . aux femmes*.

17. Aarons and Loftus, *Unholy Trinity* and *Ratlines*.

18. Gordon Thomas, *Gideon's Spies: The Secret History of the Mossad*, St. Martin's Press, New York, 1999.

19. Gunter Grau, *The Hidden Holocaust?: Gay and Lesbian Persecution in Germany 1933–45,* Fitzroy Dearborn Publishers, London, 1995.

Notes

20. Richard Plant, *The Pink Triangle: The Nazi War Against Homosexuals*, Henry Holt & Company, Inc., New York, 1988.

21, Goñi, *The Real Odessa*.

22. Carl Vaernet died in Argentina on November 25, 1965. He is buried in the British cemetery of Buenos Aires in row 11.A.120. His grandson Christian Vaernet, who still lives in Denmark, explained that while reviewing some of his grandfather's papers he found several certificates in Carl Vaernet's name issued by various Vatican departments. He also found a letter signed by Krunoslav Draganovic addressed to his grandfather, explaining the form in which "his organization" would help him escape to South America. The family donated all these documents to the National Archives of Denmark.

23. The Dachau concentration camp functioned from 1933 to 1945. During this time, 206,000 "registered" prisoners passed through its gates, of whom 31,951 were "registered" as dying there. The Oranienburg camp functioned between 1933 and 1945 as well. There are no official figures on deaths in this camp.

24. CIA Reference Operational Files, "Croatian Gold Question," February 2, 1951.

25. CIC number 5650. NARA, RG 319, 631/31/59/04, Box 173.

26. 1998 report titled *Supplement to Preliminary Study on U.S. and Allied Efforts to Recover and Restore Gold and Other Assets Stolen or Hidden During World War II*, written by William Slany, historian of the Department of Defense.

27. Aarons and Loftus, *Unholy Trinity;* and Paul L. Williams, *The Vatican Exposed. Money, Murder and the Mafia*, Prometheus Books, New York, 2003.

28. The author has proof of Holy Alliance agents' intervention in at least fifty-four escape operations for Nazi and Croat war criminals. For reasons of space, only some of these have been selected for inclusion in this book.

29. Gitta Sereny, *Into That Darkness: An Examination of Conscience*, Vintage Press, New York, 1983.

30. Report of the Foreign Office archived in the Public Record Office (PRO), FO (Foreign Office) 371.67401 R15533.

17. New Alliances (1958–1976)

1. Cahill, *Pope John XXIII*, Viking Penguin, New York, 2002.

2. Discepoli di Verità, *Bugie di sangue in Vaticano*, Kaos Edizioni, Milan, 1999.

3. Goñi, *The Real Odessa*.

4. Van Dee, *Sleeping Dogs and Popsicles*.

5. Bauer, *Espías*.

6. Ibid.

7. I Millenari, *Via col vento in Vaticano*, Kaos Edizioni, Milan, 1999.

8. The IOR (*Istituto per le Opere di Religione*), popularly known as the "Vatican Bank," was founded by Pope Pius XII on June 27, 1942.

9. Founded May 9, 1975. The most powerful, politicized, and violent of Italian secret organizations. As grand master of P2, Licio Gelli separated the lodge from the Masonic hierarchy and made it into an underground "state" within the Italian state. He recruited important figures from the political, financial, and judicial spheres, from the police and the army, and from the Church. All of them took an oath, in Gelli's presence, to destroy the democratic-parliamentary form of government of the Italian Republic.

10. In the Mexican magazine *Proceso*, October 12, 1992.

11. Short, *Inside the Brotherhood*.

12. P. Williams, *The Vatican Exposed*.

13. I Millenari, *Via col vento in Vaticano*.

14. Violation of the Pontifical Secrecy brings immediate excommunication of the violator, as well as automatic expulsion from the Catholic Church and, therefore, from the Vatican state.

15. *Ha Mossad, le Modiyn ve le Tafkidim Mayuhadim* (Institute of Intelligence and Special Operations).

16. Name by which the Mossad director is known.

17. G. Thomas, *Gideon's Spies*.

18. This text was made public after the Israeli Defense Forces' invasion of Lebanon in 1982. An Israeli unit found the document in a PLO barracks in southern Lebanon.
19. Victor Ostrovsky and Claire Hoy, *By Way of Deception*, Stoddart Publishing, Toronto, 1991.
20. G. Thomas, *Gideon's Spies*.
21. Jewish Mossad informer who did not work for the Israeli secret service as such, but did collaborate.
22. Michael Bar-Zohar and Eitan Habaer, *The Quest for the Red Prince*, William Morrow, New York, 1983.
23. Ian Black and Benny Morris, *Israel's Secret Wars. A History of Israel's Intelligence Services*, Grove Weidenfeld, New York, 1991.
24. *Kidon* means "bayonet." The name refers to the operational arm of the *Metsada*, the Mossad unit in charge of executions and kidnappings.
25. G. Thomas, *Gideon's Spies*.
26. David A. Yallop, *To the Ends of the Earth: The Hunt for the Jackal*, Poetic Products Ltd., London, 1993.
27. Ibid.

18. *"Vatican, Inc." and God's Business (1976–1978)*

1. The Vatican Bank was founded on June 7, 1929, by order of Pope Pius XI. Its capital in that year totaled $81 million, the equivalent of $900 million today. The first director of the so-called Special Administration of the Holy See was Bernardino Nogara.
2. P. Williams, *The Vatican Exposed*.
3. Charles Raw, *The Moneychangers: How the Vatican Bank Enabled Roberto Calvi to Steal $250 Million for the Heads of the P2 Masonic Lodge*, Vintage/Ebury, London, 1992.
4. Luigi DiFonzo, *Michele Sindona, el banquero de San Pedro*, Editorial Planeta, Barcelona, 1984.
5. Vatican secret services named the April 1967 operation "Tatoi" after the royal palace in Athens.
6. The reputation of the Greek officers grew worse and worse, until finally they gave up their power in 1974 after the Cyprus fiasco. That same month, Konstantinos Karamanlis returned from exile and took charge of the government. In elections that year, his party won the majority of votes. Later, a referendum approved the abolition of the monarchy.
7. David A. Yallop, *In God's Name. An Investigation into the Murder of Pope John Paul I*, Bantam Books, New York, 1984.
8. Paredes et al, *Diccionario de los Papas y Concilios*.
9. Walsh, *The Conclave*.
10. Ricardo de la Cierva, *El diario secreto de Juan Pablo I*, Editorial Planeta, Barcelona, 1990.
11. Walsh, *The Conclave*.
12. Some sources assert that the famous report was given to John Paul I by agents of the Holy Alliance or the *Sodalitium Pianum,* while others say it was Cardinal Benelli who left it in the supreme pontiff's study.
13. John Cornwell, *A Thief in the Night. Life and Death in the Vatican*, Penguin Books, New York, 1989.
14. Yallop, *In God's Name*.
15. Heribert Blondiau and Udo Gümpel, *El Vaticano santifica los medios. El asesinato del «banquero de Dios»*, Ellago Ediciones, Castellón, 2003.
16. See chapter 17.
17. Short, *Inside the Brotherhood*.
18. Yallop, *In God's Name*.
19. P. Williams*, The Vatican Exposed*.
20. De la Cierva, *El diario secreto de Juan Pablo I*.
21. DiFonzo, *Michele Sindona, el banquero de San Pedro*.
22. Monsignor Pavel Hnilica, founder of *Pro Fratibus*, was in charge of trying to recover a bag that Robert Calvi was carrying before his supposed "suicide" in London. Hnilica apparently offered millions for its return.
23. Cornwell, *A Thief in the Night*.
24. Yallop, *In God's Name*.
25. The Vatican still maintains this version today. To the Holy See it was not very "decorous" for a woman to be the first to find the body of a supreme pontiff dead in his bed. Apparently, the official version was invented by Cardinal Jean Villot, the secretary of state.

Notes

26. Yallop, *In God's Name*; Cornwell, *A Thief in the Night*; and DiFonzo, *Michele Sindona, el banquero de San Pedro*.
27. Carl Bernstein and Marco Politi, *His Holiness*, Bantam Doubleday, New York, 1996.
28. Walsh, *The Conclave*.
29. Bernstein and Politi, *His Holiness*.

19. Time of the Assassins (1979–1982)

1. Maria Guarini, *I Mercanti del Vaticano. Affari e Scandali: L'industria della anime*, Kaos Edizioni, Milan, 1998.
2. Ibid.
3. Short, *Inside the Brotherhood*.
4. Rita di Giovacchino, *Scoop mortale: Mino Pecorelli, storia di un giornalista kamikaze*, T. Pironti Edizioni, Naples, 1994.
5. Blondiau and Gümpel, *El Vaticano santifica los medios*.
6. Paolo Baffi, demoralized by the obstacles put in the way of his investigation and by threats targeting himself, his wife, and his children, decided to leave his job at the Bank of Italy in late 1979.
7. Corrado Stajano, *Un eroe borghese: il caso dell'avvocato Giorgio Ambrosoli assassinato dalla mafia politica*, Einaudi Edizioni, Turin, 1991.
8. Peter T. Schneider, *Reversible Destiny: Mafia, Antimafia, and the Struggle for Palermo*, University of California Press, Los Angeles, 2003.
9. On January 7, 1566, Cardinal Miguel Ghislieri was named supreme pontiff. As Pius V, he founded the Holy Alliance, the papal secret service.
10. Álvarez, "The Professionalization of the Papal Diplomatic Service."
11. Cornwell, *A Thief in the Night*.
12. Yallop, *In God's Name*.
13. Guarini, *I Mercanti del Vaticano*.
14. Yallop, *In God's Name*.
15. Bernstein and Politi, *His Holiness*.
16. Robert Eringer, *Strike for Freedom: The Story of Lech Walesa and Polish Solidarity*, Dodd Mead, New York, 1982.
17. Bernstein and Politi, *His Holiness*.
18. Bernstein and Politi, *His Holiness*.
19. Zbigniew Brzezinski, *The Grand Failure: The Birth and Death of Communism in the Twentieth Century*, Scribner Publishers, New York, 1989.
20. Bernstein and Politi, *His Holiness*.
21. Leopold Labedz, *Poland Under Jaruzelski: A Comprehensive Sourcebook on Poland During and After Martial Law*, Scribner, New York, 1984.
22. Christine Ockrent and Alexandre De Marenches, *Dans le secret des princes*, Édition Stock, Paris, 1986.
23. G. Thomas, *Gideon's Spies*.
24. Mehmet Ali Agca will be eligible for provisional liberty at the end of 2009 on condition of good conduct during his imprisonment.
25. Claire Sterling, *The Time of the Assassins*, Holt, Rinehart, & Winston, New York, 1983.
26. Eduard Kovaliov, *Atentado en la Plaza de San Pedro*, Editorial Novosti, Moscow, 1985.

20. The Polish Years (1982–2005)

1. Eringer, *Strike for Freedom*.
2. Bernstein and Politi, *His Holiness*.
3. After their flight from Poland, Kuklinski and his family moved to the United States. In 1990, when Walesa became president of Poland, Kuklinski decided to return, but the Poles continued to view the ex-officer as a traitor, so Kuklinski gave up the idea. Gull had forwarded nearly 35,000 pages of documents to the papal and U.S. secret services. In 1998 he stepped onto Polish soil for the first

time since his flight, but only as a tourist. He and his family returned to the U.S., where he continued to reside until his death on February 10, 2004.

4. The Exocet was developed by the tactical weapons arm of Aérospatiale. In 1974, the company produced the MM-40. The new missile was shorter than the Styx. It was much faster (800 kilometers per hour), burning solid fuel and with a range of 55 kilometers (twice that of the Styx). Its success stemmed from its ability to travel at a very low altitude, out of reach of anti-aircraft systems, and to avoid detection. By May 1982, 1,800 had been sold, which made it a weapon both popular and versatile. This missile constituted the main threat to the British Expeditionary Force sent by Margaret Thatcher to recover the Malvina Islands. During this conflict the AM-39, an airborne version of the MM-40, showed how deadly it could be.
5. Margaret Thatcher, *The Downing Street Years*, HarperCollins Publishers, London, 1993.
6. Max Hastings and Simon Jenkins, *The Battle for the Falklands*, W. W. Norton & Company, London, 1984.
7. Blondiau and Gümpel, *El Vaticano santifica los medios*.
8. Raw, *The Moneychangers*.
9. This affair was reflected in a declaration by the Sardinian entrepreneur Flavio Carboni, closely tied to the Mafia, to prosecutor Pier Luigi Dell'Osso.
10. Blondiau and Gümpel, *El Vaticano santifica los medios*.
11. Yallop, *In God's Name*.
12. Richard Hammer, *The Vatican Connection. Mafia & Chiesa come il Vaticano ha comprato azioni false e rubate per un miliardo di dollari*, Tullio Pironte Editore, Naples, 1983.
13. Blondiau and Gümpel, *El Vaticano santifica los medios*.
14. A report by the SISMI (the Italian military intelligence service) dated June 13, 1981, and sent to Viminale (the palace that housed the foreign affairs ministry) confirmed the existence of the photos and said they had been acquired by Editorial Rizzoli and Editorial Rusconi for five hundred million lire. Apparently, someone at Rizzoli informed the Vatican about the photos they had acquired. However, three of the original negatives were missing.
15. Discepoli di Verità, *All'ombra del Papa infermo*, Kaos Edizioni, Milan, 2001.
16. Discepoli di Verità, *Bugie di sangue in Vaticano*.
17. John Follain, *City of Secrets: The Truth Behind the Murders at the Vatican*, HarperCollins, New York, 2003.
18. Monsignor Luigi Poggi was raised to cardinal by Pope John Paul II on November 26, 1994, in recognition of his special services. On March 7, 1998, after many requests on Poggi's part, the supreme pontiff accepted his resignation as head of the Vatican secret services, the Holy Alliance and the *Sodalitium Pianum*.
19. Discepoli di Verità, *Bugie di sangue in Vaticano*.
20. The neighbor may have been Caroline Meyer, wife of Swiss Guard sergeant Stefan Mayer.
21. On May 4, 1959, Corporal Adolf Rückert burst into the office of Commander Robert Nünlist and shot him four times. He then tried to shoot himself, but his gun jammed.
22. Follain, *City of Secrets*.
23. The *Corpo della Vigilanza* is made up of six gendarmes, two firefighters, two telephone operators, and a number of Vatican radio technicians. These superintendents are the so-called special forces who make up the police guard that accompanies the pope. The *Corpo della Vigilanza* is part of the secretariat of state and falls under the control of Monsignor Giovanni Battista Re (raised to cardinal on February 21, 2001), Monsignor Pedro López Quintana, and Monsignor Gianni Danzi.
24. Discepoli di Verità, *All'ombra del Papa infermo*.
25. Markus Wolf and Anne McElvoy, *Man without a Face*, Times Books, New York, 1997.
26. Discepoli di Verità, *Bugie di sangue in Vaticano*.
27. Years after making this statement, Wolf retracted it, asserting that his agent was really a Dominican friar in the Vatican Scientific Commission.
28. *Panorama*, June 18, 1998. Interview by reporter Anna Maria Turi.
29. Discepoli di Verità, *Bugie di sangue in Vaticano*.
30. There is talk of the possibility that a Holy Alliance agent, Father Yvan Bertorello, was inside the

Notes

Estermanns' apartment when the shots were fired and that it was he who left the door open when he went running out.

31. The girl was found working in the Ivet travel agency on the Via della Conciliazione. She was, in fact, a Vatican state official. In 1997, the agency changed its named to Quo Vadis, having been bought by the Vatican through the *Agenzia per il Giubelio 2000*.

Epilogue: The Years to Come: Benedict XVI

1. The Argentine bishop Leonardo Sandri was raised to cardinal on November 24, 2007, by Pope Benedict XVI. The Italian bishop Antonio María Vegliò was named secretary of the Congregation of the Eastern Churches on April 11, 2001, by Pope John Paul II, a position he held under Sandri's supervision.

BIBLIOGRAPHY

Aarons, Mark, and Loftus, John, *Ratlines: The Vatican's Nazi Connection,* Arrow, New York, 1991.

———, *Unholy Trinity. The Vatican, the Nazis and the Swiss Banks,* St. Martin's Griffin, New York, 1998.

Alford, Kenneth D., *The Spoils of World War II: The American Military's Role in the Stealing of Europe's Treasures,* Birch Lane, London, 1994.

———, *Great Treasure Stories of World War II,* Da Capo Press, New York, 2001.

Alford, Kenneth D., and Savas, Theodore P., *Nazi Millionaires: The Allied Search for Hidden SS Gold,* Casemate Publishers, New York, 2002.

Allen, John L., *Cardinal Ratzinger. The Vatican's Enforcer of the Faith,* Continuum Publishing, New York, 2000.

———, *Conclave. The Politics, Personalities and Process of the Next Papal Election,* Doubleday, New York, 2002.

Álvarez, David, "The Papacy in the Diplomacy of the American Civil War," *Catholic Historical Review,* num. 69, Washington, D.C. (April 1983).

———, "The Professionalization of the Papal Diplomatic Service," *Catholic Historical Review,* num. 72, Washington, D.C. (April 1989).

———, *Spies in the Vatican. Espionage and Intrigue from Napoleon to the Holocaust,* University Press of Kansas, Lawrence, 2002.

Álvarez, David, and Graham, Robert A., *Nothing Sacred: Nazi Espionage Against the Vatican, 1939–1945,* Irish Academic Press, New York, 1998.

Anderson, Robin, *Pope Pius VII (1800–1823): His Life, Times, and Struggle with Napoleon in the Aftermath of the French Revolution,* Tan Books & Publishers, New York, 2000.

Andrew, Christopher, and Mitrokhin, Vasili, *The Sword and the Shield: The Mitrokhin Archive and the Secret History of the KGB,* Basic Books, London, 2000.

Annas, George J., *The Nazi Doctors and the Nuremberg Code: Human Rights in Human Experimentation,* Oxford University Press, New York, 1995.

Arendt, Hannah, *Eichmann in Jerusalem. A Report on the Banality of Evil,* Penguin Books, New York, 1992.

Aretin, Karl Otmar von, *El Papado and el mundo moderno,* Ediciones Guadarrama, Madrid, 1964.

Asprey, Robert, *The Rise of Napoleon Bonaparte,* Basic Books, London, 2001.

Baguley, David, *Napoleon III and His Regime: An Extravaganza,* Louisiana State University Press, Baton Rouge, 2000.

Ballester, Rafael, *Historia de los Papas,* Editorial Bruguera, Barcelona, 1972.

Balteau, J., *Dictionnaire de biographie française,* Letouzey et Ané, Paris, 1933.

Bar-Zohar, Michael, and Haber, Eitan, *The Quest for the Red Prince,* William Morrow, New York, 1983.

Bauer, Eddy, *Espías. Enciclopedia del Espionaje,* 8 vols., Idees & Editions, Paris, 1971.

Baumgartner, Frederic J., *Behind Locked Doors: A History of the Papal Elections,* Palgrave Macmillan, New York, 2003.

Bibliography

Bedeschi, Lorenzo, "Un episodio di spionaggio antimodernista," *Nuova Rivista Storica,* num. 56, Milan (May–August 1972).

Beik, William, *Louis XIV and Absolutism: A Brief Study with Documents,* Palgrave Macmillan, London, 2000.

Bergin, Joseph, *The Rise of Richelieu (Studies in Early Modern European History),* Manchester University Press, Manchester, 1997.

Bernstein, Carl, and Politi, Marco, *His Holiness,* Bantam Doubleday, New York, 1996.

Black, Ian, and Morris, Benny, *Israel's Secret Wars. A History of Israel's Intelligence Services,* Grove Weidenfeld, New York, 1991.

Black, Jeremy, *From Louis XIV to Napoleon: The Fate of a Great Power,* UCL Press, London, 1999.

Blanning, T. C, *The French Revolutionary Wars, 1787–1802 (Modern Wars),* Edward Arnold Publisher, Oxford, 1996.

Blet, Pierre, *Pius XII and the Second World War,* Paulist Press, New Jersey, 1997.

Bloch, Michael, *Ribbentrop,* Omnibus, Berlin, 1998.

Blondiau, Heribert, and Gümpel, Udo, *El Vaticano santifica los medios. El asesinato del «banquero de Dios»,* Ellago Ediciones, Castellón, 2003.

Blouin, Francis X. (ed.), *Vatican Archives: An Inventory and Guide to Historical Documents of the Holy See,* Oxford University Press, Oxford, 1997.

Bokun, Branco, *Spy in the Vatican 1941–1945,* Tom Stacey Ltd., New York, 1997.

Bonney, Richard, *The European Dynastic States 1494–1660,* Oxford University Press, Oxford, 1992.

———, *The Thirty Years' War 1618–1648,* Osprey Publishers Company, London, 2002.

Bossy, John, *Giordano Bruno and the Embassy Affair,* Yale University Press, New Haven (Connecticut), 2002.

Brooks, Elbridge S., *The Story of Our War with Spain,* Ross & Perry, Inc., New York, 2001.

Browder, George, *Hitler's Enforcers: The Gestapo and the SS Security Service in the Nazi Revolution,* Oxford University Press, Oxford, 1996.

Browning, Oscar, *Journal of Sir George Rooke, Admiral of the Fleet,* Navy Records Society, London (facsimile edition, 1897), 1998.

Bruce, George, *Dictionary of Wars,* HarperCollins, London, 1995.

Brueck, Heinrich, *History of the Catholic Church,* Benziger Brothers, Chicago, 1885.

Bruti Liberati, Luigi, *La Santa Sede e le origini dell'imperio americano: La guerra de 1898,* Edizioni Unicopli, Milan, 1984.

Brzezinski, Zbigniew, *The Grand Failure: The Birth and Death of Communism in the Twentieth Century,* Scribner Publishers, New York, 1989.

Buisseret, David, *Henry IV: King of France,* Unwin Hyman, Boston, 1990.

Burman, Edward, *Assassins: Holy Killers of Islam,* HarperCollins Publishers, New York, 1987.

Cadbury, Deborah, *The Lost King of France: A True Story of Revolution, Revenge, and DNA,* St. Martin's Press, London, 2002.

———, *The Lost King of France: How DNA Solved the Mystery of the Murdered Son of Louis XVI and Marie Antoinette,* Griffin Trade Paperback, London, 2003.

Cahill, Thomas, *Pope John XXIII,* Viking Penguin, New York, 2002.

Calvo Poyato, José, *Carlos II el Hechizado and su época,* Editorial Planeta, Barcelona, 1991.

Canny, Nicholas, *Making Ireland British, 1580–1650,* Oxford University Press, Oxford, 2001.

Carbonero y Sol, Manuel, *Fin funesto de los perseguidores y enemigos de la Iglesia, desde Herodes el Grande hasta nuestros días,* Librería y Tipografía Católica, Barcelona, 1878.

Carlyle, Thomas, *The French Revolution: A History,* Modern Library, London, 2002.

Carrillo de Albornoz, José Miguel, *Carlos V, la espada de Dios,* Editorial Biblioteca Nueva, Madrid, 2000.

Cassels, Lavender, *The Archduke and the Assassin: Sarajevo, June 28th, 1914,* Scarborough House, London, 1985.

Castiglioni, Carlo, *Storia dei Papi,* Editrice Torinese, Turin, 1939.

Cavoli, Alfio, *La Papessa Olimpia,* Editoriale Scipioni, Milan, 1992.

Chadwick, Owen, *Britain and the Vatican during the Second World War,* Cambridge University Press, Cambridge, 1987.

Chickering, Roger, *Imperial Germany and the Great War, 1914–1918,* Cambridge University Press, Cambridge, 1998.

Bibliography

Chiovaro, Francesco, and Bessiérre, Gerard, *Urbi et Orbi. I Papi nella Storia,* Gallimard, Paris, 1995.

Ciappara, Frans, *The Roman Inquisition in Enlightened Malta,* Pubblikazzjonijiet Indipendenza, Malta, 2000.

Cierva, Ricardo de la, *El diario secreto de Juan Pablo I,* Editorial Planeta, Barcelona, 1990.

Ciudad del Vaticano, Editoriale Atesina, Trento, 1971.

Coletta, Paolo Enrico, *The Presidency of William Howard Taft,* University Press of Kansas, Lawrence, 1973.

Compton, Piers, *The Broken Cross: The Hidden Hand in the Vatican,* N. Spearman, New York, 1995.

Conway, Martin, *Catholic Politics in Europe: 1918–1945,* Routledge, New York, 1997.

Coppa, Frank J., *Cardinal Giacomo Antonelli and Papal Politics in European Affairs,* New York University Press, New York, 1990.

———, *The Modern Papacy since 1789,* Wesley Longman Ltd., Essex, 1998.

———, *Controversial Concordats: The Vatican's Relations with Napoleon, Mussolini, and Hitler,* Catholic University of America Press, Washington, D.C., 1999.

Cordingly, David, *Under the Black Flag: The Romance and the Reality of Life among the Pirates,* Harvest Books, New York, 1997.

Cornwell, John, *A Thief in the Night. Life and Death in the Vatican,* Penguin Books, New York, 1989.

———, *Breaking Faith: The Pope, the People, and the Fate of Catholicism,* Viking Press, New York, 2001.

———, *Hitler's Pope. The Secret History of Pius XII,* Penguin Books, New York, 2002.

Cowley, Robert, *The Great War: Perspectives on the First World War,* Random House, New York, 2003.

Cunliffe-Owen, Marguerite, *Imperator et Rex: William II of Germany,* Fredonia Books, Amsterdam, 2002.

Daim, Wilfried, *The Vatican and Eastern Europe,* Ungar, London, 1989.

De Cesare, Raffaele, *The Last Days of Papal Rome,* Zimmern Publisher, London, 1946.

De Rosa, Peter, *Vicars of Christ: The Dark Side of the Papacy,* Poolbeg Press Ltd., Dublin, 2000.

Deacon, Richard, *The Israeli Secret Service,* Warner Books, New York, 1977.

Deavours, Cipher A., and Kruh, Louis, *Selections from Cryptologia: History, People, and Technology,* Artech House, London, 1998.

Dedijer, Vladimir, *The Yugoslav Auschwitz and the Vatican: The Croatian Massacre of the Serbs During World War II,* Prometheus Books, New York, 1999.

Delorme, Philippe, *L'Affaire Louis XVII,* Jules Tallandier, Paris, 2000.

Detzer, David, *Allegiance: Fort Sumter, Charleston, and the Beginning of the Civil War,* Harvest Books, Fort Washington, 2002.

Deutsch, Harold, *The Conspiracy Against Hitler in the Twilight War,* University of Minnesota Press, Minneapolis, 1968.

Dictionary of Beliefs and Religions, W. & R. Chambers Ltd., London, 1992.

DiFonzo, Luigi, *Michele Sindona, el banquero de San Pedro,* Editorial Planeta, Barcelona, 1984.

Discepoli di Verità, *Bugie di sangue in Vaticano,* Kaos Edizioni, Milan, 1999.

———, *All'ombra del Papa infermo,* Kaos Edizioni, Milan, 2001.

Doerries, Reinhard R., *Sir Roger Casement in Imperial Germany, 1914–1916,* Irish Academic Printed, Dublin, 2000.

Dollmann, Eugen, *Roma Nazista, 1937–1943,* RCS Libri, Milan, 2002.

Doran, Susan, *Elizabeth I and Religion, 1558–1603,* Taylor & Francis Books Ltd., London, 1993.

———, *Monarchy and Matrimony: The Courtships of Elizabeth I,* HarperCollins, New York, 1996.

Doumanis, Nicholas, *Italy (Inventing the Nation),* Edward Arnold, London, 2001.

Duchain, Michel, *Elisabeth I d'Angleterre,* Editions Fayard, Paris, 1992.

Elliott, John, and Brockliss, Laurence, *The World of the Favourite,* Yale University Press, New Haven (Connecticut), 1999.

Epstein, Klaus, *Matthias Erzberger and the Dilemma of German Democracy,* Princeton University Press, Princeton, 1959.

Eringer, Robert, *Strike for Freedom: The Story of Lech Walesa and Polish Solidarity,* Dodd Mead, New York, 1982.

Erlanger, Philippe, *St. Bartholomew's Night: The Massacre of Saint Bartholomew,* Greenwood Publishing Group, New York, 1975.

Fagle, Robert, *William of Orange and the Revolt of the Netherlands, 1572–84,* Ashgate Publishing Company, London, 2003.

Bibliography

Falconi, Carlo, *The Silence of Pius XII*, Faber, London, 1970.

Fernández Álvarez, Manuel, *Felipe II y su tiempo*, Espasa Calpe, Madrid, 1998.

Fernández Díaz, Roberto, *La España del siglo XVIII*, Anaya, Madrid, 1990.

Feuchtwanger, Edgar, *Bismarck*, Routledge Historical Biographies, London, 2002.

Fiorentino, Carlo, *All'ombra di Pietro: La Chiesa Cattolica e lo spionaggio fascista in Vaticano, 1929–1939*, Casa Editrice Le Lettere, Florence, 1999.

Fletcher, Banister, *Historia de la arquitectura por el método comparado*, part I, vol. 1, Editorial Canosa, Barcelona, 1931.

Floridi, Ulisse A., *Moscow and the Vatican*, Ardis Publishers, London, 1983.

Follain, John, *City of Secrets: The Truth Behind the Murders at the Vatican*, HarperCollins, New York, 2003.

Forssell, Nils, *Fouché, the Man Napoleon Feared*, AMS Press, New York, 1971.

Frattini, Eric, *Mafia, S. A. 100 años de Cosa Nostra*, Espasa Calpe, Madrid, 2002.

————, *Secretos vaticanos*, EDAF, Madrid, 2003.

Gabriel, Paul, *Bras de fer KGB-Vatican: dimensions spirituelle et politique du message de Fatima*, Bréchant, Société d'études personnalisées appliquées, Paris, 1989.

Gallo, Max, *Napoleón*, Robert Laffont, Paris, 1997.

Gallois, Leonardo, *Historia General de la Inquisición*, Servicio de Reproducción de Libros, Barcelona, 1869.

García Cárcel, Ricardo, and Alabrús, Rosa María, *España en 1700. ¿Austrias o Borbones?*, Arlanza Ediciones, Madrid, 2001.

Gibson, Wendy, *A Tragic Farce: The Fronde (1648–1653)*, Intellect, New York, 1998.

Gienapp, William, *Abraham Lincoln and Civil War America: A Biography*, Oxford University Press, New York, 2002.

Gilbert, Martin, *The First World War: A Complete History*, Henry Holt & Company, New York, 1996.

Giovacchino, Rita di, *Scoop mortale: Mino Pecorelli, storia di un giornalista kamikaze*, T. Pironti Edizioni, Naples, 1994.

Givierge, Marcel, *Au Service du chifre: 18 ans de souvenirs, 1907–1925*, NAF 17573–17575, Bibliothéque Nationale de France (Paris, France).

Goetz, Walter; Joachimsen, Paul; Marcks, Erich; Mommsen, Wilhelm; and Heinrich, Hans, *La época de la revolución religiosa, la Reforma y la Contrareforma (1500–1660)*, vol. V, Espasa Calpe, Madrid, 1975.

Goldhagen, Daniel Jonah, *La Iglesia Católica y el Holocausto, una deuda pendiente*, Taurus, Madrid, 2002.

Goñi, Uki, *The Real Odessa: Smuggling the Nazis to Perón's Argentina*, Granta Books, London, 2002.

Gran crónica de la Segunda Guerra Mundial, 3 vols., Reader's Digest, Madrid, 1965.

Grau, Gunter, *The Hidden Holocaust?: Gay and Lesbian Persecution in Germany 1933–45*, Fitzroy Dearborn Publishers, London, 1995.

Guarini, Mario, *I Mercanti del Vaticano. Affari e Scandali: L'industria della anime*, Kaos Edizioni, Milan, 1998.

Hamerow, Theodore S., *Otto von Bismarck: A Historical Assessment*, Heath Publisher, London, 1972.

Hamilton-Williams, David, *The Fall of Napoleon: The Final Betrayal*, John Wiley & Sons, London, 1996.

Hammer, Richard, *The Vatican Connection: Mafia & Chiesa come il Vaticano ha comprato azioni false e rubate per un miliardo di dollari*, Tullio Pironte Editore, Naples, 1983.

Hanson, Neil, *The Confident Hope of a Miracle: The Real History of the Spanish Armada*, Doubleday, London, 2003.

Hardman, John, *Louis XVI*, Yale University Press, New Haven (Connecticut), 1994.

Hastings, Max, and Jenkins, Simon, *The Battle for the Falklands*, W. W. Norton & Company, London, 1984.

Hattaway, Herman, *Jefferson Davis, Confederate President*, University Press of Kansas, Lawrence, 2002.

Hebblethwaite, Peter, *The Next Pope, a Behind the Scenes Look at How the Successor to John Paul II Will Be Elected and Where He Will Lead the Church*, HarperCollins Publishers, San Francisco, 2000.

Herman, Edward S., and Brodhead, Frank, *The Rise and Fall of the Bulgarian Connection*, Sheridan Square Publishing, London, 1986.

Hill, Henry B., *Political Testament of Cardinal Richelieu: The Significant Chapters and Supporting Selections*, University of Wisconsin Press, Wisconsin, 1964.

Bibliography

Hohne, Heinz, *Canaris: Hitler's Master Spy,* Rowman & Littlefield, London, 1999.

Housden, Martyn, *Resistance and Conformity in the Third Reich,* Routledge, London, 1997.

Howarth, David, *Waterloo: Great Battles: A Near Run Thing,* Phoenix Press, London, 2003.

Hsia, R. Po-chia, *The World of Catholic Renewal 1540–1770,* Cambridge University Press, Cambridge, 1998.

Hurley, Mark J., *Vatican Star, Star of David: The Untold Story of Jewish/Catholic Relations and the 2nd Vatican Council,* Sheed and Ward, London, 1998.

Hutchinson, Robert, *Their Kingdom Come: Inside the Secret World of Opus Dei,* St. Martin's Press, New York, 1997.

Ide, Arthur F., *Unzipped, the Popes Bare All. A Frank Study of Sex & Corruption in the Vatican,* American Atheist Press, Texas, 1987.

Inglis, Brian, *Roger Casement,* Penguin Books Ltd., London, 2003.

Inso, Jaime Do, *China,* Edições Europa, Lisbon, 1938.

Jansen, Sharon, *The Monstrous Regiment of Women: Female Rulers in Early Modern Europe,* Palgrave Macmillan, New York, 2002.

Kahn, David, *The Codebreakers: The Comprehensive History of Secret Communication from Ancient Times to the Internet,* Scribner, New York, 1996.

————, *Hitler's Spies: German Military Intelligence in World War II,* Da Capo Press, New York, 2000.

Kamen, Henry Arthur, *The War of Succession in Spain, 1700–15,* Indiana University Press, Bloomington, 1969.

————, *Spain in the Later Seventeenth Century, 1665–1700,* Longman Group, London, 1983.

————, *Philip V of Spain: The King Who Reigned Twice,* Yale University Press, New Haven (Connecticut), 2001.

Kelsey, Harry, *Sir Francis Drake: The Queen's Pirate,* Yale University Press, New Haven (Connecticut), 2000.

————, *Sir John Hawkins: Queen Elizabeth's Slave Trader,* Yale University Press, New Haven (Connecticut), 2003.

Kermoal, Jacques, *L'Onorata Società,* Éditions de la Table Ronde, Paris, 1971.

Kertzer, David I., *The Kidnapping of Edgardo Mortara,* Vintage Press, New York, 1998.

————, *The Popes Against the Jews: The Vatican's Role in the Rise of Modern Anti-Semitism,* Knopf, New York, 2001.

Kovaliov, Eduard, *Atentado en la Plaza de San Pedro,* Editorial Novosti, Moscow, 1985.

Kung, Hans, *The Catholic Church: A Short History,* Modern Library, New York, 2003.

Labedz, Leopold, *Poland Under Jaruzelski: A Comprehensive Sourcebook on Poland During and After Martial Law,* Scribner, New York, 1984.

Langley, Edward Frederick, *Henry of Navarre: Henry IV of France,* Hale Publishers, London, 1998.

Larkin, Maurice, *Church and State after the Dreyfus Affair,* Harper & Row, New York, 1972.

Le Bris, Michel, *D'or, de rêves et de sang. L'épopée de la fliguste (1494–1588),* Hachette, Paris, 2001.

Le Carré, John, *¿El traidor del siglo?,* Plaza & Janes Editores, Barcelona, 1991.

Lesourd, Paul, *Entre Rome et Moscou: Le jésuite clandestin, Mgr Michel d'Herbigny,* P. Lethielleux, Paris, 1976.

Levi, Anthony, *Cardinal Richelieu and the Making of France,* Carroll & Graf, New York, 2000.

Lifton, Robert Jay, *The Nazi Doctors: Medical Killing and the Psychology of Genocide,* Basic Books, New York, 2000.

Liversidge, Douglas, *The Day the Bastille Fell: July 14, 1789, the Beginning of the End of the French Monarchy,* Franklin Watts Inc., New York, 1972.

Lloyd, Mark, *The Guinness Book of Espionage,* Da Capo Press, New York, 1994.

Lynch, John, *The Hispanic World in Crisis and Change, 1598–1700 (History of Spain),* Blackwell Publishers, London, 1992.

MacCaffrey, Wallace, *Queen Elizabeth and the Making of Policy, 1572–1588,* Princeton University Press, Princeton, 1981.

Marshall, Samuel Lyman, *The American Heritage History of the World War I,* Bonanza Books, New York, 1964.

Martin, Colin, and Parker, Geoffrey, *The Spanish Armada: Revised Edition,* Manchester University Press, Manchester, 2002.

Bibliography

Martin, Malachi, *The Jesuits: The Society of Jesus and the Betrayal of the Roman Catholic Church,* Simon & Schuster, New York, 1988.

———, *The Keys of This Blood. Pope John Paul II versus Russia and the West for the Control of the New World Order,* Simon & Schuster, New York, 1990.

Mattingly, Garrett, *The Defeat of the Spanish Armada,* Random House, London, 2000.

Mayor, Adrienne, *Greek Fire, Poison Arrows & Scorpion Bombs: Biological and Chemical Warfare in the Ancient World,* Overlook Duckworth, London, 2003.

Means, Howard, *C.S.A.: Confederate States of America,* William Morrow Publisher, New York, 1998.

Millenari, I, *Via col vento in Vaticano,* Kaos Edizioni, Milan, 1999.

Miller, Randall, and Stout, Harry, *Religion and the American Civil War,* Oxford University Press, New York, 1998.

Minerbi, Sergio, and Schwartz, Arnold, *The Vatican and Zionism: Conflict in the Holy Land 1895–1925,* Oxford University Press, Oxford, 1990.

Monticone, Alberto, *La Germania e la neutralitrà italiana, 1914–1915,* Il Mulino Editore, Bologna, 1971.

Moote, Lloyd, *Louis XIII, the Just,* University of California Press, Los Angeles, 1991.

Morrogh, Michael, *The Unification of Italy,* Palgrave Macmillan, London, 2003.

Mousnier, Roland, *The Assassination of Henry IV: The Tyrannicide Problem and the Consolidation of the French Absolute Monarchy in the Early Seventeenth Century,* Scribner, New York, 1973.

Naunton, Robert, *Fragmenta Regalia or Observations on Queen Elizabeth, Her Times and Favourites,* Cerovski Publishers, Toronto, 1985.

Neill, Stephen, *A History of Christian Missions,* Viking Press, New York, 1994.

Nicotri, Pino, *Mistero Vaticano. La scomparsa di Emanuela Orlandi,* Kaos Edizioni, Milan, 2002.

Nouel, Élise, *Carré d'as . . . aux femmes!: Lady Hester Stanhope, Aurélie Picard, Isabelle Eberhardt, Marga d'Andurain,* G. Le Prat, Paris, 1977.

O'Brien, Brendan, *The Long War. The IRA & Sinn Fein from Armed Struggle to Peace Talks,* The O'Brien Press, Dublin, 1993.

Ockrent, Christine, and De Marenches, Alexandre, *Dans le secret des princes,* Édition Stock, Paris, 1986.

O'Dwyer, Margaret, *The Papacy in the Age of Napoleon and the Restoration: Pius VII, 1800–1823,* Rowman & Littlefield, London, 1986.

Offner, John L., *An Unwanted War: The Diplomacy of the United States and Spain over Cuba, 1895–1898,* University of North Carolina Press, Chapel Hill, 1992.

Ostrovsky, Victor, and Hoy, Claire, *By Way of Deception,* Stoddart Publishing, Toronto, 1991.

Overy, Richard, *Interrogations: The Nazi Elite in Allied Hands, 1945,* Penguin Books, New York, 2002.

Paine, Lauran, *German Military Intelligence in World War II: The Abwehr,* Stein & Day Publishers, Munich, 1984.

Painter, G. D., *Chateaubriand,* Random House, London, 1998.

Pakenham, Antonia, *King James VI of Scotland, I of England,* Random House, New York, 1975.

Palmowski, Jan, *A Dictionary of Twentieth-Century World History,* Oxford University Press, Oxford, 1998.

Paredes, Javier; Barrio, Maximiliano; Ramos-Lissón, Domingo; and Suárez, Luis, *Diccionario de los Papas y Concilios,* Editorial Ariel, Barcelona, 1998.

Paris, Edmond, *The Vatican Against Europe,* The Wickliffle Press, New Zealand, 1989.

Parker, Geoffrey, *Success Is Never Final: Empire, War, and Faith in Early Modern Europe,* Basic Books, London, 2002.

Passelecq, Georges, and Suchecky, Bernard, *Un silencio de la Iglesia frente al fascismo. La encíclica de Pío XI que Pío XII no publicó,* PPC Editorial, Madrid, 1995.

Persico, Joseph E., *Nuremberg: Infamy on Trial,* Penguin Books, New York, 1994.

Phelps, Eric Jon, *Vatican Assassins: Wounded in the House of My Friends,* Halcyon Unified Services, London, 2000.

Pichón, Jean-Charles, *Histoire Universelle des Sectes et des Sociétés Secrètes,* Robert Laffont Éditions, Paris, 1969.

———, *The Vatican and Its Role in World Affairs,* Greenwood Publishing Group, London, 1969.

Pinto, Paolo, *Vittorio Emanuele II: Il re avventuriero,* Arnaldo Mondadori, Milan, 1995.

Pipes, Richard, *Russia Under the Bolshevik Regime,* Vintage Press, New York, 1995.

Plant, Richard, *The Pink Triangle: The Nazi War Against Homosexuals,* Henry Holt & Company, Inc., New York, 1988.

Pollard, John F., *Vatican & Italian Fascism,* Cambridge University Press, Cambridge, 1985.

————, *The Unknown Pope. Benedict XV (1914–1922) and the Pursuit of Peace,* Geoffrey Chapman Publishers, London, 1999.

Poulat, Émile, *Catholicisme, démocratie et socialisme: Le mouvement catholique et Mgr Benigni de la naissance du socialisme à la victoire du fascisme,* Casterman, Paris, 1977.

Proctor, Robert N., *Racial Hygiene: Medicine Under the Nazis,* Harvard University Press, Cambridge, 1989.

Ramen, Fred, *Reinhard Heydrich: Hangman of the 3rd Reich,* Rosen Publishing Group, London, 2001.

Ranelagh, John O'Beirne, *A Short History of Ireland,* Cambridge University Press, Cambridge, 1995.

Ranum, Orest, *The Fronde: A French Revolution, 1648–1652 (Revolutions in the Modern World),* W. W. Norton & Company, London, 1993.

Raw, Charles, *The Moneychangers: How the Vatican Bank Enabled Roberto Calvi to Steal $250 Million for the Heads of the P2 Masonic Lodge,* Vintage/Ebury, London, 1992.

Rayfield, Donald, *Stalin and the Hangmen,* Viking, London, 2004.

Reese, Thomas J., *Inside the Vatican. The Politics and Organization of the Catholic Church,* Harvard University Press, Cambridge, 1996.

Renzi, William, *The Shadow of the Sword: Italy's Neutrality and Entrance into the Great War, 1914–1918,* Peter Lang Publisher, New York, 1987.

Rhodes, Anthony, *The Vatican in the Age of the Dictators, 1922–1945,* Henry Holt & Company, Inc., New York, 1974.

————, *The Vatican in the Age of the Cold War 1945–1980,* Michael Russell Publishing Ltd., New York, 1992.

Riccardi, Andrea. *Il Secolo del Martirio,* Arnaldo Mondadori Spa, Milan, 2000.

Ridley, Jasper, *Garibaldi,* Phoenix Press, London, 2001.

Robert, Denis, and Backes, Ernest, *Revelacione$, investigación en la trastienda de las finanzas internacionales,* Foca Ediciones, Madrid, 2003.

Robinson, J. G. G., *Historical and Philosophical Memoirs of Pius the Sixth and of His Pontificate,* S. Hamilton, London, 1799.

Schama, Simon, *Citizens: A Chronicle of the French Revolution,* Vintage, New York, 1990.

Schneider, Peter T., *Reversible Destiny: Mafia, Antimafia, and the Struggle for Palermo,* University of California Press, Los Angeles, 2003.

Scholder, Klaus, *The Churches and the Third Reich,* John Bowden Publishers, London, 1989.

————, *A Requiem for Hitler and Other New Perspectives on the German Church Struggle,* John Bowden Publishers, London, 1989.

Scotta, Antonio, *La conciliazione ufficiosa: Diario del Barone Carlo Monti,* Libreria Editrice Vaticana, Vatican City, 1997.

Sereny, Gitta, *Into That Darkness: An Examination of Conscience,* Vintage Press, New York, 1983.

Shane, Leslie, *Cardinal Gasquet: A Memoir,* Burns & Oates, London, 1953.

Short, Martin, *Inside the Brotherhood: Explosive Secrets of the Freemasons,* HarperCollins Publishers, New York, 1989.

Singh, Simon, *The Code Book: The Science of Secrecy from Ancient Egypt to Quantum Cryptography,* Anchor Publishers, New York, 2000.

Smith, Denis Mack, *Cavour and Garibaldi 1860: A Study in Political Conflict,* Cambridge University Press, New York, 1985.

————, *Mazzini,* Yale University Press, New Haven (Connecticut), 1996.

Soderini, Eduardo, *Leo XIII, Italy, and France,* Burns & Oates, London, 1935.

Spence, Jonathan D., *Emperor of China: Self Portrait of K'ang-Hsi,* Vintage Press, New York, 1988.

————, *The Memory Palace of Matteo Ricci,* Viking Press, New York, 1994.

————, *The Chan's Great Continent: China in Western Minds,* New York, 1999.

Stajano, Corrado, *Un eroe borghese: Il caso dell'avvocato Giorgio Ambrosoli assassinato dalla mafia politica,* Einaudi Edizioni, Turin, 1991.

La Stampa a Firenze, 1471–1550: Omaggio a Roberto Ridolfi, L. S. Olschki Rome, 1984.

Stehle, Hansjakob, *The Eastern Politics of the Vatican, 1917–1979,* Ohio University Press, Ohio, 1981.

Stehlin, Stewart A., *Weimar and the Vatican 1919–1933: German-Vatican Diplomatic Relations in the Interwar Years,* Princeton University, Princeton, 1999.

Bibliography

Steinberg, Jonathan, *All or Nothing: The Axis and the Holocaust, 1941–1943,* Routledge, London, 2002.

Sterling, Claire, *The Time of the Assassins,* Holt, Rinehart & Winston, New York, 1983.

Stevenson, David, *Cataclysm: The First World War as Political Tragedy,* Basic Books, London, 2004.

Stieber, Wilhelm, *The Chancellor's Spy: Memoirs of the Founder of Modern Espionage,* Grove Press, London, 1981.

Strachey, Lytton, *Elizabeth and Essex: A Tragic History,* Harvest Books, London, 2002.

Stradling, Robert A., *Philip IV and the Government of Spain, 1621–1665,* Cambridge University Press, Cambridge, 1988.

Strong, Roy, *Gloriana: The Portraits of Queen Elizabeth I,* Pimlico, London, 2003.

Sutherland, Norman, *The Massacre of St. Bartholomew and the European Conflict, 1559–1572,* Barnes & Noble, New York, 1996.

Thackrah, John Richard, *Dictionary of Terrorism,* Routledge, London, 2004.

Thatcher, Margaret, *The Downing Street Years,* HarperCollins Publishers, London, 1993.

Thomas, Gordon, *Gideon's Spies. The Secret History of the Mossad,* St. Martin's Press, New York, 1999.

Thomas, Jane Resh, *Behind the Mask: The Life of Queen Elizabeth I,* Houghton Mifflin, London, 1998.

Trask, David F., *The War with Spain in 1898,* University of Nebraska Press, Lincoln, 1997.

Trento, Joseph J., *The Secret History of the CIA,* Random House, Inc., New York, 2001.

Tretjakewitsch, León, *Bishop Michel d'Herbigny SJ and Russia: A Pre-ecumenical Approach to Christian Unity,* Augustinus-Verlag, Berlin, 1990.

Urquhart, Gordon, *The Pope's Armada. Unlocking the Secrets of Mysterious and Powerful New Sects in the Church,* Prometheus Books, New York, 1999.

Van Dee, Eugene H., *Sleeping Dogs and Popsicles: The Vatican Versus the KGB,* Rowman & Littlefield, New York, 1996.

Verbist, Henri, *Les grandes controverses de L'Eglise contemporaine,* Éditions Rencontre, Lausanne, 1971.

Walsh, Michael J., *The Conclave: A Sometimes Secret and Occasionally Bloody History of Papal Elections,* Sheed and Ward, London, 2003.

Weale, Adrian, *Patriot Traitors: Roger Casement, John Amery and the Real Meaning of Treason,* Penguin Books Ltd., London, 2001.

Weir, Alison, *Mary, Queen of Scots and the Murder of Lord Darnley,* Random House Ltd., London, 2003.

West, Nigel, *The Third Secret. The CIA, Solidarity and the KGB's Plot to Kill the Pope,* HarperCollins Publishers, London, 2001.

Williams, Neville, *All the Queen's Men: Elizabeth I and Her Courtiers,* Cardinal, London, 1974.

———, *A Tudor Tragedy: Thomas Howard, Fourth Duke of Norfolk,* Barrie & Jenkins, London, 1989.

Williams, Paul L., *The Vatican Exposed. Money, Murder and the Mafia,* Prometheus Books, New York, 2003.

Williamson, Murray, and Bernstein, Alvin, *The Making of Strategy: Rulers, States, and War,* Cambridge University Press, Cambridge, 1996.

Wills, Garry, *Pecado papal. Las deshonestidades morales de la Iglesia católica,* Ediciones B, Barcelona, 2001.

Wolf, Markus, and McElvoy, Anne, *Man without a Face,* Times Books, New York, 1997.

Woodward, Bob, *VEIL. Las guerras secretas de la CIA 1981–1987,* Ediciones B, Barcelona, 1987.

Yallop, David A., *In God's Name. An Investigation into the Murder of Pope John Paul I,* Bantam Books, New York, 1984.

———, *To the Ends of the Earth: The Hunt for the Jackal,* Poetic Products Ltd., London, 1993.

Youngson, Robert, *Medical Curiosities: A Miscellany of Medical Oddities, Horrors and Humors,* Carroll & Graf, London, 1997.

Zuccotti, Susan, *Under His Very Windows. The Vatican and the Holocaust in Italy,* Yale University Press, New Haven (Connecticut), 2002.

Zweig, Stefan, *Maria Stuart,* Williams Verlag AG, Zurich, 1976.

———, *Fouché,* Fischer AG, Frankfurt, 2000.

ARCHIVES CONSULTED

Active Museum of German Jewish History (Wiesbaden, Federal Republic of Germany)
Alexander Ganse Archives (www.zum.de/vvlikmla)
Archives du Ministère des Affaires Étrangères (Paris, France)
Archives Nationales (Paris, France)
Archivio Centrale dello Stato (Rome, Italy)
Archivio del Istituto per la Storia del Risorgimento Italiano (Rome, Italy)
Archivio del Ministero per i Beni e la Attivittà Culturali (Rome, Italy)
Archivio del'Accademia Ecclesiastica Napoletana di S. Pietro in Vinculis (Naples, Italy)
Archivio dell'Istituto Storico Italo-Germanico in Trento/Jahrbuch des Italienisch-Deutschen Historischen Instituts in Trient (Bologna, Italy)
Archivio della Società Romena di Storia Patria (Rome, Italy)
Archivio di Nuova Rivista Storica (Milan, Italy)
Archivio di Stato di Roma
Archivio per la Storia Ecclesiastica dell'Umbria (Italy)
Archivio Segreto Vaticano (Vatican City-State)
Archivio Storico della Sacra Congregazione degli Affari Ecclesiastici Straordinari (Vatican City-State)
Archivio Storico di Malta (Rome, Italy)
Archivio Storico per le Province Napoletane (Naples, Italy)
Archivio Trentino (Trento, Italy)
Archivo General de Indias (Seville, Spain)
Archivo General de Simancas (Valladolid, Spain)
Archivo Histórico Nacional (Madrid, Spain)
Archivos de la Comisión de Esclarecimiento de las Actividades Nazis en Argentina (CEANA) (Buenos Aires, Argentina)
Archivum Historicum Societatis Iesu (Rome, Italy)
Arnold Daghani Collection
Bibliothèque Nationale de France (Paris, France)
Catholic Historical Association (Washington, D.C., U.S.A.)
Catholic Historical Review Archives (Washington, D.C., U.S.A.)
The Catholic University of America (Washington, D.C., U.S.A.)
Center for German-Jewish Studies, University of Sussex (Sussex, Great Britain)
Christ Church Cathedral Dublin Ireland Library and Archives (Dublin, Ireland)
David M. Cheney Archives (www.catholic-hierarchy.org)
Institute of Documentation in Israel for the Investigation of Nazi War Crimes (Haifa, Israel)
National Archives and Record Administration (Washington, D.C., U.S.A.)
The National Archives of Ireland (Dublin, Ireland)
National Library of Ireland (Dublin, Ireland)

Archives Consulted

Public Record Office (London, Great Britain)
Public Record Office, Kingdom of Scotland (Edinburgh, Great Britain)
Royal Geographical Society (London, Great Britain)
Ruhr-Universität Bochum (Westphalia, German Federal Republic)
Uniwersytetu Jagiellonskiego (Kraców, Poland)

INDEX

Index

Index

Index

ABOUT THE AUTHOR

Eric Frattini spent several years as a Mideast correspondent, living in Beirut (Lebanon), Nicosia (Cyprus), and Jerusalem (Israel).

During his twenty-five-year career as a journalist, he has interviewed figures including Nelson Mandela, the Dalai Lama, Yitzhak Rabin, Ariel Sharon, Yassir Arafat, and Tony Blair, to mention a few.

Frattini is the author of nearly twenty books, including *Osama bin Laden, la espada de Alá / Osama bin Laden: The Sword of Allah* (2001); *Mafia S.A. 100 Años de Cosa Nostra / Mafia Inc.: 100 Years of Cosa Nostra* (2002); *Secretos Vaticanos / Vatican Secrets* (2003); *ONU, historia de la corrupción / The U.N.: A History of Corruption* (2005); *La Conjura, Matar a Lorenzo de Medici / Conspiracy: Killing Lorenzo de Medici* (2006); *CIA. Joyas de Familia / The CIA: "Family Jewels"* (2008); *Los Espías del Papa / The Pope's Spies* (2008); and a quartet on the history of the most famous spy services (the CIA, KGB, Mossad, and MI6). He recently published his first novel, *El Quinto Mandamiento / The Fifth Commandment.*

His works have been published in the United States, Australia, Great Britain, Spain, France, Portugal, Brazil, Poland, Italy, Romania, and Russia. He works as an international politics analyst for several television channels and as a professor of investigative journalism at the University of Madrid.

Eric Frattini lives in Spain with his family, devoting his free time to participating in classic-car races throughout Europe when he is not writing or traveling the world with his wife and son.

www.ericfrattini.com